ARTHUR J MARDER was a meticulous researcher, teacher and writer who, born in 1910, was to become perhaps the most distinguished historian of the modern Royal Navy. He held a number of teaching posts in American universities and was to receive countless honours, as well as publish some fifteen major works on British naval history. He died in 1980.

BARRY GOUGH, the distinguished Canadian maritime and naval historian, is the author of *Historical Dreadnoughts: Arthur Marder, Stephen Roskill and the Battles for Naval History*, recently published by Seaforth Publishing.

ADMIRAL SIR JOHN JELLICOE
First Sea Lord, December 1916–December 1917

[Painting by Sir Arthur Cope:
by permission of the second Earl Jellicoe

FROM THE
DREADNOUGHT
TO
SCAPA FLOW

The Royal Navy in the Fisher Era 1904–1919

VOLUME IV
1917: YEAR OF CRISIS

ARTHUR J MARDER
INTRODUCTION BY BARRY GOUGH

Naval Institute Press

Annapolis

Seaforth
PUBLISHING

THE MAPS
Large-scale versions of the maps located at the back
can be downloaded from the book's page
on the publishers' websites.

Copyright © Arthur J Marder 1969
Introduction copyright © Barry Gough 2014

This edition first published in Great Britain in 2014 by
Seaforth Publishing,
Pen & Sword Books Ltd,
47 Church Street,
Barnsley S70 2AS

www.seaforthpublishing.com

Published and distributed in the
United States of America and Canada by the
Naval Institute Press,
291 Wood Road, Annapolis,
Maryland 21402-5034

www.nip.org

British Library Cataloguing in Publication Data
A catalogue record for this book is available from the British Library

Library of Congress Control Number: 2013937405

ISBN 978 1 84832 201 1

Printed and bound in Great Britain by CPI Group (UK) Ltd, Croydon, CR0 4YY

Introduction

IN HIS PREVIOUS volume in this series on the Royal Navy in the Fisher Era, *Jutland and After*, Marder had wound up his narrative and analysis with a bold indication of what would come in this current installment, *1917: Year of Crisis*. He had outlined the German submarine peril, the costs to Allied shipping, and the failure of the anti-submarine campaign to the end of 1917. All the while that British fortunes apparently turned on the fates of the Grand Fleet the German U-boat arm was rising to a challenge that the German High Seas Fleet could not undertake – a war against Allied shipping on which the lifeblood of the United Kingdom and the endeavours of the Allied armies on the Western Front depended. The Germans sensed that victory was within their grasp.

To the year 1914 the threat posed by U-boats had been underrated in the Admiralty. The submarine was regarded as a damned un-English weapon. Senior British statesmen denied that the enemy would use it against innocent shipping, particularly against British liners plying North Atlantic routes, the Western Approaches, or even inshore British waters. The *Lusitania* tragedy of May 1915 exploded that myth and also awakened American interest. Moreover, right from October 1914 with the loss of the 'live-bait squadron' in the Broad Fourteens south of the Dogger Bank and the cruiser *Hawke* (and other vessels) to the torpedoes carried by U-boats on the prowl, the German *guerre de course* had been successful. It only required a political decision by the German high command to unleash unrestricted U-boat warfare for the hitherto unimaginable crisis to come upon the British.

The war waged by the Germans in underwater warfare, principally by the submarine, caught the Admiralty, both in policy-making and in mentality, totally unprepared. Furthermore, technological capabilities for countering the U-boat menace had not been developed, with science and technology unharnessed for the purposes of U-boat hunting. Meanwhile, the German submarine arm continued to do massive damage to Allied shipping. The matter became a major political one in Whitehall, in Parliament and the press. While all of this was happening the great armies were locked in mortal combat on the Western Front in what amounted to siege warfare. In April 1917 it looked very possible that the Central Powers might win out in the end. The Royal Navy therefore had to fight an unexpected war and one for which they were ill equipped both in terms of mentality and material.

The volume begins with a look at naval aviation. The Royal Naval Air Service was tied up with everything except providing air support for the Grand Fleet, and the Germans undoubtedly had better scouting capability. The production of British airships was slow and uncertain. Moreover, carriers capable of carrying seaplanes or aeroplanes, and able to keep station with the Grand Fleet or the Battle Cruiser Fleet, were ill suited to their intended tasks. The sad fact, Marder recounted, was that the Grand Fleet did not have a single effective aircraft carrier while hostilities were on. Yes, there were carriers – six of them in 1917–18 – but none of them could be called efficient. In terms of offense, the Sopwith Camel 2F.I was flown from carriers, its main function being the interception of Zeppelins. The torpedo plane, with all its vast potential, was largely in its operational infancy, though an indication of its brilliant future had already been revealed.

Admiral Sir David Beatty hoisted his flag in the *Iron Duke* on 29 November 1916, succeeding Admiral Sir John Jellicoe, who had been summoned to the Admiralty to put a stop to the growing shipping crisis. Many measures were tried. Jellicoe had no solution. Neither it seems did many others serving in the Admiralty or afloat. The Grand Fleet under Beatty (as previously under Jellicoe) remained at the heart of British naval strategy with the responsibility of safeguarding lines of communication. But British naval resources were stretched thin in such places as the Narrow Seas and in Irish waters. Real weaknesses were apparent off Queenstown, in the waters covered by Dover Patrol, and in North American waters where U-boats with extended cruising capabilities could hunt merchant shipping and sow mines.

Even changes at the Admiralty brought no new perspective, and Marder explores its serious shortcomings, particularly exposing its failure to make a serious study of trade protection. Only Admiral Sir Alexander Duff, head of the Anti-Submarine Division, came fully to grips with the issue – and at the last moment, and under political pressure from the Prime Minister, Lloyd George, and cabinet member Lord Curzon (the latter was keeping the statistical data on shipping losses) the convoy was introduced as a trial measure. Colonel Maurice

Hankey at the War Cabinet office was pressing for convoy. Marder, caught between the role of a prosecuting attorney and defender of the Admiralty's traditions and suspicion of change, manages to explore both sides of the matter. Jellicoe was pessimistic about the prospects of curbing the U-boats. He could see no effective counter-measures, which irked the Prime Minister. Even bringing Jacky Fisher out of retirement was regarded as a possibility, at least in *his* mind. The idea of concentrating merchantmen under warships on convoy duty had much opposition. Merchant captains and merchant shipping companies did not want to be held back in their sailings. There was anxiety about port congestion, while worries about being entangled in minefields were expressed. The War Cabinet began to think about making a peace overture.

Marder worked strenuously to show that it was the Admiralty that finally introduced convoy (even if on a trial basis) and not Lloyd George, who on 25 April threatened to visit the Admiralty with a view to changing the policy if Their Lordships did not take action. On the 26th Duff submitted detailed proposals for a trial ocean convoy from Gibraltar. The next day the Admiralty so approved. The convoy sailed without incident, though delays ensued on general implementation of convoys. In reference to the Admiralty Marder says that their hearts were not in it. He writes (p189): 'They regarded convoy as the last shot in their lockers, were skeptical of its success, and had a lingering preference for a trade protection system based on patrolling.' Besides, there was a lack of escorts. The United States Navy was against convoy, too, though Rear-Admiral William Sims, USN, who was in London at this time and closely in touch with naval affairs and discussions, saw convoy as not only essential but as a form of warfare of the offensive. Almost everyone else was thinking of convoy as a defensive measure. Jellicoe, though he realised that it was the last and only hope, had no confidence in the success of the system. Even Duff was reluctant: the need of fifty-two cruisers for ocean escort and seventy-five torpedo boat destroyers for danger zones could not seemingly be met. By 4 May 1917 the first six US destroyers had arrived at Queenstown, and many more were to follow.

Heads continued to roll. The Prime Minister lost faith in the First Lord of the Admiralty, Edward (later Lord) Carson, and he was dismissed. But at the root of the issue was Lloyd George's opinion of Jellicoe, who exhibited unbounded pessimism. Lloyd George wanted optimism and he wanted good results in difficult times. Marder draws wonderful character sketches as he moves inexorably through the various tragic sequences that were being played out in Whitehall. The politicians warmed to their task, striking committees of investigation. Jellicoe attempted to maintain the Admiralty's independence, but the fates and the circumstances were against him. Sir Eric Geddes was brought in to succeed Carson. Now he had to deal with Jellicoe. On Christmas Eve Jellicoe was dismissed at 6pm as First Lord of the Admiralty.

Marder examines 'the war behind the war' in great detail. This is the feature of his work that had so strongly attracted the readers of Volume II. That was the one that dealt with the events of late 1914, when Churchill was First Lord of the Admiralty and Battenburg the First Sea Lord, but soon to be replaced by Fisher. But whereas that story was generally well known, that of the shake-ups of 1917 was largely new material. Political direction was now compelling Admiralty responses in a hitherto unimaginable way. Jellicoe's dismissal was only a matter of time, though the manner in which it was done smacks of cruelty. The reader follows all the action knowing the inevitable. Always in the background are the statistical details: tonnage losses are noted and so are U-boat losses. Only gradually was an advantage being gained over the U-boats. But the convoy successes told all. Marder concluded that the sinkings fell in almost direct proportion to the increasing number of ships under convoy. By October, at last, convoys could be proclaimed as a successful measure of warfare.

Marder had no special training in economic history or in matters of maritime trade. It was thus fortuitous that Lieutenant Commander David Waters, who had compiled a confidential document on trade defence in the First and Second World Wars, gave him aid in these matters. Researched and written during the Cold War, Marder's discussion of the 'politics' of convoy adoption, implementation and success squared nicely with the frequent appeal for ocean escorts to maintain transatlantic links during a war that might come. Pages of the *United States Naval Institute Proceedings* and the *Journal of the Royal United Services Institute for Defence Studies* commonly appealed for a better appreciation of the importance of convoy and the necessity to maintain a strong merchant marine. The lifeblood of NATO depended on sea power. Marder did not specifically write at such length in Volume IV, *1917: Year of Crisis*, as a lesson to be learned by NATO statesmen and member states. But the link was obvious.

Marder tells the stories from such sources as the Admiralty manuscripts, and the Beatty, Jellicoe and Asquith papers. In many cases he was the first to use these sources. The Admiralty Librarian might be charged with giving Marder preferential treatment. In fact, at every turn Marder had to make application to use the Admiralty documents in question, and readers will note he gives no specific file numbers. These documents are now at the National Archives, Kew. But in Marder's time they were fast under lock and key. The success of his volumes aided his future search for documents hidden from view in the Admiralty 'cage'. In addition, his manuscript had to pass the censors before being released for publication.

Marder exploited every living contact that could shed light on the subject at hand, and he was to gain privileged information from his many informants. His acknowledgments list all those who helped him. Many true friendships developed in the course of Marder's inquiries. But with *1917: Year of Crisis* Marder had special thanks to pay to Lady Duff, widow of the admiral who had headed up the A/S Division at the critical hour. Marder had been led to her by one of the many personal recommendations given by naval officers, or their wives, who knew of his zeal and his reliability, also of his competence as an excellent writer of history. Marjorie Duff had always expressed a keen interest in her husband's work and the Navy's obligations and practices. When Marder came to see the Admiral's papers Marjorie was always faithfully at his elbow, pointing out this and that, explaining the particulars of the war at sea. Here was a classic case of one of the 'Women Behind the Fleet.' Marjorie became a devoted servant of Marder's work. When in late 1968 this volume appeared she gave Marder a running commentary on booksellers who should have been stocking the book and pointing out how she had instructed them to make sure Marder's books were on display.

With the close of the year 1917 the Royal Navy stood in a commanding position against its German challenger. The great crisis had come and gone, though it had taken much longer to contain the U-boat menace than imagined. Indeed, Marder makes clear that the U-boat threat remained strong, if diminished, until the end of the year. Once again British sea power had exerted influence not in decisive battle but in long-range actions. The sea-keeping demands of the Fleet and all those engaged in U-boat hunting was wearing on those concerned. While the politicians and the press called for decisive action and immediate results the Admiralty was grappling with a set of problems hitherto unimagined by even the most competent senior officers. In Marder the Navy found an historian who would give these problems every appreciation. Yet it is fair to say that he was invariably critical of the Admiralty's failure to grasp these demands for, or necessities of, change.

BARRY GOUGH
Victoria, BC, Canada

Preface

This was to have been the concluding volume of a tetralogy. Instead it is the penultimate volume of a quintuplet, my Publisher having graciously opted for two moderate-sized tomes in preference to one formidable one. The second should follow during 1970.

The present volume is the story of the Royal Navy from December 1916 through December 1917: from Jellicoe's arrival at the Admiralty to cope with the U-boat menace until his dismissal a year later. This was the most critical period of the war. It was a time of strategic stalemate so far as the main British and German fleets were concerned. The big issue was whether the Navy could defeat, or at least contain, the submarine menace. On its ability to do so depended the outcome of the war at sea and with it the whole Allied cause.

Again it is a pleasure to acknowledge with my profound thanks the assistance of officers whose expertise has been indicated in earlier prefaces and who gave the manuscript a careful and constructive reading (to say nothing of their helpful replies to a flood of queries): Admiral Sir William James, Vice-Admiral Sir Peter Gretton, Rear-Admiral W. S. Chalmers, Captains John Creswell and Stephen Roskill, and Lieutenant-Commander P. K. Kemp. For Part I: the late Commander M. G. Saunders; the chapters dealing with the U-boats and trade defence: Lieutenant-Commander D. W. Waters; the Grand Fleet (Chapter II): Admiral Sir Angus Cunninghame Graham, who served in the Grand Fleet, 1917–18; the Mediterranean material: Admiral J. H. Godfrey, who was on the staff of the C.-in-C., Mediterranean, 1917–18; naval aviation (Chapter I): Air Chief Marshals Sir Ralph Cochrane, Sir Christopher Courtney, and Sir Arthur Longmore, Marshal of the Royal Air Force Sir William Dickson, and Group Captain H. A. Williamson, all of them pioneers in the development of the R.N.A.S. Needless to say, none of the afore-mentioned are responsible for errors of any sort in this volume.

I owe an extra measure of thanks once more to Captain Creswell for overseeing with care and skill the preparation of the maps and charts, and to Mr. N. Atherton for the cartographic work itself.

In addition to those whose permission to examine collections of papers was acknowledged in previous volumes (some of which materials were needed for this volume as well), I owe warm thanks to Mrs. John Marsden-Smedley, for the papers of her father, Admiral Sir Alexander Bethell; Lord Salter, for important material pertaining to trade defence; and the second Baron Hankey, for the privilege of examining his father's diary for 1917 and 1918. Mr. Norman Macleod, Private Secretary to successive Civil Lords, 1913–19 (and from August 1914 till May 1915 to the Fourth Sea Lord as well) kindly prepared a memorandum on members of the wartime Boards of Admiralty. I am grateful also to these gentlemen: Commander W. B. Rowbotham and Mr. J. D. Lawson, for helping to tie together countless loose ends; Dr. Ives Hendrick, for permission to quote from Rear-Admiral W. S. Sims's *The Victory at Sea*; and, for assistance of various kinds, the late Vice-Admiral Sir Geoffrey Blake, the second Baron Maclay, Lord Hurcomb, Professors Robin Higham, G. Waterhouse, and L. A. Willoughby, Dr. Douglas H. Robinson, Sir Edward Beharrell, the staff of the Public Record Office, and the staffs of the Air Historical Branch, the Naval Historical Branch, and the Naval Library, Ministry of Defence. My belated thanks are due to Messrs. David Woodward and Anthony Sainsbury for bringing to my attention collections of papers important for Volumes ii and iii. Miss Cathy Smith bore with extraordinary patience and good humour the burdens of preparing a neat typescript from a mass of hieroglyphics. The financial assistance of the University of California and the American Philosophical Society once again eased my labours.

I wish to thank the following publishers for their kind permission to quote from the copyright material indicated: George Allen & Unwin, Ltd., and The Macmillan Co., from Lord Hankey's *The Supreme Command*; Beaverbrook Newspapers Ltd., from the *War Memoirs of David Lloyd George*; Cassell & Co. Ltd., and Lord Jellicoe, from Admiral of the Fleet Earl Jellicoe's *The Submarine Peril*; Chatto & Windus, Ltd., from David W. Bone's *Merchantmen-at-Arms*; Christy & Moore, Ltd., from Admiral Sir Lewis Bayly's *Pull Together!*; Constable & Co. Ltd., from R. H. Gibson and Maurice Prendergast's *The German Submarine War, 1914–1918*; Eyre & Spottiswoode, Ltd. (and for the Keyes title E. P. Dutton

& Co., Inc.), from *The Private Papers of Douglas Haig, 1914–1919* (Robert Blake ed.), *The Naval Memoirs of Admiral of the Fleet Sir Roger Keyes*, and Lady Wester Wemyss's *The Life and Letters of Lord Wester Wemyss*; G. T. Foulis & Co. Ltd., from Robin Higham's *The British Rigid Airship, 1908–1931*; The Hamlyn Publishing Group Limited and Charles Scribner's Sons, from Winston Churchill's *Thoughts and Adventures*; Her Majesty's Stationery Office, from Sir Julian Corbett and Sir Henry Newbolt's *History of the Great War. Naval Operations*, W. K. Hancock and M. M. Gowing's *History of the Second World War. British War Economy*, and Sir Walter Raleigh and H. A. Jones's *History of the Great War. The War in the Air*; Hodder & Stoughton, Ltd. and Rear-Admiral W. S. Chalmers, from the latter's *The Life and Letters of David, Earl Beatty*; Hutchinson Publishing Group, Ltd., and the executors of the estate of Admiral Sir Reginald Bacon, from the Admiral's *The Dover Patrol, 1915–17*, *The Concise Story of the Dover Patrol*, and *From 1900 Onward*; Lieutenant-Commander P. K. Kemp, from his *H.M. Submarines*; E. S. Mittler & Sohn, from The Official German History *Der Krieg zur See*: Captain Otto Groos and Admiral Walther Gladisch's *Der Krieg in der Nordsee* and Rear-Admiral Arno Spindler's *Der Handelskrieg mit U-Booten*; John Murray (Publishers) Ltd., from C. Ernest Fayle's *History of the Great War. Seaborne Trade*, and Sir Archibald Hurd's *History of the Great War. The Merchant Navy*; Oxford University Press (London), from Sir Norman Hill, *et. al.*, *War and Insurance*; Sampson Low, Marston & Co., Ltd., from Captain John Creswell's *Naval Warfare*; Anthony Sheil Associates, Limited, from Desmond Young's *Rutland of Jutland*; H. F. & G. Witherby, Ltd., from Admiral Sir William James's *A Great Seaman: the Life of Admiral of the Fleet Sir Henry F. Oliver*. Unpublished Crown copyright material is published by permission of the Controller of Her Majesty's Stationery Office. I would also like to express my sincere thanks to Lieutenant-Commander D. W. Waters for the privilege of quoting from certain of his restricted writings.

As in the previous volumes I have made good use of the pertinent articles in the *Naval Review*, but without citing this restricted journal, in accordance with its long-established policy.

The collections of papers cited in footnotes and their present whereabouts are as follows:

Admiralty MSS.: Public Record Office, London.

Balfour MSS.: British Museum.

Barley-Waters MSS.: Naval Historical Branch, Ministry of Defence.

Beatty MSS.: the second Earl Beatty.

Bellairs (Roger M.) MSS.: Naval Library, Ministry of Defence.*

Carson MSS.: Public Record Office of Northern Ireland, Belfast; the Hon. Edward Carson. Referred to in footnotes as 'Carson MSS. (Belfast)' and 'Carson MSS.', respectively.

Dewar (K.G.B.) MSS.: National Maritime Museum Library, Greenwich.

Duff MSS.: National Maritime Museum, Greenwich, and for certain papers outside the main collection, Lady Duff.

Evan-Thomas MSS.: British Museum.

Frewen MSS.: British Museum.

Geddes MSS.: Admiralty MSS., Public Record Office, London (Adm. 116/1804–1810).

German Ministry of Marine MSS.: Militärgeschichtliches Forschungsamt, Freiburg im Breisgau.

Graham Greene MSS.: National Maritime Museum, Greenwich.

Hankey MSS. (diaries): the second Baron Hankey.

Jackson MSS.: Naval Library, Ministry of Defence.

Jellicoe MSS.: British Museum.

Keyes MSS.: Churchill College, Cambridge.

Lloyd George MSS.: The Beaverbrook Library.

Oliver MSS.: National Maritime Museum, Greenwich.

Sturdee MSS.: Captain W. D. M. Staveley, R.N.

Tyrwhitt MSS.: Lady Agnew.

U.S. Navy Department MSS.: National Archives, Washington, D.C.

Windsor MSS.: Royal Archives, Windsor Castle.

Irvine, California ARTHUR J. MARDER
Trafalgar Day, 1968

---

* Unaccountably missing when this preface was written. They may have been mislaid or lost when the Library was moved from Whitehall to Earls Court in 1963.

Abbreviations Used in the Text
(whether official or in common Service usage)

A.C.N.S.   :   Assistant Chief of Naval Staff

A/S   :   Anti-Submarine

A.S.D.   :   Anti-Submarine Division

A.D.O.D.   :   Assistant Director of Operations

B.C.F.   :   Battle Cruiser Force

B.C.S.   :   Battle Cruiser Squadron

B.S.   :   Battle Squadron

C.I.G.S.   :   Chief of the Imperial General Staff

C.M.B.   :   Coastal Motor Boat

C.O.S.   :   Chief of the Admiralty War Staff (to May 1917) (also Chief of Staff to a Flag Officer Commanding)

D.A.S.D.   :   Director of the Anti-Submarine Division

D.C.N.S.   :   Deputy Chief of Naval Staff

D.N.C.   :   Director of Naval Construction

D.N.I.   :   Director of Naval Intelligence*

D.N.O.   :   Director of Naval Ordnance

D.O.D.   :   Director of Operations Division

D. of P.   :   Director of Plans

D.T.D.   :   Director of Trade Division

G.F.B.I.s   :   Grand Fleet Battle Instructions

G.F.B.O.s   :   Grand Fleet Battle Orders

G.F.   :   Grand Fleet

H.S.F.   :   High Seas Fleet

I.W.C.   :   Imperial War Cabinet

L.C.S.   :   Light Cruiser Squadron

M.L.   :   Motor Launch

N.I.D.   :   Naval Intelligence Division

* The title of pre-War Staff days (—1912), revived in 1918. As in Volumes ii and iii, I use this in place of 'D.I.D.' (Director of the Intelligence Division), which was the official title, 1912–18.

R.A.F.	:	Royal Air Force
R.F.C.	:	Royal Flying Corps
R.N.A.S.	:	Royal Naval Air Service
S.M.	:	Submarine
S.N.O.	:	Senior Naval Officer
T.B.D.	:	[Torpedo-Boat] Destroyer
V.A.	:	Vice-Admiral
W.C.	:	War Cabinet
W/T	:	Wireless telegraphy

Contents

CONTENTS

PART II. EBBING OF THE TIDE:

the Jellicoe-Geddes Period

July 1917–December 1917

CHAPTER VIII. A REVOLUTION AT THE ADMIRALTY
(July 1917–October 1917)

war operations and ship movements—Broader significance of
the changes—Wemyss is elevated to Deputy First Sea Lord—
The consequences of the appointment—A capsule summary of
the story of Jellicoe's dismissal.

CHAPTER X. THE CONVOY SYSTEM IN OPERATION
(July 1917–December 1917)

—Improvement of the situation as regards mines—The high German hopes for unrestricted U-boat warfare are shattered—The cautious optimism at the Admiralty—But there is no general awareness that the worst is over—Reservations on convoy: it is a 'defensive' measure—Winter conditions and German battle-cruiser raiders promise to reduce the efficacy of convoy.

List of Illustrations

(The rank and titles held in 1917 are given)

Admiral Sir John Jellicoe, First Sea Lord, December
1916–December 1917   *Frontispiece*
(*From the painting by Sir Arthur Cope, by permission of the second Earl Jellicoe*)

Facing page

I. Admiral Sir David Beatty, Commander-in-Chief, Grand
Fleet, from November 1916   40
(*From the painting by Sir William Orpen; reproduction by permission of the photographer, Paul Laib*)

II. 1. Vice-Admiral Sir Rosslyn Wemyss, Deputy First Sea
Lord, September–December 1917   41
(*Photograph: by permission of the Hon. Mrs. F. Cunnack*)

2. Rear-Admiral Alexander L. Duff, Director of Anti-
Submarine Division, Admiralty War Staff, December
1916–May 1917, Assistant Chief of Naval Staff from
May 1917   41
(*Photograph: by permission of Lady Duff*)

III. Acting Vice-Admiral Sir Henry Oliver, Chief of
Admiralty War Staff, November 1914–May 1917,
Deputy Chief of Naval Staff from May 1917   56
(*Photograph: by permission of Dame Beryl Oliver*)

IV. 1. Rear-Admiral Sir Osmond de B. Brock, Chief of
Staff to the C.-in-C., Grand Fleet, from November
1916   57
(*From the painting by Sir Arthur Cope, by permission of Mrs. John Davie*)

2. Admiral Sir Charles Madden, Second-in-Command,
Grand Fleet, from November 1916   57
(*From the painting by Sir Arthur Cope, by permission of Admiral Sir Charles Madden, 2nd Bt.*)

xxiii

List of Maps and Charts
at end of book

PART I

The Crisis of the Naval War:
The Jellicoe–Carson Period
December 1916 – July 1917

I

In the Background:
The Rise of Naval Aviation

This is a war in which we want new ideas, new weapons, and the courage of young men to handle them.

COMMODORE MURRAY F. SUETER
(Superintendent of Aircraft Construction, Admiralty)
in a paper of 20 December 1916.

Air supremacy may in the long run become as important a factor in the defence of the Empire as sea supremacy.

REPORT OF THE PRIME MINISTER'S COMMITTEE ON AIR ORGANISATION
AND HOME DEFENCE AGAINST AIR RAIDS, 17 August 1917.

I. AIRSHIP POLICY

THE war saw important developments in all branches of naval aviation that promised to revolutionize warfare at sea. The beginnings were modest enough. When the war broke out, the R.N.A.S. had 7 airships (non-rigids), 52 seaplanes (only half of them in flying condition), 39 aeroplanes (landplanes), and a personnel strength of approximately 140 officers and 700 men. Although the R.N.A.S. in the first part of the war bombed Zeppelin sheds at Düsseldorf and Friedrichshaven (from bases in France and Belgium) and carried out anti-submarine and anti-Zeppelin patrols over the sea, its main concern, until the R.F.C. took over this function early in 1916, was the air defence of Great Britain, the Thames estuary in particular. Captain Macintyre's judgement on one consequence of the Admiralty responsibility for Home air defence is worth recording, though not beyond dispute: 'There can be little doubt that this large and expensive commitment adversely affected the development of a ship-borne air arm. The delays to which this development was subjected were to cause the part that naval aviation had to play in battle to be lightly considered.'[1] This is an important reason why, despite the

[1] Donald Macintyre, *Wings of Neptune: the Story of Naval Aviation* (London, 1963), p. 20.

3

promising start in July 1913, when aircraft participated for the first time in the annual naval manœuvres, the Fleet had little assistance from the R.N.A.S. through 1916. In January 1917 Beatty, the new C.-in-C., Grand Fleet, asked the First Lord what air support the Grand Fleet could expect to have during the war, as at present 'for all practical purposes it had no assistance from the Air Service: whereas the Germans have six seaplane carriers, besides Zeppelins, to assist their naval operations in the North Sea. . . .'[2] The C.-in-C. wanted every effort to be made to develop the use of naval aircraft for fleet purposes. Otherwise, the Grand Fleet would be at a disadvantage whenever the High Seas Fleet came into the North Sea, since the latter would emerge for operations only when the weather was suitable for Zeppelins and seaplanes. He had a particular interest at this time in airships.

Jellicoe held the strongest opinion of the value of airships for fleet reconnaissance. 'One Zeppelin is worth a good many light cruisers on a suitable day', he had asserted in 1913. War experience strengthened this faith: the Germans owed their escape on 1 June and 19 August 1916, *in his belief*, to their Zeppelins. 'Unless we can compete with Germany in this respect on favourable terms our Fleet is greatly handicapped in its operations' (6 April 1917). Beatty agreed with this evaluation, especially after exercises in October 1916 and July and September 1917 had demonstrated the great value of airship reconnaissance to the Fleet. It was a source of constant annoyance to him that the Germans still had 'the monopoly of the best air scouting in good weather, when one Zeppelin can do as much as five or six cruisers'.[3] In a conference with the Deputy First Sea Lord, Wemyss, on 10 October 1917, the C.-in-C. reminded him that airships (by which he meant rigids) would undoubtedly be of immense value to the Grand Fleet and would permit him to hold back his heavier-than-air machines until the last moment. At that time only the Sopwith 'Baby' seaplane could be carried in light cruisers. They had a Service ceiling of

[2] Carson, 'Memorandum of Conversations with the Commander-in-Chief of the Grand Fleet on Board H.M.S. *Iron Duke* on the 8th and 9th of January, 1917'; Beatty MSS. The German naval rigid airships were either Zeppelins or Schütte-Lanz airships, mostly the former, but in popular parlance 'Zeppelin' covered all the German rigids. It must be remembered that the Germans had had at least four years' start over Britain in the development of these big rigid airships.

[3] As reported by Repington, the Military Correspondent of *The Times*, on 10 October 1917; Lieutenant-Colonel Charles à Court Repington, *The First World War, 1914–1918* (London, 1920, 2 vols.), ii. 13.

10,000 feet (that is, the maximum height at which manœuvrability for operational purposes is possible); but while their speed was 15 to 18 knots in excess of that of a Zeppelin, their endurance was but 2¼ hours. Otherwise, Beatty had only non-rigid airships operating with the fleet, and their performance was disappointing: they were unable to keep up with the fleet.

A paper of 1917 that probably reflected high Admiralty views spelled out the advantages of rigid airships to the fleet:

> A Rigid Airship with its speed and endurance and range of vision can search an area and provide the Admiral in Command of a Fleet with full information as to whether the enemy's vessels are present, in far less time than would be taken by a number of cruisers. For it must be remembered that from a height of only about 2,000 feet—provided the visibility be good—the range of vision is 60 miles. The latest types of Rigids are of a range of approximately 2000 miles and can be used far beyond the limits of heavier-than-air craft. They are, therefore, unquestionably more effective for extended Naval reconnaissance than any other type of craft, whether surface or air. In fine weather a long range Rigid can effectively search an area of over 100,000 square miles in from 40 to 50 hours . . . the only safe policy is to press on with a type of weapon which has proved of so great use to the enemy forces and of such discomfort to our own.[4]

Unfortunately, airships that could do the job for the Fleet were not to hand. Let us go back.

The start of the war found the Navy without a single rigid airship. There were seven small non-rigids, only two of which the R.N.A.S. were able to use operationally in the first stage of the war: they patrolled the Channel during the passage of the Expeditionary Force to France. Their lack of ceiling made them too vulnerable for offensive operations.

Churchill, First Lord of the Admiralty since 1911, continued to put a damper on the building of airships. (In other respects he was a great supporter of naval air power.) In February 1915 he ordered the suspension of work on the one rigid under construction, *No. 9*, on which progress had been very slow. (She belonged

---

[4] 'The Uses of Airships for the Navy (British)', 20 September 1917; Air Ministry Historical Branch. The same paper answered the criticism of the airship's vulnerability to aeroplane attack, with its consequent liability to catch fire, by stating that the Americans were about to supply Britain with helium, a non-inflammable gas, which would be used in place of hydrogen. Helium is, of course, an inert gas, but it is double the weight of hydrogen.

to a 1913 programme of two rigids and six non-rigids and semi-rigids, of which only *No. 9* and two non-rigids eventually joined the Navy.) As a partial set-off, in the spring of 1915 under Fisher's stimulus the Admiralty began to construct small fairly fast non-rigid airships for A/S patrol: the 'S.S.' (Submarine Scout) airships and the later improved versions, principally the 'Coastal', 'North Sea', and 'C-Star' ('Coastals' with a bigger and better envelope) classes. Of the more than 200 non-rigids constructed in 1914–18, 98 were in commission on 1 November 1918. 'Coastals', 27 of which were delivered to the Navy in 1916, were used as scouts with the Grand Fleet, working mainly from Scottish shore bases. They had a maximum speed of about 50 m.p.h. and a cruising endurance of twenty-four hours. Successful experiments in towing and refuelling a 'Coastal' by a light cruiser in May and September 1916 increased their possible range for A/S patrol or fleet reconnaissance. Further trials from March 1917 'were successful, but they made it clear that a towed airship was difficult to control and that the consequent strain on the airship crew was high. It was therefore decided that when "Coastals" were required for work in co-operation with the fleet, they should be flown out and taken in tow for refuelling as necessary, but that towing for other reasons should not be undertaken.'[5] Despite this advance, the serious disadvantages inherent in all the non-rigid airships if used with the Fleet remained. They lacked the necessary strength and range to work effectively with the Fleet as scouts and they were no match for Zeppelins in speed or armament. The main work of the non-rigids was patrol in search of minefields and U-boats, and in convoy escort.

Towed kite balloons (non-rigids), which were gradually introduced into capital ships, then light cruisers, and destroyers and other small craft, in 1916, were useful for spotting the fall of shot and observing enemy movements. They proved no answer, however, to the reconnaissance problem, as Beatty for long hoped they would. They were difficult to manœuvre, were liable to break away in squally weather, and they revealed the presence of British ships to enemy submarines and surface craft.

[5] Walter Raleigh and H. A. Jones, *History of the Great War. The War in the Air* (London, 1922–37, 6 vols. and a volume of Appendices, all but vol. i by Jones), iv. 42. The 'North Sea' airships were also used with the Grand Fleet, though not very successfully.

Rigid airship prospects had brightened when Balfour, an air enthusiast, succeeded Churchill at the Admiralty in May 1915. In August 1915 the new Board of Admiralty ordered *No. 9* to be recommenced and three rigids of an improved class to be built—what came to be the '23' class. Progress was slow: the three '23s' were ordered in October 1915; and five more in January 1916, of which only one was completed. There was a misreading of the work of the Zeppelins in the three most important naval actions of 1916. 'It is,' asserted the Admiralty airship paper already quoted, 'no small achievement for their Zeppelins to have saved the High Sea Fleet at the Battle of Jutland, to have saved their Cruiser Squadron on the Yarmouth [Lowestoft] raid, and to have been instrumental in sinking the *Nottingham* and *Falmouth* [19 August 1916]. Had the positions been reversed in the Jutland Battle, and had we had Rigids to enable us to locate and annihilate the German High Sea Fleet, can anyone deny the far-reaching effects it would have had in ending the war?' The Zeppelins had been responsible for none of these achievements. But the myths of 1916 did quicken interest in rigids.

Then, on the night of 23–24 September 1916, the Zeppelin *L33*, a six-engine ship, made a forced landing in Essex. Study of her design proved a shocker for the airship constructors at the Admiralty. It was all too clear that the *No. 9* was woefully outdated and the '23' and '23X' classes not comparable. (The designs of the latter, improved '23s', had been approved in June.) The *No. 9*— the first British rigid to be completed—did not fly until 27 November 1916, and then it had to be returned to the makers for changes and was not operational until April 1917. Used occasionally for training flights and patrolling in 1917, she then lay idle and was finally deleted in June 1918. The Admiralty did proceed with the '23' class. Four were commissioned in the autumn of 1917: *No. 23*, *No. 24*, *No. 25*, and *R26*, the first airship to have the prefix 'R'. As direct consequences of the study of *L33*, however, the Admiralty in January 1917 cancelled two 23X-class ships that had not yet been laid down (the other two were completed in June 1918: *R27* and *R29*, the latter the only rigid to engage a U-boat, attacking three of them and helping to sink two), and copied the *L33* design for the new 33-class. The Admiralty eventually proposed (August 1917) to build sixteen '33s'. Since their size cut shed capacity in half, the War Cabinet would only authorize eleven. In the end, only two were completed: *R33* and *R34*, the first really successful British rigids; but they were not ready for service until March 1919. (In July 1919, *R34* made the first airship crossing of the Atlantic.) There were also the two wooden rigids of the '31' class: the *R31*, commissioned as the war was ending, and the *R32*, commissioned in September 1919.

At the Armistice the Navy did not possess a single rigid capable of long-range reconnaissance. A mere five rigids were in service, and four of these (the '23s') were only suitable for training and experiment, though occasionally used for escorting convoys. The two '23X' (*R27*, *R29*) and the *R31* could have been useful to Beatty as scouting airships capable of accompanying the Grand Fleet during sweeps, though not up to the standard of the latest Zeppelins. *R27*, however, was burned in August 1918, less than two months after commissioning, and *R31* was commissioned only five days before the Armistice and was in damaged condition when the war ended. The Grand Fleet had to rely, so far as airships were concerned, on the *R29* and 'Coastal' non-rigids, and the latter, as pointed out, lacked the radius of action for really useful fleet work.

By comparison, the High Seas Fleet had eight rigid airships when the war ended, despite the heavy mortality. (70 had been built.) Equally revealing is a comparison between the British best and the German best in service before the war ended. The *R31* had a service ceiling of 9,500 feet, a maximum speed of $65\frac{1}{2}$ m.p.h., and a maximum range of 2,215 miles. The *L53*, the standard German type in the North Sea during most of the last year of the war, had a ceiling of better than 20,000 feet, a (trial) speed of 66 m.p.h., and a maximum range of 3,000 miles.

The fact is that the Admiralty never had a rigid-airship policy during the war, but 'merely', as J. D. Scott puts it, 'a series of reactions to German successes'. The products of these reactions, copying, more or less, successful Zeppelin designs, were obsolescent by the time they flew. An authority on the saga of the British airships has analysed the reasons for the weak airship policy:

The reason why the Royal Navy had so few rigid airships in commission at the time of the Armistice was that policy and design underwent constant refinements. This left the manufacturers without consistent experience, reusable dies, jigs, and parts, and without a stable work force skilled in the mass-production of a standard design. *R26* of the 23-class was the only British rigid airship to be duplicated by the same builder, whereas the Zeppelin company commonly mass-produced classes . . . every new ship or group of vessels had to have Cabinet approval, and this provided further delay. It becomes apparent that the good old habit of muddling through had not been discarded, while at the same time the Rigid Airship Committee had made the perfectly understandable mistake of attempting to catch up with the Germans, rather than to gain sound experience and then leap ahead of them. But Sueter and the other pioneers were hamstrung by their memories of *Mayfly* and a consciousness that they were carrying the banner of a cause as well as a programme. One cannot but help feel sorry for them in their constant dilemmas.[6]

As it happens, the Royal Navy, like the High Seas Fleet, had an exaggerated opinion of the value of rigid airships as scouts for the Fleet. Their inability to navigate with any accuracy, and storm, fog, and low-cloud conditions, so common in the North Sea, reduced their effectiveness considerably. And yet, as an astute historian of the Zeppelin reminds us, 'The indispensability of the airship as an aerial scout in the early days of aviation is generally conceded. With low-powered and unreliable motors, the aeroplane could not lift from the ground enough fuel to fly for extended periods. Using its engines only for forward motion, the airship, supported in the air by buoyant gas, could carry quantities of fuel and, cruising with engines throttled back, had an endurance of several days.'[7] This was no longer the case by the last year or so of the war, when the development of heavier-than-air craft surpassed the performance of the airship.

Although Beatty never let up in his efforts to speed up the supply of long-range airships to the Grand Fleet, in 1917–18 he turned increasingly to ship-borne aircraft for the solution of both his reconnaissance and Zeppelin problems. It was the latter, the activities of the Zeppelins in reconnaissance over the North Sea, which threatened to nullify the effectiveness of his endeavours to bring the High Seas Fleet to action by eliminating the possibility of surprise, that now made the development of ship-borne aircraft an urgent requirement. (Note that the Grand Fleet never feared

---

[6] Robin Higham, *The British Rigid Airship, 1908–1931* (London, 1961), pp. 146–7. Cf. the contrasting German methods in building Zeppelins, *ibid.*, p. 147. The *Mayfly* was a large experimental airship, which owing to structural weaknesses had her back broken by a strong cross wind (September 1911) when she was being hauled out of the shed for her maiden flight.

[7] Douglas H. Robinson, *The Zeppelin in Combat* (London, 1962), p. 348.

a Zeppelin attack. The officers rather thought them, and the little bombs they carried, funny.) Since the Zeppelins navigated by making their call signs so that the D.F. (direction-finding) stations could send them their position, 'Room 40', the Admiralty's secret intelligence section, was able to plot them from the time they rose out of their sheds until they were back in their sheds. There was, therefore, ample warning in the Grand Fleet of their arrival. Warship guns could not expect to drive off the Zeppelins, since the latter would rise far out of gun range. What were needed were aircraft that could be depended upon to climb above a reconnoitring Zeppelin.

2. THE EVOLUTION OF THE CARRIER

Two important pre-war events pointed the way to the development of another new dimension in naval air warfare. Immediately responsible for both was Lieutenant C. R. Samson, described by Vice-Admiral Richard Bell Davies as 'the best known naval pilot of those early days, a very strong personality . . . his performance in the air together with his truculent, black-bearded, piratical appearance combined to make him good copy . . .' On 10 January 1912 Samson made the first successful flight off the deck of a ship when he flew a Short modified 'S27' biplane fitted with flotation bags (a forerunner to the seaplane proper) off an improvised launching platform on the battleship *Africa*, at anchor off Sheerness, and safely landed in the sea. The first British flight from a ship when under way occurred on 2 May 1912, when Samson flew a Short modified 'S27' from the battleship *Hibernia* off Portland. These experiments demonstrated the possibility of flying off a ship that was either stationary or under way, so long as it faced into the wind. But it was evident that a solution had, first of all, to be found to the problem of carrying air scouts in surface craft without impairing their efficiency as fighting ships.

The answer at first appeared to be in the provision of efficient aircraft carriers—ships able to carry seaplanes or aeroplanes and to keep station with the battle fleet or the Battle Cruiser Fleet. Because the seaplane was at first regarded as the most suitable naval scout—it was able to take off from, and alight on, the sea— the first carriers were seaplane carriers. In May 1913 Jellicoe had a flying-off platform fitted on the forecastle of the old cruiser *Hermes*, from which, on 28 July, a Caudron amphibian 'G.III' flew off in the naval manœuvres and was hoisted inboard. In these manœuvres a Short seaplane was hoisted in and out of the *Hermes* and successfully launched from the water on several occasions when the heavy swell permitted. The *Hermes* was paid off at the end of 1913. When war broke out, the Royal Navy was without a single carrier. The *Hermes* was quickly fitted with a launching deck for aeroplanes and recommissioned, but she was torpedoed by a submarine in the Straits of Dover on 31 October 1914. The Admiralty commandeered three cross-Channel steamers on 11 August and rapidly fitted them out as pure seaplane carriers: the *Empress*, *Riviera*, and *Engadine*, with improvised hangars to accommodate four seaplanes, but without a flight deck. These three small carriers, each carrying three Short seaplanes, launched seven of them in the well-known raid of Christmas Day, 1914, which did minor damage to the German dockyards at Cuxhaven. (They had not located the Zeppelin sheds, their primary objective.) These and other early seaplane carriers were unsuited for duty with the Grand Fleet, being severely handicapped by their inability to keep station with the fleet. The principal difficulty was that, lacking take-off facilities, they had to stop when hoisting their seaplanes over the side (they took off from the sea) or picking them up. When loaded with bombs, the seaplanes could only get off in a calm sea because of the fragility of their floats. All Jellicoe's experiments with seaplanes in the first year of the war showed that 'the chances are about a hundred to one against it being suitable for them to rise from the water'.[8] Their performances in six operations during 1915 against Zeppelin bases (they were transported in light cruisers or carriers) were exercises in futility, as they proved themselves unable to operate in the open sea.

A short forward flying-off deck was added in the second generation of seaplane carriers: the redesigned cargo steamer *Ark Royal* (commissioned in December 1914, the first vessel to be fitted out exclusively as a seaplane carrier), the 20,000-ton ex-Cunarder *Campania* (April 1915), the ex-Isle of Man steamers *Vindex* (September 1915) and *Manxman* (December 1916). However, this deck was not much used for flying-off and never for landing, as the seaplanes ordinarily took off from the water.

On 11 June 1915, for the first time in history, planes scouted with a fleet at sea. Seaplanes, working with the *Campania* in Grand

[8] Jellicoe to Beatty, 7 August 1915; Beatty MSS.

Fleet exercises, observed the movements of the 'hostile fleet'. The C.-in-C. concentrated on the effort to have the *Campania*'s seaplanes rise from the deck. (She had a 120-foot flying-off deck stretching from the navigating bridge to the bows.) The seaplanes would then alight on the sea and have their crews rescued. On 6 August 1915 a successful experiment of this theory was made. A Sopwith 'Baby' seaplane, her floats resting on wheeled carriages which fell into the sea when the seaplane was airborne, was flown off the deck of the *Campania* while she was steaming into the wind at 17 knots. (This was followed by the first landplane take-off: a Bristol 'Scout' from the deck of the *Vindex* on 3 November 1915.)

The seaplane reconnaissance flight made from the *Engadine* in the Jutland daylight action, 31 May 1916, though it achieved nothing remarkable, stimulated interest in new carrier construction. The *Argus* and the converted *Furious* were immediate results. (See below.)

Experience proved that aeroplanes were preferable to seaplanes for fleet use, having a greater speed, superior climb, and higher ceiling, and, fitted with airbags, being safer on the water than were the Sopwith 'Baby' seaplanes. Jellicoe was pressing for aeroplanes in carriers as early as August 1915. By the end of 1916 the Admiralty were convinced of the marked superiority of aeroplanes to seaplanes in performance. Aeroplanes generally replaced seaplanes for ship use throughout the Grand Fleet in 1917–18.

A major flying problem had yet to be solved. Whereas aeroplanes could take off quite easily from catapults and short platforms, the strong upcurrent of air directly behind the superstructure of a ship made attempts to alight on the afterdeck uncertain and hazardous. The only practicable way to get back to the ship was to fit flotation bags beside the landing wheels and to land alongside in the water and be recovered quickly. But the planes often sank before they could be hoisted aboard. The solution, which proved much more difficult than the problem of launching aircraft, became pressing in 1917, when the Admiralty became so anxious about the capabilities of the new Zeppelins.

The Senior Flying Officer of one of 'Fisher's Follies', the converted light battle cruiser *Furious*,[9] was Squadron-Commander

---

[9] In the spring of 1917, when she was completing, her forward 18-inch turret was removed and a hangar installed whose top was extended to the ship's bow to form a flying-off deck 228 feet long and 50 feet wide. She was commissioned in July 1917.

E. H. Dunning, one of the ablest pilots in the Service. He thought that he had the answer. 'He reasoned that if a [Sopwith] Pup could be flown at thirty to thirty-five knots, then it should be possible to come in and sit over the flying-off deck while the ship was steaming to produce this air-speed. There would be no relative movement between the plane and ship. On touching down it would be seized and held by a ground crew.'[10] There were no arrester devices at this period. Dunning made history on 2 August 1917 by skilfully manœuvring his 'Pup' round the superstructure and funnel of the *Furious* while she was under way in Scapa Flow and making a successful landing on the carrier's flight deck. A fellow air pioneer had written to Dunning at the time that 'it was a fine show as a stunt and had proved it could be done by an expert pilot, but what we wanted was a flush-deck carrier to make it a practicable proposition. I concluded by hoping that he would not try it again, but alas! he did so five days later.'[11] When Dunning came in on this occasion, a stalled engine brought the plane down heavily on its starboard wheel, its tyre burst, and the plane cartwheeled over the starboard side into the sea. The gallant Dunning was drowned—a great loss.

Flight-Commander Rutland, who succeeded Dunning in command of the air squadron in the *Furious*, gave up these deck-landing trials in favour of a quite different approach. This persistent, outspoken, self-confident young pilot, who, his biographer tells us, 'liked to be the first to try out any new idea', pushed hard for a flush deck in the carrier, that is, one totally clear—a flying deck along the full length of a ship. This would have converted the *Furious* from a half-carrier, half-battle cruiser hybrid (she still retained a single 18-inch gun in her stern) into a full-fledged carrier. Her Captain (Wilmot Nicholson), to say nothing of Beatty, wanted to preserve her remaining gun armament so as to keep her a fighting ship in part at least. The future lay with the flush-deck carrier, which gave the best conditions for landing on: a continuous flight deck was necessary to obtain smooth air flow, so vital for safe landings. But such a deck would have interfered with the ship's guns. Rutland had to be satisfied with a compromise. The *Furious* was sent to the builders in November 1917 for the removal of her after 18-inch turret and the installation of a 284-foot long, 70-foot

[10] Desmond Young, *Rutland of Jutland* (London, 1963), p. 59.
[11] Air Chief Marshal Sir Arthur Longmore, *From Sea to Sky* (London, 1946), p. 69.

wide landing deck above the quarter-deck and various devices for slowing down a plane (none of them satisfactory), including longitudinal wire cables, on to which a hook beneath the plane's fuselage was meant to catch. The altered *Furious* rejoined the Grand Fleet in March 1918. She was not a success, as the air currents set up by the funnels and superstructure when the ship was steaming at high speed made landings extremely dangerous. All but three of the trial landings ended in a crash. There was nothing for it but to abandon the landing-on attempts, and for the last months of the war aircraft only flew *off* the *Furious*. She was, nevertheless, the one carrier to launch a major air action in the war. On 19 July 1918, seven Sopwith 'Camels' (fighter aeroplanes) flew off the carrier to bomb the Zeppelin sheds at Tondern in Schleswig-Holstein. They set one of the large sheds on fire, and one of the aircraft, piloted by Captain B. A. Smart, destroyed two Zeppelins, *L54* and *L60*, in another shed. The success of the raid seems to have awakened the Sea Lords, albeit a little late in the day, to the potentialities of air power as no other event or development had.

The unsatisfactory experience of the *Furious* led to the first carrier with a flush flying-deck stem to stern, the first in which both take-off and landing-on were practicable. The principle was introduced into the Italian liner *Conte Rosso*, which had been purchased in August 1916, when still on the stocks, and reconstructed from the waterline up as the first real carrier, the *Argus* (15,750 tons), with a flight deck 550 feet long and 68 feet wide. Beatty expected to have her by the end of 1917; she was not launched until December 1917 and was not ready for service when the war ended. Neither were the *Eagle* and the new *Hermes* ready at the Armistice. The *Eagle*, formerly the battleship *Almirante Cochrane*, building for Chile at Armstrong's, was taken over in July 1917 and launched in June 1918. She was the first 'island' carrier (26,400 tons): funnels and superstructure moved to one side of the deck, forming a streamlined island and leaving a full-length flying deck. She did not join the Fleet until 1922. Also an island-type carrier, the new *Hermes* (12,900 tons) was the world's first vessel designed and built from the keel up as an aircraft carrier. Laid down in July 1917, she was not in commission until 1923. Completed in August and September 1917 were the *Pegasus* and *Nairana*, small converted merchant vessels provided with a flying-off deck forward.

Finally, commissioned only in October 1918, was the *Vindictive* (10,000 tons), the ex-light cruiser *Cavendish*, which was converted into a carrier in *Furious* style, with a flying-off deck forward and a landing deck aft of the superstructure. Although considerable problems remained—island versus flush-deck type of carrier and how to 'arrest' a landed aircraft—the first stage of the carrier's evolution was complete and the bright future of carrier-borne air power was assured.[12]

The sad fact remains that the Grand Fleet did not have a single effective aircraft carrier while hostilities were on—a situation closely paralleling that in rigid airships. None of the six carriers attached to the Grand Fleet in 1917–18 could be called efficient. Reconnaissance planes could be flown off the *Campania* only in smooth water; the restricted radius of action of, and lack of speed in, the *Manxman*—she could barely do 17 knots—made it unlikely that she would be present with the Fleet during an action; the *Engadine* had no launching platform and was not reliable except in a fairly calm sea. By the spring of 1918, the *Campania* had been relegated mainly to training duties, and the *Engadine* and *Manxman* were operating in the Mediterranean. That left the fast carriers *Furious*, *Pegasus*, and *Nairana* with the Grand Fleet. The first-named had her troubles, and the latter two were mainly used for training pilots in deck-flying for service in light and battle cruisers. They were unsuitable for work with the Grand Fleet, not being fast enough.

One other method was developed of using aircraft at sea: flying them off from the decks of small lighters towed at high speeds by a destroyer. The original purpose was to transport flying boats across the North Sea in order to increase their radius of action in the Heligoland Bight. It was discovered in 1918 that lighters

---

12 Flight-Commander H. A. Williamson had in the summer of 1915 submitted the design for an 'island'-type carrier. (What he had in mind was the conversion of an ocean-going liner.) The idea was too revolutionary for the time, and Sueter was persuaded to accept the *Argus* design—the flush-deck type of carrier—in 1916. Williamson is confident that 'had the proposal been adopted and production turned over to a man with the drive displayed by Beaverbrook in the 1939–45 war, we should have had a practical carrier in 1916. Then all the protracted tests of flying off, and on to, a carrier would have been unnecessary.' Group Captain H. A. Williamson's memorandum of 22 July 1968 for the author. The *Hermes* was designed very much as Williamson had proposed; but this came late in the war. The island-type carrier design was eventually adopted by all navies. For giving the Admiralty this design for carriers Williamson received a handsome official award of £500!

could also be used with 30-foot-long take-off platforms for launching single-seater fighters. Flight-Lieutenant S. D. Culley made the first successful take-off, in a Sopwith 'Camel', on 31 July 1918. Repeating this technique on 11 August, during a sweep by the Harwich Force in the waters north of Terschelling, he destroyed the Zeppelin *L53*. As the squadron, after a suspenseful wait of an hour, saw in the far distance a light high up in the east descending rapidly, with a trail of smoke behind—obviously the Zeppelin—Tyrwhitt (commanding the Harwich Force) signalled the ships: 'Your attention is called to Hymn No. 224, Verse 7' (*Hymns Ancient and Modern*). This verse reads:

> Oh happy band of pilgrims,
> Look upward to the skies,
> Where such a light affliction
> Shall win so great a prize.

If the future of naval aviation lay in the evolution of the aircraft carrier, the most important development in the last year of the war was the provision of aircraft in fighting ships (battle cruisers, light cruisers). Early in 1918 Beatty realistically observed that 'if aircraft were not carried in fighting ships there would usually be none available with the fleet in present circumstances, owing to the lack of speed of the carriers hitherto provided. It remains to be seen how far it will be affected by the completion of *Furious* and *Cavendish*. The probable tendency of the future will be towards increasing the demand for machines with the fleet.'[13] This prediction was about to come true.

One of the recommendations (5 February 1917) of the Grand Fleet Aircraft Committee set up by Beatty in January 1917 was that some of the light cruisers be provided with their own aeroplanes for anti-Zeppelin use. The Committee arranged for aeroplane experiments to be made in the light cruiser *Yarmouth*, which was fitted with an extemporized 20-foot platform over her conning tower and forward gun. In June 1917 the indefatigable Rutland made the first of his three historic flights when he successfully flew a Sopwith 'Pup' off this platform when the ship was at sea. Two months later, Flight Sub-Lieutenant B. A. Smart took off in a 'Pup' from the *Yarmouth* (operating with the 1st Light Cruiser Squadron, which was covering a minelaying operation off the

[13] Minute of 5 February 1918; Admiralty MSS.

Danish coast) and shot down the Zeppelin *L23*. Smart alighted on the sea; he was picked up, but it was too risky in those U-boat infested waters to attempt to salve the aeroplane.

These successes resulted in the fitting of the *Yarmouth* type of platform to every light cruiser that could take it. The C.-in-C. refused to have planes carried in battleships and battle cruisers. He dreaded the prospect of having to turn his capital ships head to wind to fly-off their aeroplanes when an action was imminent, since the ships would have to break station with the fleet. This indeed was the fundamental drawback of flying planes from any type of ship, aircraft carrier or fighting ship. Rutland worked out a solution. Undeterred by the fears of his pilots and of the flying officers at the Admiralty, who were certain that he was courting suicide, he scored another first. On 1 October 1917 he flew a 'Pup' off a platform mounted on the 15-inch fore gun-turret of the battle cruiser *Repulse*. Whereas the original platforms had been fixed, this one was on a turntable, which device enabled the 'Pup' to be launched into the wind without any change in the ship's course. (The idea must be credited to the Gunnery Officer of the *Yarmouth*, Lieutenant-Commander C. H. B. Gowan.) On 9 October, again without mishap, Rutland flew off a platform that had been installed on the after turret. There were two advantages: the superstructure forward of the turret afforded the plane some protection, and the ship could carry *two* planes. On 4 April 1918, Captain F. M. Fox, R.A.F., successfully flew a Sopwith '1½-Strutter' off a turret platform in the battle cruiser *Australia*, demonstrating that the system could accommodate two-seater aeroplanes.

The turntable system made it possible for aeroplanes to fly off a ship without affecting the ship's course and without unduly interfering with the turret guns. The latter consideration meant the preservation of the full gun armament of any ship that adopted the system, and this helped to convert the 'gun-conscious objectors' to ship-borne aircraft.

It is no exaggeration [writes Rutland's biographer] to say that these three experimental flights by Rutland—flying off the short twenty-foot platform in *Yarmouth*, flying off the fore turret in *Repulse* and then flying off the after turret—coupled with the success of his persistent advocacy of aeroplanes against seaplanes—revolutionized the fleet aircraft policy of the day.

In due course every capital ship carried two aircraft—one a fighter [a single-seater aeroplane on the after turret platform for attacks on Zeppelins], the other for reconnaissance [a two-seater aeroplane on the forward turret platform]—the Commander-in-Chief accepted them as part of the Fleet's normal equipment and their employment became an integral part of Fleet battle orders. It was a remarkable advance in the short time since the Battle of Jutland, when *Engadine* was left to hobble behind and *Campania* was forgotten in harbour.[14]

Turntable platforms were also designed for light cruisers. By the end of the war the ship-carried aeroplane had come into its own: Grand Fleet ships (other than carriers) fitted with flying-off platforms, including twenty-two light cruisers, were carrying over a hundred aircraft. Armed with bombs, they had both defensive and offensive capabilities. Already, by the spring of 1918, the crack Sopwith 2F.1 'Camel' fighting aeroplane with which the battle cruisers and light cruisers, as well as the carriers, were equipped had largely reduced the usefulness of the Zeppelins, few of which now ventured out of sight of their own coast. German seaplanes were unable to take over the Zeppelin's distant reconnaissance duties: they could not stand up to the 'Camels'. We should also note the great development in 1917–18 of the flying-boat, a long-range seaplane, which played a useful role in reconnaissance (especially of the mined areas in the southern part of the North Sea) and as a U-boat killer.

Gone, then, by the spring of 1918 was the German command of the air in the North Sea. The immediate practical benefit to the Grand Fleet was that it had no longer to face the possibility of a Zeppelin reconnaissance that might enable enemy minelayers to sow the path of the Fleet with mines.[15] Also, the Grand Fleet now had a much better chance to surprise the High Seas Fleet if it should venture far from its bases. Finally, Beatty could count on air superiority in any North Sea naval operations not within effective range of German shore-based aircraft. This pleasant prospect

---

[14] Young, *Rutland of Jutland*, p. 55. Planes carried in individual ships landed ashore or, if too far out, just flopped down alongside a destroyer and hoped to be salvaged.

[15] The idea that minelaying directed by Zeppelins in the open sea was a serious danger seems to have been something of an obsession. The Zeppelins doing 60 knots might find the Grand Fleet, but the minelayers could not keep company with them, so to speak. The Grand Fleet attitude might have stemmed from the loss of the *Audacious* in 1914 and an unrealistic idea of how much water minelayers could cover at short notice. They ought to have thrown off this fear of mines by 1917–18, particularly now that the whole fleet was equipped with paravanes. But no doubt it was nice to feel as safe as possible.

sharpened his desire for an aggressive strategy, as did the prospect of an effective torpedo-carrying plane in the last year of the war.

3. EVOLUTION OF THE TORPEDO PLANE

Speaking broadly, three types of naval aircraft had become recognized by 1918: reconnaissance (and A/S patrol), fighter, and torpedo planes. The dominant type of reconnaissance plane prior to 1917 was the seaplane. (Originally known as 'hydro-aeroplanes', they were rechristened by Churchill in 1913. 'That's a beastly word,' Flight-Commander R. B. Davies heard him say. 'Let's give them a better name; let's call them seaplanes.') It was replaced, beginning in the spring of 1916, by the two-seater '1½-Strutter' aeroplane, which was employed from carriers and battle cruisers. The two-seater version had a maximum speed of 106 m.p.h. and a service ceiling of 13,000 feet. Fighter aeroplanes had as their principal duty the interception of enemy aircraft. Fighters were hardly used with the Fleet until it began to get the single-seater Sopwith 'Pup' in the last months of 1916. The more powerful and faster single-seater Sopwith 'Camel 2F.1' (124 m.p.h. maximum speed, ceiling, 17,300 feet), which began to join the Fleet in large numbers in the early summer of 1917, largely superseded the 'Pups'. They were flown from both carriers and fighting ships and their main function was the interception of Zeppelins.[16] The torpedo plane, which was intended to be used with carriers, merits a more extended discussion because of the Navy's great expectations of this machine.

As early as 1912 the pioneers of naval aviation recognized that the torpedo, which could hit its target below the water line, had vast offensive potentialities if it could be carried and launched by swift aircraft. Experiments in dropping torpedoes from aircraft began in 1913. In the lead was an officer of enthusiasm and energy, and full of ideas, who got the maximum of loyalty from all

[16] The one success of warships against Zeppelins was on 4 May 1916: the light cruisers *Galatea* and *Phaeton*, assisted by the submarine *E-31*, brought down the *L7* ten miles south of Horns Reef. The R.N.A.S. accounted for 7 Zeppelins; the R.F.C., 5; R.A.F. (from 1 April 1918), 4; A/A gunfire, 4. Total attributable to British action: 21. The Germans lost six others not attributable to English action, but directly or indirectly as a result of raids on England. Of the R.N.A.S. total, ship-borne aircraft accounted for three—a Sopwith 'Pup' from the *Yarmouth* on 21 August 1917, and two from the *Furious* in the Tondern attack of 19 July 1918.

who worked under him—Captain Murray F. Sueter (successively Director of Air Department and Superintendent of Aircraft Construction at the Admiralty, 1914–16). He is the 'Father' of British naval aviation, if anyone deserves that title. Unfortunately, like another maverick in the Navy, Herbert Richmond, Sueter's intolerance of the views of others often hurt his cause. On 28 July 1914, at Calshot (one of the early naval air stations, at the entrance to Southampton Water), Squadron-Commander A. M. Longmore, responding to a challenge by Churchill, made the first successful torpedo drop from the air in a Short seaplane. Sueter was now convinced that torpedo-dropping aircraft were 'a practical proposition'. In the spring of 1915 he secured Admiralty approval to send a flight of Short '184s', torpedo-carrying seaplanes of 225 h.p. (later known as Short '225s') to the Dardanelles in the makeshift carrier *Ben-My-Chree* to test them against surface vessels. On 12 and 17 August 1915 two of the seaplanes, launched from the sea, made three attacks, each with a 14-inch torpedo of 1,000-yard range slung under its fuselage. They took off from the carrier, flew in low against the land to avoid detection, attacked under fire, and torpedoed and sank three Turkish ships at anchor (a merchantman, a tug, and an ammunition ship). This was the first time that torpedo-carrying aircraft had been used successfully in war. The gallant pilots (Flight-Commander C. H. K. Edmonds and Flight-Lieutenant G. B. Dacre) showed the Navy that such aircraft could be developed into a weapon of great range and power.

Despite this exploit, and the belief of air enthusiasts like Sueter that Jutland might have had a quite different outcome had torpedo planes been present and succeeded in reducing the speed of the High Seas Fleet (the Admiralty had turned down his proposal at the end of 1915 that 200 torpedo planes be built), the development of torpedo craft was slow. This is not surprising, considering the difficulties and uncertainties. The basic technical difficulty was that until 1917 the R.N.A.S. used only seaplanes as torpedo-carriers. Experience demonstrated that the Short '225', carrying a 14-inch torpedo, would often not rise in the North Sea. The 14-inch torpedo, moreover, was not regarded as effective against larger warships. A torpedo seaplane of much greater range and power was evolved in 1916: the Short 310-h.p. machine (increased to 320 h.p. when it went into production in 1917), capable of carrying an 18-inch torpedo of 1,000 lbs. and with a 2,000-yard range. This seaplane had (with torpedo) a maximum speed of 72½ m.p.h., a service ceiling of 3,000 feet, and a radius of 100 miles, which limited its utility. The first of two prototype machines carried out its trials in October 1916. The performance of the new type in practice attacks from Felixstowe (Harwich) was promising. During the last three months of 1916, out of twenty-one torpedo runs there were only five failures, two of which were due to small mechanical defects, two to the insufficient training of the pilots, and one to the torpedo being fired in too shallow water. The other sixteen ran well, four out of ten fired at ships actually hitting.

Sueter was, nevertheless, anxious to develop a torpedo-carrying aeroplane, capable of operation from a flying deck. He was at this time Superintendent of Aircraft Construction at the Admiralty. With the aid of T. O. M. Sopwith, the aircraft designer and manufacturer, in October 1916 he designed a plane for which he confidently predicted a great future: the 'Cuckoo', a 200-h.p., single-seater, carrier-borne (and, after the war, shore-based) torpedo-carrier (one 18-inch torpedo). With a service ceiling of 12,000 feet, a maximum speed of 103 m.p.h., and a radius of about 160 miles, its performance was far superior to the Short '225' and '320'.

Obviously, it would be some time before there would be sufficient torpedo landplanes available for large-scale operations. On 20 December 1916 Sueter proposed that a strong torpedo-seaplane force attack the German Fleet at Wilhelmshaven and the Austrian Fleet in its Adriatic harbours. For the first operation he would have the machines transported across the North Sea in a ship, or towed over on a lighter, to within striking distance. 'We know by experience that the weather must be very fine to enable a seaplane to get off in the open sea, but if the operation is timed in conjunction with the Admiralty weather forecasts no great difficulties are presented in Summer.' As regards the Austrian Fleet, there were 'enormous possibilities open to half a dozen torpedo-carrying seaplanes based near Rimini: Trieste, Pola, and Fiume would be within easy reach. . . . Immediate action is necessary if it is decided to tackle these two objectives next Summer.' The Admiralty liked Sueter's plan for an offensive use of torpedo seaplanes. They saw no great scope for torpedo planes used defensively, which only locked up a number of pilots and machines for the possible eventuality of enemy warship raids on the British coasts. The Third Sea

Lord (Tudor) made this recommendation: 'I see no reason why even eventually ships in German harbours should not be attacked but as a more immediate possibility, the Adriatic holds out greater hopes of success . . . orders for new Torpedo Seaplanes of the most advanced types should be placed forthwith, and that the Torpedo aeroplanes should be pushed on with vigorously.' The First Sea Lord (Jellicoe) approved this policy at the end of January 1917.[17] Orders went out early in February for 25 Short '320s', the immediate dispatch to the Mediterranean of eight Short '225s', and the establishment of a seaplane station at Otranto with Sueter in command. He was to prepare for the operation against the Austrian Fleet, relying upon Short '320s' when the machines and trained pilots were available. (The torpedo aircraft offensive planned against the Austrians took the form of an attack, 2 September 1917, on the submarines lying at Cattaro. It was a failure, as a sudden gale made the sea too rough for the six '320s' to take off. The operation was never repeated.)

With Sueter's departure for Italy official interest in the Sopwith 'Cuckoo' waned. Wing-Commander Longmore spotted the unfinished prototype during a visit to Sopwith's in February 1917. At his instigation the plane was completed in June. It passed its trials in July, and a hundred of these efficient machines were ordered. Additional orders, for a total of 350, were placed in 1918 in response to Beatty's appeal in September 1917 that 200 'Cuckoos' be put in hand forthwith and assigned to the Grand Fleet, and in anticipation of satisfactory trials of the aircraft carriers *Furious*, *Eagle*, and *Argus*. The C.-in-C. was to be grievously disappointed. In the first place, the torpedo plane was never popular with pilots because its great weight made it slower in manœuvre and hence more vulnerable. Again, the new R.A.F., its gaze fixed on the Western Front, had little interest in promoting torpedo aircraft, the successful experiments at Calshot in February 1918 notwithstanding. (On that occasion four Short '320s' had released 40

[17] Sueter's paper and the Admiralty minutes are in a docket entitled 'Policy to be Followed as Regards Development and Use of Torpedo Carrying Seaplanes'; Admiralty MSS. Strangely, only Rear-Admiral C. L. Vaughan-Lee, the mediocre Director of Air Services, who was not an airman himself, was cool to the idea of using torpedo planes offensively. He claimed that it was 'one thing to torpedo a comparatively unarmed vessel and quite a different matter to torpedo a fast ship under weigh with guns manned, particularly when it is borne in mind that the seaplane has to descend within a few feet of the water . . .'

torpedoes fitted with dummy heads. Only three were lost.) For Beatty the crusher was the serious delays resulting from the award of the bulk of the 'Cuckoo' orders to inexperienced firms. The first of them were not delivered until May 1918; at the Armistice only 90 were in service. Unhappily, existing carriers lacked the space for the storage of torpedo-carrying aeroplanes, unless they sacrificed some of their reconnaissance and fighting machines. The first carrier from which these planes could operate, the flush-deck *Argus*, did not begin her trials until October 1918. A squadron of 18 'Cuckoos', the first torpedo-carrying aeroplanes in a carrier, was embarked in the *Argus* on 19 October. Since she was not in service until after the Armistice, the war ended before the 'Cuckoos' could be used operationally and the Navy could demonstrate the offensive power of torpedo attacks made by aircraft.

In 1917–18 naval aviation was in its infancy; yet the Royal Navy was responsible for the first torpedo drop and the first aircraft carrier. The employment of aircraft in naval operations was largely confined to use in defensive air combat, in reconnaissance, and in convoy escort. If the development of maritime air power was not more spectacular, it was due, first, to the technical difficulties the pioneers faced in having to solve problems without precedent, and that while a war was on (with the subsequent developments in aircraft, we are apt to forget how near 1914–18 was to the beginning of flying); second, to the excessive Admiralty concern with non-naval aspects of air warfare, of which a conspicuous instance was the establishment in 1916–17 of an R.N.A.S. wing in France to participate in the bombing of Germany; third, to the cramping influences displayed by anti-airminded senior naval officers and, particularly in the first two years and more of the war, by the Sea Lords of the Admiralty and the War Staff. Admiral Sueter's *Airmen or Noahs* brings out clearly the lengths to which the naval authorities went in order to block naval air development. Admiral Mark Kerr remembered one Lord of the Admiralty having 'observed that four lieutenants had been taken from the Navy for the Royal Air Service, and that was four too many . . .'[18] Such 'blimps' were the exception, yet there can be no denying the lack of vision in higher naval circles. I have no doubt, moreover, that this anti-air policy was a factor in the decision to form the R.A.F. in April 1918.

[18] *Land, Sea, and Air : Reminiscences of Mark Kerr* (London, 1927), p. 281.

Squadron-Commander Douglas Hyde-Thomson's poem, written in 1917, reflects the mood of many of the R.N.A.S. officers. It begins:

The Navy is our Father (in the strictly legal sense
That binds an obligation just of shillings, pounds and pence)
A parent so neglectful of us children of the Air,
That had not hope maintained us we'd have died of sheer despair,
For our Father didn't want us and he didn't want to know
What it was we wanted or the way, the why or wherefore . . .

Those were the days in which an R.N.A.S. officer described the senior Admirals as being 'solid ivory from the jaws up, except for a little hole from ear to ear to let useful knowledge go in and out'.

Only the most farsighted and enthusiastic officers were alive to the possibilities of naval aviation—pioneers like Sueter, Samson, Williamson, Rutland, Dunning, Longmore, Clarke-Hall, and some of the senior officers, Beatty, Phillimore (Rear-Admiral, Aircraft Carriers), and Richmond, for example. But apart from the gunnery officers, who were interested in the Fleet air arm because by the end of the war the Navy had evolved an effective system of air spotting for naval gunfire, the average naval officer was not concerned or interested. Generally speaking, the Navy regarded aeroplanes as of uncertain value owing to their limited range and the inexperience of the pilots—mostly young men with little or no knowledge of ships and the sea. Nor did they appreciate the potential in the aircraft carrier. The first true ones, we must remember, were not ready until after the war. Finally, there was a psychological factor that influenced some officers at least and was but a reflection of the Admiralty contempt for the air: 'the dislike of blue water sailors for the noisy and smelly machines which desecrated the decks and paintwork of the ships—and for the unconventional and outspoken young men who flew them'.[19]

Beatty, despite all the delays and disappointments that hampered the development of naval air power, had the vision to assign a prominent role to aircraft and aircraft carriers in his strategic and tactical thinking when C.-in-C., Grand Fleet. This will help to explain the revived Grand Fleet interest in, and optimism about, a more aggressive strategy and tactics in 1917–18.

[19] Captain S. W. Roskill, 'The Role of Maritime Forces: Lessons of World War I and II', an unpublished lecture of March 1960 at the Imperial Defence College.

II

The Grand Fleet under Beatty

The Grand Fleet is the centre and pivot on which all naval operations depend. It is true that its activity is confined to the North Sea, but on its very existence depends the possibility of carrying out the all-important operation of safeguarding our lines of communications.

JELLICOE in a memorandum for the War Cabinet, 18 November 1917.

I pray, not for tranquillity nor that my tribulations may cease, but for opportunity and strength to overcome adversity and make use of opportunity when it comes. They always say opportunity makes the man, but what is more to the point is that man makes the opportunity, and that is where I am beat. I cannot see my way to make the opportunity.

BEATTY to Lady Beatty, 27 April 1917.

His [Beatty's] 2½ years' period of command [as C.-in-C., Grand Fleet] was not crowned by the great naval victory he expected, hoped for, and worked for, but during those 2½ long years of waiting and anxiety he maintained by his resolution, example, and wonderful personality the morale and efficiency of the Fleet at its highest state.

ADMIRAL OF THE FLEET SIR ERNLE CHATFIELD's letter in *The Times*, 13 March 1936.

I. BEATTY AS COMMANDER-IN-CHIEF

BEATTY had hoisted his flag in the *Iron Duke* as C.-in-C., Grand Fleet, on 29 November 1916. (He transferred it to the *Queen Elizabeth* in mid-February 1917.) His leading traits were, as ever, dash, a touch of swagger, and self-confidence. He welcomed suggestions from all his officers; he never resented any criticisms. Of his work habits, his biographer writes: 'He was an exceptionally quick thinker, and had the invaluable faculty of being able to pick out at a glance essential points in a paper and give the required decision. In consequence his "IN" basket was usually empty, but he had another basket labelled with an abbreviation for "Balderdash", to which he committed all ill-conceived schemes or excuses.'[1] Nor was he one to immerse himself in detail. The new

[1] Rear-Admiral William S. Chalmers, *The Life and Letters of David, Earl Beatty* (London, 1951), p. 205, writing of Beatty as C.-in-C., Battle Cruiser Fleet, but this passage applies equally well to the C.-in-C., Grand Fleet.

C.-in-C. quickly found himself staggering under an impossible work load, which seemed only to increase. 'There are so many questions which have been allowed to pass and they have accumulated to such an extent that it seems impossible to overtake them. The Augean stable will require an immense amount of cleaning, and I work up to 1.30 every morning.'[2] At first Beatty had difficulty keeping afloat in the ocean of paper that surrounded him. 'There seems at present to be such an enormous amount of time wasted on details which can be much better performed by others than by me and so free me for the more important things. I fancy the late C.-in-C. loved detail and messing about finicky things, and consequently the big questions got slurred over or overlooked altogether.'[3] Jellicoe did love detail. Beatty preferred to have his Secretary (Frank T. Spickernell) handle this aspect of his job, leaving him 'free for other things of greater importance'.

Beatty had to come to terms with two unpleasant situations. A long-standing one was his unfortunate marriage with a glamorous American millionairess, a neurotic woman of strong character. Lady Beatty thought her husband selfish because he was so wrapped up in his work and had so little time for her! Of course, there was only a war going on. Sir Shane Leslie, who knew the Beattys well, writes of her 'utterly unpredictable moods' and of how 'she trifled with the laws of marriage and thought nothing of it'. She 'tried her Lord beyond all that any other man would have stood'. The Admiral described certain nights with his wife as 'worse than Jutland'. He found it impossible to reason with her. Yet he would never contemplate divorce and he loved her and remained devoted to her until the end.[4] Officers who served under Beatty say that he never showed the least emotional stress and carried on his job with serenity and full concentration. But nobody who has examined the hundreds of wartime letters he wrote to her can doubt for a moment that he was engaged in a two-front war—with the High Seas Fleet in the North Sea, on the one hand, and with Lady Beatty at Aberdour, on the other—and that this must have imposed a very severe mental strain upon him which was all the more burdensome because he kept it locked up within himself. Paradoxically perhaps, it was a great relaxation for him to get away to their house at

[2] Beatty to Lady Beatty, 29 December 1916; Beatty MSS.
[3] Beatty to Lady Beatty, 5 December 1916; Beatty MSS.
[4] Leslie, *Long Shadows* (London, 1966), pp. 209-12.

Aberdour, seven miles outside Rosyth, with a view of the Firth. There he found relaxation in playing strenuous tennis and mixing with the company, mostly naval, that Lady Beatty had collected.

The other unpleasant situation was the long-standing mental gulf between the officers of the Grand Fleet proper, or main fleet, and the Battle Cruiser Fleet. (The latter became the Battle Cruiser Force on 28 November 1916.) The battle cruisers were based nearer the enemy, had fought three battles, and had most of the excitement that the war had provided. Indeed, the younger officers regarded the officers of the Grand Fleet at Scapa Flow with some pity. They felt that they had little to learn about close action from the Grand Fleet and could teach them a lot. Perhaps the younger officers in the Grand Fleet were a bit envious of the greater opportunities of the battle-cruiser men. To this mental gulf Jutland added a rift. Jellicoe and Beatty, like Nelson, had that remarkable gift for drawing utter loyalty and great affection from their juniors. When controversy over the battle began, the officers almost instinctively rallied round their Admiral. It is no small measure of Beatty's success as C.-in-C. that he greatly improved the relationship between the Grand Fleet and the Battle Cruiser Force. As the onetime Battle Cruiser Fleet Commander he was in an ideal position to bring about this change.

The changeover in the high command was smooth. This was partly due to the excellent organization that Jellicoe had bequeathed his successor, thanks to which Beatty exulted a week after taking over, 'Everything goes like a clock.' Even more important was Beatty's staff, which served him so well. That superb all-rounder, Ernle Chatfield, continued as his Flag-Captain, commanding the flagship and with a special responsibility for co-ordinating and standardizing Grand Fleet gunnery. The charming and popular 'Tommy' (the Hon. Hubert) Brand, with his boyish appearance, twinkling eyes, and high sense of humour, made a splendid Captain of the Fleet (in succession to Halsey), responsible for administration and supply. Approachable, tactful, and full of common sense, Brand served as an effective buffer between the C.-in-C. and visiting officers. He had a soothing influence on angry senior officers who came to the flagship with complaints for the C.-in-C. If not particularly brainy, he knew how to make the best of the brains and abilities of others of all grades. Beatty had an ideal complement in his Chief of Staff, the former commander of the 1st Battle Cruiser Squadron, the youthful-looking Rear-Admiral O. de B. Brock—brilliantly clever, erudite (he had a wealth of accurate, detailed knowledge on every kind of subject—art, poetry, philosophy, history, etc.), impatient, careless about his dress. He kept a library of classical books in his cabin, but devoured paperback thrillers in spare moments on the bridge. The C.-in-C. told this delightful story about the recently married Brock: 'I have had to send O. de B. down to London to attend a conference on my behalf. . . . When he departed, I said you had better telegraph to your Lady and she can meet you in London. He said, Oh no, he had lots of friends in London!! He certainly is a quaint soul. I am not sure that the lady won't repent herself for her bargain after all. I am very fond of O. de B., but I wouldn't marry him if I were a woman if there wasn't another man in the world.'[5] Beatty thoroughly appreciated his talents. 'O. de Brock has developed a tremendous capacity for work, and is perfectly excellent, clear as a bell, and is of the greatest assistance in the most unexpected ways.'[6]

The only commanding officer who disappointed Beatty, the more so because he was directly responsible for the appointment (and 'had a deuce of a fight to get him his appointment at all'), was Pakenham—the aloof, immaculately dressed, patrician 'Paks', Rear-Admiral Commanding the Battle Cruiser Force. After six months: 'I am rather disappointed with old Paks . . . he does not seem to possess quite the right flair or be quick enough in grasping the situation and at high speeds it makes such a difference. But for the life of me I don't know a soul who would do it better. I can only go on instilling (or trying to) into him the right principles by which he must be governed.'[7]

The flag officers who had been closely associated with Jellicoe

[5] Beatty to Lady Beatty, 27 June 1917; Beatty MSS.
[6] Beatty to Lady Beatty, 23 December 1916; Chalmers, *Beatty*, p. 285.
[7] Beatty to Lady Beatty, 22 May 1917; Beatty MSS. Some of Pakenham's troubles stemmed from the one serious weakness of his Flag-Captain. Roger Backhouse was charming, hard-working, brilliant, but, as a contemporary has remarked, 'Never did a man have the centralizing bug so virulently as Roger Backhouse.' His devotion to detail and his habit of doing everything himself and never using a staff eventually led to a physical breakdown when he was First Sea Lord and to his premature death (1939). The battle-cruiser squadron commanders were: 1st B.C.S., Rear-Admiral Richard F. Phillimore (*vice* O. de B. Brock), and 2nd B.C.S., Rear-Admiral Arthur F. Leveson (*vice* Pakenham). We have met both, the former briefly. 'Fidgety Phil' Phillimore was a highly competent sea-officer with a good war record, which included the command of the *Inflexible* at the Falklands and in the Dardanelles operations.

(Acting Admiral Madden, Vice-Admiral Sturdee, and Rear-Admiral Evan-Thomas[8]) at first regarded their new Chief with some reserve and even mistrust, whether through a mistaken sense of loyalty to their old Chief, or to sincere doubts about Beatty's fitness for the succession (there were many Grand Fleet officers who in November 1916 must have echoed Lord Fisher's reaction to Beatty's appointment: 'LORD! HELP US!'), or because (especially in the case of Madden and Evan-Thomas) they were temperamentally so different, or because Beatty's promotion to Acting Admiral when he became C.-in-C. (he was only 45) had taken him over the heads of eight Vice-Admirals. It was a noteworthy achievement of Beatty's that it was only a matter of months before he had the full confidence of the fleet. Witness this gleeful report: 'Everything as far as the Fleet is concerned is going like hot cakes and all my admirals are in good humour and think the Fleet has improved in morale 50 per cent. This is an uncalled for remark by our old friend Sturdee, and was supported by Madden this evening, so naturally perhaps I am feeling elated, I hope not unduly so. But everybody is pulling together in the Fleet. There is no friction and no jealousies, and they all tell me they think we are more efficient. I must not buck about it or shall have a heavy fall, but can't help being puffed.'[9] Sturdee had been a special problem. He was, initially, very bitter over Beatty and Madden being put over his head and did not disguise his feelings from the C.-in-C. as regards Madden. He quickly got over his bruised feelings and was anxious to help Beatty and Madden in every way.

There was a general recognition that the C.-in-C. was an exceptionally fine and inspiring leader, one who, as Madden testified, 'is always ready and willing to receive criticisms and very approachable'. Also, Beatty won confidence when it became abundantly clear within a few months that his strategic and tactical ideas were fundamentally sound. '. . . he is very shrewd and *takes no risks*,' Madden noted with satisfaction. 'Responsibility is a great steadier.'[10] What made a great appeal to the 'Young Turks'

[8] Respectively, Jellicoe's able onetime Chief of Staff (ensuring continuity of policy as Second-in-Command and Admiral Commanding, 1st B.S., in succession to Burney), and the Commanders of the 4th and 5th Battle Squadrons. The remaining battle-squadron commanders were Vice-Admiral John de Robeck (*vice* Jerram), 2nd B.S., and Vice-Admiral Herbert L. Heath (*vice* de Robeck), 3rd B.S. (in the Thames).

[9] Beatty to Lady Beatty, 1 April 1917; Beatty MSS.

[10] Madden to Lady Jellicoe, 17 February 1918; letter in possession of the late Dowager Countess Jellicoe.

(of whom more elsewhere) was the C.-in-C.'s great breadth of view. 'It is refreshing,' Richmond noted, 'to find a naval officer who sees so much beyond his own arm.'[11] Tyrwhitt, who had just spent three days at Rosyth, left singing Beatty's praises. '. . . he impresses me more every time I meet him. He has a wonderful grasp of the situation and absolutely fills me with confidence and hope of the future.' Four months later, after another three-day visit to Rosyth: 'It fills me with admiration the way he has captivated everybody and the absolute faith that everybody has in him. There's no doubt that he is the right man in the right place.'[12]

2. GRAND FLEET TACTICS

Beatty intensified fleet interest in tactics by proposing that when the Grand Fleet was in harbour, 'periodical (say, weekly)' meetings be organized in each battle-fleet division, each battle-cruiser squadron, and each destroyer flotilla for the discussion of tactical and other problems. This would 'counter-balance to a certain extent the lack of opportunity for constant fleet exercises . . .'[13] Apparently this scheme was carried out.

Under Beatty's new battle orders, dated 12 March 1917, the G.F.B.I.s (two printed sheets of Grand Fleet Battle Instructions) were attached to the G.F.B.O.s (Grand Fleet Battle Orders) as an introductory statement of strategical and tactical principles. (In naval parlance, *orders* were to be carried out literally, whereas *instructions* were guidelines on how the admiral wanted a job to be done, but allowed discretion to commanding officers to modify them in the light of circumstances.) The G.F.B.O.s proper were 'in amplification of the Battle Instructions'—detailed instructions to cover every conceivable contingency. They were modified and altered throughout 1917. On 1 January 1918 (coming into force on 19 February) the G.F.B.O.s became two series—G.F.B.I.s and G.F.M.O.s (Grand Fleet Manœuvring Orders), the former with a revised prefatory exposition of principles, dealing with battle only, the latter dealing with cruising formations and change of dispositions when cruising.

[11] Diary, 22 September 1917; Arthur J. Marder, *Portrait of an Admiral : the Life and Papers of Sir Herbert Richmond* (London, 1952), p. 274. (Hereafter cited by title.)
[12] Tyrwhitt to Keyes, 18 February, 22 June 1917; Keyes MSS.
[13] Beatty's memorandum, 'Tactical Investigations', 6 June 1917; Sturdee MSS.

Beatty's lament after Jutland, 'There is something wrong with our system,' did not lead to a revolution in tactics when he became C.-in-C.; he saw no need to go far beyond the post-Jutland modifications in the G.F.B.O.s,[14] and this remained just as long a document and its provisions almost as precise. On the three main points which had given rise to so much discussion after the battle—decentralization of command *v.* centralization, divided tactics *v.* concentration of the battle fleet, and a fleet turn *towards v. away* from a massed torpedo attack—Beatty came down on the side of greater decentralization, maintenance of concentration, and more aggressive anti-torpedo tactics, all with qualifications, however.

As regards centralization, the G.F.B.I.s state:

The Commander-in-Chief during the approach and prior to deployment will control the movements of the whole battlefleet, when accurate station keeping is essential. . . . When action is joined the Flag Officers commanding battle squadrons [1 January 1918: 'and divisions'] have full discretionary power to manœuvre their squadrons ['or divisions'] independently whilst conforming generally to the movements of the Commander-in-Chief. He will control the squadron ['division'] in which the fleet flagship has taken station and will make the necessary signals ordering the movements of this squadron or of the division which he may be leading. Such signal will convey the Commander-in-Chief's intentions to the Flag Officers of other squadrons or divisions, and they should conform to his movements as the situation demands. Notwithstanding the decentralisation of command indicated above, the Commander in Chief will retain the power to order the movement of the whole fleet by a general signal. Such a movement may be necessary owing to information known only to him and in order to ensure decisive results. (Paras. 4, 11, 12.)

Among the conditions under which independent action on the part of commanders of squadrons or divisions was permissible were these (all in force at Jutland and afterwards): '(i) Minelaying, or a threat of minelaying, ahead of the line of battle. The Flag Officer in the van may be in a position to see this whilst the Commander-in-Chief may not; the Flag Officer has full discretion to act. (ii) A movement of the Commander-in-Chief's division carried out

---

[14] See *From the Dreadnought to Scapa Flow*, iii. 221–7; for the G.F.B.O.s in force at the time of Jutland, see *ibid.*, pp. 4–32. The G.F.B.I.s and G.F.B.O.s quoted below, unless otherwise indicated, are from those of 12 March 1917. Substantive differences in the G.F.B.I.s of 1 January 1918 are indicated in footnotes.

without signal or before a signal has got through to all ships in the line. (iii) A movement of one of the enemy divisions necessitating a counter on our part, such as an attack on the rear, or attempt to close for the purpose of firing torpedoes, etc.'[15] It is difficult to note any significant difference between Jellicoe's views (post-Jutland, particularly) and Beatty's on how much scope ought to be allowed to individual initiative.

Nor did their ideas on concentration differ noticeably. Beatty had thoughts of taking the fleet into action in some other formation than single line, but in face of stiff resistance from his flag officers to any 'loss of cohesion' and consequent danger of being defeated in detail, he decided to stick to the established practice. He hardly needed any convincing on this point. He made it clear that he had no intention of employing divided tactics until the battle had reached an advanced stage—that is, in Dreyer's words, not 'until he had knocked the stuffing out of the enemy'. As stated in the G.F.B.I.s:

> *British main fleet to remain concentrated.* As a general principle the British battlefleet will be kept together until the defeat of the enemy has been ensured. Attacks by a division or squadron separately on a portion of the enemy are until then to be avoided. . . . An exception to the above may occur if the rear is not in gun range and the Admiral commanding considers it improbable that the general conditions will allow of his co-operating with the main body of the fleet. In this case, he may detail a portion of his squadron to deal with enemy ships which fall out. (Paras. 14, 15.)

The C.-in-C.'s intentions were summarized in these terms: 'The present day armament, the introduction of steam, and the freedom with which heavy units can be manœuvred, do not permit the repetition of the breaking of the line tactics. All tactical exercises, and even exercises on the tactical board have shown that any large division of the fleet in the approach almost invariably results in a failure for all parts of the fleet to come into action together, and therefore gives the enemy the opportunity to concentrate on a portion of the fleet. For this reason an initial division is not contemplated. . . . A division of the fleet may finally result as the enemy's resistance is overcome and as detached enemy units fall out and

[15] G.F.B.O.s of 16 April 1917 (VII: 17).

32

have to be dealt with by various squadrons of the British fleet. Discretionary power is allowed to Flag Officers to meet these circumstances as soon as the enemy fleet is disorganized.'[16]

Younger officers like Richmond were unhappy with this conservatism in tactics. 'We can't,' he groused, 'trust divisional leaders to handle their division and not get lost. It is fairly pitiful that the British Navy, which prides itself on being so "practical", cannot undertake tactical movements because they are too difficult!'[17]

Beatty was more willing than Jellicoe had been to accept the torpedo menace in order to be able to inflict serious punishment on the German line of battle. He recognized that the enemy's turn-away tactics (the retirement of his line of battle by a 'turn together'), which the Germans were likely to adopt, under cover of smoke screens and destroyer attacks, were the most difficult tactics for the British fleet to counter. Exercises at sea and on the Tactical Board proved this. The C.-in-C. was prepared under certain conditions to counter these evasive tactics by having the fleet turn *towards*, instead of, as at Jutland, *away*, from such torpedo attacks. The G.F.B.I.s state:

Torpedo menace from the Enemy main fleet. If the British fleet, owing to a turn away on the part of the enemy or other reason, finds itself in a position of torpedo disadvantage, provided visibility and other conditions admit, and the enemy can be kept under gunfire, it is the intention of the Commander-in-Chief to keep outside the line 15,000 yards from the enemy's course measured along the normal. If, however, this procedure would entail the loss of gunfire, the torpedo menace will be accepted and the fleet turned towards the retiring enemy, keeping at the limit of

[16] 'Notes for Meeting of Captains', summarizing 'the Commander-in-Chief's intentions' (mid-1917); Bellairs MSS. The likeable, cheerful, and brainy Commander Roger M. Bellairs was Beatty's War Staff Officer. There is a similarity in all this to the constant discussions on this point in the eighteenth century. The general view of the experienced tacticians was the same as Beatty's—stick together till the main body of the enemy 'be disabled or run'. There were some distinguished Admirals (Anson, Boscawen) who thought otherwise. They were not concerned with any question of divided tactics before joining action, but they wanted to press the occasions on which the stuffing had been knocked out of individual ships without waiting for the stuffing to be knocked out of the enemy fleet as a whole. They were prepared to forgo the advantages of concentration once the battle was under way. However, their consequent alterations to the Fighting Instructions were subsequently cancelled—emphatically by Hawke, for example, though he was as vigorous a thruster as one could wish for.

[17] Diary, 29 June 1917; *Portrait of an Admiral*, p. 263.

torpedo range and formed so as to present a narrow target to the probable tracks of enemy torpedoes. (Para. 17.)[18]

'The point to be emphasized,' explained the G.F.B.O.s, 'is that only by keeping the enemy fleet engaged can the initiative remain with the British fleet and a decision be obtained.'[19] The C.-in-C. had a difficult job 'establishing the idea that Torpedo Menace under certain circumstances *must* be accepted. It is not a popular conception, but I am convinced it is right, but it is difficult to upset ideas that have been absorbed for so long.'[20]

The above modifications to Jellicoe's G.F.B.O.s illustrate the new offensive spirit in Beatty's tactics. Like the G.F.B.O.s of 1914–1916, Beatty's stressed the long-range gunnery duel on parallel courses (16,000 yards was envisaged as the opening range for the van ships) as 'the form of action likely to give the most decisive results'; but they stated the doctrine of the tactical offensive more clearly and forcibly. He impressed on his Captains: 'So soon as action has been joined, it is a fundamental principle that contact should be maintained and the action continued until the enemy is defeated; no considerations such as darkness coming on will modify this rule.' And in the G.F.B.O.s: 'The main principle which should govern the action of all vessels is that the enemy must be pursued and the utmost damage inflicted on him. This does not imply that the pursuit is to be reckless, nor that the possibility of being drawn over minefields or submarines is to be overlooked by large vessels.'[21]

There was provision for a closer range in the later stages of an action (as noted above), a concentration of gunfire on a portion of the enemy's fleet, a more aggressive use of torpedoes, the acceptance of a night action *if necessary*, and a full use of submarines and aircraft with the fleet.

The C.-in-C. intended to obtain his gunnery concentration as

---

[18] Omitted in the 1 January 1918 G.F.B.I.s are the words after 'retiring enemy', and this statement is added (taken from the G.F.B.O.s of 16 April 1917): 'Circumstances may also arise during action in which the need for a rapid decision is imperative. Under these conditions the signal "Engage the enemy more closely" may be expected, by which it is to be understood that the torpedo menace is to be disregarded and every effort made to close to decisive gun range.'

[19] G.F.B.O.s of 16 April 1917 (VII: 10).

[20] Beatty to Tyrwhitt, 26 May 1917; Tyrwhitt MSS.

[21] Respectively, 'Notes for Meeting of Captains' and G.F.B.O.s of 25 August 1917 (XIII: 4).

soon as action was joined. 'The necessity for obtaining this concentration, adopting thereby the principles of Rodney and Nelson of overwhelming a portion of the enemy with the whole power of the British fleet, is a matter which requires the serious attention of the armament officers. Until the armament is able to achieve this concentration as opposed to being able to fire only at opposite-number ships in the line, the principle of overwhelming a part of the enemy by superior fire of the British cannot be obtained.'[22] Chatfield was responsible for the introduction in 1917–18 of methods for, and extensive training in, the effective concentration of fire on a portion of the enemy fleet, thereby smashing it to bits.

Concerning the more effective use of torpedoes, 'In the attack on the enemy fleet with torpedoes, the maximum rate of torpedo fire is to be developed by all vessels as early as practicable. The number of enemy ships which will be damaged by torpedoes will chiefly depend on this rate of fire, and the importance of ensuring that no favourable opportunity of discharging torpedoes is missed cannot be too strongly emphasised.'[23] A more offensive role was assigned to the flotillas. Whereas in the G.F.B.O.s in force at Jutland the primary duty of the destroyers was to prevent the enemy destroyers from delivering an attack on the battle fleet (taking advantage of their heavier gun armament), now 'Should enemy flotillas attack first, British flotillas are to proceed to beat them off, and after meeting and engaging them are, if the situation is favourable, to press on and attack the enemy battle line with torpedoes in preference to turning back to re-engage the enemy flotillas, which should be dealt with by the supporting light cruiser squadrons and the secondary armaments of heavy ships.'[24]

The G.F.B.I.s of 1 January 1918 had this to say about a night

[22] 'Notes for Meeting of Captains'. The same principle is found in the G.F.B.I.s of 12 March 1917. It is repeated and at the same time modified in the G.F.B.I.s of 1 January 1918. The emphasis is now on attempting to destroy the whole of the German battle fleet initially. 'The general fighting principle is to bring to action the whole force of the enemy in order to annihilate him. The possibility of effecting this depends upon "Time available". When it is apparent that owing to failing light or the vicinity of minefields it will be impossible to annihilate the whole main force of the enemy, every endeavour will be made to annihilate a part of it rather than to continue to engage the whole. In such circumstances the signal will be made at the critical moment to concentrate the fire of the fleet on a part of the enemy, probably the rear, leaving the remaining enemy ships unfired at' (1: 3).

[23] G.F.B.O.s of 22 November 1917 (XXVIIa: 1).

[24] G.F.B.I.s of 1 January 1918 (8: 3). Cf. the post-Jutland G.F.B.O.s (*From the Dreadnought to Scapa Flow*, iii. 225), which seem to be just as aggressive.

action: 'Owing to the risk incurred from torpedo fire, it is undesirable for heavy ships to engage at night if it can be avoided. If, however, it is decided to engage, the general principle to be followed is that searchlights are to be switched on, and the maximum volume of gun and torpedo fire opened simultaneously, ships turning as necessary.' (13: 2.) Jutland pointed to the need for maintaining contact with the enemy during the night. Accordingly, we find this provision: '*The attack at night.* One or more light-cruiser squadrons will be detailed to locate the enemy after dark if touch has been lost, and they will be accompanied by destroyer flotillas, which are to attack when the light-cruisers have gained touch with the enemy (this force will be known as the *Attacking Force*).'[25]

Beatty supported the use of submarines in a tactical role which had been a feature of Jellicoe's G.F.B.O.s in 1915–16. Lord Fisher had had the idea of developing a submarine with sufficient surface speed to accompany the battle fleet as an advance striking force against the High Seas Fleet. Such a craft appeared to make sense, given the prevailing tactical idea of fleet actions based on the long battle line of capital ships and the desperate need to find some way of 'fixing' the enemy battle fleet, that is, of discouraging it from breaking off action. The conception of the new type, the 'K' class, may have been sound, but despite a remarkable achievement in giving a submarine so high a surface speed, this was probably not enough for battle needs.[26] Beatty, nevertheless, continued to have high hopes for their tactical use. Four submarine flotillas were attached to the Grand Fleet with two of them definitely assigned to proceed to sea with the fleet, 'taking part in any operations as a unit of the fleet'. Thus, in March 1917: 'We had the K's out the last 2 Exercises and they did well on every occasion. Were able to

---

[25] G.F.B.O.s of 26 March 1917 (XXVII: 13). This provision goes back to Jellicoe's revision of 26 October 1916. See *From the Dreadnought to Scapa Flow*, iii. 226. Night fighting technique, however, was scarcely improved.

[26] The Navy commissioned 17 'K' boats between August 1916 and May 1918 (*K-18* became *M-1*). These twin-funnelled, steam-driven boats were of revolutionary design, the biggest and fastest submarines built during the war. They were a sort of submersible destroyer: a submerged displacement of 2,560 tons, 338 feet in length, two 4-inch, an anti-aircraft gun, eight torpedo tubes (18-inch), and capable of 24 knots on the surface and $9\frac{1}{2}$ submerged as compared with the 19 knots on the surface and the $9\frac{1}{4}$ submerged of the fastest conventional diesel-engine boats of the war period. (These were the 'J' class, which began to join the Fleet towards the end of 1916. The 'L' class, which joined the Fleet in 1918, had a surface speed of $17\frac{1}{4}$ knots, a submerged speed of $10\frac{1}{2}$.)

get into a position to make a good attack. For Fleet purposes they will be very valuable . . .'[27] Yet in the end they proved a disappointment for various reasons. Among these was a very large turning circle when submerged, which deprived them of the handiness needed for torpedoing ships in a main fleet action fought at 21 knots or thereabouts, with the ships manœuvring at high speed and with frequent changes of course. Nor did their surface speed give them enough excess over the battle fleet. Even destroyers doing 30 or more knots often took a long time getting to good attacking positions on the enemy's engaged bow, and that the 'K' boats would ever get to the disengaged bow, which was where they were wanted, was highly unlikely. They were never put to the test of battle.

Beatty, a naval air enthusiast, allocated a definite role to his aircraft in a fleet action. The airships with the fleet were, on deployment, 'to scout on the disengaged bow and right ahead of our fleet and give early warning of the approach of further enemy vessels'. Those not with the fleet were 'to patrol the approaches to the Firth of Forth, Humber and Scapa during a fleet action'. The heavier-than-air craft attached to the Grand Fleet, which operated from aircraft carriers, were classified as 'fighting machines' and 'reconnaissance machines', whose respective duties were 'to locate and destroy hostile aircraft and to locate and report the enemy's fleet'. Nothing is said about the former aircraft attacking enemy ships, only: 'Every effort must be made to prevent hostile aircraft from locating the fleet. . . . Their duties will be to destroy enemy aircraft and to defend our reconnaissance machines and airships from attack by hostile aircraft.' This defensive function is emphasized by the nature of the weapons carried by the aircraft: 'Both reconnaissance and fighting machines are to be armed with machine guns. Bombs are not to be carried unless specially ordered.'[28] This is not to say that Beatty was oblivious to the offensive potentialities of aircraft, for, as noted, both he and a number of officers in the Grand Fleet and at the Admiralty saw interesting possibilities in the development and use of torpedo-carrying aeroplanes.

There are other respects in which Beatty profited from Jutland. Take the problem of communications and intelligence. His recollection of what had happened to his critical signal of 2.32 p.m.,

[27] Beatty to Jellicoe, 26 March 1917; Jellicoe MSS.
[28] G.F.B.I.s of 1 January 1918 (12: 12, 13, 16, 17).

31 May (it had not got through to the 5th Battle Squadron for some precious minutes), prompted these instructions to repeating ships: 'The duty of a repeating ship attached to a squadron is not only to repeat all signals made by the senior officer of the squadron, but also to make every endeavour to see that such signals are seen and understood, and repeating ships should, if necessary, leave their station for the purpose of getting signals through, so long as they remain within effectual visual signalling distance of the flagship to which they are attached.'[29]

Remembering the unhappy incidents at Jutland when flag officers waited upon an executive signal to be made before carrying out an order, Beatty instructed: 'The Fleet is to be guided generally by the movements of the division led by the Commander-in-Chief, which should be considered as the rallying point. The movements of the Commander-in-Chief must therefore be very carefully watched and his wishes if possible anticipated. Signals may either be indistinguishable or they may take too long to get through a large fleet. This does not mean that they will not be made, but the movement signalled may be commenced before the executive is given.'[30]

The G.F.B.I.s of 1 January 1918 detailed a 'Challenge Procedure' to obviate the repetition of some of the incidents during the night of Jutland. As late as the Second War, however, the Royal Navy had not produced a satisfactory challenge-and-reply system. In both wars the Germans had the advantage of knowing that any ship sighted was either an enemy or neutral.

Again, with Jutland in mind, Beatty enjoined the importance of the C.-in-C. being in possession of all information on the whereabouts of the enemy. 'It is vital that the Commander-in-Chief should obtain reliable information of the bearing, distance and course of the enemy main force at the earliest moment; such information should also be passed simultaneously by visual to all adjacent ships. In order that it may be plotted correctly relative to the position of the Commander-in-Chief, it should be based on the Commander-in-Chief's reference position which must therefore be passed out to all ships immediately on receipt. To admit of in-

[29] G.F.B.O.s of 16 April 1917 (VII: 24).
[30] *Ibid.* (VII: 4). In the G.F.B.I.s of 1 January 1918 (2: 1) the last two sentences are combined to read: 'Signals may be indistinguishable, and in any case the movement signalled may be commenced before the executive is made.'

formation and reference positions being rapidly passed, advanced forces must be linked to the battlefleet by linking vessels which are in certain visual touch.'[31] Similarly with regard to the movements of the enemy in an action: 'Reports of movements, *provided they are made in good time*, may be of great value, and any ship in a position to see clearly what is occurring, when it is probable that the Commander-in-Chief cannot, should not fail to make a report.'[32]

At Jutland the cruisers tended to consider they had done their job after locating the enemy. We now find, for example, that when contact with the enemy was gained, it was the duty of the advanced light cruisers of the Battle Cruiser Force: '(a) When the enemy is superior, to maintain touch; (b) When the enemy is equal or inferior, to engage him.'[33] Probably with Jutland in mind, Beatty further instructed that light-cruiser strength be economized 'so that more ships *do not concentrate at any one point than are necessary to accomplish their object*.'[34]

Jutland was directly responsible for the revival of these provisions: 'Whenever junior Flag Officers or captains find themselves without special directions during an action, either from inability to make out or receive the Admiral's signals or from unforeseen circumstances rendering previous orders inapplicable, they are to act as their judgment shall dictate in making every effort to damage the enemy.'[35]

The Scarborough action of 17 December 1914, which had caused Beatty so much grief, prompted this paragraph: 'If, when in actual touch with the enemy, the senior officer or the captain of a ship acting singly, receives an order from a higher authority which it is evident may have been given in ignorance of the conditions of the moment, and which, if obeyed, would cause touch with the enemy to be lost, discretion must be exercised by the junior officer as to obeying the order and an early opportunity taken of representing the real facts; a signal made under such conditions is in the nature of an instruction.'[36]

[31] G.F.B.I.s of 1 January 1918 (5: 8).
[32] G.F.B.O.s of 9 August 1917 (XXIV: 14).
[33] G.F.B.O.s of 24 July 1917 (XXII: 3).
[34] *Ibid.* See *From the Dreadnought to Scapa Flow*, iii. 56.
[35] G.F.B.O.s of 16 April 1917 (VII: 28), incorporated in the 1 January 1918 G.F.B.I.s (1: 19) with these changes: 'Whenever Flag or Commanding Officers . . . inability to make out or receive signals . . .'
[36] G.F.B.I.s of 1 January 1918 (5: 10). See *From the Dreadnought to Scapa Flow*, ii. 139–40.

More aggressive tactics and improved communications and intelligence were fine; but of what use were they unless there was contact with the High Seas Fleet? Aye, there was the rub of the matter.

3. GRAND FLEET STRATEGY

There was a basic disagreement between Jellicoe and Beatty on the importance of the blockade of Germany. Beatty viewed the blockade as 'at the present moment, the only offensive policy apparently carried on', and he felt that the 10th Cruiser Squadron (the Northern Patrol), 'the one unit that could *win us the War*, if up to the fullest strength', must not be weakened. '*Great Britain* [he wrote to the First Lord] is trying to strangle Germany by means of the Blockade maintained by the 10th Cruiser Squadron, which is made possible by our Command of the Sea by *Surface Vessels. But* this Blockade is being EASED UP by the detachment of certain ships of the 10th Cruiser Squadron, which also makes it simpler for the Enemy to pass out raiders to assist the Enemy's Blockade. The *Enemy* are trying to strangle the *Entente* by means of the Blockade maintained by their Submarines. This Blockade is being TIGHTENED UP by the employment of more and more Submarines, as rapidly as they can be built. Which side will be strangled first?'[37] The Admiralty found it impossible to bring the 10th Cruiser Squadron up to full strength. The needs of A/S warfare were paramount. The controversy over the blockading squadron (January–February) culminated in a sharp exchange. 'There are two things,' Beatty claimed, 'which are going to win or lose this War and nothing else will affect it a damn. Our Armies might advance a mile a day and slay the Hun in thousands, but the real crux lies in whether we blockade the Enemy to his knees, or whether he does the same to us. Our Blockade rests on the 10th Cruiser Squadron, the enemy's on his submarines.' Jellicoe's position was directly opposite. 'I think you are quite wrong in assuming that the blockade will ever cause the enemy to give in. That certainly is not the opinion of those who are in a position to know. We may cause them a good deal of suffering and discomfort by the blockade, but

[37] Beatty to Carson, 13 January 1917; Beatty MSS. He had already expressed himself forcibly on 'the right policy', which was to keep the squadron as strong as possible. Carson's 'Memorandum of Conversations with the Commander-in-Chief . . . 8th and 9th of January, 1917'. Beatty raised the same point in his conversations with Carson on board the *Iron Duke* on 15–16 February.

PLATE I

ADMIRAL SIR DAVID BEATTY
Commander-in-Chief, Grand Fleet, from November 1916

[*Painting by Sir William Orpen :*
reproduction by permission of the photographer, Paul Laib

PLATE II

2. REAR-ADMIRAL
ALEXANDER L. DUFF

Director of Anti-Submarine Division, Admiralty
War Staff, December 1916–May 1917; Assistant
Chief of Naval Staff from May 1917

[Photograph: by permission of Lady Duff

1. VICE-ADMIRAL
SIR ROSSLYN WEMYSS

Deputy First Sea Lord,
September–December 1917

[Photograph: by permission of the Hon. Mrs. F. Cunnack

we shall not win the war by it. The war will not be won until the enemy's armed forces are defeated—certainly on land, and probably at sea—and therefore it is essential to get our troops to France and keep our communications open.'[38] The controversy, in which *both* Admirals were right, became academic two months later.

This bone of contention was removed when blockade policy was vastly simplified. This occurred when the United States, with the Northern neutrals the chief source of contraband, declared war on Germany, 6 April 1917. Britain then frankly returned to her policy of the Napoleonic Wars, prohibiting all trade destined for the enemy either directly or through neutral ports, under pain of confiscation of ship and cargo, unless the neutral ship voluntarily submitted to examination at a British or Allied port. At the same time, since few ships were now coming to Kirkwall, there was virtually no need for a blockade fleet, the 10th Cruiser Squadron, to intercept and examine suspected cargoes. The Customs officers in Atlantic ports did the work for them. In June 1917 the Admiralty decided that they ought to be able to do without the squadron. Gradually, this splendid force was weakened, and in the autumn of 1917 it was no more.

This issue apart, Jellicoe and Beatty saw eye to eye on the larger strategic aspects of the war at sea. This was certainly true as regards the use of the Grand Fleet. It was assumed in the country at large, and to some extent in the Fleet, that on the long and fierce controversy on the question whether the Navy's task was to hold the seas and wait for the Germans to come out, or whether the Navy should adopt a more provocative policy and lure the High Seas Fleet to its destruction, the new C.-in-C. stood for the latter strategy. This was to misunderstand Beatty. As Lord Chatfield reminds us, 'He was no reckless and light-hearted swordsman, as he has sometimes been represented to be, but was always imbued by the need of a wise balancing of risks, realizing the responsibility of his valuable command . . .'[39] That he was no mere 'go at 'em' boy is evident in his official correspondence and memoranda. Beatty's strategic policy was as cautious as Jellicoe's had been. At no time, either as Commander of the Battle Cruiser Fleet or now as C.-in-C., did he suggest any fundamental change in the naval strategy of the war. He was no more in favour of so-called offensive

[38] Beatty to Jellicoe, 27 January, Jellicoe to Beatty, 4 February 1917; Jellicoe MSS.
[39] Lord Chatfield's letter in *The Times*, 13 March 1936.

operations than Jellicoe ever had been as C.-in-C. There was indeed a basic agreement on broad strategy between the C.-in-C. and the Admiralty. The exceptions will be noted as we proceed.

One reason for a cautious strategy was the constant inroads into Grand Fleet personnel and destroyers for the A/S campaign and, later, the convoy system. The needs of the former seriously diluted fleet personnel with untrained manpower, and the latter left the fleet weak in screening craft. For example, in July 1917, of the 100 destroyers and 9 flotilla leaders attached to the Grand Fleet, 46 were absent on A/S duties and 29 were refitting. Initially, however, Beatty's principal anxiety was the weakness of his light-cruiser screen. This type of craft was especially important to the fleet because at the beginning of his command it had no airships for scouting, and they were absolutely essential for protection against minelaying. In mid-February he had only 20 light cruisers (not counting the so-called large light cruisers *Courageous*, refitting, and *Glorious*), with two more refitting; the High Seas Fleet had at least 14. The Admiralty could not bring home any light cruisers from the Mediterranean, as Beatty suggested, because of commitments to the Italians and the need to counter the German light cruiser *Breslau* (at Constantinople).

Beatty was as concerned over his battle-line superiority as Jellicoe had ever been. Not that he worried about his margin in dreadnoughts, even allowing for the three ships which under normal circumstances were being repaired. According to Admiralty reckoning, in March 1917 the Grand Fleet had 32 against the 21 in the High Seas Fleet, with each fleet due to add one by February 1918.[40] The calamity that befell the *Vanguard* at Scapa on 9 July 1917 (she blew up at anchor, 'probably due to defective cordite', thought Beatty), with the loss of a thousand men, reduced the Grand Fleet superiority in the line, but in the existing margin of battleship superiority the effect of the loss was minimal. Any doubts Beatty may have had about his superiority in dreadnoughts were removed by the arrival early in December 1917 of four American dreadnoughts. They came in response to an Admiralty request made in July for four coal-burning dreadnoughts (oil-burning dreadnoughts could not be supplied) to replace the five

---

[40] Two sister ships of the *Baden* had been laid down in 1914: the *Sachsen* and *Württemberg*, eight 15-inch, launched in November 1916 and June 1917, respectively. Neither was completed.

'King Edwards' that were being paid off in order to provide officers and ratings for light cruisers, destroyers, submarines, etc. The American ships, under their own Admiral, formed an integral portion of the Grand Fleet as the 6th Battle Squadron.

It was the 'growing relative weakness' in battle cruisers that deeply concerned Beatty throughout 1917 and beyond, as it did the Admiralty, for it promised to put the battle fleet at a disadvantage on joining action with the High Seas Fleet. Statements prepared by the First Sea Lord (21 July, 26 August) and by the Rear-Admiral Commanding, Battle Cruiser Force (29 October) showed that the German battle cruisers were much superior in protection (this point was stressed), their guns had considerably greater range than the British, and the slowest units were 2 knots faster than the slowest British battle cruisers. The Admiralty credited Germany with four battle cruisers (*Von der Tann, Moltke, Seydlitz, Derfflinger*), with two (*Manteuffel* and *Hindenburg*) expected to be added by February 1918, one (*Mackensen*) late in 1918, and two in 1919. Only the *Hindenburg* (October 1917), as it happens, was ever completed.[41] Britain had nine by the summer of 1917, a figure that included the fast but weakly protected *Repulse* and *Renown*, which were not regarded as fit to occupy a place in the battle-cruiser line. The *Hood* (eight 15-inch), laid down in September 1916, was not expected to be ready for service until the end of 1918. (In fact, she was not launched until August 1918.) Her three sister ships (*Rodney, Howe, Anson*) were still in the projected stage, preliminary work having been stopped on them in February 1917.

To correct the approaching imbalance in battle-cruiser forces, the Admiralty asked the War Cabinet (26 August 1917) to have the Foreign Office sound out the Japanese Government on the sale of two of their battle cruisers. This was done. On 5 October the Japanese Foreign Minister informed the British Ambassador: 'Japan had only four battle cruisers; that public took greatest pride and interest in these and that Government would be unable to defend themselves in Parliament or before the public if they consented to part with any of them.' The Admiralty now suggested

[41] The true situation—*Mackensen*: laid down, 1914, launched, April 1917; *Graf Spee*, 1915, September 1917; *Prinz Eitel Friedrich*, 1915, March 1920; *Fürst Bismarck*, 1915, not launched; Ersatz *Yorck*, Ersatz *Gneisenau*, Ersatz *Scharnhorst*, 1916, not launched. The last three were to have eight 15-inch, the earlier ships, eight 14-inch. The *Hindenburg* carried eight 12-inch.

(15 October), as second best, that the Japanese be invited to attach two of their battle cruisers to the Grand Fleet for the duration. The War Cabinet approved. The Japanese answer, conveyed by their Ambassador in London in a memorandum (14 November), was a polite refusal. It was evident to Balfour, the Foreign Secretary, that

the real reason was political. The Japanese Government, in their weak parliamentary position, did not feel themselves strong enough to resist the attack which the Opposition would not fail to make upon them if they diminished the strength of their battle-cruiser fleet in Asiatic waters. It was on this fleet that the Japanese mainly relied for home defence. It had been laboriously brought into being under many difficulties. It constituted an organic whole which would be seriously maimed if there were detached from it on distant service two of its constituent units; and no such procedure would be tolerated by Japanese public opinion.

I asked the Ambassador what naval peril Japan anticipated in Eastern waters where she proposed to bottle up her fleet. She had just concluded a friendly arrangement with America; she was united by treaty with Great Britain; she was fighting on the side of the Allies. The only fleet, therefore, she had to fear was the German fleet; and I pointed out to him that, if that were so, the best position in which Japanese ships could find themselves was one in which there was some chance of their meeting, under favourable conditions, the only naval enemy from which they had anything to fear.

He did not reply to this argument, but contented himself with insisting again upon the strength of Japanese public opinion, and with dwelling upon the magnitude of the naval services that had been, and still were being, performed by Japan for her Allies.

I did not pretend to be satisfied either with the course pursued by his Government or by the arguments with which that course was justified; but his instructions were formal, and for the moment at least there was clearly nothing to be done.[42]

The Government and the Admiralty now had further cause for uneasiness over Japan's post-war intentions in the Far East. And Beatty continued to worry about his battle-cruiser strength.

Also dictating a cautious strategy was Beatty's knowledge of the *matériel* weaknesses of his fleet—the structural weaknesses of the ships and the poor quality of the shell.[43] Most of the defects

---

[42] Balfour to Sir Conyngham Greene (Ambassador in Tokyo), 15 November 1917 (printed for the War Cabinet); copy in Admiralty MSS.

[43] See *From the Dreadnought to Scapa Flow*, iii. 215–19. The first lot of the new shell, able to penetrate armour and explode in a ship's vitals, arrived in the Grand Fleet in April 1918: a 30 per cent supply to the more important units.

revealed by Jutland had been at least partially remedied by the middle of 1917, yet they continued to give Beatty cause for concern.

Finally, and the crux of the matter, was Beatty's conviction, as it had been Jellicoe's, that there must be no gambling with the Navy: the whole Allied cause was based on the latent power of the Grand Fleet.

For these reasons, above all the last named, Beatty was as strongly opposed to such bold offensive schemes as an attack on Heligoland as his predecessor had been, and again, like Jellicoe, he would not seek an engagement except in favourable circumstances. Favourable circumstances did *not* include a fleet action in the Hoofden (the southern part of the North Sea), where the occupation and fortification of Zeebrugge and Ostend and the proximity of the enemy's main naval bases gave the Germans great advantages. It was a very different matter north of the latitude of Horns Reef.

Early in 1917 Beatty discussed with the First Lord 'the question of naval policy and how far it could and ought to be an offensive policy. He considered the offensive at sea only possible in regard to Blockade and anti-submarine measures.'[44] Six months later his policy had not changed. 'The role of the Navy is to keep its head and not be bounced into attempting impossible things by irresponsible and ignorant cranks, and we shall come out on top in the end.'[45] In some respects he was more cautious than Jellicoe, as when, at the time of Third Ypres (Passchendaele), he disagreed with the Admiralty's projected landing of Rawlinson's troops on the Ostend front.

This is not to say that ideas for offensive action were absent from Beatty's thinking. He itched for action and encouraged his officers, no matter how junior, to come up with promising ideas that might at least keep the High Seas Fleet busy. Thus, he did not hesitate to send to the Admiralty (May 1917) a scheme for the bombardment of Zeebrugge evolved by a gunnery lieutenant which seemed to promise excellent results. Early in 1917 he asked Tyrwhitt

to consider the feasibility, when the weather is suitable, of an operation or series of operations on the Enemy's Coast. . . . When we have stirred them up in the past, we have always fetched something out, but have

[44] Carson, 'Memorandum of Conversations with the Commander-in-Chief . . . 8th and 9th of January, 1917'.
[45] Beatty to Lady Beatty, 9 July 1917; Beatty MSS.

invariably gone away *too soon*. Stir them up one day and be there the next, when they have really woken up, is my theory, and stir them in more places than one at the same time is my idea. What do you think?

Your Zeebrugge scheme I return. I am not very well qualified to give an opinion, but I am all for doing something and we must use our imagination, and for that reason I like it . . . we must keep them busy. Any move on our part makes them nervous, and they will not be so concerned about sending their S.M.s away if they think they are likely to be wanting them for defensive purposes. Therefore we must become offensive if it is only make believe.

The time of the year is against us just now, but we must be prepared for a generally more active development when the spring comes, and let it synchronize with our Army's offensive when it begins. But if anything is to be gained, I am ready *now*. Let me know what you think. Any ideas are very welcome, the wilder the better. One can always tame them down. What we lack is imagination.[46]

Beatty waited with diminishing hope that the High Seas Fleet would put to sea. To a man of his temperament this was most irksome. At first he thought that the probability of the United States declaring war on Germany might induce the enemy to try a fleet action on well-prepared ground before the American Navy could reinforce the British Navy. By March 1917 he was less confident: the Grand Fleet was too strong for the High Seas Fleet. '. . . three months I have been in command of the Grand Fleet and we have not struck the enemy a severe blow yet. We have got some submarines, but that is not what is required to satisfy the longing to do something. I keep on saying to myself patience, just have patience, but it is hard to act up to that.' 'Six months I have commanded the Grand Fleet now, and we haven't met the enemy yet. How many months are we to wait? I would not mind how many if I knew at the end we would get them, but it is the haunting fear that we never shall, and the Grand Fleet will never be able to justify itself, that is the fly in the ointment.' 'I never allow myself to think or speak of such a possibility, but at the back of my mind

---

[46] Beatty to Tyrwhitt, 16 January 1917; Tyrwhitt MSS. Sir Reginald Tyrwhitt, commander of the Harwich Force (light cruisers, destroyers) throughout the war, was under the orders of the Admiralty, but was to co-operate with Beatty if they were out together. This situation would arise if the High Seas Fleet were reported at sea north of latitude 53° N. and a fleet action were probable. Tyrwhitt had to wait till January 1918 to achieve flag rank (Acting Rear-Admiral). He was still a bit of a tartar, yet always had the full respect and devotion of his officers and men. The Zeebrugge reference in the letter is to Tyrwhitt's scheme for sinking a ship in the lock there.

it is always there like a nightmare.'[47] Until the end of 1917 he was not entirely without hope that, spurred by the growing necessity to break the British blockade and open up the oceans to German shipping, as well as by the need to boost the national morale, the High Seas Fleet would gamble on a victory. He could not have known, any more than the Admiralty, that in its pursuit of limited objectives, above all, of supporting the submarine warfare, which took priority once unrestricted U-boat warfare started, the High Seas Fleet would not risk destruction. Its Cs.-in-C. realized that if their battle fleet suffered defeat, it would be impossible to use the Bight. Only its support enabled the German mine-sweepers to carry out their important task in safety, and it stood in the way of a close British blockade of the U-boat bases. If the High Seas Fleet were seriously weakened in a fleet action, the submarine campaign would collapse with it, or so the Germans believed.

Jellicoe and Beatty were in agreement that the Grand Fleet must be held ready for a new Jutland. This attitude was not to change until the turn of the year 1917–18. Since, however, Grand Fleet strategy was to accept battle with the High Seas Fleet only if the situation were favourable, that is, if the action took place in waters remote from the German bases, and since the prevailing doctrine in the High Seas Fleet was that the large-scale battle, if fought at all, should be accepted only if circumstances were advantageous, that is, if it took place in waters comfortably close to German bases, the prospect was for the continued employment of both Fleets as 'fleets in being'. Not that, as Geddes (then First Lord) reminded the House of Commons on 1 November 1917, the Royal

---

[47] Beatty to Lady Beatty, 1 March, 24, 31 May 1917; Chalmers, *Beatty*, pp. 289, 316–17. Jellicoe was no more sanguine about the likelihood of meeting the High Seas Fleet. It was likely to adopt a 'strictly defensive attitude during the present phase of the war, and if it moves into the North Sea its object will probably be to entice our capital ships into dangerous and prepared areas, thus bringing about a process of attrition by mines and submarines. The most obvious way of doing that is by raiding, or pretending to raid, the east coast . . . the way to deal with [these raids] is to retain the Grand Fleet somewhere north of the latitude of Horns Reef until the enemy has committed himself to some operation which will afford a good chance of intercepting him on the way back.' Jellicoe's memorandum for the War Cabinet, 'British Naval Policy' (G.T.-1272), 1 July 1917. All cited memoranda for the War Cabinet (G.T. series) or the War Committee (G. series) are from the Cabinet Office Papers in the Public Record Office (Cab. 24). The Admiralty MSS. and other sources contain memoranda for the War Committee or the War Cabinet which are not in these series.

Navy did not retain its old tradition of seeking to bring the enemy Fleet to action, as well as to keep open the trade routes and protect British and Allied commerce. The frontiers of England, he said, were still the coasts of the enemy.

In practice, so far as the main fleets were concerned, the strategical situation in the North Sea was one of stalemate. No important movements were made on either side until the autumn of 1917, although the light forces were constantly active, the British in offensive sweeps or covering minelaying operations. With the Germans staking everything on an endeavour to circumvent the power and pressure of the Grand Fleet through an unrestricted U-boat offensive against trade, the most urgent task facing the Royal Navy was the defeat, or at least the containment, of the submarine menace.

III

New Strategy and New Men: Pless and Whitehall

(December 1916 – January 1917)

With the unrestricted U-boat campaign we had probably embarked on the most tremendous undertaking that the world-war brought in its long train. Our aim was to break the power of mighty England vested in her sea trade in spite of the protection which her powerful Fleet could afford her. . . . if we did not succeed in overcoming England's will to destroy us then the war of exhaustion must end in Germany's certain defeat. There was no prospect of avoiding such a conclusion by the war on land. . . . *In such a situation it was not permissible to sit with folded hands and leave the fate of the German Empire to be decided by chance circumstances.*

ADMIRAL REINHARD SCHEER, *Germany's High Sea Fleet in the World War.*

The nation grumbled, and another combination was tried. This time Sir John Jellicoe and Sir Edward Carson, both sound men; but both of rather a pessimistic temperament. There was none of the fiery optimism of Lord Fisher about Admiral Jellicoe. He viewed things from the sober standpoint, which, it must be confessed, was at that time rather a cheerless one; and his First Lord was temperamentally the exact opposite to Mark Tapley [the invariably cheerful character in Dickens's *Martin Chuzzlewit*].

ADMIRAL SIR REGINALD BACON,
Lord Fisher of Kilverstone.

I. THE LAUNCHING OF UNRESTRICTED U-BOAT WARFARE

THE conduct of U-boat operations was a much disputed question throughout the war, leading to serious differences within the German Government and between the Government and the Army and Navy High Commands. The cardinal question was always whether U-boats operating under existing international regulations, as favoured by the Government because of political considerations, could be really effective. The worsening economic situation of the Central Powers in 1916, the result of the continuing British blockade and of such internal factors as the inability of

49

German agriculture to expand its food output, made an early victory more urgent than ever. There was encouragement in the excellent results achieved by the restricted U-boat campaign of the autumn of 1916: 146,000 tons of British shipping sunk in October, 145,000 in November, and 109,000 in December were the actual figures, though the Germans were claiming more. Under these circumstances the Army High Command, Field-Marshal von Hindenburg and General Ludendorff, pushed vigorously for the abandonment of cruiser warfare (that is, the submarine campaign in accordance with prize rules) for an unrestricted U-boat campaign, sinking without distinction and without warning. Because of the favourable military situation, the Generals were prepared to accept the risk of United States entry into the war.

The Chief of the Naval Staff, Admiral von Holtzendorff, buoyed by this firm support, produced a memorandum on 22 December that argued for 'an early opening of the unrestricted campaign' on these grounds: 'A decision must be reached in the war before the autumn of 1917, if it is not to end in the exhaustion of all parties, and consequently disastrously for us. Of our enemies, Italy and France are economically so hard hit that they are only upheld by England's energy and activity. If we can break England's back the war will at once be decided in our favour. Now England's mainstay is her shipping, which brings to the British Isles the necessary supplies of food and materials for war industries, and ensures their solvency abroad.' Holtzendorff's reckoning was that Britain was fed and supplied by only $10\frac{3}{4}$ million tons of shipping ($6\frac{3}{4}$ million British, 900,000 captured enemy shipping, and 3 million neutral). Judging from the experience gained in 1915–16, when the U-boats operated under cruiser conditions, unrestricted warfare should account for 600,000 tons of British shipping each month; and at least 1,200,000 tons of neutral shipping would be frightened away. After five months, shipping to and from Great Britain would be reduced by some 39 per cent. 'England would not be able to stand that . . . I do not hesitate to assert that, as matters now stand, we can force England to make peace in five months by means of an unrestricted U-boat campaign. But this holds good only for a really unrestricted campaign . . .' It did not matter if an unrestricted campaign resulted in a breach with the United States, since the U-boats would have brought Great Britain to her knees before American power could be brought to bear. He pressed for the commencement of this campaign no later than 1 February 1917, the latest date possible, if the campaign were to be successful.[1]

Only the opposition of the Chancellor, Bethmann Hollweg, and, to a lesser degree, of the new Foreign Secretary, Zimmermann, held up the official approval of an unrestricted campaign. At a meeting at General Headquarters in Pless on 9 January, attended by the Emperor, Holtzendorff, Hindenburg, Ludendorff, and the Chiefs of the Military and Naval Cabinets, the Chancellor withdrew his opposition. The Emperor thereupon sent Scheer, the C.-in-C., High Seas Fleet, a telegram through Holtzendorff commanding that the unrestricted submarine campaign begin on 1 February 'with the utmost energy'. The die had been cast. 'Submarine warfare is the last card' was the Chancellor's comment. For Admiral Müller, the Chief of the Naval Cabinet, it was the 'last shot in our locker'. On 31 January the German Government notified the United States of their intention to open the unrestricted campaign the next day, sinking at sight all Allied and neutral shipping approaching British or French coastal waters. The prohibited zones covered the English Channel, the western half of the North Sea, the western coasts of Scotland, Ireland, England, and France, and extended about 400 miles west into the Atlantic. The Mediterranean was forbidden to shipping, except for narrow passages south and east of Spain, around the Balearics, and a narrow corridor to Greece.[2]

Prior to 1 February 1917, U-boat sinkings without warning had been the exception rather than the rule. The usual method of attack on merchant ships was for a surfaced U-boat to 'bring them to' by gunfire, then, having made sure of the enemy nationality of the vessel, to close in for the kill by gun, torpedo, or bomb. This practice at least gave an armed merchantman a chance to protect herself and escape. It seems clear that this was due less to feelings of humanity than to the fear of complications with the United States in the event of incidents involving the loss of American lives. This is evident from the fact that most of the sinkings without warning had taken place in the Mediterranean, where Allied trade

[1] The more important parts of the memorandum are in Admiral Reinhard Scheer, *Germany's High Sea Fleet in the World War* (London, 1920), pp. 248–52.

[2] The Admiralty had got wind of German intentions earlier. 'It is now certain (very secret information) that Germany will proclaim a blockade of all our coasts on Feb[y] 1st and they will sink everything found in an area to be defined by them.' Jellicoe to Beatty, 25 January 1917; Beatty MSS.

was confined to a fixed route, distinct from the usual traffic routes. What had been the exception would now be the general practice.[3] The British attitude at the time and since has never altered. As expressed by the Official Historian of the merchant navy: 'The Germans now utterly disregarded the rules and obligations of maritime warfare previously observed by civilized nations. Throughout the Napoleonic wars it had been a point of honour to rescue from drowning those seamen whose ships had been taken or destroyed. . . . It was reserved for the twentieth century to witness in the German submarine campaign the deliberate jettisoning of all such obligations hitherto considered sacred, and the casting to the winds of the most elementary dictates of humanity.'[4] The German argument has always been the simple one that if they had not embarked on unrestricted warfare, they would never have had a chance of strangling the British war economy.

Germany began her unrestricted campaign with approximately 142 submarines (154 was the average number of U-boats in commission during February), which is about what the Admiralty credited her with. The figure is deceptive, since the number of *Frontboote* (U-boats assigned to operational flotillas) on 10 February 1917 was 111 (average for the month: 121). These 'war-front' or operational boats were distributed as follows: 49 with the North Sea flotillas (based on North Sea ports), 33 in Flanders (based on Zeebrugge and Ostend), 24 in the Adriatic (based on Pola), 3 at Constantinople, and 2 in the Baltic. The average number of operational boats actually at sea in February was only 36, but this represented an increase of 11 over the January average and 19 over the monthly average of 17 in 1916.

For the entire period of unrestricted submarine warfare, February 1917–October 1918, using monthly averages, the maximum number of boats in commission was 184 (October 1918), the maximum number of operational boats available, 139 (September 1917), the average of the operational U-boat fleet, 127, and the

---

[3] Of the 544 British ships sunk from 29 January 1915 until 1 February 1917, 269 had been torpedoed, of which number 148, or 27 per cent of the total, had been sunk without warning. R. H. Gibson and Maurice Prendergast, *The German Submarine War, 1914–1918* (London, 1931, 2nd ed.), p. 123. Jellicoe gives the percentages of U-boat sinkings without warning for 1915 and 1916 as, respectively, 21 and 29, and for the first four months of the unrestricted campaign, 64. Jellicoe, *The Crisis of the Naval War* (London 1920), p. 38.

[4] Sir Archibald Hurd, *History of the Great War. The Merchant Navy* (London, 1921–9, 3 vols.), iii. 17.

average number of operational boats at sea, 46, or not quite a third of the boats available at any one time. The others were undergoing refits or repairs or resting their crews. The highest number of U-boats at sea on any one day was 70 on 13 October 1917.[5]

Admiral von Capelle, who had succeeded Tirpitz as the Secretary of the Navy in March 1916, was averse to embarking on any crash programme of U-boat construction. 'Put in a nutshell,' as Gibson and Prendergast neatly sum up the situation, 'the whole effort was to be a gigantic "smash and grab" raid: the brittle glass of the world's shipping was to be shattered, so that the U-boats could grab the gems of victory and decamp before Policeman America could lay a hand upon them.' U-boats that would not be ready in 1917 would not be of much help. Fifty-one new boats were ordered in February 1917; in June 1917, 95 more, of which 21 were in commission when the war ended. None of a large batch of 120 boats ordered in December 1917 was ready when the war ended. At that date 226 boats were under construction. A further 220 boats were ordered in January 1918. It was too late. Asked after the war why, in January 1917, no larger submarine construction programme was ordered at the commencement of the unrestricted campaign, Commander Gayer replied, 'There is no doubt that the opinion of the Chief of the Naval Staff [Holtzendorff] that the U-boat warfare would achieve its goal within 6 months had a restricting effect on all measures. Furthermore, it was believed that industry would be unable to cope with a heavier burden.'[6] Another factor was the opposition of Germany's military leaders to the release of enough skilled workmen from the front for a really large

---

[5] Average monthly totals of U-boats in commission (not including boats paid off because of lengthy repairs), average monthly totals of *Frontboote*, average number of operational boats at sea daily during each month, and the greatest number of boats at sea on any one day during a month are all from the statistical data compiled by or for Spindler, the German Official Historian of the U-boat warfare, from the daily *Admiralstab* lists, 'Standort- und Bereitschaft der Kriegs- und Hilfsschiffe', for the whole war period. (Copy in Naval Historical Branch, Ministry of Defence.) This material (cited below as Spindler, 'Hand-Material') was probably intended for the final volume (v) of his *Der Handelskrieg mit U-Booten*, which he never lived to complete properly. The totals and breakdown of operational boats at sea (always given for the 10th of the month) in Gibson and Prendergast, *The German Submarine War*, pp. 354-5, are taken from the German authority Vice-Admiral Andreas Michelsen, Senior Officer U-boats, 1917-18 (*Der U-Bootskrieg, 1914-1918*, Leipzig, 1925), and are in line with the Spindler 'Hand-Material'.

[6] Undated paper in the Levetzow Papers; German Ministry of Marine MSS. Gayer was a U-boat flotilla commander and later a department head in the U-Boat Office of the Ministry of Marine.

construction programme. It was not until the last months of the war that the Generals agreed to co-operate with the German Admiralty.

At first (31 January 1917) the Admiralty grossly overestimated the size of the German programme, believing that 316 boats would be available by January 1918 (the actual figure at the beginning of 1918 was 165), and that 130 would likely be added during 1918 (80 was the actual number of U-boats built). On 24 March Jellicoe estimated the submarine construction rate at 15 a month. In fact, the average monthly building rate, according to Spindler, was not quite eight boats in 1917 (the Anti-Submarine Division at the Admiralty put it at about eight) and eight for the first ten months of 1918.

The British had suffered serious mercantile losses earlier in the war. These had come mainly from enemy surface craft. But in 1915 and 1916 the submarine, which had been a fragile thing at the beginning of the war, had developed into a desperately dangerous instrument of destruction. It was evident as 1917 opened that the whole issue of the war would depend on the success or failure of the new unrestricted campaign. A new régime at the Admiralty was called upon to meet the terrible blow that was about to fall.

2. NEW FACES AT WHITEHALL

Sir Henry Jackson's resignation as First Sea Lord on 3 December 1916, and the reconstitution of the Coalition Government when Lloyd George succeeded Asquith as Prime Minister on 7 December, had involved a thorough shake-up of the key personnel at the Admiralty. Succeeding Arthur Balfour as First Lord was Sir Edward Carson, Conservative M.P. for Dublin University since 1892 and member of a very old family of south-of-Ireland Protestants. As the pre-war champion of Ulster's resistance to Home Rule, he had earned the sobriquet, the 'uncrowned King of Ulster'. He had also established a great reputation as a clever lawyer with an almost uncanny ability to sway a jury. His only experience as a minister had been five months as Attorney-General in the first Coalition Government (May–October 1915). Yet the new First Lord possessed formidable assets apart from his supreme gift for arguing a case. He had a keen mind and a powerful personality, and, in contrast to his aloof, rather detached predecessor, to whom the Service had never warmed, he was a very understanding man. This, with his gentle manner and kindly ways (belied by his 'dark eyes brooding above the heavy mouth and brutal chin'), quickly endeared him to the Navy. His periodical tours to the naval bases (a practice Balfour had shunned) and monthly visits to the Grand Fleet also help to explain his rapid acquisition of the confidence and regard of the Service, as does his obvious love for the Navy, pride in being its head, and anxiety to master his new duties. Oliver, the longtime Chief of the Admiralty War Staff, who was never lavish with his praise, recollects how the new First Lord 'came round to the various offices and told us that he was going to learn the way the Admiralty was organised and how it worked before he made changes, and he used to send for heads of Departments in the afternoons and discuss their work and office organisation . . .' For such reasons Oliver rated Carson as 'a very good First Lord'.[7]

Frankly admitting he had no technical knowledge, Carson sternly refused to interfere in technical matters. The principle he publicly adopted (at an Aldwych Club luncheon, 8 March 1917) was that he would not interfere with the seamen so long as he was at the Admiralty, nor would he (in a warning intended as much for the Prime Minister as for anybody) permit anyone else to do so. He added, good-humouredly, 'I entered the Admiralty in a state of extreme ignorance. Someone asked me the day I went there how I felt, and I said, "My only qualification is that I am absolutely at sea." ' (Laughter.) 'I confined myself,' he wrote later, 'to the chief duty of a Minister in his Department which is to hold the scales impartially, and to see that every officer and man in the service has justice and fair treatment.'[8] He had no intention, he told a friend in his first week at the Admiralty, of becoming 'an amateur in naval strategy or tactics'. Essentially, he was the mouthpiece of the Admiralty, its defender against attack, and the arbiter in controversial issues—an excellent arrangement from the point of view of the sailors.

Carson made an ideal political chief, quickly establishing a cordial working relationship with the First Sea Lord and the C.-in-C., Grand Fleet. An ideal political chief is not necessarily an ideal First Lord of the Admiralty. Lord Beaverbrook has suggested as much. 'He placed himself at once at the disposal of his expert

[7] Oliver MSS.
[8] Interview in the *Morning Post*, 24 September 1934.

advisers. He became to a marked degree dependent on the advice and guidance of his department. And he resisted any inclination to develop his own ideas of Naval strategy.'[9] This comes out very well, we shall see, in the role he played during the convoy controversy. Lloyd George points to the dilemma from which Carson could not escape. He could have obtained an abundance of advice from other officers in the Service, men who were not part of the Admiralty hierarchy, but his legal training and sense of propriety made such a procedure distasteful to him and he therefore continued to rely solely on the very men whose opinion he had begun to distrust.[10] In short, Carson's self-imposed restraint, his lack of assertiveness—to say nothing of his lack of administrative gifts—largely nullified his powerful assets of energy, courage, independence, and intolerance of complacency.

As regards the other civilian members of the Board of Admiralty, the tireless Sir W. Graham Greene, the Secretary ('Permanent Secretary', strictly speaking) since 1911, remained on. Ernest G. Pretyman replaced the Earl of Lytton as Civil Lord—a good appointment, as he was familiar with Admiralty procedure, having been Civil Lord in 1900–3 and Parliamentary and Financial Secretary in 1903–6. Not perhaps the most congenial of men, he was, nevertheless, the ablest of the four wartime Civil Lords. The most important of the civilians, apart from the First Lord, was the Parliamentary and Financial Secretary, Thomas J. Macnamara, who held this post from 1908 till 1920. He belonged to the Radical wing of the Liberal Party and was closely attached to Lloyd George. Macnamara was a very effective platform speaker, less effective in Parliament, and not an especially competent administrator. Although the Financial Secretary was not formally a member of the Board until 1929, he ranked in practice above the Civil Lord. In the absence of the First Lord, the Financial Secretary was the principal representative of the Admiralty in the Commons.

The Naval Secretary to the First Lord was a good choice: Commodore Allan F. ('Ev') Everett, a genial, level-headed, hardworking officer of independent mind and considerable professional attainments.

The new First Sea Lord was Jellicoe. A serious shortcoming was his inclination to do too much himself. That he over-centralized is

[9] Beaverbrook, *Men and Power, 1917–1918* (London, 1956), p. 150.
[10] *War Memoirs of David Lloyd George* (London, 1933–6, 6 vols.), iii. 1170–1.

PLATE III

ACTING VICE-ADMIRAL SIR HENRY OLIVER
Chief of Admiralty War Staff, November 1914–May 1917,
Deputy Chief of Naval Staff from May 1917

[*Photograph : by permission of Dame Beryl Oliver*

PLATE IV

2. ADM. SIR CHARLES MADDEN
Second-in-Command, Grand Fleet,
from November 1916
[Painting by Sir Arthur Cope : by permission of

1. REAR-ADM. SIR O. DE B. BROCK
Chief of Staff to the C.-in-C.,
Grand Fleet, from November 1916
[Painting by Sir Arthur Cope : by permission of Mrs. John Davie

a point which has been made by Admiral Wemyss, Paymaster Rear-Admiral Manisty, and Lord Hankey, among others. 'Paper work is my curse, the same as with you,' he had written when C.-in-C. 'I can't get away from it.'[11] This remained his 'curse' when he went to the Admiralty, and, at a time when, owing to constant attendance at meetings, he had less time than ever before for paper work. He quickly found himself 'overwhelmed with work'. 'War Councils waste $\frac{1}{2}$ my day', he complained to Beatty. The combination of his natural propensity for making all the decisions himself and the demands on his time gave him few opportunities to reflect on the higher strategy of the war at sea. 'The Imperial War Cabinet meets 3 times a week, besides the ordinary War Cabinet daily, and I find as a consequence very little time for the work of the war. The waste of time is abominable, but I cannot be away or something may get settled to which I should object.'[12] This was all the more reason why he should have confined himself to *policy* and the other things that really mattered rather than on petty problems. In practice, there were few papers he did not see. His time was absorbed in such routine matters as writing minutes on a paper in which the Director of Statistics asked that shipping loss figures be obtained from him instead of the Ministry of Shipping. When the Commander of the Dover Patrol complained that the coastal motor-boat committee had been appointed without a representative from his staff, Jellicoe wrote a long minute on this.[13] The First Lord advised Jellicoe not to work so hard over so many details. 'Sit in a chair, put your feet up, and think.' This excellent advice made no impression on the Admiral and only distressed Lady Jellicoe. 'The First Lord does not understand my Jack', she told Lady Carson over the tea cups.[14] Jellicoe never understood that there was but one way for a high war administrator not to be worn out before his time, and that was for him to concentrate on formulating policy and to leave the details to subordinates.

There was a second main reason why Jellicoe was not entirely successful at the Admiralty. His new appointment brought him into regular contact with the politicians, particularly in the War Cabinet. A First Sea Lord had to have many of the talents of a

[11] Jellicoe to Admiral Sir Henry Jackson (First Sea Lord), 8 October 1916; Jackson MSS.
[12] Jellicoe to Beatty, 26 March 1917; Beatty MSS.
[13] Diary entries, 12 July, 21 September 1917; Dewar MSS.
[14] Lady Carson in a conversation with the author, 23 February 1960.

politician to survive in this jungle of wily manœuvrers and clever debaters. Jellicoe, soft-spoken, not forceful, not given to the parry and thrust of debate, incapable of manœuvring, was out of his element. Lord Fisher put the matter perfectly when he said Jellicoe was 'not the man to stand up against a pack of lawyers clothed with Cabinet garments and possessed of tongues that have put them where they are!'[15] Beatty, as he afterwards proved when First Sea Lord (1919–27), and as Fisher had realized in November 1916, was much better endowed with the non-naval talents needed for success as professional head of the Navy. Moreover, Beatty was much younger than Jellicoe, had a more flexible mind, was more receptive to new ideas, and exploited to the full the brains of his staff. For these reasons alone he would have been the better man to deal with the submarine menace.

Busy though Jellicoe was, his fundamental humanity never deserted him. Thus, one officer writes of how he 'will never forget the little figure in mess undress who used to come into Room 40 nearly every night to hear the latest news and cheer us with appreciative words'. The strength and weakness of the man are revealed by Admiral Sir Lionel Preston, who, as Director of the Minesweeping Division at the Admiralty, attended the Staff meeting every morning at which Jellicoe usually presided. 'He was always quietly confident, prompt and logical in every decision he made, and if he had any fault, it was too much consideration for those serving him. He could not be ruthless. I never remember him showing anger or raising his voice.'[16]

Beatty appraised the new régime at Whitehall this way: 'I fancy you will find Jellicoe will stop there much longer than you think. I certainly hope he will, as he knows the Grand Fleet conditions, and if Carson supports him strongly, he will do. The trouble with him, i.e. J., is that if Carson doesn't support him, he, Jellicoe is not strong enough in character to make him.'[17] The C.-in-C. need not have feared. Jellicoe and Carson hit it off very well. Few First Sea Lords, indeed, have been so staunchly supported by their civilian Chief.

As for the men around Jellicoe, Cecil Burney, who succeeded

---

[15] Fisher to E. G. Pretyman, 27 December 1916; Arthur J. Marder, *Fear God and Dread Nought: the Correspondence of Admiral of the Fleet Lord Fisher of Kilverstone* (London, 1952–9, 3 vols.), iii. 408. (Hereafter cited by title.)

[16] Admiral Preston's letter to the author, 8 January 1963.

[17] Beatty to Lady Beatty, 15 December 1916; Beatty MSS.

Gough-Calthorpe as Second Sea Lord, was concerned with the personnel of the Navy, the manning and training of the Fleet, services and appointments of officers, and so forth. His uncertain health (he suffered constantly from arthritis) was not his only handicap. Graham Greene, who had ample opportunities to size up Burney's talents, wrote of him:

He was not a man of strong and decided character and had not the gift of independent judgment, but his knowledge of the details of the Naval Service was deep and his advice on all that concerned the routine and inner life of officers and men afloat was very valuable. His qualities made him an admirable supporter of men, like Lord Fisher [he had assisted Fisher in carrying out his personnel reforms], who possess enterprise and vision, but he himself would never supply the initiative and force of character necessary to the accomplishment of any great action or policy. . . .

As Second Sea Lord during the war his administrative functions did not call for much display of special abilities. My recollection is that he was a very useful member of the Board and carried out his duties in an efficient manner, but the executive direction of the Fleet and naval operations was centred in the hands of the First Sea Lord and the War Staff, and Burney's share in this was small. . . .

In character Burney was amiable and very easy to work with . . .[18]

Senior officers had no high opinion of Burney. Beatty's estimate was representative of Service opinion. 'I hear Jellicoe is very seedy and has had to go away for a rest. What a situation with an old mummy like Burney to do his work.'[19] He, nevertheless, possessed Jellicoe's entire confidence.

Tudor, an officer of superior talents, stayed on as Third Sea Lord, in charge of all *matériel* matters. Sueter describes him as 'a very able scientific gunnery officer and most capable Controller of the Navy'.

Lionel Halsey, who had been Captain of the Fleet, was the new Fourth Sea Lord, in succession to C. F. Lambert. His department was concerned with the transport service, the superintendence of naval stores, fleet coaling and victualling services, prize questions, pensions, allowances, medals, and similar miscellaneous matters. He was a delightful, outgoing, frank person of vitality and great

[18] Graham Greene's memorandum, 'Admiral of the Fleet Sir Cecil Burney', 23 January 1935; Graham Greene MSS.
[19] Beatty to Lady Beatty, 4 June 1917; Beatty MSS.

charm of manner, universally popular in the Service. His ships were all 'happy ships'. Richmond could pass him off as 'a very good chap, but as mutton-headed as he can be', and another contemporary describes him as 'not a very serious sailor—a very nice man of little weight'. Most of Halsey's peers, however, rated his intelligence and professional ability highly.

Until this time air matters had been divided among the Sea Lords. The Second Sea Lord included air personnel in his domain, the Third Sea Lord was responsible for aerial construction, and so on. The Director of Naval Air Services was not a member of the Board. A Fifth Sea Lord for Naval Air Duties was now added (11 January 1917): Commodore Godfrey Paine, a thickset, forthright man with much drive, who was one of the earliest officers who had qualified as a flyer. On 22 December 1916 the second (Cowdray) Air Board had become in effect a ministry, with the Admiralty represented on it by the Fifth Sea Lord.

When the war started, every able-bodied captain and commander had done his best to get to sea. The result was that the Admiralty was manned principally by 'retired officers, the hurt, and the maimed'. The situation righted itself very slowly. It was not until Jellicoe became First Sea Lord that the best brains of the Navy found their way to the Admiralty. He brought a large party of officers from the Grand Fleet to augment the War Staff. It rather amused Oliver and his people, since, while Jellicoe was C.-in-C., he had regarded any Admiralty raiding of Grand Fleet personnel as a *casus belli*. There was a distinct improvement in the quality of War Staff officers. There were now fewer retired officers who had been hunting or keeping chickens for years, and more men fresh from the sea, a number of them of exceptional ability.

'Dummy' Oliver, that strong silent man, was kept on as Chief of the Admiralty War Staff, as Jellicoe found that he could not at once lose this vast accumulation of knowledge. Richmond's estimate of Oliver is not far off the mark: 'He is intensely shrewd and hard-working, full of common sense, but deficient in knowledge of war. . . . He is one of the finest seamen in the Navy, but seamanship & strategy do not necessarily accompany each other. . . . He is by nature a man who does everything for himself, even to his own typing, & is unable to decentralise & use subordinates.'[20]

Among the 'mob' from the north were selected officers for the

[20] Diary, 5 June 1917; *Portrait of an Admiral*, p. 256.

Anti-Submarine Division of the Staff, which Jellicoe established almost at once. He placed Rear-Admiral A. L. Duff in charge of the Division, with Captain F. C. Dreyer as Assistant Director. (Captain H. T. Walwyn relieved Dreyer when the latter succeeded Morgan Singer as D.N.O. on 1 March 1917.) Duff was a most attractive person—6' 2" tall and with an 'indefinable princeliness' about him. One who knew him well in China after the war wrote: 'At the mere sight of him, the Homeric epithet "Agamemnon, King of Men" instinctively rose in the mind.' Duff was a torpedo specialist who had flown his flag in the *Superb* at Jutland as Second-in-Command of the 4th Battle Squadron. He was a most competent officer, as testified by Jellicoe's earmarking him in the spring of 1916 to be his C.O.S. if anything happened to Madden, and by now choosing him from all the junior flag officers to organize the anti-submarine campaign. As D.A.S.D., he had to organize his department out of nothing, virtually.

The Acting Director of the Trade Division since October 1914, the kindly and charming Captain Richard Webb, was retained. He was strangely old-fashioned in many ways, as, when commanding the flagship *Ariadne* on the West Indian Station in pre-war days, he forbade gin in the wardroom as not being a gentleman's drink! But he was well suited to his job, having all the gifts of an outstanding staff officer: an encyclopedic mind, 'a gift for analysing a complicated situation, and summing it up from its various angles', and a hatred of not being 'stood up to'. Also kept on was Captain Reginald Hall, the D.N.I. (promoted to Rear-Admiral in April 1917), considered by many as one of the few great brains of the war, which, indeed, he was.

So much for the new régime at Whitehall. On the whole, it was more youthful, and one that promised a more vigorous administration.

A note on the War Cabinet will not be amiss at this point. On Lloyd George's becoming Prime Minister, the Cabinet and the War Committee were merged into a single body, the War Cabinet, thus combining 'in itself the powers of decision of the former Cabinet with the systematic procedure of the Committee of Imperial Defence' (Hankey). The main defects of the War Committee, as experience had brought out, were its size (it had grown from eight to thirteen) and the fact that many of its members were overburdened with departmental responsibilities. The War Cabinet did not have these defects. The number of members was reduced to five; it never exceeded seven. As Lloyd George told the Commons (19 December 1916), 'You cannot run a war with a Sanhedrin.' One advantage of small size was that the War Cabinet could meet more frequently—over three hundred times in 1917 alone. The original members were the Prime Minister (Chairman), Bonar Law, Arthur Henderson, and Lords Curzon and Milner. Lloyd George was, of course, a Liberal, Henderson represented Labour, and the others were Conservatives. With the exception of Bonar Law, the Chancellor of the Exchequer and Leader of the House of Commons, they were Ministers without departmental responsibilities, therefore free from heavy administrative and Parliamentary duties, and able to devote all their time and energy to the larger problems of the war. It seems extraordinary that the First Lord, the War Secretary, and the Foreign Secretary were not regular War Cabinet members. Cabinet Ministers (with their experts if they wished) attended when matters concerning their own department were under discussion, but only during that time. In this way, Carson, and later Geddes, attended on occasion. Arthur Balfour, as Foreign Secretary, though not officially a member, 'claimed and exercised the right of attending any meeting', Hankey informs us. The C.I.G.S. and First Sea Lord attended at the beginning of each meeting, reporting on the military and naval situations and leaving after all military and naval questions on the agenda had been disposed of. This points up another difference between the War Cabinet and the War Committee. The former kept minutes and worked to an agenda paper. When attended by the Prime Ministers and other representatives of the Dominions (March–May 1917, June–December 1918), the War Cabinet became known as the Imperial War Cabinet. The incomparable Sir Maurice Hankey, with his many fine qualities, among them an exceptional memory, agile mind, tact, patience, and loyalty, was the Secretary of the War Cabinet.[21]

---

[21] The minutes of the War Cabinet and Imperial War Cabinet meetings will be found in the Cab. 23 class at the P.R.O. Material from this source will be identified merely by 'W.C.' or 'I.W.C.' number of meeting.

IV

Fighting the U-boats

(December 1916 – April 1917)

The first phase of the naval war was the tacit submission of the German sea-going fleets to the superior strength of Britain. There supervened upon this from October, 1916, with ever-growing intensity, the second phase, namely the life-and-death struggle of the Royal Navy with the German U-boats. It was a warfare hitherto undreamed-of among men, a warfare at once more merciless and complicated than had ever been conceived. All the known sciences, every adaptation of mechanics, optics, and acoustics that could play a part, were pressed into its service. It was a war of charts and calculations, of dials and switches, of experts who were also heroes, of tense, patient thought interrupted by explosions and death; of crews hunted and choked in the depths of the waters, and great ships foundering far from port without aid or mercy. And upon the workings of this grisly process turned the history of the world.

WINSTON CHURCHILL, *Thoughts and Adventures*.

I. MEASURES TO EASE THE SHIPPING SHORTAGE

FOUR remedies for the shipping shortage were continually under discussion: (1) an increase in the home-grown supply of food, as well as an economization in the consumption of food, in order to release shipping for the war effort; (2) building more merchant ships; (3) relieving the squeeze on shipping; (4) reducing the destructiveness of the U-boats. The first, the food problem, was of no direct concern to the Admiralty. In 1913 Britain imported 18·1 million tons of food; in 1918 she imported only 11·4 million tons, or about 63 per cent as much. The difference, 6·7 million tons, represented the amount of shipping saved by the increase in agricultural production and the introduction of voluntary food restrictions and, by July 1918, of rationing on a national basis.

Turning to merchant shipbuilding, we find that the Board of Trade had been responsible for this until the end of 1916, but there was no department which *controlled* merchant shipping. There was only a Shipping Control Committee (set up in January 1916),

63

which decided how best to use the shipping available. It lacked full executive powers to do its job effectively. In December 1916 Lloyd George appointed the canny Scottish shipowner Sir Joseph Maclay as Shipping Controller, with a seat in the Cabinet and wide and undefined powers. Maclay was a strong personality with a reputation for not being guided—or hampered—by precedents. Hankey describes him as a man who 'knew his job inside and out', and Lord Hurcomb, who worked with him in those days, says that he 'found him a most wise and understanding chief, and the bigger the issue, the more this stood out'. The duties of the new ministry, whose organization was completed by April 1917, included the direction of mercantile shipbuilding, the control of port facilities in Great Britain, and, after it had absorbed the Transport Division of the Admiralty (following a showdown with the Sea Lords in the War Cabinet in February 1917), the allocation of tonnage for the needs of the Service and other ministries.

In 1915, 651,000 tons of merchant shipping had been built in the United Kingdom. The figure dipped to 542,000 tons in 1916, or 43 per cent of the British tonnage lost that year. As the New Year opened, and certainly from February, it was obvious that output had to be stepped up considerably if the anticipated much higher rate of loss was to be made good. Maclay at once grasped the essential fact that ships had to be built faster than the enemy was sinking them. Upon expert advice he decided 'to proceed at once with an extensive building programme of cargo ships of simple design and as far as possible of standard types with respect to both engines and hull'. Four standard designs had been approved by the end of February 1917. In all about twelve types were selected in 1917. By the end of 1918, 76 per cent of the ships building were 'Standard Ships'. Among other methods adopted to increase shipbuilding output was the prevention of the further depletion of the labour force. In January 1917 the Government exempted from military service all men employed in shipbuilding and marine engineering shops prior to 29 March.

New United Kingdom tonnage for the first quarter of 1917 was 246,000 tons gross, or 326,000 tons, if we include the whole Empire. This figure was quite an improvement over any quarter in 1916: the output for the last quarter of 1916 was 213,000, or 220,000, including the Empire. Yet it was about 18 per cent below the Shipping Controller's target for the United Kingdom, which itself was not enough to replace the British shipping that was being destroyed after 1 February 1917. The future did not look bright, since the main reasons for the lagging building rate promised to continue indefinitely: the labour shortage and the dearth of steel. Figures submitted to the Government on 26 April showed that, to increase the output to 1,800,000 tons a year, or 50 per cent above the Shipping Controller's original estimate, it would be necessary to find 35,000 more skilled (or 44,000 unskilled) workers and to increase the weekly steel supply allotted to merchant shipbuilding from 13,000 to 22,000 tons. But even were 1,800,000 tons possible, it would replace only about a third of the British tonnage that was being destroyed. An almost frenzied programme of purchases from neutrals might help. 'The world's ports were ransacked for tonnage', writes the Official Historian Fayle. 'Decrepit steamers fetched fabulous prices, and even old sailing-vessels, derelict or used as harbour hulks, were reconditioned and sent out to sea again.' Another War Cabinet measure was to have the Admiralty curtail their programme of capital-ship construction. Jellicoe preferred to see all four battle cruisers that were building proceeded with; but when the Admiralty stated that it would be impossible to complete any of them, except the *Hood*, before the spring of 1919 at the earliest, the War Cabinet decided (February 1917) to halt the building of all the battle cruisers except the *Hood*, as well as five light cruisers.

The results of all the Government's measures to increase the building rate were dismal. Total United Kingdom mercantile tonnage output was 495,000 in the first half of 1917 (631,000, including Empire output), and 668,000 in the second half (676,000, including Empire output), for a total of 1,163,000 (1,307,000). With the purchase of foreign tonnage (mainly Japanese) new British shipping for the year totalled a little under a million and a half tons, which was far below expectations.

There were, in the third place, attempts to relieve the squeeze on shipping. Thus, on 16 February 1917 the War Cabinet approved the recommendations of the inter-departmental Import Restrictions Committee for the monthly reduction of 500,000 tons of imports over the 1916 figures. There was some improvement in the spring in relieving the chronic port congestion. The discharge of cargoes was speeded up, where possible, by providing extra equipment and accommodation at the ports, and by making a fuller use of the Transport Workers' Battalions authorized in December 1916. These men rotated between their military training and work at the ports. By mid-April over 10,000 workers were enrolled in these battalions, with an average number of 4,702 employed daily during April in discharging cargoes. The figure rose to 5,760 in June.

The Admiralty had their own programme for easing the shipping shortage. One of the first problems with which Jellicoe had to deal was the strain placed upon the Navy by military operations, particularly in distant theatres of war. In December 1916 some two million and a quarter troops were being maintained overseas. It was becoming increasingly difficult to provide the immense amount of shipping for the transport of troops, munitions, and stores for the various overseas operations, to say nothing of the tax on war vessels for escort duty. The light craft were more urgently needed for guarding trade in Home waters, and a reduction of overseas military commitments would also free a large number of merchant ships for use in bringing in essential imports. At the end of March 1917, 631 ships of over two million tons were tied up in supplying the requirements in troops and stores of France, Mesopotamia, East Africa, Salonika, and Egypt.[1] The Allied demands for supplies aggravated the situation as France and Italy became more and more dependent upon Britain for shipping.

Jellicoe alluded to the problem in memoranda for the War Cabinet on 14 December 1916 and 21 February 1917. In the latter he pointed out that the position was 'exceedingly grave' and could only be met by a radical change in the policy with regard to overseas operations. It was evident from the figures of shipping losses of 1–16 February through submarines and mines (243,000 tons of British, Allied, and neutral shipping, including sailing and fishing vessels) that there were not enough patrol vessels for the efficient protection of both transports and other merchant shipping in all the areas where losses were taking place. Drastic and immediate action was required to relieve the demand upon the limited supply of A/S vessels. The 'only practicable method' was by reducing the number of transports, supply ships, etc. requiring escort which were employed in supplying the operations in Mesopotamia, Salonika, Egypt, and East Africa. This meant, of course, as Jellicoe

[1] Admiralty paper for the Imperial War Cabinet, 'A General Review of the Naval Situation' (G.T.–277), 24 March 1917.

clearly stated, a reduction of some or all of the overseas forces.[2] A Jellicoe minute sent to the War Cabinet on 2 March pointed to the great danger of an eventual food shortage as the result of merchant ship losses and the strain on naval resources imposed by the Cabinet decision to continue the advance in Mesopotamia. An Admiralty paper circulated to the Imperial War Cabinet on 24 March asserted that without very drastic changes in policy the available mercantile tonnage would be utterly insufficient to carry out Britain's requirements.

For instance, it is estimated that in the period from April to August (inclusive) of this year there will only be available from 60 per cent. to 70 per cent. of the total shipping tonnage required to carry the food and other imports necessary for civilian requirements and for munitions. This does not take into account the tonnage required for the import of the 2,000,000 tons of wheat which is wanted by the Food Controller to build up a reserve. It is known that the store of wheat is very low (at the end of July it will only be six or seven weeks), and that the reserve of stores and food for our armies abroad is measured by days and not by weeks. It is impossible to over-estimate the gravity of the situation under these conditions. The position is rendered still more critical by the inadequacy of our shipping resources for the supply of coal to France and Italy up to the amounts required.[3]

Persisting in their campaign to reduce the immense strain on shipping resources and protecting vessels by reducing Allied commitments in secondary theatres of war, the Admiralty sent to the War Cabinet on 12 April a War Staff paper warning against falling in with the French proposal to invade Greece. If this campaign materialized, there would be an increase in the losses of transports, etc., a reduction in tonnage available for carrying essential supplies, and an increase in shipping losses in Home waters, due to the withdrawal of patrol craft and minesweepers for use in the Mediterranean.

On 1 May the War Cabinet received a grave memorandum from Jellicoe which had the unanimous endorsement of the Board of

---

[2] 'Naval Policy in Relation to Mercantile Shipping Losses from Submarine Warfare, and the Effect on the Strategical Situation'; Admiralty MSS. There were 37 destroyers, 35 sloops, and 183 trawlers in the Mediterranean, all employed on escort and patrol work. 'The withdrawal of the troops would not of course permit the whole number of these vessels to be withdrawn as a proportion would still be required for the protection of trade and the escort of Men-of-War and valuable ships, etc.' *Ibid.*

[3] 'A General Review of the Naval Situation' (G.T.–277).

Admiralty. It was the most despairing plea yet made on the subject of secondary military operations, a veritable *cri de coeur* that Newbolt calls an 'ultimatum':

> . . . I have urged time after time [on the War Cabinet] the absolute necessity that exists for reducing the number of lines of communication which the Navy is called upon to safeguard and for increasing the protection of those lines of communication which remain. So far the only result of my efforts has been increased calls upon the Navy without any sort of reduction of liabilities and with no appreciable increase of our resources. During the last three months, for example, we have been asked to import large numbers of native labourers from all parts of the world and, by the recent actions of the enemy, we are also called upon to escort all our hospital ships except those in far distant waters. . . .
>
> I feel certain that the Navy will indubitably fail in the near future to satisfy the demands made upon it by the present policy of H.M. Government unless—(a) we at once withdraw the whole of our force from Salonica, as this is the quarter which taxes our resources most heavily and, from the military point of view, gives no promise of a successful offensive. . . . (b) We realise that we cannot continue to bring reinforcements of troops into this country unless they are conveyed in ships carrying other essentials from the Colonies, such as food, etc., as we cannot afford to provide the necessary escorting ships. (c) The policy of importing labour is at once abandoned for the same reason. (d) The import of everything that is not essential to the life of the country is ruthlessly and immediately stopped.[4]

The Prime Minister had to do something. At an Allied conference held in Paris on 4–5 May, he argued against a big offensive at Salonika and declared that the essential needs of the civilian populations of the Allied countries could be met only by gradually reducing the Salonika force to the size required to hold its position, and he announced that Britain would pull out one British division and two cavalry brigades. Jellicoe, who was present, asserted that they could not continue to tie up 150 ships of 600,000 tons to 'carry out the requirements of the War Office at Salonica'. The tonnage was badly needed elsewhere. 'It was even more important to release patrol vessels to guard the home routes.' He was convinced that 'unless the Salonica force was evacuated before the

---

[4] Jellicoe's memorandum for the War Cabinet, 'The Naval Situation with Reference to the Submarine Danger' (G.T.-611), 27 April 1917. Haig, C.-in-C. of the British Army in France, and Robertson, the C.I.G.S., had been influential in converting Jellicoe into a thorough 'Westerner', yet it should be clear from the foregoing that the Admiral had good and sufficient naval reasons for espousing that policy.

end of the year it would starve there . . . unless a beginning were made at once to reduce, it would be too late. A little later there would be no ships to take the troops away.'[5] The French objections made no impression on Lloyd George. In June–July one British division and two mounted brigades were withdrawn and sent to Egypt, and were joined by another division early in September, again over Allied opposition. There were no further withdrawals: four divisions remained at Salonika. Moving troops from Macedonia to Egypt made no practical difference in the mercantile tonnage required and the Navy's responsibilities in the area. And so Jellicoe's hopes of reclaiming 400,000 tons of shipping in that direction were dashed. He did eventually recover the 400,000 tons, after the adoption in the summer of Sir Leo Chiozza Money's suggestion (he was Parliamentary Secretary to the Ministry of Shipping) early in May that there be a concentration upon the North Atlantic routes—that the Allies draw all necessary supplies from the United States and Canada, so releasing shipping normally employed on the longer routes. This was, as Fayle used to impress on the officers at the Staff College after the war, one of the most important decisions of the war.

The fourth possible remedy to ease the shipping shortage was through anti-submarine warfare, and this was, of course, the special province of the Admiralty.

2. NAVAL MEASURES OLD AND NEW[6]

The Anti-Submarine Division had come into being on 16 December 1916. Prior to Jellicoe's coming to the Admiralty, no one division dealt with the submarine menace as a single problem. The Trade, Operations, and Intelligence Divisions and the Submarine Committee all had a hand in it. These branches of the Admiralty War Staff were now co-ordinated by the A.S.D., which also absorbed the duties and personnel of the old Submarine Committee; it had been concerned with technical measures against the U-boat. The overall charge of the A.S.D. was to co-ordinate existing, and to devise new, measures and devices in the A/S campaign. The

[5] I.C.-21 (Cab. 28 class at the P.R.O.: Allied war conferences—proceedings and resolutions.)
[6] It will be convenient to discuss in this section all the more important measures in use during 1917–18. On the 1914–16 A/S measures, see *From the Dreadnought to Scapa Flow*, ii. 349–64.

A.S.D., as Admiral Dreyer has explained, 'did not actually *design* mines or depth-charges or smoke apparatus or any other weapon; but "fathered" the trials of all anti-submarine weapons and got in touch with the departments whose duty it was to invent them to meet our requirements!'[7] The A.S.D. relieved the Operations Division of control of all ships and aircraft engaged in A/S work. It co-operated with the Chief of the War Staff, but worked directly under the First Sea Lord. 'As a result,' says Dreyer, 'any measure we could propose which was worth trying would get a strong shove from Jellicoe.'

The first weeks of the A.S.D. were inevitably a period of grand confusion. A young officer from the 3rd Battle Squadron who had visited the Admiralty informed Richmond that 'apparently things are quite chaotic as far as the new submarine department is concerned. Nothing organised, no principles, everyone scratching his head and wondering what to do.'[8] The newcomers did settle down, and by the time the unrestricted U-boat campaign began, there was, thanks to Jellicoe's foresight, initiative, and prodding, an organization at the Admiralty, staffed by experts, whose entire efforts were devoted to defeating the U-boats. The A.S.D., incidentally, was the first important wartime instance of decentralization at the Admiralty.

Jellicoe was disgusted with the Admiralty 'apathy' during the year and a half of the Balfour-Jackson administration, thanks to which he had inherited a serious situation. 'There were,' as he summarized the problem, 'only three ways of dealing with the submarine menace. The first, naturally, was to prevent the vessels from putting to sea; the second was to sink them after they were at sea; and the third was to protect the merchant ships from their attack.' He quickly decided that the second was the most promising approach, and that, accordingly, the most pressing need was a great increase in A/S craft, weapons, and devices. The problem could be stated this way. The Germans had lost 22 submarines during the year 1916 (and two more in January 1917). Even if we disregard the fact that of these 22, four had been sunk through accident (blown up on their own mines or stranded) and two others through Russian action (mined or sunk by a patrol), the

---

[7] Admiral Sir Frederic Dreyer, *The Sea Heritage: a Study of Maritime Warfare* (London, 1955), p. 215.
[8] Diary, 9 January 1917; *Portrait of an Admiral*, p. 228.

Royal Navy could not hope to accomplish much against the U-boat campaign with an average monthly destruction rate of less than two.[9] Urgently needed, therefore, were new methods of counter-attack and an improvement of older methods.

In essence, the A/S campaign was based on what one officer has called the 'thousands scheme'—thousands of patrol craft, thousands of mines, thousands of nets, etc. Three principal A/S weapons were developed or improved for attacking the submarine under water (the arming of merchant ships having had the effect of driving the submarine below water)—depth charges, bomb howitzers and throwers, and mine nets—and their manufacture in quantity ordered. The depth charge, which had been evolved during 1915 and was distributed to the Fleet from January 1916, was a bomb that was exploded at a predetermined depth. Originally, the depth charges were dropped overboard from chutes—by hydraulic gear operated from the bridge or by an ordinary slip operated by hand and were fired by a hydrostatic pistol with 40- and 80-ft. settings. In use from August 1917 was the depth-charge thrower, operating on the howitzer principle, which could project depth charges some 40 yards on the beam of the attacking vessel. Until June 1917 two depth charges were usually supplied to each A/S vessel. The allotment was increased to four in July and to six in August. Later, in 1917–18, as the usefulness of the weapon became more evident and production now permitted, P-boats (patrol boats, really small destroyers) and sloops operating outside the North Sea and Dover areas were each given 30 to 50 of them. Whereas the peak monthly production of depth charges prior to 1917 had been 732 (December 1916), and was less than 600 as late as July 1917, it was over 2,000 in October 1917, and over 5,000 a year later. Two types had been used; but during 1917 the heavier Type 'D' (300 lb. charge of TNT) replaced Type 'D*' (120 lb.) in all craft fast enough to be

[9] The statistics and other data on U-boat losses in this volume are derived from: Historical Section, Admiralty, 'Chronological List of German U-boats Sunk in First World War, 1914–1918', ca. 1954 (this is the final approved list; there is a copy in the Naval Historical Branch of the Ministry of Defence); Gibson and Prendergast, *The German Submarine War, 1914–1918*; Erich Gröner, 'Schiffsverluste der Kaiserlichen Marine, 1914–1918', *Marine Rundschau*, February 1964 (a reprint of the official list issued by the German Admiralty in 1934); the official work by Rear-Admiral Arno Spindler, *Der Krieg zur See, 1914–1918. Der Handelskrieg mit U-Booten* (1932–66, 5 vols.), iv and v covering 1917–18; and Robert M. Grant, *U-Boats Destroyed* (London, 1964). Needless to say, the authorities are not always in agreement.

clear of the heavier jolt when the charge exploded. By the end of the year the pistol was capable of firing at 50, 100, 150, or 200 feet. A/S craft could now use the 300-lb. bomb (set to 100 feet or more) and no longer had to have a lighter charge. During 1917 the Navy expended between 100 and 300 depth charges a month in attacks upon the U-boats; during the last six months of the war, the average monthly number used was 2,000.

The depth-charge has been described as a compound of 'applied chemistry, synthetic earthquake and sudden death', and as the most effective of all the A/S measures, whether used by a merchant vessel or a warship. In Jellicoe's opinion, there was 'no doubt that the increased use of the depth-charge was a great factor in the defeat of the submarine menace. German submarine officers themselves have stated the nerve-shattering effect that this method of attack had on them. . . . The convoy system alone could not possibly have defeated the submarines had it not been accompanied by an ever-increasing expenditure of depth-charges by the escort vessels. *The ability to use depth-charges in larger numbers enabled the submarine [convoy] escort to use offensive measures against the attacking submarines.*'[10] Although depth charges proved to be the most effective of all the weapons used against submerged U-boats, they were no panacea. Even when the Navy possessed huge quantities of depth charges and released them on the slightest provocation, they seldom found their mark. To destroy a U-boat it was necessary to explode the 'D'-type charge within 14 feet of her, and, to disable her and force her to the surface, within about 28 feet.

It had [writes an officer who served in torpedo craft] proved itself an effective weapon against a submarine that, by attack or otherwise, revealed her presence close at hand. The greater the number that could be provided for destroyers and patrol craft the greater were the chances of showering these missiles round any submarine that showed herself. But the trouble was that a well handled submarine refrained from showing herself when a war-vessel was near, and we could not, or thought we could not, arrange to have patrol craft in close company with every merchant ship. Submarines that were inefficient or unfortunate were sometimes destroyed, but our shipping losses continued to increase.[11]

[10] Jellicoe, *The Submarine Peril* (London, 1934), p. 14.
[11] Commander John Creswell, *Naval Warfare* (London, 1942, 2nd ed.), p. 157.

Closely related to the depth charge was the bomb fired by a howitzer (rifled gun) or bomb-thrower (smooth-bore gun) to explode under water. Trials and experiments were carried out late in 1916 and the first types went into production in April 1917: a 3·5-inch bomb-thrower which fired a 200-lb. bomb to a distance of 1,200 yards, and a 350-lb. bomb, 650 yards. Later developments produced howitzers and bomb-throwers ranging up to 13·5-inch. Bomb howitzers and throwers were being issued to various types of A/S craft as well as to merchant ships by the summer of 1917. Over 1,200 had been mounted by the end of the war. They were in a way the ancestors of the 'Hedgehog' and 'Squid' of World War II, although these were *ahead*-throwing weapons.

Indicator nets and E.C. (electro-contact) mine nets were old weapons which had become standardized by 1917 and whose use was now extended. Indicator nets were wire nets moored in long lines to buoys which by their movement indicated the submarine's presence, or they were towed in various lengths by patrol craft. Already by 1916 it was discovered that the most effective use of nets was with electro-contact mines which studded the nets at frequent intervals. 'As the enemy tried to plough his way through the obstruction—the use of net cutters having somewhat nullified the utility of the net *per se*—the net would trail aft, the mines exploding on contact with the submarine's hull. These nets were laid in various areas in the supposed track of submarines and to the seaward sides of the tracks of convoys, and besides claiming several victims, acted as a deterrent against submarine attack in several localities where the enemy either presumed or feared their presence, especially on the East Coast of England.'[12]

A moored mine-net barrage across the Straits of Dover was laid down from the southern end of the Goodwin Sands to the Ruytingen Bank in the autumn of 1916 and extended to the Snouw Bank (off Dunkirk) in February 1917. This barrage, called the 'Cross-Channel Barrage', consisted of mine nets (two E.C. mines in each net) with the nets clipped to a jackstay which was secured

[12] Technical History Section, Admiralty, Monograph TH 7 (1919), *The Anti-Submarine Division of the Naval Staff, December 1916–November 1918*, p. 20. The Technical History Monographs are to be found in the Naval Library, Ministry of Defence. Although various authorities, including Newbolt (*Naval Operations*), the Naval Staff Monograph, etc., refer to 'indicator mine nets' in the 'Cross-Channel Barrage' (the discussion of which follows), the evidence is that these nets did not have indicator (breakaway) buoys attached to them.

between buoys moored about 500 yards apart. The pressure of the tide on the nets was so great that nets of only 40 or 60 feet in depth were practicable. As compensation for the shortness of the depth of the nets, three rows of moored mines were laid deep half a mile to the westwards of the nets. Secret gaps, periodically changed, were left in the net barrage to allow British craft to proceed safely to the Belgian coast. The Dover Patrol, under Vice-Admiral Sir Reginald Bacon, had among its many responsibilities the task of patrolling the net barrage. A comparatively few ships (drifters, mostly unarmed, supported by armed yachts and trawlers) watched this barrage, and were assisted by light-buoys placed at intervals along the barrage.

The Cross-Channel Barrage was not a success. The bad weather made it difficult to maintain the efficiency of the mine nets. The mine barrage was no more effective, apart from the inefficiency of the mines themselves (see below). The mines dragged their moorings and fouled the nets, becoming by May 1917 a menace to the vessels maintaining or patrolling the barrage. There was nothing for it but to lift the western portion of the barrage (to Outer Ruytingen) and sweep up the mines (May–July 1917). The mine nets in the western portion were relaid, with strengthened moorings, to the south-west of their old position to clear any remaining mines. In short, the Cross-Channel Barrage presented little more than an inconvenience to the U-boats going to or coming from their Flanders or North Sea bases by way of the Channel.

The High Seas Fleet boats (that is, the larger boats operating from bases in the Heligoland Bight) had not been allowed to attempt the passage through the Dover Straits since April 1915, and had had to use the north-about route. Now, in December 1916, the interdiction was lifted. The advantages to the seboats were great. Passage through the Straits saved the North Sea boats at least ten days for the double journey to and from their patrol area. The U-boats had little trouble in crossing the net barrage at night, normally by drifting over the nets at high tide. From the beginning of 1917 until the middle of November they made 253 passages; only six boats were sunk in the Dover Straits area in this time, and of those only one hit a mine. Only occasionally would a U-boat encounter a net, and even then she would usually break through without exploding a mine. 'So through this defile poured one long stream of submarines, to spread themselves over the western approaches, where they could extirpate all seaborne trade as it flowed in from the outer world.' Admiral Bacon had to admit: 'There is no doubt that this Barrage never stopped submarines passing. . . . But this does not mean that the Barrage was useless. It was an undoubted deterrent to destroyers. In fact, we had unfortunate proofs of its efficiency in the accidents to more than one of our own boats.'[13] How he arrives at 'undoubted deterrent', I cannot say. The barrage does not seem to have caused the Germans any particular inconvenience in their raid on 20–21 April (see below, pp. 107–8). The net barrage would, no doubt, restrict the freedom of movement of their destroyers, but not to any great extent.

The production of the explosive paravane ('high-speed submarine sweep') was increased and all destroyers were fitted with it.[14]

What appeared at the time to be the most important of the A/S devices, as distinct from weapons, was the hydrophone, a microphone that detected the beat of a submarine propeller at some distance. There were two main types. One was fixed on the sea-bottom and connected generally with shore stations. The other was for use at sea, being suspended over the ship's side. Trials began in November 1914, the device had emerged from the experimental stage by the autumn of 1915, and various shore hydrophone stations were established in 1916. But the immense amount of opposition, principally from the *Vernon* (the Torpedo and Mining School at Portsmouth) and the technical experts at the Admiralty, delayed its general adoption as a sea-service instrument. It began to be supplied to patrol vessels in the latter part of 1916, and after more obstruction (mainly, Beatty claimed, from the Commodore (S), S. S. Hall), it was fitted to submarines in 1917. Some destroyers and P-boats also received them. Their principal use was by hunting flotillas of small craft, which depended entirely on the hydrophone to detect a submerged U-boat, whereupon they would close for a depth-charge attack.

The early hydrophones had serious limitations for ship use. Mounted for harbour defence, the hydrophone usually could detect an approaching submarine. At sea it could only be used from a stationary, or nearly stationary, vessel, since otherwise the noise

[13] Bacon, *The Dover Patrol, 1915–17* (London, 1919, 2 vols.), ii. 399.
[14] For details and methods of use, see *From the Dreadnought to Scapa Flow*, ii. 351.

of the ship's engine and of the sea washing against the hull drowned the noise made by a U-boat. Yet a stopped vessel was a perfect target for a U-boat's torpedo. Another handicap was that the listening vessel could not expect to hear a submarine if she were lying on the bottom. (U-boat commanders quickly learned to escape detection by lying motionless on the bottom, though this was not possible at depths much below 120 feet.) And if the enemy submarine were moving slowly, the range had to be very close for the listening vessel to hear it. Another disadvantage of the early hydrophones was that they were not accurately directional, being able to pick up sound but giving no indication of the position of its source. It was necessary to sight the submarine, or follow up a torpedo track, in order to attack her. In the spring of 1917 a hydrophone with directional qualities was invented, but it was effective only when suspended over the side when the ship was stopped. This undesirable limitation pointed to the need for an instrument that could be used at any time without stopping the ship. Experiments were now carried out with directional hydrophones fitted into streamlined bodies towed astern. In October 1917 the Admiralty began to produce the towed, directional 'Nash Fish' (named after the inventor). A much improved towed directional type, the 'Porpoise', was being produced and issued by the summer of 1918. Great things were hoped from, and sometimes claimed for, the American K-tube of 1917–18, despite the fact that, like the earliest hydrophones, it could only be used when the vessels working with it were stopped. A drawback of acoustic hunting that could not be overcome was that these devices were least effective where traffic was heaviest, and they were practically useless in the vicinity of convoys.

The introduction of the hydrophone 'marked the beginning of a new era in anti-submarine warfare', Gibson and Prendergast assert. It did nothing of the kind.[16] There was much exaggerated optimism at the time. Captain Creswell, who was acquainted with some of the anti-submarine hydrophone enthusiasts during the war, discounts the value of the hydrophones entirely and maintains 'they were more useful to the hunted [enabling them both to elude their pursuers and to find targets] than to the

[16] Gibson and Prendergast (*The German Submarine War, 1914–1918*, pp. 186–7) claim too much for the early hydrophones. The stress on their 'moral and psychological effect' on the U-boat crews is nonsense.

hunters!'[16] The onetime Admiralty's German Navy expert bears
out this opinion:

> To avoid detection by hydrophones, the U-boat would proceed at
> 'silent running speed', i.e., on electric motors at about 1 to 2 knots, at
> depths ranging from periscope depth to 100 or 120 feet, depending on
> the situation, and heading away from the enemy on varying courses.
> Our hydrophone equipment in W.W. I was rather primitive, and until
> relatively late in the war the U-boat captains did not have to worry too
> much about being chased, although they always credited us with a
> greater capacity to hunt them than we ever possessed. The fact is that
> the U-boats used their own hydrophones to much greater effect on their
> targets [than British A/S craft could].[17]

There were not many occasions when a hydrophone brought
about, or at least contributed to, the destruction of a U-boat.
Official figures show that, through October 1918, 3 U-boats were
known to have been sunk due to hydrophones (including one
through a hydrophone detector minefield); probably sunk, 1;
probably seriously damaged, 5; possibly slightly damaged, 17.[18]
Post-war trials finally condemned this equipment; hydrophones
were abolished in 1921.

One submarine-detection device that offered great promise came
too late in the war: a method devised for the transmission and
reception of supersonic sound waves. Experiments beginning in
June 1917 demonstrated that the device could be used to locate

---

[16] Captain Creswell's letter to the author, 24 October 1962. Hydrophones were also
fitted in British submarines to locate surface vessels or Diesel-engined U-boats on the
surface when outside periscope range or diving below periscope depth. These hydrophones were fixed to plates, one of which was mounted in a hole on each bow, so that
some idea of the direction of the enemy vessel could be obtained by swinging the
submarine until the noise was equalized. One hears of a submarine enthusiast who
thought he could aim his torpedoes by hydrophone instead of using his periscope!

[17] Commander M. G. Saunders's letter to the author, 19 February 1963.

[18] A.S.D., 'Monthly Report No. 18, October 1918', 1 November 1918. These reports
are in the Naval Library, bound in a volume, Anti-Submarine Division, *Monthly
Reports, 1917–18*. The results did not include the 'Fish' flotillas (the specially organized hunting flotillas, on which see below), nor the 'Porpoise' hydrophone. An analysis of 49 Fish hydrophone hunts, May–September 1918, revealed that on the 31
occasions when attacks were made, three submarines were 'possibly slightly damaged'.
Plans Division, 'Analysis of Fish Hydrophone Hunts', 12 October 1918; Dewar
MSS. A Plans Division paper gives three as the wartime total of submarines credited
to the hydrophone. 'Future Anti-Submarine Policy with Special Reference to Hunting Tactics', 30 October 1918; Admiralty MSS. Experiments in using seaplanes,
flying boats, and airships for the detection of submerged submarines by means of the
hydrophone gave poor results.

submarines and other vessels. The object was 'attained by the echo effect, the hull of the distant vessel acting as a reflector and thus producing an echo, and since the speed of sound waves is accurately known the distance can be accurately computed'. The Admiralty Experiment Station at Harwich succeeded in the spring of 1918 in securing supersonic echoes from a British submarine at a range of a few hundred yards. They named the apparatus they used 'ASDIC', after the Allied Submarine Detection Investigation Committee, which had initiated the project. The war ended before any of the equipment was in a sufficiently advanced state to be fitted into ships and operated at sea. ASDIC was developed into an operational device, but of considerably limited capabilities, between the wars. (In 1943 the term was replaced by the newer, United States-originated, SONAR, which derives from Sound Navigating and Ranging.)

The scientists employed by the Admiralty were entranced with the idea of training sea lions, taking advantage of their long hearing and other qualifications to track U-boats. In May 1917 the Admiralty, without conviction, approved of trials being carried out in the Solent. 'Valuable time, personnel, and money had in fact to be wasted to prove the futility and childishness of this contention', declared Admiral Duff in 1931. Commander Kemp tells the story of 'Queenie' and Co.

Experiments with two trained animals in a circus were first carried out in a Glasgow swimming bath. Men stationed at various points on the sides of the bath rang little bells and the sealions swam to the source of the sound. On arrival they were rewarded with a fish. After they got used to the sound of a bell, a submerged oscillator was tried, and it was found that they responded equally well. One slight drawback was they eventually got rather sluggish and fat from earning so many fish as rewards.

From the Glasgow swimming bath they were taken to Lake Bala in Wales, where longer range trials were carried out. Other sealions were obtained from the zoo and a team of five now put into training. The prize animal, named Queenie, several times managed a run of three miles and there were high hopes of success.

From Lake Bala, the sealions went for their final trials in the Solent, but here, alas, they met their Waterloo. They seemed to be unable to distinguish between the sound of a submarine's propellers and those of any other ship. They followed liners, cruisers, destroyers, motor boats, with reckless abandon, but not a submarine. They also found sufficient fish in the Solent waters to satisfy their appetites without having to swim long distances after a noise in order to earn one. The experiments broke down at this stage and had to be abandoned.[19]

There were also experiments with a similar idea involving sea-gulls. Perhaps the most fantastic suggestion of all (it emanated from a private source outside the Admiralty) was the one sent to Jellicoe in 1917, that the U-boat problem would be solved by fill-ing the North Sea with barrels of Eno's Fruit Salt. They would be opened by the shore control when U-boats were suspected in the area, the fruit salt would effervesce upon striking the water, and the resulting streams of bubbles would force the submarine to the surface, where she could be disposed of!

In use by January 1918 were flares of high power, at first burned from kite balloons, later from surface ships. Under optimum at-mospheric conditions the flares illuminated the surface of the water for four to five miles all around. The device had a measure of night-time usefulness in the Dover area and other narrow waters. The flares forced the U-boats to dive to escape detection and often drove them on to the minefields. The daily output of flares was 1,000 in the spring of 1918. By the end of hostilities over 100,000 had been manufactured.

We have considered weapons and detection devices, and now we turn to the main A/S operational resources—that is, the attack on the U-boats by surface craft, aircraft, and submarines. Coastal motor-boats (C.M.B.s, a new type of craft, 55-ft. boats of 34–38 knots, carrying a torpedo, depth charges, and a Lewis gun) were allocated for U-boat work in the English Channel.

The Technical History claims that 'An outstanding feature of the Anti-Submarine campaign was the work of the Auxiliary Patrol',[20] whose small, slow surface craft (armed yachts, trawlers, drifters) hunted U-boats in focal areas near the coast. It was hardly 'an outstanding feature', despite the tremendous numbers of craft employed.[21] During 1916 the A.P. had accounted for seven boats in about a hundred engagements with the U-boats, 'so that when an encounter took place, the U-boat captain's chances of

---

[19] P. K. Kemp, *H. M. Submarines* (London, 1952), pp. 102–3. And see *Portrait of an Admiral*, pp. 276–7, also below, p. 162.

[20] Technical History Monograph *The Anti-Submarine Division of the Naval Staff*, p. 9. The A.P. organization comprised at the time of the Armistice 27 separate areas or commands with bases round the coast.

[21] See *From the Dreadnought to Scapa Flow*, ii. 357, iii. 273–4.

escaping were about fourteen to one'.[22] The A.P. had no more luck in 1917, although the arrival of the U.S. submarine-chaser in European waters did increase its effectiveness in the last year of the war.

At a number of bases the Admiralty established special 'hunting units' or 'hunting patrols' of available destroyers and P-boats under the local S.N.O.s for hunting U-boats on the approach routes (on which see below). Destroyers, with their speed and manœuvring powers, were the ideal craft, but the call on them for Grand Fleet needs and convoy escort work for particularly valuable ships, and later for ocean convoy escort, resulted in a great paucity of hunting craft and an increasing use of smaller craft for 'hunting' work.

A complementary measure to the hunting patrols was the organization of hydrophone patrols. With the introduction of the directional hydrophone and its general supply to A.P. bases, a decision was reached to establish submarine-hunting flotillas of trawlers or drifters equipped with hydrophones and depth charges and trained to work together as a hunting unit. The system, first tried in the Aegean in February 1917, was in full operation by the end of the year. The idea was extended to the M.L.s or motor launches. This was a new type of craft that went into service at the end of 1916: 50 feet long (the later ones were 80 ft.), at least 19 knots, armed with depth charges and a specially designed 13-pdr. Q.F. with short barrel and long recoil, so as to reduce the strain on their rather flimsy structure. They were the forerunners of the larger and more seaworthy American submarine-chasers of 1918. In June 1917 four M.L. Hunting Flotillas (six motor launches in each) were formed at English Channel ports. When the experiment appeared successful, similar flotillas were formed all round the coast in the spring of 1918, generally in groups of three motor launches.

'The U-boat,' writes the Official Historian of the merchant navy, 'would first be located on the hydrophones by means of cross-bearings, and depth-charges would then be dropped. Even if he was not always destroyed, the experience certainly inflicted on the enemy a good deal of "moral damage" and tended gradually to wear him down until, as actually happened on some occasions,

---

[22] Sir Julian S. Corbett and Sir Henry Newbolt, *History of the Great War. Naval Operations* (London, 1920–31, 5 vols., iv and v by Newbolt), iv. 348.

the submarine came to the surface glad to surrender.'[23] Possibly two U-boats—probably none—were sunk by hydrophone hunting flotillas. Apart from the inherent shortcomings of the hydrophone, the flotillas achieved little because low speed handicapped the trawlers, and bad weather, the M.L.s, on account of their size.

A large increase was made in the Special Service Ships (Q-ships)—there were 78 in July 1917. These decoy ships tried to lure the enemy submarines to destruction. The law of diminishing returns had, however, begun to operate by 1917, as was realized at the Admiralty by the autumn. The introduction of convoy clinched their departure: U-boats were highly suspicious of a ship out of convoy. Moreover, a Q-ship had little chance against a submerged U-boat, the torpedo having replaced the gun as her chief weapon.

Despite the extensive network of coastal air patrols established in 1916, the results had been disappointing. No U-boats were destroyed as a result of surface and air hunts, and U-boat attacks on shipping in coastal waters, although only a percentage were made without warning, were not curtailed. The creation of the A.S.D. led to a great increase in the activities of all types of A/S aircraft—aeroplanes, seaplanes, and airships. Their operations were re-organized, systematized, and co-ordinated with other U-boat counter-measures. The A.S.D. also initiated an ambitious scheme of naval air expansion for A/S work. Prior to the introduction of convoys in 1917, A/S aircraft were employed exclusively on patrol work. Until 1917 the emphasis was on lighter-than-air craft, in the form of non-rigid airships. They were capable of more extensive operations under favourable weather conditions than were aeroplanes and seaplanes, whose low performance and limited endurance relegated them to inshore work. By the end of 1916, 50 S.S. (submarine scout) airships were in operation and 27 improved 'C' (Coastal) types had been commissioned. Hitherto heavier-than-air A/S operations had been concentrated off the East Coast and in the mid- and eastern stretches of the Channel. West of Portland there were only airship stations. It was now appreciated that the decisive theatre of U-boat operations was in the Western Approaches to the English Channel, where the oceanic shipping converged on the British Isles and where defence by dispersion was proving impracticable. It was therefore decided to supplement the existing patrols with seaplanes, and by February 1917, seaplane stations had been established at Plymouth, Newlyn (Cornwall), in the Scillies, and at Fishguard—but not at Queenstown and Berehaven, owing to Admiral Bayly's lukewarm attitude to aircraft. In April, to meet the demand for more air patrols, as no seaplanes were available, aeroplanes were brought into use, airfields being opened in the vicinity of the seaplane stations. Systems of routine patrols by airships, seaplanes, and aeroplanes, were established by which the main areas in the St. George's Channel, Bristol Channel, and Western Approaches, and in the Channel itself, were covered. Off the East Coast seaplanes and airships operated similar patrols, and later in the year aeroplanes were also brought into use here. By September 1917 there were 21 aeroplane or seaplane stations, with 190 planes, on the East Coast and in the English Channel, and 10 airship stations, with 50 airships, on the East Coast and in the English and Irish Channels. These air patrols supplemented the numerous surface patrols operating in the coastal areas and in the Western Approaches.

During the whole of 1917, aeroplanes and seaplanes sighted 135 U-boats and attacked 85 of them; airships sighted 26 and attacked 15. All this busy work was singularly unproductive. Except for *UB-32*, which may have been sunk by a seaplane bomb (22 September), *not a single U-boat sunk during 1917, or indeed during the war, was definitely accounted for by aircraft.* These results are not difficult to explain. Airships proved too sluggish as attackers of U-boats sighted, and the vast majority of the aeroplanes and seaplanes used in A/S work were old trainers with an unreliable engine, very limited endurance, and capable of carrying in addition to the pilot only an observer or a bomb load. Forward view was very limited from these aircraft, there was no method of sighting for bomb-dropping on U-boats, and the 100-lb. A/S bomb was often defective, and in any case proved to be too light to cause lethal damage. Moreover, its fuse setting ($2\frac{1}{2}$-second delay action) was found to be too deep for shallow-dived U-boats and too shallow for deep-dived ones. All the same, aircraft played a useful role in the convoy system, as we shall see.

Kite balloons, flown by destroyers and other craft employed on A/S work, were a new method of air patrol. A kite-balloon operation involving Grand Fleet destroyers claimed *U-69* as a victim on 12 July. Kite-balloons were at best an auxiliary aid, even if the

London Naval Conference of September 1917 agreed that the best all-round offensive measure was the destroyer–kite-balloon combination.

There had always been opposition to the use of submarines against U-boats on the ground that their possible achievements would not be sufficiently great to justify the risk of mistaken identity and resulting damage to friends. The results of sporadic use of submarines against surfaced U-boats were not especially encouraging. Through 1916, British submarines on patrol had established contact with U-boats fifty-six times, had made only six attacks, five of them with success—two of these by a submarine working with a decoy ship, a trawler towing a submarine. This method had been abandoned by the end of 1916. Submerged submarines towed by specially fitted Q-ships were tried in 1917 and abandoned in October of that year. Difficulties were encountered in the towing, and the effectiveness of the scheme was not proved. It became apparent, indeed, that the U-boats were fully aware that British decoy ships and submarines were working together.

Beatty, a strong believer in using submarine against submarine, did not feel that British submarines were being employed to the best advantage. The conditions of submarine warfare had entirely changed since the outbreak of war. The submarine was built to sink the enemy's heavy ships, but since it was now the U-boats that threatened Britain's existence, the British boats should consider them their primary target. The Navy had three distinct types of submarines: the fleet submarines with the battle fleet, the patrol submarines engaged chiefly in watching enemy exits, and the coastal submarines distributed on the East Coast as part of the defence scheme. 'These dispositions', explained the C.-in-C., 'are chiefly for offensive or defensive purposes against the enemy heavy ships; they therefore do not fulfil the requirements of the moment.' The fleet boats were too large for effective A/S work. It was the patrol and coastal boats that he would like to see used primarily for A/S work in the North Sea.[24] In June he strongly recommended an acceleration of submarine construction and an increase in the projected programme of a little over four a month, because he was, the new Controller reported, 'firmly convinced that the only real

[24] Beatty to Admiralty, 6 February 1917; Bellairs MSS. He had made his views known earlier in conversations with the First Lord on board the *Iron Duke*, 8–9 January 1917.

reply to the Submarine menace is that wherever a German Sub-marine is, there must be also a British Submarine . . .'[25]

After some hesitation, the Admiralty came round to the view that the submarine flotillas might be used to advantage offensively against the U-boats. Beginning in February, 'C' class submarines, previously limited to coast-defence duties, were employed as submarine patrols in the North Sea. Encouraged by what was regarded as their success (three 'certainties' reported on 10 March, 7 April, and 1 May, of which the first and third, *UC-43* and *U-81*, were actual kills), in May submarine patrols were established in the Channel and were gradually extended to all areas in which the U-boats operated, particularly after American boats became available. Experience showed that surface patrols were dangerous and not very effective, and a diving patrol accordingly became by May the normal procedure, the hope being to catch the U-boats on the surface. By the autumn of 1917 submarine patrols constituted an important facet of A/S warfare. Sixty-odd submarines were being used in the North Sea and on the West Coast of Ireland as diving patrols which tried to intercept U-boats in passage.

Submarine *v.* submarine produced few successes. The inherent difficulty of successful attacks was never overcome, as shown by

[25] Sir Eric Geddes's notes on a 'Visit to the Commander-in-Chief, Grand Fleet, 16 June, 1917', 18 June 1917; Admiralty MSS. Duff, who was a strong believer in submarine *v.* submarine, spelled out some of the advantages in the use of submarines in A/S patrols. 'The enemy submarine can never be sure that he is not being stalked, and consequently he must either:—(a) keep diving, or (b) keep continually under way at a moderate speed (8–10 knots) and zig-zag. If (a) is chosen our object is attained. If (b):—(i) His personnel is under continual tension. (ii) His engines are continually being used, which means in effect a longer time laid up between cruises. (iii) The time he can remain out is limited by his increased consumption of fuel. (iv) He is much more likely to be sighted than if at rest on the surface, and so avoided. Whenever he makes an attack, whether successful or not, he will always have the feeling that unseen submarines may be closing him, and this will act as a strong inducement to remain submerged and safe.' Duff's minute of 25 March 1917 on a Bayly memorandum, 'Protection of Sea-Going Trade . . .', 15 March 1917; Admiralty MSS. The morale effect was supposed to have been particularly noticeable during the last year of the war. The Technical History cites as evidence reports of prisoners from the *UC-38* (successfully depth-charged by a French destroyer escort in the Ionian Sea, 14 December 1917). 'Several prisoners gave clear evidence of the fear inspired by the possible presence of enemy submarines submerged when they themselves were on the surface. Besides the probable result of this method of attack, the apprehension of it constitutes a seriously demoralising influence.' Technical History Monograph TH 1, *Submarine v. Submarine* (1919), p. 14. It is interesting that this sort of thing was reported and recorded, but it was misplaced optimism. As long as the captain of the submarine was staunch, it mattered little that odds and ends of prisoners had felt frightened.

these figures: submarines operating against U-boats in the latter's 'operational areas' had but a remote chance of success—1:122 (destructive hits to contacts); those operating against U-boats on passage had a much better chance of success—1:39, or 1:21, if hits which failed to destroy were counted.[26] There were six kills in 1917, another six in 1918, for a wartime total of 17 U-boats sunk by British submarines (a French submarine accounted for another in 1917) of the 178 German war losses. A more efficient torpedo would have given them a higher score. A U-boat was not in any case an easy target because of the difficulty in estimating her course and speed, the small target offered, and the uncertainty of the depth at which to set the torpedo. Early in September 1917, for instance, a British submarine reported firing four torpedoes at a U-boat 600 yards away; all had missed. 'This is frequently happening', the Admiralty reported at that time to the Allied Naval Conference in London, 'but although we only occasionally get a submarine, it has considerable moral effect on enemy submarines in cramping their activities.'

During 1917–18 the most important work of the Submarine Service was against the U-boats. Experience pointed to low under-water speed as a principal hindrance to the achievement of better results. In the autumn of 1917 designs were prepared for a special class of 'hunter-killer' submarine, the 'R' class, in which high submerged speed was the main consideration. The 16 knots submerged speed ($7\frac{1}{2}$ knots surface) attained in these small boats (160 feet long, 420 tons displacement on the surface) on their 'K' class batteries and motors was high for those days. They were fitted with hydrophones and six bow 18-inch torpedo tubes. Approval was given to build 12 of the class; five had come into service when the war ended. The one contact they made (R-7, 13 October, in the Irish Sea) might have been successful (the British boat had used her high underwater speed to place herself 3 points on the bow of the enemy at 2,500 yards, a highly advantageous position) but for the untimely arrival of a merchant ship, which caused the U-boat to dive before the attack could be completed.

Another anti-submarine tack was the prevention of the exit of

---

[26] Paper No. 7, 'Chronological List of U/Bs Sunk by British S/Ms'; Barley-Waters MSS. We also have these figures: in 1917–18 there was a total of 564 contacts and 19 hits, or 29·7 contacts per hit. Technical History Monograph TH 1, *Submarine v. Submarine*, p. 15.

U-boats from their North Sea bases by extensive mining in the Bight. (Mining the Kattegat, to prevent the emergence of the U-boats at Kiel, was out of the question, as this would have infringed Scandinavian neutrality.) This had been mulled over since the start of the war. A close blockade of enemy ports by light craft had been considered and rejected. Such craft would need to be supported against a sortie in force by a strong squadron of heavy ships, which would have exposed the latter to submarine attack and to submarine-laid mines. Also discussed and rejected was the laying of mines close in to enemy harbours: such minefields could readily be swept up by minelayers supported by the fleet and shore guns. Little more feasible was a policy of mining the Bight. The Chief of the Admiralty War Staff summed up the difficulties: 'A permanent [mine] barrier to stop submarines getting out of Heligoland Bight would have to be defended to prevent its removal. It would entail Auxiliary Patrol Vessels with Destroyers to protect them, Light Cruisers to protect the Destroyers, Battle Cruisers to protect the Light Cruisers, and the Grand Fleet to protect the whole, with about 90 additional Destroyers to protect it. The Destroyers would want relief every 48 hours and the Grand Fleet every 4 days.'[27] As matters stood, the Bight was foul with mines, British and German. The Germans constantly swept ways out, and the British, upon discovering these channels, put mines in them.

This did not discourage Beatty from suggesting (January 1917) a very extensive semi-circular mine barrage (shallow and deep mines forming a vertical barrier) across the entrance to the Heligoland Bight from the Rote Kliff Bank to Ameland, *to be patrolled continuously by light craft and submarines*. That was the key element. This proposal, he maintained, 'went to the root of the submarine danger, as if effective, it would largely hinder the submarines coming or returning in safety'. He wanted '80,000 mines as close as can be got to Heligoland'. If the Admiralty were not turning out mines in sufficient quantity (Jellicoe gave 3,000 a month as all they could expect to produce), the C.-in-C. deemed the matter so important that they should entrust the production to the Munitions Department, 'as being the most highly organized

[27] Oliver's memorandum of 10 November 1916; Admiralty MSS. Hankey had several times in 1915–16 urged a vast North Sea mine barrier: the forerunner of the Northern Barrage of 1918, which was *not* a huge success.

Department we have ever created'.[28] Jellicoe was never the mining enthusiast Beatty was. He did not consider that laying mines close in was correct policy, 'and has been proven so hundreds of times during the war. The proper place to lay them is where they cannot be swept up without the enemy sweepers being risked to a greater extent than they care to risk them, that is, well away from German bases. You have too exaggerated a view of the value of mines against submarines. This is proved by the ease with which submarines pass the Dover barrage, which consists not only of mined nets but four rows of deep mines. Your ideas in regard to the facility with which mines or anything else can be produced in this country at the present time are far too optimistic . . .'[29]

The Admiralty's objective in the Bight was the enemy sweepers and patrol craft more than his heavy ships or submarines. All that could be done at the time (January) was to lay seven independent minefields (712 mines) in the Bight. 'These fields accounted for some half-dozen enemy trawlers; they did not cause the loss of a single outgoing or incoming submarine, and were always discovered after fairly short intervals.'[30] The policy of laying fields 'in driblets' (as Beatty called it) continued into the summer. The chronic shortage of mines, quite apart from Jellicoe's attitude, prevented a more ambitious mining policy. Only seventeen fields and 1,782 mines had been laid in the Bight during 1916, and a total of 6,320 mines in the war through 1916. On 22 January 1917 there were, Jellicoe informed the War Cabinet, only 1,100 mines —that is, fit for laying. 'It is nothing less than a national scandal', moaned Hankey. Four days later the War Cabinet authorized the Admiralty and Ministry of Munitions to provide 100,000 mines 'as soon as possible . . . in view of the great urgency of this question.'

It was not only that the supply of mines at the time was grossly inadequate. Although the war had been on for two and a half years, the Admiralty had not evolved an efficient mine, whether against submarines or surface craft. British mines were still a joke. The shortcomings of the mines were varied. Since, as mentioned,

---

[28] Carson, 'Memorandum of Conversations with the Commander-in-Chief . . . 8th and 9th of January, 1917', and Beatty to Jellicoe, 22 January 1917; Beatty MSS. On 31 January Beatty revised his 80,000 figure downwards—to 54,000 moored and 5,700 ground mines, constituting a 155-mile barrage about 50 miles from the Jade, with a double line of mines laid at 30–60 ft. depths, 40–50 ft. apart.

[29] Jellicoe to Beatty, 4 February 1917; Beatty MSS.

[30] Newbolt, *Naval Operations*, iv. 343.

mining policy had the German sweepers and patrol craft mainly in view, rather than the U-boats and heavy ships, the mines were laid near the surface. This made them vulnerable to wave action, and a large percentage broke adrift in the first gale after laying. Most of the mines failed to explode when struck by a submarine and often they failed to keep their intended depth and would pop up on the surface. In some trials with a British submarine running against a number of British mines fitted with small charges, only a third of the mines exploded! At one point, as late as April 1917, only 1,500 mines of the stock of 20,000 available were fit for laying, that is, could be depended upon not to come to the surface when laid. In December 1917 Jellicoe was still complaining of 'mines that come to the surface as soon as laid'.[31] A turning point came with the commencement in the spring of 1917 of the production of a simple expedient, which Beatty (also Lord Fisher) had long urged, of copying the reliable German contact ('E-') mine, which had proved its efficiency. They took up and maintained an accurate depth and went off when hit. (They contravened the Hague Convention of 1907 by being dangerous when adrift.) By the autumn this reliable type, the Mark H-2, was becoming available in quantity, making an intensive mining programme practicable. (Actually, Jackson, the First Sea Lord, had ordered the manufacture of an exact copy of the German mine in the spring of 1916, but a year had been lost by the departments concerned in attempts to improve on it.)

3. SHIPPING DEFENCE

So far I have been discussing the offensive aspects of the A/S campaign, which were in the hands of the A/S and Operations Divisions of the War Staff. A defensive category of A/S measures was concerned with protective measures for merchant ships. This was the responsibility of Captain Webb and the Trade Division of the Staff.

---

[31] The quality of British torpedoes also still left something to be desired. The removal of Captain Dumas, the Assistant Director of Torpedoes (whom Madden considered 'a very active obstructionist'), at the end of February 1917 helped. In April a new department of Torpedoes and Mines was organized, with Rear-Admiral the Hon. Edward Fitzherbert as Director, responsible to the Fourth Sea Lord. It took time to evolve an efficient torpedo. As late as August 1917 the torpedoes were so bad that, when a submarine commander had a 'sitting shot' at a U-boat, 'his torpedoes ran like porpoises, jumping up and down, and finally diving under the hostile craft.' Repington, *The First World War*, ii. 18.

Two types of smoke-producing apparatus were designed late in 1916 for use by merchant ships when attacked by U-boat gunfire. One type was fixed on board, and the other was for throwing overboard.

Elaborate schemes of camouflage known as 'dazzle' painting were perfected during 1917 and brought into general use, beginning in May, as a substitute for the neutral grey colour in which the ships had been painted since 1915. This purported to make it more difficult for an attacking submarine to judge her target's course and apply the correct deflection when firing her torpedo. A false bow wave was sometimes included in the artistic make-up, but it is doubtful if any U-boat was ever deceived thereby, for you could not paint in a false wake! The official verdict claims too much: 'Though from the nature of the case it is quite impossible to produce statistics or even evidence, it would be safe to say that dazzle-painting was among the most successful of the devices for securing immunity from destruction.'[32]

The 'Otter', a mine-protecting device similar to the paravane for warships, was fitted to merchant ships from the latter half of 1917, 900 having been so fitted by 1 December 1917. This gear proved of considerable service by sweeping up mines and keeping them away from contact with ships' hulls. The Otter had its disadvantages: it proved fragile, especially in a rough sea, necessitating frequent replacement, and it (allegedly) reduced speed by half a knot or more. It was never popular with masters, who often neglected to use it, the regulations notwithstanding.

Trials during 1916 with towed nets as an anti-torpedo protection for merchant ships under way eventually resulted in the evolution of the 'Actaeon' net (after the *Actaeon* Torpedo School ship) in the winter of 1917–18. The principle of the net was 'to hang up the torpedo—not to explode it—and its action is dependent on the ship travelling through the water, which brings the meshes across the torpedo as it tries to pass through'. The war ended just as the net was beginning to be supplied to a large number of merchant vessels.

[32] 'A Report of Shipping Control during the War. The Work of the Transport Department and Ministry of Shipping up to the Armistice, 11th November, 1918' (n.d.); copy in Lord Salter's possession. The report of a committee on dazzle painting (31 July 1918) concluded that it had not afforded protection to ships so treated, but that the moral effect on crews justified its continuance. Admiralty, 'Statistical Review' (see below, p. 102, n. 2), p. 21.

The defensive measures for the merchant fleet also included the alteration as necessary of the trade routes to avoid areas in which U-boats were known to be operating, the provision of trained guns' crews, and the adoption of the zig-zag manœuvre: a ship proceeded on a course by a series of tacks eastward and westward, say, of her real objective; this often threw off a U-boat which, having sighted a merchant ship, submerged to attempt to cut her off. Jellicoe had Merchant Navy training schools set up to teach zig-zagging and other A/S work to the masters and officers, to train guns' crews for the merchant ships, and to instruct wireless operators.

The Admiralty put their greatest faith in defensive armament for the merchant ships. This policy, inaugurated at the start of the war, had been lagging somewhat. An important reason was the opposition of the Army, because the guns were needed, they said, for other purposes. The War Committee (predecessor of the War Cabinet) had decided on 13 November 1916 that the arming of merchant ships should be a first charge on artillery resources, a decision not implemented until the new Government and new Board of Admiralty took over in December. The work of defensive arming now proceeded at top speed, the weapons being obtained from diverse sources—France and Japan, the War Office, and the stripping of the secondary armament of older warships, in addition to the intensified production of guns. By 22 February 1917, 2,899 merchant ships had been armed since the beginning of the war; by November 1918, 4,203 ships had been fitted. Both figures exclude those sunk from any cause. Including the 1,684 ships fitted with defensive armament which had been sunk, a grand total of 5,887 ships were fitted. Approximately a thousand ships were unarmed —for the most part those operating outside the danger zone and vessels under repair. With the heavier gun-power of the U-boats in the last years of the war (the later boats carried up to 5·9-inch guns), in September 1917 the Admiralty established this standard for ships under construction: one or two guns from 3-inch (12-pdr., 18-cwt.) to 6-inch, depending on the gross tonnage and the size of the ship's complement. Guns being useless against submerged U-boats, 7·5-inch howitzers to combat these were supplied from October 1917 to merchant ships of over 3,000 tons.

The growing proportion of defensively armed merchantmen proved to be no solution to the problem. Whereas the merchant ship could afford to be hit several times, the submarine could run no risks. One hit might sink her or so seriously damage her as to prevent her from submerging. Accordingly, the more general arming of merchant ships from the end of 1916 drove the U-boat more and more below the surface, and the German declaration of 31 January 1917, stating their intention to sink ships on sight, signified a change in the method of attack. In January about 60 per cent of the vessels sunk by U-boats were accounted for by gunfire; in April the same percentage held for sinkings through the torpedo. The arming of merchant ships had thus limited the power of attack of the U-boat by contributing to driving her below the surface, as well as limiting the fruitfulness of her patrol to the number of torpedoes she carried. But at the same time it had also decreased the chances of destroying U-boats by gunfire.

It was a straw in the wind that down to the last months of 1916 the number of armed merchantmen destroyed was modest. Then the figures began to rise—to 12 in December 1916 and 20 in January 1917. The figures soared under conditions of unrestricted submarine warfare. By the spring of 1917 it had become uncomfortably apparent that the U-boat was establishing a definite ascendancy over the armed merchant ship. Whereas 68 per cent of the armed merchantmen attacked during the last quarter of 1916 had managed to survive attack, this percentage dropped to 49 in the first three months of the unrestricted campaign, and to 43 in April. 'Whereas, in the earlier period, just over half the steamers of all classes attacked succeeded in reaching port, it had now to be reckoned that, in spite of the spread of defensive armament, only four steamers out of every ten attacked would escape destruction. It was obvious that defensive armament, though it might mitigate the perils of a voyage, no longer afforded any reasonable prospect of keeping down the rate of loss to a bearable level . . .'[33]

Shipping defence also took the form of the routeing of ships. In the early days of the war the direction of merchant shipping movements by the Admiralty was limited to the issue of general advice as to the policy of evasion and dispersion recommended on the report of a U-boat threat to a particular route (or if all routes were threatened, a recommendation for the entire suspension of traffic until the U-boat was accounted for), and to the communication of information regarding areas prohibited on account of mines.

[33] C. Ernest Fayle, *History of the Great War. Seaborne Trade* (London, 1920–4, 3 vols.), iii. 96–7.

The growth of enemy submarine operations in the Western Approaches towards the end of 1915 led to the issue of more particular advice in regard to making and leaving the British coasts, but except for a few specially valuable ships there was no individual treatment. Experience gained, particularly the lessons learned from the operations of the enemy surface raider *Moewe* early in 1916, showed that general advice was not enough, and that the necessary dispersion and evasion could only be controlled generally from the Admiralty. An elaborate system of routeing ('approach routes') was therefore developed, from March 1916, for merchant ships approaching Home waters from the Atlantic. By the end of 1916 all British vessels were receiving individual detailed and explicit instructions in regard to the routes to be followed. Allied vessels and neutral vessels trading in Allied interests could obtain similar instructions in the form of advice.

The first detailed and definite system of approach routes, issued on 2 March 1917, allowed for four areas of approach for homeward-bound ships. These areas were cone-shaped zones with their apexes at Falmouth, on the south-west coast of England, Berehaven, on the south-west coast of Ireland, Inishtrahull, off the north coast of Ireland, and Kirkwall, off the north coast of Scotland. Each zone covered about 10,000 square miles and was 90 to 150 miles wide at its mouth, which was about 150 miles from the coast (an average night's run). Steamers were routed to enter a zone on the base line as widely dispersed as possible on a certain degree of longitude. The protection inside the zone was furnished by patrol craft— mainly sloops, Q-ships, trawlers, and an occasional destroyer. On making the apex of a cone, vessels were routed along the coast to their destinations. Jellicoe admitted that the approach areas 'were necessarily of considerable length, by reason of the distance from the coast at which submarines operated, and of considerable width, owing to the necessity for a fairly wide dispersion of traffic throughout the area. Consequently, with the comparatively small number of patrol craft available, the protection afforded was slight, and losses were correspondingly heavy.'[34] Changes and improvements in the system, suggested by experience, were frequent. Approach routes were altered and new approach routes were established.

The approach-route system only accentuated the inefficiency of patrolling. Under this system A.P. craft patrolled the coastal

[34] Jellicoe, *The Crisis of the Naval War*, pp. 43-4.

traffic lanes as far as their numbers permitted. The 'hunting patrols' did likewise on the approach routes. The criticism against the patrolling of threatened areas with destroyers, patrol boats, sloops, armed trawlers, and Q-ships is succinctly summarized by Admiral K. G. B. Dewar: 'Patrols could not protect ships scattered over large areas. The S. W. Approaches, where many of the sinkings occurred, alone covered well over 100,000 square miles. Their chances of sighting much less destroying submarines were negligible. By the time the patrols reached the scene of an attack, the U-boat was often hundreds of miles away. The most they could hope to do was to rescue the shipwrecked crew.' Again, the U-boats were able to locate the traffic routes by the mere presence of the patrolling vessels. They could see the patrols long before they could themselves be seen, and they had only to dive until the patrol had passed, and then resume their lookout for merchantmen. The patrolled traffic routes were, as Fayle says, little better than 'death-traps'. Patrol and hunting measures also left the initiative with the enemy, and, although often referred to as systems, were not that at all—they were inherently unsystematic.

4. THE CAMPAIGN IN THE MEDITERRANEAN

The A/S campaign in the Mediterranean calls for separate treatment. Few areas there lent themselves to Allied mining, because of the great depth of water and the danger to traffic. Only two areas were mined extensively, the northern Adriatic and the approaches to the Dardanelles. The major efforts were, as before, connected with attempts to close the Straits of Otranto, since the German submarines that were causing most of the trouble were still working from the Adriatic—the Austrian ports of Pola and especially Cattaro. The mobile barrage of indicator nets and trawlers, which ran from the Italian coast to Fano Island, a distance of 44 miles, was protected by the British Taranto-based flotilla (motor launches and net drifters), which was nominally under the C.-in-C. of the Italian Fleet at Taranto (the main base of the Italian battle fleet). Reinforcing the Taranto flotilla were a few Italian submarines working above the line of nets, and a few French submarines to the south of it. In the spring of 1917 a seaplane wing of the R.N.A.S., based on Taranto, was added to the A/S forces.

'The inefficiency of this barrage', Oliver had written in December

1916, 'is the root of all the submarine trouble in the Mediterranean.' The Allied defences annoyed the U-boats, no more. They continued to pass to their hunting ground without much restraint, when bad weather prevented the drifters from keeping guard, or diving beneath the nets at other times. Only two enemy submarines had been destroyed in 1916 while trying to pass the barrage. The first U-boat kill in 1917 did not come until 24 May, when *UC-24* was torpedoed by a French submarine off Cattaro. On 15 May 1917, after the drifter patrol had begun to inconvenience the U-boats, three Austrian light cruisers, supported by destroyers and submarines, raided the Otranto Barrage, destroying part of the drifter line, sinking a number of drifters, damaging the British light cruiser *Dartmouth* with a torpedo, and sinking a French destroyer with a mine laid by a U-boat.

A glaring weakness of the barrage was the Italian policy with regard to their destroyers. As described by Newbolt, 'In England, wherever a net line had been operated it was considered that an integral part of the barrage must consist of destroyers constantly present with the double object of forcing submarines to dive and of engaging them if they should be caught in the nets. But the Italian destroyers nominally appropriated to the Otranto net remained, as a rule, at anchor in harbour, the idea being that if signals for assistance should be received from the drifters the destroyers would then get up their anchors and proceed to sea.'[35]

The Admiralty considered various possible naval offensives in the Adriatic that would curb U-boat activity: the capture of Cattaro or Curzola Island, or even the main Austro-Hungarian naval base of Pola. The report of the War Staff dampened any enthusiasm for such a project. The capture of Cattaro was 'almost impossible of attainment'. It would take a very large-scale joint operation in view of the heavy guns sited high above the sea, which would outrange bombarding ships, and the very mountainous and difficult surrounding country. 'Ships by themselves would accomplish nothing.' The capture of Pola from the sea was in the same category—'not feasible'. Curzola might be taken by surprise, though troops and artillery would be required to hold lines across the island.[36] The subject was not pursued seriously.

[35] Newbolt, *Naval Operations*, iv. 288–9.
[36] Oliver's memorandum, 'Question of a Naval Conference between France, Italy and Great Britain', 29 December 1916; Admiralty MSS.

Once in the Mediterranean, the U-boats had little to fear from the Allied naval forces. (In mid-April 1917 eight Japanese destroyers under a rear-admiral with his flag in a light cruiser arrived to work as an independent escort force, though in co-operation with the British. This force, up to a cruiser and twelve destroyers by the end of the war, rendered valuable assistance in A/S operations and escort duties.) The congeries of independent commands in the Mediterranean was very much to the advantage of the U-boats, since there was anything but perfect co-operation between the patrol forces of adjacent zones. Each Admiral did the best for his own area and cared little about his neighbour's problems. (The French, who nominally held the supreme command in the Mediterranean proper, were directly responsible for the areas between France and Algeria, around Tunisia, south and west of Greece, and the eastern Mediterranean around Cyprus; Britain controlled the Aegean and the waters east of Gibraltar, and between Malta and Egypt; the Italians managed the waters around their coasts and a zone around Tripoli.) Always working in favour of the U-boats operating in the Mediterranean was the long coastline, with its narrow channels and safe hiding places on the mainland and in the innumerable islands.

The actual method of shipping protection, patrolling fixed traffic routes, was inefficient. The routes in the Mediterranean were very long and the number of patrol craft hopelessly inadequate.[37] More important, as indicated above, the patrol system was inherently an inefficient one. The British (with Allied approval at the London Naval Conference of 23–24 January 1917) experimented with a system of dispersed routes, in place of fixed routes (in operation since March 1916), for British armed steamers early in 1917: ships sailed independently, each on its own prescribed, unpatrolled track. This led to a temporary improvement in the situation.

Very nearly the only positive British achievement in the whole Mediterranean theatre in the early part of 1917 was Jellicoe's success at the Allied naval conference in London in getting Allied

[37] The Allied forces in the Mediterranean early in 1917 were impressive in numbers. The vessels that could have been usefully employed against submarines included 147 destroyers, 75 torpedo-boats, 200 trawlers, 68 submarines, and 79 sloops, gunboats, armed boarding steamers, etc. But a large proportion of these light craft were immobilized so far as fighting U-boats was concerned: as integral parts of the Allied fleets, they were engaged in watching the considerably inferior Austrian and Turkish Fleets.

consent to the withdrawal of five of the eight old British battleships in the Mediterranean (there were four at Taranto and four in the Eastern Mediterranean), which were locking up some 9,000 officers and men. As Carson had written prior to the conference: 'It is high time that an effort was made to put an end to the anomalous position in which British battleships are kept tied up with their valuable officers and men, in assisting two combined allied fleets to contain the Austrian fleet which is inferior to either of them.'[38] The battleship crews, officers and men, were badly needed to man the destroyers and light cruisers to be completed in 1917 to augment the A/S forces in Home waters. Although the French agreed to keep a battle squadron at Corfu to compensate the Italians for the detachment of the old British battleships at Taranto, the Italians accepted the decision to withdraw the British ships with poor grace and only after a very voluble protest. They had flourished in Jellicoe's face the Anglo-Italian Naval Convention signed in Paris on 10 May 1915, under which the British had promised to keep four old battleships in the Adriatic. Under the new arrangement only the *Queen* remained in the Adriatic, as parent ship for the drifter flotilla, but with a care and maintenance party. Her crew was shipped home. In the Eastern Mediterranean only the two 'Lord Nelsons' remained, with the two being withdrawn to be replaced by two old French battleships. None of this, of course, improved the situation *vis-à-vis* the U-boats in the Mediterranean.

*　　*　　*

An analysis of the A/S measures in effect in the spring of 1917 (the balance of the war saw qualitative improvements, refinements, and greater production, but little that was new in weapons and devices), shows that, with an exception or two, they were along the old lines. Oliver had some reason for his complaint: 'Since all the new brooms came to the Admiralty I have been very fully occupied. The place swarms with bright people full of new ideas from the north, but sad to relate all the ideas are chestnuts, which have been in use for long and telling them these things without hurting their feelings takes a good deal of my time . . .'[39]

Basically, where the Admiralty had gone astray was in their

---

[38] Carson to Beatty, 15 January 1917; Beatty MSS.
[39] Admiral Sir William James, *A Great Seaman: the Life of Admiral of the Fleet Sir Henry F. Oliver* (London, 1956), p. 158.

emphasis upon the system of patrol—the use of A/S craft in the enemy's areas of operations. A War Staff paper of February 1917 on 'Submarine Warfare, 1917', emphasized that 'too much stress cannot be laid on the necessity of enemy submarines being constantly harried and hunted and never allowed to rest.' The First Sea Lord early in February 1917 and again on 22 April urged upon the War Cabinet the construction of a larger number of patrol vessels as the key to the solution of the problem. The serious shortage of vessels available for offensive action against the U-boats is suggested by these figures of February 1917: excluding the East Coast, where the situation was 'by no means satisfactory', there was a shortage of about 240 trawlers (251 were available) and 60 destroyers or P-boats (17 were available) on the Coastal Patrol, and about 60 sloops or similar ships (12 were available) for the Ocean Patrol (which commenced where Coastal Patrol terminated) on the numbers considered necessary to give adequate protection to merchant shipping round British coasts. This allowed for protection only to a distance of 250 miles to sea.[40] The Admiralty had lost no time in placing orders for, and expediting the construction of, large numbers of patrol vessels. The difficulty was that so many of the light craft were absorbed by the needs of the Grand Fleet, the Harwich Force, and the Dover Flotillas, or were engaged in convoy escort work for particularly valuable ships like transports and ammunition ships, that there could be no reasonable hope of constructing sufficient destroyers, P-boats, and sloops to patrol effectively the traffic lanes and approach routes.[41]

The cumulative effect of all the A/S measures was to make the U-boat's life uncomfortable without finding the actual remedy. 'In Home waters and the Mediterranean [February 1917],' Newbolt relates, 'about three thousand destroyers and auxiliary patrol vessels were engaged in combating the submarine menace, either directly

[40] Appendix to Jellicoe's paper for the War Cabinet of 21 February 1917, 'Naval Policy in Relation to Mercantile Shipping Losses from Submarine Warfare, and the Effect on the Strategical Situation'; Admiralty MSS.

[41] These were the only effective vessels for this purpose. P-boats were small 20-knot destroyers (573 tons) carrying one 4-inch, one 2-pdr. pom-pom, and two 14 inch tubes. Sloops were 17-knot, 1,250-ton craft carrying two 12-pdrs. at first, and later two 4-inch guns. They were excellent sea boats. The armed trawler was able to force a U-boat to dive but was too slow to conduct a rapid attack. (A larger and faster class of trawler, the 13-knot escort trawler, was adopted early in 1917, but construction delays permitted the delivery of only one in 1917.) Motor launches (there were over 500 at the beginning of the year) were not suited to patrol work in winter.

or indirectly; so that every German submarine was diverting some twenty-seven craft and their crews from other duties by pinning them to patrol areas and forcing them to spend their time in screening, searching and hunting operations which very rarely ended in success.'[42]

Shipping defence through the arming of merchant ships, routeing of ships along approach routes, and 'offensive' patrolling had proved to be no answer to the problem.

[42] Newbolt, *Naval Operations*, iv. 347–8.

V

Failure of the
Anti-Submarine Campaign

(February 1917 – April 1917)

Everything [in April 1917], indeed, combined to show that the Allies were really within sight of disaster. The lists of sinkings, the numbers of successful attacks, the increasing use of the torpedo, the moderate rate of German submarine losses all told the same story. Admiral von Holtzendorff's prophecy of victory was apparently verging towards fulfilment, and only a change in our system of defence could turn the tide.

Sir Henry Newbolt, Naval Operations.

In war nothing counts but success. A Board which sinks German submarines is a good Board. A Board which allows the submarines to sink 55 British ships in a week need expect no gratitude.

Daily Mail, 27 April 1917.

I should like to scream at times when I think of all the sacrifices that have been made, the gallant efforts of our glorious army, and the navy is losing the war as fast as the army is winning it. We are sitting on top of a volcano which will blow the Admiralty, the Navy and the Country to hell if we don't pull ourselves together.

Beatty to Carson, 29 April 1917.

I. SURFACE RAIDERS AND U-BOATS

CONCURRENTLY with the vigorous activity of the U-boats, German minelayers (large U-boat minelayers and UC boats) intensified their efforts, dropping their deadly cargoes as far afield as the west coast of Ireland. The great depths and wide spaces of the Mediterranean still discouraged extensive minelaying there. During 1917 British minesweepers were kept busy almost to the nerve-breaking point; 3,989 moored mines were swept up in Home waters. In April alone 515 mines were swept up, which was considerably more than the total in any previous *quarter*.

Surface raiders (German merchant ships fitted out as auxiliary cruisers) were active on the trade routes in the outer seas once more, three of them having broken out in the last weeks of 1916. In Newbolt's opinion, this offensive was 'probably designed as a preliminary' to the unrestricted submarine warfare, and was intended to divert sizeable British cruiser forces from the protection of shipping in the Atlantic and Home waters. First to sail was the ex-banana ship *Moewe*, on her second cruise. She left Kiel on 22 November, disguised herself as a Swedish steamer, broke through the Northern Patrol, passed between Iceland and the Faeroes, and was now loose on the North Atlantic trade routes. She worked there for a couple of weeks, then continued her marauding in the South Atlantic. The *Moewe*'s cruise ended at Kiel on 20 March 1917. In four months she had sunk 122,000 tons (all but 10,000 British). The Admiralty knew she was out on 7 December, and every effort was made to intercept her. About 24 British cruisers and auxiliary cruisers and an unspecified number of French ships were employed in a fruitless search in the North and South Atlantic. 'One single armed merchantman defied the power of the combined Navies because of the fundamental difficulty of locating ships on the wide expanse of the ocean.'

Next it was the turn of the ex-Hansa liner *Wolf*, disguised as a tramp steamer, which left Kiel on 30 November on what developed into a nearly fifteen-month epic cruise of 64,000 miles. Her task was, first, to mine the approaches to the most important British Indian and South African ports, and the interconnecting trade routes, and then (from 4 September 1917, as it turned out) to concentrate on the attack of shipping in the Indian Ocean. The *Wolf* reached Germany and a deserved hero's welcome on 19 February 1918, having accounted for 120,000 tons of shipping, three-quarters of it British, through captures and minelaying. The Allied measures adopted against the *Wolf* (the first definite information that she was out was not received until 5 March 1917) were similar to those adopted for the other raiders. At one period, in the spring of 1917, a host of British, French, and Japanese naval craft were involved in the fruitless hunt—21 cruisers, 14 destroyers, 9 sloops, etc.

Finally, there was the *Seeadler*, a full-rigged sailing ship, which left on 21 December 1916, disguised as the Norwegian ship *Hero*. This was the first use of a sailing ship as a raider. She was under the command of Count Felix von Luckner, who won praise and fame for the chivalry with which he conducted his cruise. After successfully evading the blockade, the *Seeadler* operated for over two months in an area between the bulges of South America and Africa, then passed around South America into the South Pacific. She was eventually wrecked upon a coral reef in one of the Society Islands (2 August 1917), though not until she had captured 16 vessels (six of them British) of nearly 18,000 tons. She was the last of the surface raiders, since the Germans had decided that U-boats were more economical in men and *matériel*.

The three raiders had earned their keep, for, apart from the destruction they wrought, they had seriously delayed shipping in various parts of the world, impeded the movement of troopships, and attracted to themselves a large number of British and Allied warships.

But it was the U-boats which did the principal damage. By 1917 they had greatly increased in size (from the 500 to 675 tons surface displacement of the boats available at the outbreak of the war to the 808- to 857-ton boats of the newer classes available in 1917), and consequently in endurance. The earlier types had a surface endurance of up to about 5,000 miles at 8 knots, the later types, better than 7,000 miles at 8 knots. The more powerful torpedo armament (from the four tubes and six to ten torpedoes of 1914 to the six tubes and ten to sixteen torpedoes of 1917) and gun armament (from the one or two 1·9 or 3·4 of 1914 to the one or two 5·2 of 1917), as well as the stronger pressure hulls, made the newer boats formidable adversaries. What is more, as of 17 January 1917 the U-boats were under definite instructions to pass through the Dover Straits, so as to give them more time for work. On 7 March the commanders were given the option of proceeding to western waters by the Channel or the northern route. On 1 November 1917 the Straits became compulsory once more.

In February (using average figures for the month), of the 121 operational boats 36 were at sea (maximum in any one day, 44), and of the 126 in March, 40 were at sea (maximum, 57). In the climacteric month of April 1917, of the 128 operational boats a mere 47 were at sea on the average (maximum, 58). (The Admiralty estimate at the time was that between 30 and 40 were operating in waters surrounding the British Isles and the French coast.)[1]

---

[1] Few though the U-boats at sea were, they represent a marked increase over 1914–16, when the largest number at sea (daily average over the month) was 30 (October 1916), or a monthly average of 12 for the thirty months, August 1914–January 1917.

These few boats were responsible for a veritable slaughter on the shipping lanes:

British Shipping Losses in 1917
(Number of ships in parentheses.)[2]

	By Mines	By Surface Craft	By Submarines	Total
January	24,254 (8)	19,304 (6)	109,954 (35)	153,512 (49)
February	28,413 (12)	28,679 (7)	256,394 (86)	313,486 (105)
March	26,938 (13)	42,893 (11)	283,647 (103)	353,478 (127)
April	28,888 (14)	—	516,394 (155)	545,282 (169)

Britain's Allies suffered tonnage losses during these four months of 76,882, 84,280, 81,151, and 134,448. In the same period the neutrals lost 126,905, 135,090, 165,225, and 189,373. The grand totals, British, Allied, and neutral, were:

	By Submarines	By All Forms of Enemy Action
January	291,459 (145)	357,299 (171)
February	464,599 (209)	532,856 (234)
March	507,001 (246)	599,854 (281)
April	834,549 (354)	869,103 (373)

It is interesting to compare these figures with the Admiralty forecasts of British, Allied, and neutral losses. It was 'not improbable that they may reach and even surpass' these tonnage totals:

January	320,000
February	350,000
March	380,000
April	400,000

The February–December 1917 monthly average was 46, and for January–October 1918, 44. The maximum number of boats at sea in any one day prior to February 1917 was 49 (October 1916); thereafter, 70 (13 October 1917). The spectacular rise in shipping losses in the first months of unrestricted U-boat warfare would seem to have been closely related to the size of the U-boat force at sea rather than to the nature of the warfare, restricted or unrestricted. See the maps on shipping losses in Chart 3, at the end of this volume.

[2] Compare these and the following figures with the statistics for the last months of 1916 in *From the Dreadnought to Scapa Flow*, iii. 270. Shipping losses cited in this volume are mainly from the invaluable 'Statistical Review of the War against Merchant Shipping', by the Director of Statistics, Admiralty, 23 December 1918. (Hereafter cited as Admiralty, 'Statistical Review'. There is a copy in the Naval Library.) The official works by Hurd (*The Merchant Navy*) and Fayle (*Seaborne Trade*) relied upon this study. Its figures are identical with those in Parliamentary Paper 199 of 1919, 'Merchant Shipping Losses', except that the 'Statistical Review' goes only to 31 October 1918, whereas the Parliamentary Paper takes the results up to 11 November 1918 and includes the names of the ships sunk. This means that the latter has one extra ship of 1,622 tons sunk by surface forces, two extra of 10,195 tons sunk by submarine, and one extra of 3,030 tons sunk by mine.

for a total of 1,450,000 tons as against the actual figure of 2,359,112 tons.[3]

If the British underestimated the extent of the shipping losses by over 50 per cent, the Germans, with less justification, made consistently and increasingly exaggerated claims (sent out monthly by wireless) regarding world tonnage sunk:

	Admiralty figures (Gross tonnage)	German claims (Gross tonnage)	German exaggeration (Per cent)
First Six Months, February–July 1917	3,843,765	5,454,000	41·9
Second Six Months, August 1917–January 1918	2,305,526	4,095,000	77·6
Third Six Months, February–July 1918	1,750,156	3,706,000	111·8
Two Months, August–September 1918	467,073	860,000	84·1

The exaggeration rose from 24·7 per cent in April 1917 to 135·6 per cent in September 1918, and for the whole period, February 1917 to September 1918, it was 66 per cent. In September 1918 the Germans claimed to have destroyed 11,220,000 tons of British shipping, and 19,220,000 tons of British, Allied, and neutral shipping, from the start of the war to August 1918. The Admiralty figures were 8,050,000 and 13,050,000, respectively, representing a German exaggeration of 39·3 per cent and 47·2 per cent, respectively. 'It is obvious that the German records of tonnage sunk before the commencement of unrestricted submarine warfare were considerably more accurate than the claims issued subsequent to February 1917.'[4] One cannot cavil at this British judgement. The German estimates were grossly excessive, especially in 1918. As to the question of how deliberate the exaggerations were, I have

[3] Jellicoe's paper for the War Cabinet, 'Shipbuilding Programme to 1918', 28 January (printed on 31 January) 1917; Carson MSS. His estimate for May was 420,000 tons; the true figure was 593,206. On 24 March his estimate for June was 'possibly 700,000 tons'. The actual figure was 683,325; but by then the convoy system was beginning to operate.

[4] Admiralty, 'Statistical Review', p. 9. Appendix F. (p. 24) has all the figures. The Admiralty tonnage figures cited show slight discrepancies as compared with those given in Appendix A. Cf. the figures of what the Germans *believed* they were sinking in Scheer, *Germany's High Sea Fleet in the World War*, p. 261. This book was completed in September 1919, before the true British or Allied figures of shipping losses were available to the Germans.

found no evidence to support the idea that there was any 'fiddling' with the figures. Certainly, both the British and the Germans 'cooked' their figures for propaganda purposes, but whereas the British admitted this after the war, the Germans have never, so far as I know, investigated this aspect of their statistics of the U-boat warfare. My own view is that there was a lot of wishful thinking in them, but that they were not deliberately 'cooked'. And certainly there was an important extenuating factor during the time of the convoy system. The U-boat commander had no difficulty in recording the identity, and with it the size, of an attacked ship sailing independently. Now single ships became rarer. The German Official Historian of the U-boats writes of the consequences:

The U-boat commander who, after the firing of a torpedo, immediately brought his boat down to greater depths to escape the expected depth-charge attack by the convoy escorts, had no other choice than to estimate the size of his target through his periscope as accurately as possible and to consider the sinking of the ship as achieved once he heard the detonation of the torpedo. The conditions were even more unfavourable in this connection during night attacks, which U-boat commanders always preferred in order to avoid the always present danger of depth charges during the daytime. While approaching for a surface attack at night, the size of the target ship is even harder to estimate than through the periscope of the submerged U-boat during the day. Thus, the inaccuracies in computing the monthly figures of sunk ships were increased for the naval authorities.[5]

Significant was the steep rise in the monthly average of the world's merchant tonnage sunk by submarines. Whereas U-boats had accounted for 52·3 per cent of the tonnage sunk during the first year of the war (August 1914–July 1915), the figure for the second year (August 1915–July 1916) was 77·5 per cent, for the next six months (August 1916–January 1917), 85·8 per cent, and now, for February–April 1917, a startling 90·2 per cent.

The situation was more perilous than any of the figures cited would suggest, for they do not include the many ships damaged and hence contributing nothing for a time to the cargo-carrying service. In the three months ending in April 1917, mines and torpedoes (mainly) damaged 272,000 tons of British shipping of 500 tons gross and upwards, or 321,000, including foreign tonnage.

[5] Spindler, *Der Handelskrieg mit U-Booten*, iv. 511.

Nor do the figures of actual sinkings indicate that the mere threat created by the underwater marauders often caused delay in the movements of shipping, thereby seriously reducing its usefulness. Nor do they show the effect of the paralysis of neutral shipping induced by the declaration of unrestricted U-boat warfare. At the end of February 1917 over 600 neutral vessels in Allied ports had refused to sail. Shipping entering British ports during February and March was only about a quarter what it had been a year earlier: 299 ships (1,000 tons net) against 1,149. The clearances were little better: 660 v. 2,293. Fayle remarks, 'But for the enterprise and courage displayed by the Norwegian shipowners and seamen the comparison would have been far more unfavourable; indeed it was only under the Norwegian flag that any considerable volume of [neutral] trade continued to be carried.'[6] Moreover, the effectiveness of British tonnage was diminishing because of the longer time needed to load and discharge, as more and more men were called up from the docks, harbours, railways, etc.

In March 1917 it was estimated that in the period from April to August inclusive there would be available only from 60 to 70 per cent of the total shipping tonnage required for food and civilian requirements, and for munitions.[7] The U-boats posed a serious threat to more than the food supplies and other requirements of the home front. The Allied forces in East Africa, the Middle East, and Salonika had to be continuously supplied with fresh troops, food, and military stores. Large supplies of war *matériel* were going to Italy by sea. One or more of these operations might have to be abandoned or at least reduced if the U-boats continued on their merry way.

There was no offset to these losses in the sinkings of U-boats, although Jellicoe could speak in the middle of March of 'compensations' for the various serious mercantile losses in the list of U-boat successes since the beginning of the year. From the start of the war through December 1916, 47 U-boats had been accounted for (49 through January 1917), or an average of fewer than two per month of the war. In the first three months of unrestricted warfare against shipping, 10 more boats were destroyed. (Of these, 7 boats were destroyed by British action, one was stranded on the Dutch coast and interned, another had struck one of her own mines, and a

---

[6] Fayle, *Seaborne Trade,* iii. 52, and tables on p. 53.
[7] See above, p. 67.

third had been lost through unknown causes). This improvement was not nearly enough, as the Germans were building an average of seven boats a month during 1917 (the Admiralty put it at about eight) and eight a month in 1918. The Admiralty, of course, did not have the exact figures on U-boats destroyed and under construction; but they did know that the boats were not being sunk faster than new ones were being completed. They were, as a matter of fact, quite close to the actual statistics. The figure of about 54 U-boats known to have been captured or sunk as of mid-April was only four under the correct figure.[8] But the crux of the matter was the sharply rising curve of shipping losses.

* * *

An aspect of the German trade warfare was the series of tip-and-run destroyer raids on the Dover Straits from Zeebrugge. They were intended primarily to weaken or break up the British defence system in the Straits and thereby ease the passage of U-boats to the Atlantic via the shortest route. The last previous attack on the Straits had been on 25 October 1916. On 25 February 1917 the Germans took advantage of an overcast night to send strong flotilla forces in three detachments to attack the patrol craft and merchant shipping in the Downs (the anchorage in the English Channel off Deal), raid the drifters keeping watch on the Goodwins-Snouw net barrage across the Dover Straits, and attack the trade route between England and the Netherlands, off the Maas. The results were practically nil. The raiders achieved nothing in a ten-minute attack on the Downs, except the killing of two children and a woman, when their shells fell in Margate; the detachment that attacked the Dover barrage withdrew rapidly after a hot ten-minute fight with the Dover Patrol; and the destroyers off the Maas saw nothing. In their next effort, a destroyer raid on the barrage and the northern entrance of the Downs on the night of 17–18 March, the Germans fared better, despite the fact that the Admiralty had

[8] The figure of 54, from official British sources, was cited in a cable from Admiral Sims to the Secretary of the Navy, 14 April 1917; Rear-Admiral William S. Sims, *The Victory at Sea* (London, 1920), p. 374. On 17 March Jellicoe stated that 11 U-boats had been 'certainly sunk' since 1 January; the true figure was 10. Ten more were rated 'probably sunk'. 'I never pin much faith in the probables, and only count as certainties those from which we get prisoners or where we locate the wreck of the SM.' Jellicoe to Beatty, 17 March 1917; Beatty MSS. The official statistics classified U-boat losses as: 'Known', 'Probable', 'Possible', 'Improbable', and 'Not for submarine losses return' (or 'Not classified').

known that some movement was afoot in the Hoofden. The attack on the Downs was ineffective: a coastal bombardment did little serious damage, a small British steamer was sunk, and an armed drifter was heavily damaged. The attack on the barrage netted one destroyer and damage to a second. Bacon still had no solution to these raids. 'The enemy,' he reported, 'need only keep a rigid lookout, when close to the straits, for one hour, and fire a torpedo at everything he sees and run away. . . . The enemy can vary the time of attack at will and choose their night. They can predetermine whether to "shoot and scoot" or to carry out a more or less prolonged attack.'[9] All he could do was to change the dispositions for the patrol of the barrage; the forces were now more concentrated.

The most famous of the destroyer raids on the Straits took place on the night of 20–21 April. The object of the raiding force (twelve destroyers in two detachments of six each) was the destruction of patrol vessels on the barrage, and, if possible, a heavy bombardment of Calais and Dover. Conditions were favourable: the sea was calm, the night was black. Bacon had at his disposal a total of 16 destroyers, 2 flotilla leaders, 2 light cruisers, and a monitor. The barrage itself was patrolled by four destroyers and the flotilla leaders *Swift* (Commander A. M. Peck) and *Broke* (Commander E. R. G. R. Evans). In the early morning hours of the 21st, the *Swift* and *Broke*, patrolling the western end of barrage, seven miles east of Dover, encountered six of the raiders at 600 yards, steaming in an easterly direction towards the middle of the barrage. The British vessels closed. In the wild mêlée that followed, the *Swift* missed her ramming target (and just missed being rammed herself) when Peck was temporarily blinded by the flash of the 6-inch fo'c'sle gun. She fired her torpedoes, scoring a hit, and her guns, was badly holed by a shell, and, with her wireless out of action and her stokers' messdeck flooded, went off in pursuit of a fleeing destroyer. The *Broke* had an even wilder time as she concentrated on a second enemy destroyer. Her first torpedo hit, and this was followed by a withering fire of her 4-inch guns, ramming at 27 knots, and then the repelling of boarders by cutlasses, fixed bayonets, pistols, and 'throwing cups of hot cocoa at the enemy'. 'It was like an excerpt from a Marryat story, an echo of the spar-to-spar combats at Trafalgar', writes Evans's biographer, Reginald Pound. 'By then

[9] Newbolt, *Naval Operations*, iv. 368.

the stern of the *G42* was well down and the *Broke* rode in triumph over her.' By this time the *Broke* was in a bad way; a cordite fire was blazing, all her guns but one were out of action, and many of her crew had been killed or wounded. Yet she went on to complete a good night's work by disposing of another destroyer with torpedoes and gunfire. The official communiqué stated that two, 'possibly three', enemy destroyers had been sunk; two was correct.

This historic engagement discouraged further German destroyer raids into the Straits until February 1918, gave the country a new naval hero in the high-spirited 'Teddy' Evans, 'Evans of the *Broke*', as he was now known in the country (the equally gallant Peck for some reason never caught the public imagination), and gave the national morale a badly needed fillip.

2. THE POT SIMMERS

Jellicoe used the occasion of his admission to the Fishmongers' Company (11 January), his first public appearance as First Sea Lord, to make a long and important statement on the naval position. The passage which attracted the greatest attention ran: 'The submarine menace to the merchant service is far greater now than at any period of the war, and it requires all our energy to combat it. It must and will be dealt with: of that I am confident.' This was very comforting to public opinion, though it was opposite to what Jellicoe really felt. (See below.) On 26 January, Carson and Jellicoe received deputations from the Executive Committee of the Navy League and the Cardiff and Bristol Channel Incorporated Shipowners' Association, who were accompanied by four M.P.s. They appealed for more vigorous measures of repression of U-boats and left satisfied with the assurances that everything possible was being done. Beresford raised a debate in the Lords, 13 February, on the submarine campaign. None of the chief speakers sought to minimize the danger, although they were confident that it could be overcome. Beresford declared his 'absolute and complete faith in the ability of the present Board of Admiralty successfully to combat the German submarines and destroy the ferocious barbarities of these assassins of the sea', and predicted that 'in from six weeks to two months the submarine menace will be really well in hand'. Lytton (the Additional Parliamentary Secretary of the Admiralty) announced that the countermeasures taken had already met with 'very considerable success', and Curzon added some calming statistics: the enemy had succeeded in diminishing the British mercantile tonnage a mere 5 or 6 per cent of the gross tonnage: from 16,850,000 tons gross in July 1914 to just under 16,000,000 on 31 January 1917. In general, press opinion on the debate was that the Admiralty were not asleep.

On 21 February Carson delivered his maiden speech in the Commons as First Lord. Jellicoe sat in the distinguished strangers' gallery; Fisher, in the peers' gallery, was very still and attentive. It was a masterly speech, full of restrained drama and powerful sincerity, which did not seek to minimize the seriousness of the submarine menace. 'It is grave. It is serious. It has not yet been solved.' Although he suggested that 'no single magic remedy exists, or probably will exist', he expressed his confidence that 'in the development of measures which have been and are being devised its seriousness will by degrees be greatly mitigated'. One passage in particular was listened to with rapt attention. The First Lord announced that since 1 February there had been no fewer than forty armed encounters with U-boats. 'The fact that we have got into grips with them forty times in eighteen days is an enormous achievement.' He made no claim that there had been forty kills, but he left the impression that the Admiralty were pleased with the way the A/S campaign was going. Carson's lucid and straightforward review of the submarine situation was distinctly reassuring to the country. Declared the *Morning Post* (22 February), 'Not merely the matter but the spirit of the statement was well calculated to inspire public confidence . . . the country imposes an absolute confidence in the Board of Admiralty and in the Admirals at sea. The country is right, for never has it been better served.' The First Lord's statement, the *Spectator* commented (24 February), 'turned on the electric light in a dark room. It was thoroughly informing, bracing, and reassuring . . .'

The honeymoon of the country and the new Board of Admiralty, which had reached its peak on 21 February, gradually came to an end during the spring as the shipping situation worsened. The published weekly reports on the U-boats' harvest (number, though not tonnage, of British merchant vessels sunk) made grim reading. Here and there a newspaper or periodical, like the *Westminster Gazette*, *Morning Post*, and *Naval and Military Record*, or an individual, like Beresford or Archibald Hurd, the naval journalist, refused to panic or to withdraw the faith reposed in the Admiralty earlier in the year. But the voices of these few journals and individuals were drowned out by the rumble of uneasiness and criticism that began to mount in April and that reached its full volume in the first two weeks of May. The 'reptile press' (Madden's term) was led by Northcliffe's *Daily Mail* and by the naval journalist A. H. Pollen in the weekly *Land and Water*.[10] The Admiralty were slow in appreciating the position, it was said; they were conducting a defensive war: 'passive resistance' would never defeat the U-boat; they would solve the problem only by finding out the wasps' nests and destroying them (a favourite theme of the *Spectator*); Carson's appointment was a disaster for the country; and so forth and so on. A *Daily Mail* leader of 30 April carried the heading in large capital letters, 'What We Want From The Sea Lords'. The sub-heading read: '*Results, and no excuses*'. It was not only that the submarine menace was widely regarded as being nearly out of hand. The effects of the Russian Revolution of March thickened the gloom, as it was clear by May that the Russians would not be capable of a sustained military effort for some time to come. The United States had entered the war on 6 April, but it would be many months before they had a sizeable army in France.

Even before public opinion had taken this nasty turn there was the inevitable demand that Lord Fisher be recalled to the councils of the Admiralty as the only man with the originality and boldness of conception to deal with the menace. He touched the imagination of a very large public, which could not understand why the Government persisted in 'wasting' him. Some of what the *Daily Mail* called 'the steadily rising murmer of "Fisher, Fisher" throughout the country' may have been due to a naïve belief that the old Admiral had a secret plan or device up his sleeve by which he could sink all the enemy's submarines. Fearing that 'the submarine business is of course going to get worse', Fisher's great friend and admirer, the energetic Editor of *The Observer*, pleaded with Carson to make use of this 'man of genius—astonishingly vital despite his

---

[10] Pollen had been very biased against Jellicoe for some time. 'It fell to me,' wrote Jellicoe after the war, 'to turn down his inventions on more than one occasion.' The reference is to certain fire-control instruments invented by Pollen in the pre-war decade and which were, after trial, found unacceptable by the Admiralty. In fairness to Pollen it should be mentioned that he received £30,000 from the Royal Commission on Awards and Inventions for the Argo Clock, which the Admiralty cribbed in 'Captain F. C. Dreyer's Fire Control Tables' (1912).

age'.[11] C. P. Scott, the Editor of the *Manchester Guardian*, was more specific: Fisher should be put in Duff's place; he would accept, since he was anxious to help in any way, 'down to sweeping a crossing in Berkeley Square'.[12] George Lambert, the onetime Civil Lord of the Admiralty (1905–15), clamoured in the House of Commons (15 February) for Fisher's recall to the Admiralty: he was the only man capable of dealing with the U-boats.

Although Fisher had ardent supporters in the press and a following in the Service, he was anathema to certain organs (the *Morning Post* on 7 February delivered a shamelessly malicious attack on him) and to a large number of sailors who were dead set against his return. Admiral of the Fleet Sir Hedworth Meux, M.P., spoke his mind to his constituents at Plymouth (17 February), and Madden wrote to his brother-in-law: 'Beatty told me how dangerous the Fisher cabal has become . . . I do hope this catastrophe can be averted. B. said he [Fisher] was anxious to become Controller. Of course once he got a footing [he] would intrigue to push you or Sir E. Carson out or both.'[13] Indeed, Fisher had on 31 January offered to serve under Jellicoe as Third Sea Lord and Controller, an office he had filled with conspicuous success in 1892–7, for the specific purpose of annihilating the U-boat menace. The Prime Minister would have been willing, Carson, too (though he foresaw difficulties), but, after a fortnight's consideration, Jellicoe turned down the proposal as not being 'practicable'. 'There are only two posts which, in my opinion, you could hold here—those of First Lord or First Sea Lord. In any other position, I cannot help feeling that difficulties are bound to arise.'[14] It was 'the most bitter disappointment!' of Fisher's life—and at the hands of the man whom he had in the pre-war decade groomed for the highest positions in the Navy. Fisher never recovered from this blow. Henceforth the frustrated seadog was an even more outspoken critic of the new Board of Admiralty than he had been of the old.

For Fisher the problem had become, 'Can the Army win the

[11] J. L. Garvin to Carson, 24 January 1917; Carson MSS.
[12] Scott to Lloyd George, 29 January 1917; Lloyd George MSS.
[13] Madden to Jellicoe, 21 February 1917; Jellicoe MSS. The worst of the anti-Admiralty campaign, thought Beatty, was the 'danger of Fisher returning on the top of a wave. I wouldn't mind if he was ten years younger, but he is gaga now and could not serve any good purpose.' Beatty to Lady Beatty (April 1917); Beatty MSS. But see below, p. 173, for Beatty's *volte-face* in May.
[14] Jellicoe to Fisher, 13 February 1917; *Fear God and Dread Nought*, iii. 428.

War before the Navy loses it?' (This was also the view of Repington, Military Correspondent of *The Times*.) Hankey was afraid
that they would 'lose at sea without winning on land'.[15] No less a
personage than the C.-in-C., reflecting Grand Fleet sentiment, was
losing faith in the ability of the 'stupid Admiralty' to meet the
situation. Less than a month after the new Board had taken over
he was writing: 'These cursed submarines of the enemy are doing
untold damage, and will continue to do so until they [the Admir-
alty] take the question in the right way, and if they don't we shall
very shortly be brought to our knees.'[16] He became even more
critical. Thus, in February:

I am afraid the Enemy submarines are inflicting upon us immense
losses and all the Admiralty do is to make bombastic announcements
and yet fail to take the most elementary precautions. I have written and
wired until I am sick of it. Unfortunately the sphere of their activity is
outside my domain and I am reduced to hurling insults at them. But
the matter is serious. I am glad to say they are adopting some of my
suggestions, but the provision of certain essentials is so inadequate that
it will take a long time before we can really expect a satisfactory return.
Still I suppose better late than never, if we don't lose all our mercantile
marine in the meantime.

A couple of months later: 'It is a thousand pities that Jellicoe is
not stronger in his dealings with the S.M. menace. . . . Everything
at present is given up to the defensive attitude, and even that is not
being well done.' At about this time he remarked of the 'determined' anti-Admiralty campaign 'brewing' in press and Parliament: 'They have brought it entirely upon themselves by their
inane methods and lack of concrete ideas.'[17] Beatty was far from
being the only critic in the Fleet. It was a widely held opinion

[15] Fisher to Hankey, 23 April 1917, *ibid.*, p. 454; Lord Hankey's diary, 29 April 1917,
Hankey, *The Supreme Command* (London, 1961, 2 vols.), ii. 650.
[16] Beatty to Lady Beatty, 1 January 1917; Chalmers, *Beatty*, p. 286. Admiral Chalmers
has written of Jellicoe and Beatty: 'Like all great men, they had their differences,
but no one could question Beatty's loyalty to his chief while he served under his
command, and afterwards.' Beatty was often outspokenly critical of Jellicoe over
Jutland, but I especially question the 'and afterwards', which glosses over Beatty's
increasingly critical attitude towards Jellicoe during 1917 on account of the First Sea
Lord's alleged fumbling A/S policy and the lack of the offensive spirit generally at
Whitehall. Beatty's views got back to Jellicoe. On the other hand, Beatty would
never lend himself to any intrigues aimed at forcing Jellicoe out.
[17] Beatty to Lady Beatty, 6 February, 25, 27 April 1917; Beatty MSS.

among Grand Fleet officers that the Admiralty were doing a poor job in meeting the U-boat problem.

Jellicoe frequently emphasized that there was no sovereign remedy against the submarine threat—that it was the cumulative effect of every measure and every device that would solve the problem. The counter-measures in operation by April would never by themselves have done the job, quite apart from the fact that a number of them needed many months to be developed. The cumulative effect of the action taken was to make the life of the U-boats uncomfortable, without finding the actual remedy. By the end of March, Carson had to admit that the continued sinkings gave him 'grave anxiety and I do not see any daylight in our efforts to combat this menace'.[18] Jellicoe was even more doleful about the prospects. Indeed, he had been pessimistic from the very start. 'The shipping situation is by far the most serious question of the day. I almost fear it is nearly too late to retrieve it. Drastic measures should have been taken months ago to stop unnecessary imports, ration the country and build ships. All is being started now, but, as I said, it is nearly, if not quite, too late.'[19] This pessimism only worsened when the U-boats began their unrestricted campaign. A War Cabinet paper by Jellicoe (21 February) admitted that 'up to the present no complete and practicable cure for the submarine menace has been, or is likely to be, discovered short of the destruction of the bases, which is obviously a military measure of great magnitude'.[20] An Admiralty appreciation of the end of March struck a grave note:

> Even if we could rely on the average number of enemy submarines operating during the next six months as not appreciably exceeding that of last month, it must be recognised that, with the advent of longer days and finer weather, the offensive capacity of the submarine will greatly increase. As a matter of fact, we are faced with the certainty of an increase month by month in the number of hostile submarines. . . . It is evident, therefore, that we must be prepared for the menace assuming a still more acute stage, unless we are able to sink many more enemy submarines than is at present the case. . . . the introduction of new measures and the use of additional resources cannot be relied on to affect the situation during the next two or three months, and in the

[18] Carson to Beatty, 26 March 1917; Beatty MSS.
[19] Jellicoe to Beatty, 23 December 1916; Beatty MSS.
[20] 'Naval Policy in Relation to Mercantile Shipping Losses from Submarine Warfare, and the Effect on the Strategical Situation'; Admiralty MSS.

meantime we must be prepared for greater losses in tonnage than we have yet experienced.

The paper went on to give as a 'not unreasonable estimate' of mercantile losses, British, Allied, and neutral, in March of 500,000 tons, 'increasing possibly to 700,000 tons in June. From that month onwards some amelioration of the situation may be expected.'[21] Here was a blunt admission by the Admiralty that the defence had not caught up with the offence, and could not be expected to for some months anyway, during which time the country would have to accept huge mercantile losses. All that the Admiralty could offer was the perfection of existing A/S devices, continued reliance on patrol and hunting tactics, and the multiplication of A/S craft.

The prospect was so gloomy as spring arrived that, on General Smuts's initiative, a full Imperial War Cabinet discussion took place on 23 March 'on the question of the possibility of exploiting such moderate degree of military success as was likely to be achieved this summer in order to secure a reasonable peace. . . . It was agreed [among various considerations], on the one hand, that the submarine campaign and the possibility of deflection [defection?] among our Allies might render the situation very uncertain after this year . . .' But the decision reached was to put forth the whole of their military strength to achieve victory in 1917—and, if not successful, in 1918.[22]

The Naval High Command at Whitehall would not consider some fresh method even when it was obvious as early as February 1917 that only some drastic change of A/S policy, some as yet untried method of trade protection, could save the situation. This fresh method, it was evident to many, lay in a reversion to the method of the sailing era of forming ships into groups protected by armed escorts.

---

[21] Admiralty paper for the Imperial War Cabinet, 'A General Review of the Naval Situation' (G.T.-277), 24 March 1917.
[22] I.W.C. 3.

VI

The Introduction
of Mercantile Convoy

(December 1916 – April 1917)

The institution of a general system of Mercantile Convoy is commonly regarded as the turning point in the Submarine campaign and salvation of the country. I have no fault to find with this view with the qualification that the success of the system depended entirely on the right moment being chosen for its introduction.

ADMIRAL SIR ALEXANDER DUFF in a private memorandum of 1931.

He [Jellicoe] withstood Mr. Lloyd George's visionary schemes until America entered the War; then Atlantic convoys became feasible and were instituted as quickly as possible.

ADMIRAL SIR REGINALD BACON, *The Life of John Rushworth, Earl Jellicoe.*

I propose now to deal with the story of the amazing and incomprehensible difficulties encountered in inducing the Admiralty even to try the convoy system. . . . in the teeth of the fact that other methods were proving futile and disastrous, and our sinkings were increasing at an alarming rate, the Admiralty stubbornly refused to consider adopting the convoy system and thus extending to the mercantile marine the same guardianship as that upon which they relied for their own safety in the Grand Fleet. . . . Thus, on the one hand we had a confident Germany launching its deadly offensive against our shipping, and on the other hand we had a palsied and muddle-headed Admiralty declaring that nothing effective could be done to counter it.

LLOYD GEORGE, *War Memoirs.*

I. FORCES AND ARGUMENTS IN OPPOSITION

THE story of the introduction of the convoy system has given rise to a controversy almost as heated as Jutland. Lloyd George, in Volume iii of his *War Memoirs*, tells us that the Admiralty persistently and stubbornly fought the introduction of the convoy system, which had in the end to be forced upon them. This is also the position of the Official Naval Historian of the Second War, Captain Roskill, and of the late Vice-Admiral K. G. B. Dewar, among others. If we are to believe the opposing school, best represented in published form by Newbolt (*Naval Operations*, v)[1] and Admirals Bacon (*Jellicoe*) and Dreyer (*The Sea Heritage*), the delay in introducing convoy was unavoidable and the system was instituted as soon as conditions, notably America's entry into the war, made it practicable. What *are* the facts?

First, a definition. Convoying consists in the dispatch of merchant ships in organized groups accompanied by an escort of one or more warships. 'Convoy' refers to the ships being escorted. It had been the traditional British way of sailing a large proportion of merchant shipping and military transports in time of strained relations and of war since the early thirteenth century. It had proven its worth repeatedly over the centuries, most recently during the wars of the French Revolutionary and Napoleonic era. The results in this period (1793–1815) were nothing short of sensational. (The system was compulsory from 1798.) Thus, of 132 recorded convoys between 1793 and 1797, which convoyed 5,827 ships, 1·5 per cent were attacked and 35 ships, or 0·6 per cent, were taken. Of 16 recorded convoys and the 564 ships convoyed in the period August–December 1814, during the Napoleonic wars and the American War of 1812–14, only three stragglers were taken, a convoy loss rate of 0·53 per cent, or an estimated one-tenth of the loss rate of independent ships. At the end of the nineteenth century Mahan had drawn the only possible answer from history—that convoy was the only effective answer to commerce raiders. Writing of the Napoleonic wars, he had concluded: '. . . the result of the convoy system . . . warrants the inference that, when properly systematized and applied, it will have more success as a defensive measure than hunting for individual marauders,—a process which, even when most thoroughly planned, still resembles looking for a needle in a haystack.'[2]

---

[1] Newbolt's original version went through quite a few changes before it saw the light of day. As Churchill once remarked, 'Important personages in the story have clearly applied their pruning knives and ink-erasers with no timid hand.' Thus, it is instructive to examine Jellicoe's post-war notes for the Admiralty, 'Errors in *Naval Operations*, Vols. IV & V,' in the Jellicoe MSS. They consist of his comments on the draft chapters of iv and v (1927?), 'General Remarks on Revised Chapter I [of Vol. v] on the Submarine Campaign' (30 July 1928), comments on the re-revised Chapter I (4 April 1929), with Newbolt's minute on the same, and remarks on Newbolt's minute (8 August 1929). Note that *Naval Operations*, iv, was published in 1928, and v, in 1931.

[2] Captain Alfred T. Mahan, *The Influence of Sea Power upon the French Revolution and Empire, 1793–1812* (Boston, 1894, 2 vols.), ii. 217.

And yet, by the outbreak of war in 1914 an amazing metamorphosis in naval thought had relegated convoy to the scrap heap of outmoded naval strategy. During the hundred years' peace of the nineteenth century the lessons of the old wars were forgotten, which is not surprising, since the study of history was generally regarded as a waste of time. And the strange dogma had emerged in the pre-war generation that to provide warship escorts to merchant ships was to act essentially 'defensively' (because it protected ships from attack), which was *ipso facto* bad, and that to use naval forces to patrol trade routes, however futile the result, was to act 'offensively' against the warships of an enemy, and this was good. It was, therefore, a retrograde policy to divert warships from 'offensive' action to 'defensive' action. Moreover, U-boat attacks on shipping were somehow looked upon as a totally new kind of *guerre de course*, with past principles of defence no longer applicable. 'It was not appreciated,' as Commander Barley tells us, 'that in all the old wars nearly all the capturing of, or the destruction of, our merchant shipping had been done by small elusive craft conveniently classified under the title of privateers which, despite all attempts at close blockade of the enemy's ports and bases, eluded the fleets and cruisers and swarmed in the western approaches to Europe and in the eastern approaches to the Caribbean, snapping up independent ships and stragglers. No-one, in other words, recognized the U-boats as the ancient enemy dressed in a different guise.' Even the great lay expert on naval warfare, Julian Corbett, considered it 'doubtful whether the additional security which convoys afforded is sufficient to outweigh their economical drawbacks and their liability to cause strategical disturbance'.[3]

Since a convoy system was considered fundamentally unsound, there were, naturally, no plans at the Admiralty for initiating one when war came. For trade protection the Admiralty relied on a distant blockade of the High Seas Fleet, supplemented by patrols and hunting forces, the arming of merchantmen, and the dispersion of shipping in waters where enemy warships or mines were suspected through a system of advisory routeing before the ships sailed. Until 1917, merchant ships outside of coastal waters sailed independently as 'single' ships, setting their speeds and courses and conforming only to the general route instructions issued by the Admiralty. They depended for safety on their defensive armament,

[3] His classic *Some Principles of Maritime Strategy* (London, 1911), p. 274.

zigzagging, and smoke screens. Escorts were in use, though only on a small scale—for troop transports, munition ships, ships carrying cargoes of gold, and other especially valuable ships, which were wastefully escorted one at a time or in small convoys by a cruiser or merchant cruiser on an ocean voyage and by one or more destroyers when passing through the submarine danger zone.

Convoy, nonetheless, had its advocates from the beginning of the war. They were cognisant of the great and obvious tactical advantage of forcing the U-boats (or surface raiders, for that matter) to act in known positions where means of attacking them, armed escorts, could be provided—or, as Captain Roskill has put it, 'that raiders of no matter what type are as certain to be drawn to their quarry as bees to honey; and if the quarry has an armed escort, the opportunity for a vigorous counter-attack at once arises'. Moreover, convoy forced the submarine to attack submerged and by torpedo (whose supply was limited), not by gun.

The Flag-Captain of the 10th Cruiser Squadron (Northern Patrol) suggested in October 1916 that the enemy's submarine campaign would be 'considerably reduced' were convoy adopted. They frequently met straggling lines of merchantmen all of whom had apparently left port by the same tide. He submitted that these vessels should sail in close formation, escorted by a number of fast and powerful trawlers accompanied by a few destroyers. 'The suggested convoying system would entail the necessity for enemy submarines having to operate in the vicinity of anti-submarine craft.' A covering letter by Tupper, Vice-Admiral Commanding the 10th Cruiser Squadron, recommended that convoy be given a trial if enough fast trawlers and destroyers could be found for escort duties. The proposal was poorly received at the Admiralty. The D.O.D., Thomas Jackson, flatly declared that the vessels called for were not to be had, and the C.O.S., Oliver, concurred, adding, 'Ideas are of no use if they entail the employment of vessels which cannot be obtained.'[4] A number of officers supported a convoy system following Jellicoe's appeal to the Grand Fleet (9 November 1916, when still C.-in-C.) for suggestions on how to defeat the U-boat. At this time the head of Donald Macleod and Co., the ship-brokers, took the liberty of repeating a suggestion that he had sent to the First Lord some months back, 'viz. that so far as the shipowner and

---

[4] Captain H. H. Smith to Admiralty, 21 October 1916, and Admiralty minutes of 6 November 1916; Admiralty MSS.

the cargo is concerned there is only one way of saving both surely and that is by a system of CONVOY'. The necessary escort vessels would be found by building several hundred standardized light, unarmoured fast vessels, or by converting a number of 'FREE ships of the Mercantile Marine' into armed vessels suitable for the work.[5] In February 1917 a conference of British admirals at Malta (Vice-Admiral Commanding Eastern Mediterranean, C.-in-C. East Indies, and S.N.O. Malta—respectively, C. F. Thursby, R. E. Wemyss, and G. A. Ballard) recommended to the Admiralty that an 'escort system should be adopted [in the Mediterranean] as far as resources permit'. The Vice-Admiral Mudros (A. H. Christian) backed up this proposal. The First Sea Lord showed no interest.[6]

From the beginning of 1917 Beatty kept urging the adoption of convoy. After the Longhope conference (see below), he felt more strongly than ever that 'some form of convoy' had to be instituted for the 'Western Trade and approaches to the British Isles. . . . A system which permits of 9 vessels being sunk in a small area in the course of 6 days cannot be a good one: In fact it is deplorably bad.'[7] Beatty had the support of a few senior flag officers like de Robeck. From early in 1917 the Ministry of Shipping and the Shipping Controller warmly upheld the proposals of the naval officers who wanted to give convoy a trial.

Despite the strong current of opinion in favour of a general mercantile convoy system, the idea had little support at the Admiralty, where it was regarded as impracticable. The objections raised at the Admiralty were practical ones, or so they honestly considered them. Theirs was a reasoned opposition, not the obstructionist, obscurantist policy that Lloyd George and the Ministry of Shipping (Maclay, Norman Leslie, Norman Hill) believed at the time.

When the War Committee asked him (2 November 1916) if it would be wise to adopt a convoy system, Jellicoe had replied in the negative. 'Such knowledge as was then at my disposal led me to

[5] Donald Macleod to Admiralty, 6 November 1916; Admiralty MSS.
[6] S.N.O. Malta and Vice-Admiral Mudros telegrams to Admiralty, 2, 4 February 1917, Jellicoe's telegram to S.N.O. Malta, 3 February 1917; Admiralty MSS. Ballard told Richmond after the war that from the beginning of his time in the Mediterranean (September 1916) he had urged the adoption of convoy, saying he would require no extra small craft. '. . . he got nothing but snubs in reply, & eventually what amounted to reprimands.' Diary, 11 March 1919; *Portrait of an Admiral*, p. 362.
[7] Beatty to Carson, 29 April 1917; Beatty MSS. And see Beatty to Carson, 30 April 1917; Chalmers, *Beatty*, p. 448.

think that the objections to a general convoy system *at that time* would be insurmountable. I knew that we were very short of cruisers and destroyers for escort work and was doubtful about merchant ships in convoy being kept in sufficiently accurate station to ensure safety by a comparatively small number of escorting destroyers.'[8] A full knowledge of the facts when he arrived in Whitehall did not alter his fundamental objections to convoy. He minuted a paper on 29 December 1916: 'Convoy is impossible as a protection against submarines.'[9] Jellicoe did show a glimmer of interest in adopting the system for the protection of the Atlantic trade against the *Moewe*, which had just broken out. What were the difficulties? he wanted to know. The D.T.D., Webb, raised these, apart from the question of the availability of vessels for this service. It is a neat résumé of the whole of the Admiralty case against convoy, and the arguments were to be repeated *ad nauseam* in the next four months.

(a) The fact that unlike the convoys of the old wars vessels are now proceeding to so many destinations that it would involve a large number of different convoys, assuming the raider might be met with anywhere in the North or South Atlantic.

(b) The delays consequent on collecting the vessels for the various convoys.

(c) The alternating congestion and slack time at the ports of loading and discharge.

(d) The considerable delays imposed on the faster vessels of the convoy.

[8] Jellicoe, *The Submarine Peril*, p. 7. Newbolt (*Naval Operations*, v. 3) claims that 'Among other subjects the question of a possible convoy system was discussed. . . . He [Jellicoe] did not approve of convoys, as they offered too big a target.' Newbolt's original draft of the discussion in the War Committee included a remark by Jellicoe that 'practically they would want [in a convoy system] a destroyer for each ship, and this would come to the same thing as sending ships singly, which was a better arrangement.' This verbatim statement was taken from the report made by Colonel Dally Jones from his notes taken at the time. Claiming that he had no recollection of having made this remark, and that Jones's notes were never submitted to him, Jellicoe insisted, with Hankey's backing, that they were not quotable. 'If it is insisted that quotations should remain I consider it should be stated that my reason for X [the Jones quote above] was the difficulty merchant ships should have in keeping station.' Jellicoe, 'Errors in *Naval Operations*'. The offending passage disappeared in Newbolt's final draft.

[9] Naval Staff Monograph No. 33 (1927), *Home Waters—Part VII. From June 1916 to November 1916*, p. 240 n., which does not identify the author. But Newbolt did so in his minute on Jellicoe's critique of the draft chapters of *Naval Operations*. Jellicoe, 'Errors in *Naval Operations*'.

(e) The dislocation of service in the case of Mail Steamers, and other vessels which run to a fixed itinerary.

The delays refered to in (b), (d) and more particularly (c) above would still further aggravate the present very serious loss of carrying capacity of the Mercantile Marine. The present delays in discharging at U.K. Ports are now very considerable, and in the case of French Ports this is still more so. This in spite of the fact that trade is arriving comparatively normally and not in batches as would be the case with convoys.

Also, convoys arriving at ports such as Buenos Aires would be delayed there until the last vessel of the convoy was loaded. This in the case of, say, 20 ships in the convoy would mean a delay to the first ship loaded of perhaps 30 days. . . .

Oliver was no more favourable. His memorandum stressed that

The provision of men-of-war for convoys seems to be beyond our resources having regard to the volume of traffic. . . . The monthly sailings from Atlantic U.S.A. ports are estimated to be 304 or roughly the average of 10 ships sailing every day. If convoys were made up at Halifax and consisted of 20 merchant ships to one man of war, a convoy would have to sail every second day. The passage to England would take about 11 days at 10 knots. The man of war would require 8 days in port to clean boilers at one end and 4 days in port at the other end, roughly about 34 days for the round trip. Fifteen men of war would be required to start every month from Halifax. The West Indian trade and the large volume of trade from South America and the Cape would also have to be provided for and would take a large number of ships owing to the much greater distances. A number of our older cruisers would not stand the continuous steaming and a very few trips would put them in Dockyard hands. We have comparatively few cruisers which can steam all the way from Sierra Leone to England . . .[10]

At about this time (21 December) Duff was objecting to convoy on such grounds as the variation in speed of merchant ships, their inability to zigzag, and tendency to straggle.[11] And in January 1917 the Admiralty War Staff issued a revised handbook on trade defence that condemned convoy in explicit terms. 'Wherever possible, vessels should sail singly, escorted, as considered necessary. The system of several ships sailing in company, as a convoy, is not recommended in any area where submarine attack is a possibility.

[10] Jellicoe to Webb and Oliver, 24 December 1916, and their memoranda of 26 December 1916 and 6 January 1917, respectively; Admiralty MSS.
[11] Naval Staff Monograph, *Home Waters. From June 1916 to November 1916*, p. 240.

It is evident that the larger the number of ships forming the convoy, the greater the chance of a submarine being enabled to attack successfully, and the greater the difficulty of the escort in preventing such an attack.'[12]

We must now examine these arguments more closely to determine their validity. The overwhelming objection of the decision-makers at the Admiralty to a system of regular ocean convoy was the alleged dearth of escorting ships. Wrote Jellicoe, '. . . the insuperable difficulty at that time was that the number of escorting vessels available *was totally insufficient to adopt the system.*'[13] The argument that he, Oliver, and Duff emphasized then and afterwards was that vessels could not be spared from other duties (the needs of the Grand Fleet and the armies in France, Salonika, Mesopotamia, and East Africa) to undertake the escort of convoys. To start the system prematurely, with inadequate protection for convoys, would be to give the U-boats sitting ducks as targets. Convoy was introduced, to continue the argument, as soon as it became possible to provide the necessary fast vessels (destroyers, sloops, or, with slow convoys, trawlers) to escort the convoys through the submarine zone, and the necessary ocean-going vessels for ocean escort (cruisers, specially armed merchant ships, and perhaps old battleships) as protection against attacks by a surface raider.

The Admiralty estimated early in 1917 that about 12 cruisers or armed merchant ships would be needed for the outward-bound trade and about 50 more for the homeward-bound trade; the needs of the escorting flotillas were reckoned at 81 destroyers or sloops for the homeward-bound Atlantic trade alone, and 44 more for the outward-bound Atlantic trade. (The trawlers were useful only for escorting the slow ships on the Gibraltar to Great Britain trade.) At this period there were available for ocean escort, according to Admiralty reckoning, only 18 vessels, which would have been provided by stripping the North Atlantic of cruisers. The destroyer-sloop situation was, as they saw it, equally unpromising: only 14 destroyers (Devonport) and 12 sloops (Queenstown) were nominally available for the protection of shipping—'nominally', because

---

[12] Operations Division, Admiralty War Staff, 'Remarks on Submarine Warfare, 1917'; Technical History Monograph TH 14 (1919), *The Atlantic Convoy System, 1917–1918,* p. 3. Jellicoe's annotations on a proof copy in the Admiralty records show that he had seen the handbook and accepted its conclusions.

[13] Jellicoe's autobiographical notes; Jellicoe MSS. Similarly, in his *The Submarine Peril,* p. 111.

most of them were engaged in the protection of specially valuable ships like troop ships. During February, six minesweeping sloops were transferred from the North Sea to Queenstown, and eight destroyers were detached from the Grand Fleet for patrol and escort work in southern waters.[14] Consequently, the Admiralty could have scraped together a total of 40 destroyers and sloops at the end of February.

Let us turn in greater detail to the situation in the early spring. The crux of the matter was the destroyer situation, for it was primarily these craft that could do the job in the danger zone. It was now considered at the Admiralty that about 72 destroyers would be needed to start a general convoy system. During April the average nominal distribution in Home waters was:[15]

Grand Fleet (Scapa and Rosyth)	99
Harwich Force	28
Dover Patrol	37
Scapa, Rosyth (the Forth), and Cromarty	11
Humber and Tyne	24
The Nore	8
Portsmouth	32
Devonport	44
Queenstown	8

Twelve of the boats (the eight at Queenstown and four of those at Devonport) were detached from the Grand Fleet but are also included with the Grand Fleet's nominal strength, as they were supposed to be 'on loan'. The net total was, therefore, 279.

To have detached any large additional number of destroyers from the Grand Fleet would have had the effect of partially immobilizing it, especially when we consider that 8 of its boats were at Lerwick (for the escort of the Scandinavian convoys) and 21 were under repair. If Jellicoe angered the C.-in-C. by withdrawing too many destroyers, he provoked the Prime Minister by not

---

[14] Jellicoe, *The Crisis of the Naval War*, pp. 111–12. Newbolt, *Naval Operations*, v. 6–7, spells out the destroyer situation as it looked to the Admiralty at the beginning of the year.

[15] The figures are from Newbolt, *Naval Operations*, v. 387–8. They represent the average number of vessels allotted daily, not the actual strength on the spot, and make no allowance for the boats that were repairing or refitting (though Newbolt gives this figure): 54, or about 20 per cent of the total. Nor do they include flotilla leaders or destroyers attached to submarine flotillas.

withdrawing enough. Lloyd George intimates that the Grand Fleet could have spared more of its destroyers for the A/S war, when an attack by the German High Seas Fleet upon the vastly stronger Grand Fleet was, in his view, an extremely remote possibility. So long as there was even a remote possibility of meeting the High Seas Fleet, Jellicoe and Beatty regarded the denuding of the Grand Fleet still further of its indispensable destroyer escort, without which it could not move, as too hazardous a gamble.

If not from the Grand Fleet, from where would the 72 destroyers come? The Harwich Force could not be weakened further. It had, Newbolt reminds us, 'ceased to be a concentrated force and had become a sort of pool for miscellaneous service in the Flanders Bight and the Dover Straits'. And the effective striking force at Harwich, about half its nominal strength, was busy escorting the Dutch convoys. (See below, p. 138.) The large force at Dover could not be tampered with, in view of the recurring destroyer raids in the Straits. The Admiralty would not consider detaching boats from the Local Defence Flotillas at Scapa, Cromarty, the Forth, the Humber and Tyne, the Nore, Portsmouth, and Devonport (a total of 32 boats). They considered the risk from U-boats in the approaches too great. Besides, many of these boats were also engaged in essential escort (of transports, supply ships, etc.) and trade-route patrol and submarine-hunting duties. Moreover, the figures in the above table include 13 of the Humber and Tyne destroyers and seven of those in the north (Scapa, the Forth, Cromarty) that were detached for Scandinavian convoy on 24 April.

Jellicoe deemed that he could not have scraped together enough destroyers to start anything like a comprehensive scheme in the Atlantic. At best the maximum number of destroyers that could have been used for convoy work as late as the end of April was 24: 10 each from Portsmouth and Devonport, and four from Queenstown. In Jellicoe's opinion, it would have served no useful purpose, and would indeed have increased the danger to the rest of the trades, if the Admiralty had introduced a partial system of convoy.

. . . at the best it was only possible to start in April a *partial homeward bound convoy*. If all the escort destroyers were taken for this purpose what would become of the other homeward bound and all outward bound vessels? Obviously protection was still needed for them, and that protection had to be afforded by the old means, which are stated to have failed. They failed it is true to save very heavy losses, but had all protection been withdrawn in order to start a homeward convoy system at this period, the losses would certainly have been infinitely heavier. . . .

Even by mid-July, *by which time we had been reinforced by 18 U.S. destroyers and no doubt by some of our own vessels by that time completed,* even so we were only able to provide anti-submarine escorts for 4 homeward bound convoys every 8 days from New York, Sydney, and Hampton Roads. Outward trade was still unconvoyed as was the South Atlantic and Mediterranean trade. Is not this an indication that in April the difficulty of starting the system was almost insuperable? Further, the matter of the provision of ocean escorts was a very real problem.

Newbolt's reaction was sharp and very much to the point: 'The "impossibility" of convoy, and the "difficulty of starting" are two different things. The fact is that in spite of the difficulty the start was not impossible, for it was made.'[16]

This leads us to another way of looking at convoy escort requirements—the number of vessels actually used when convoy began: 14 ocean escorts and approximately 90 A/S escorts for the partial system, and 50 and 170, respectively, when the system was in full operating order. The question is: could these vessels have been available for convoy escort early in 1917 without giving up or jeopardizing other operations? The answer, it seems to me, is *yes*, if only Duff, Oliver, and other high naval authorities had not believed that every convoy would need twice as many escorts as there were merchant ships in the convoy—an utterly impracticable ratio—and if they were not so wedded to patrol and hunting measures.[17] They did not realize the utter ineffectiveness of patrolling the Western Approaches and would not abandon their clichés

---

[16] Jellicoe, 'Errors in *Naval Operations*'. The figure of 18 U.S. destroyers, moreover, was incorrect. See below, p. 275, n. 25.

[17] As regards the former, Duff remarked in his minute of 19 April on the Longhope conference recommendations (4 April) for a Scandinavian trade convoy system (see below, p. 143), '. . . a not uncommon opinion is that a very slender escort is sufficient to act as a deterrent against submarine attack. My opinion is diametrically opposed to this, and I believe that an escort to be effective must number two escorting vessels to every ship in the convoy. . . . An insufficiently guarded convoy passing daily over the same area must prove the easiest of preys to the submarine.' Admiralty MSS. Newbolt wrote (*Naval Operations*, iv. 383): 'The opinion which at the time prevailed at the Admiralty was that, if merchantmen were placed under convoy, then the escort would have to be twice as numerous as the ships escorted. The Admiralty's advisers did not share the view, which was then not uncommon, that a comparatively weak escort would suffice.' Jellicoe objected strongly to this (or a very similar) statement in Newbolt's draft manuscript. 'This statement is made because Admiral Duff

about patrolling being offensive, whereas convoy was defensive, and only offensive measures could defeat the U-boat. The average number of ocean-going ships entering and leaving the United Kingdom per week was 120 to 140 each way. Not much more than 150 destroyers or sloops were required to convoy them through the Western Approaches, where most of the sinkings occurred. The Navy had *over 400 of these vessels* (about 350 destroyers and 60 sloops), and there would have been no great difficulty in providing the necessary A/S vessels if a large number, about 60 destroyers alone, had not been wastefully employed (except for the rescue of shipwrecked crews) patrolling wide expanses of water and escorting single valuable ships. And there were more than enough old cruisers and old battleships available for ocean escort—60 and 24, respectively, but tied up on ineffective patrolling. 'The problem,' as Admiral Dewar has summed it up, 'was not so much lack of escorts as the more efficient use of those we had.' In the end, ample craft were made available for escort by taking them from the patrols.

Weighing just as heavily with the Admiralty as the escort problem were the strongly adverse opinions of mercantile officers. Most ship masters feared that the zigzagging together and accurate station-keeping required under the system were beyond their capabilities, since sailing in company was quite outside the experience of merchant service officers. (Close station was necessary to reduce the area covered by a convoy and therefore the size of the escort required.) At an Admiralty conference on 23 February 1917 between Jellicoe, War Staff representatives, and ten masters of merchant ships lying in the London docks, the masters emphatically stated that good station-keeping, a *sine qua non*, was impossible, particularly at night without navigation lights, because of the limited sea experience of the majority of the officers—so many of the experienced deck officers (R.N.R. officers) and men had been taken by the Navy. Other obstacles, they pointed out, were the

---

in one minute did say [this] . . . It does not in the least follow that he was expressing the "Admiralty view" in this minute. He certainly was *not* doing so.' Duff's opinion, moreover, 'appears to refer to the Scandinavian convoy as he mentions a convoy *passing daily over the same area.* . . . Atlantic convoys obviously would not *pass daily over the same area.*' Newbolt stood by his guns. Jellicoe's comment 'cannot be sustained: Admiral Duff gave it [his minute] no such limited interpretation in the interviews with the Historian, at which Lord Jellicoe himself was present.' Jellicoe, 'Errors in *Naval Operations*'.

inferior quality of the coal, which would make it difficult to keep a regular speed, and the poor communications system between bridge and engine-room. Two or three ships were the maximum that 'might be able' to sail together and keep station. 'The Masters who were assembled were firmly of opinion that they would prefer to sail alone rather than in company or under a convoy.'[18] The Admiralty consulted the masters on other occasions but could never win their support; they insisted that the inexperience of officers and men, coupled with the 'impossibility' of making ships keep station in convoy when they had so many different speeds, would result either in the ships straggling during the night, or a bunching up and consequent collisions. Their unanimous demand was: 'Give us a gun and let us look out for ourselves.' The objections of the merchant skippers were undoubtedly a powerful factor in the Admiralty's reluctance to adopt convoy.

Equally decisive was Service opinion. Wrote Admiral Duff, in a résumé of the inception and development of the convoy system: 'The introduction of a system of convoy was fully considered early in 1917, but not proceeded with owing to strongly adverse criticism from both Naval and Mercantile Officers. The more experienced the Officer the more damning was the opinion expressed against mercantile convoy.'[19] In his autobiography Admiral Bayly asserted, 'Considering that in our past wars the necessity and value of convoys were so clearly recognized, it is difficult to see why they were so long delayed in the Great War.'[20] One reason is that many senior officers *like himself* were not at that time thinking of convoy as an answer to the problem.[21] On the naval side the arguments against convoy were of two kinds. It was considered that station-keeping would at best be so rough-and-ready, and straggling so much the rule, that the main advantage of sailing in convoy would not be achieved. Further, the provision of the necessary escorts, ocean and danger zone, appeared to be out of the realm of the possible. Even after the decision had been taken to give convoy a trial, Beatty's Second-in-Command wrote: 'It is probable that a

[18] Report of 'Meeting Held at Admiralty on 23rd February, 1917', Bellairs MSS; minutes of W.C. 91, 8 March 1917.
[19] Duff's paper of 19 August 1918; Duff MSS.
[20] *Pull Together! The Memories of Admiral Sir Lewis Bayly* (London, 1939), p. 239.
[21] In March we find Bayly advocating a few, fixed, heavily patrolled trade routes—no mention of convoy. Bayly's memorandum, 'Protection of Sea-Going Trade Leaving and Approaching British Isles', 15 March 1917; Admiralty MSS.

system of convoys will become a necessity, at least for the more valuable ships; if submarines torpedo at sight, it seems to be the only way of protecting ships in open waters. This policy cannot be generally adopted, however, for lack of escorting vessels.'[22] The naval opposition to convoy probably stemmed in part from an unconscious motive. Naval thought was focused too exclusively on battle and too little on the protection of shipping, hence there was a tendency to reserve destroyers and skilled personnel for the main fleet and to view shipping protection as a matter of secondary importance. It does not appear to have been fully realized that lack of shipping could lose the war without a single major engagement at sea.

The fears adumbrated by the masters and by naval officers proved to be quite groundless, for (as the evidence of the many successful troop convoys since August 1914 should have indicated), when straggling all over the place would make their ship a gift to a U-boat, the masters quickly learned the art of sailing in a tightly packed formation. They maintained station without undue hardship and were capable of zigzagging and altering course together. Soon after the introduction of convoy, moreover, the decision was reached to group ships according to speed, although ships with a speed exceeding 16 knots ordinarily sailed independently without escort. This minimized the problem of straggling. It also helped that convoys sailing eastward across the Atlantic had the advantage of at least five to six days' practice in keeping station before entering the dangerous areas.

Another consideration that swayed the Admiralty against convoy was the hostility of most of the shipowners to the idea, and the apparent soundness of their argument that convoy meant delays in turnover, which would be bad for the war effort, as well as financial loss incurred by demurrage. Concerning the latter, the shipowners had a good thing in the war (Lloyd George in his *War Memoirs* branded the 'inflated' shipping rates as 'a scandalous example of war profiteering'), and undoubtedly there were unscrupulous ones among them who did not hesitate to use their influence to oppose a system of shipping protection that seemingly

---

[22] Madden to Beatty, 1 May 1917, sent by Beatty to Duff for the First Sea Lord's information; Admiralty MSS. The same objection, the paucity of suitable escort vessels, had been raised by senior Grand Fleet officers at a dinner party given by Burney on 13 November 1916. Commodore G. von Schoultz, *With the British Battle Fleet: War Recollections of a Russian Naval Officer* (London, 1925), p. 227.

would threaten their swollen profits, or at least delay them. Of course, the consideration that impressed the Admiralty was the anticipated grave loss in carrying power. The full argument ran along these lines: sailing alone and able to load and turn round swiftly, the merchant vessel was a more efficient vessel than it would be as a member of a convoy compelled to wait for the assembly of its escorts, often ten days or a fortnight, and to sail at the speed of the slowest vessel of the convoy. Moreover, it was said, the arrival of a large convoy would inevitably lead to port congestion by overtaxing the port loading and unloading facilities, with a consequent reduction in carrying power.[23]

The Admiralty strategists lost sight of the serious delays experienced by independent sailings owing to frequent detention in ports because of a reported U-boat in the vicinity until the port approach was supposed to be clear (or, more often, until the congestion reached the point where the shipping simply had to move!), and to diversions and closure of routes for days at a time until a 'safe route' could be reported. In contrast, convoys could disregard the submarine situation in particular areas, sail at fixed dates, and use a direct route. As an example, the ships of the first convoy which left Gibraltar (10 May 1917) arrived home two days earlier than if these ships had followed the devious routes prescribed for independent sailings. The delays of independently routed ships were, in fact, as important a reason for introducing convoy as the necessity of reducing shipping losses: the suspensions had a serious effect on the available tonnage, particularly with the start of the unrestricted campaign. For instance, the total duration in hours of interruption (partial or total) of English Channel traffic, January–March 1917, was 300, in the Irish Sea, 443, and in the Bristol Channel, 400.

The port-congestion factor merits special attention, since the reduction in imports through port delays meant a diminution of available tonnage that was greater at certain periods than that due to destruction of shipping.

No really thorough attempt was made [write two scholars] to calculate how far British imports might under war conditions be limited by

---

[23] Jellicoe afterwards asserted that the speed-of-the-slowest-ship and port-congestion factors were the main causes in the delay in the introduction of convoy. Jellicoe, *The Crisis of the Naval War*, p. 102. Actually, the scarcity of escort vessels and the opposition of the masters and of the Navy bulked larger in Admiralty calculations at the time.

shortage of port capacity. One of the major factors determining the carrying capacity of a ship is the time she spends in port—in loading or discharging cargo and in other port operations. . . . Between 1914 and 1917 [before the institution of convoy] the times spent in port had been so much extended that, as a result of the difference, the United Kingdom almost certainly lost more imports, in any single year, than the submarines sank. In 1917 the United Kingdom imported (excluding petroleum products) some 34 million tons of commodities. In the first four months of the year, at the peak of the U-boat effort, cargoes were being sunk at a rate of about five million tons a year. At the same time the loss from delays in port, taking peacetime performance as a standard, was between four and five million tons. It must of course be remembered, in comparing the losses from sinkings with port delays, that sinkings are cumulative and port delays are not: ships sunk in one year mean so many the less the next.[24]

The unpredictability of shipping movements that resulted from the precautionary detentions of vessels and sailing large numbers of ships independently were the primary causes of the serious port congestion. This uncontrollable bunching threw off the railways, the main distributors of a ship's cargo, since the efficiency of a railway system depends upon the predictability of the movements of the trains operated over it. This situation intensified the port congestion.[25] (The railway companies, strangely, were not enthusiastic over convoy, feeling that so many cargoes arriving at the same time would result in congestion at the ports and on the railways themselves.) The port congestion was aggravated by such other factors as the siphoning off of dock labour by the Services and by the phenomenon of wartime imports being much heavier in relation to bulk (approximately 65 per cent) than peacetime imports, hence the damage done by an ever diminishing delivery rate. Port congestion, it was proved, could be prevented, or, where it had developed, cured, only by systematic sailings, that is, by convoying ships. This made possible the systematic controlled movement of

[24] W. K. Hancock and M. M. Gowing, *History of the Second World War. British War Economy* (London, 1949), p. 124.
[25] The railways in England were then regional private enterprise organizations (though the Government took over control of them immediately war was declared); the idea of one integrated railway system was quite foreign. Similarly, the ports and many of the wharves in many of the ports were privately owned and 'tied' to shipping lines. Here again the idea of an integrated port system was alien. These facts, together with the draining of skilled dock labour into the forces, all contributed seriously to a drop in shipping delivery as soon as the peace-time rhythm, such as it was, was violently disturbed with the outbreak of war.

large numbers of ships with a high probability that they would sail and arrive to schedule. This made it feasible to plan unloading and transport from the harbours more efficiently than was possible with independently sailed ships.

Another difficulty ('the dominant difficulty', according to Newbolt) arose in connection with the assembly of a convoy in a neutral port. This could be done under international law. 'But statesmen . . . may refuse to allow their ports to be used for such a purpose—on the ground that it will attract foreign combatants to their national waters. Even though they do not forbid it outright, they can raise such administrative difficulties that the work of collecting and routeing a convoy from a neutral harbour becomes impossible. The attitude which the American Government would adopt seemed doubtful. Even when they had broken off diplomatic relations with Germany, they were still neutral. The President on 3 February announced that he hoped to remain so. Their active or passive opposition might make the whole system unworkable.'[26] This consideration undoubtedly counted for something at the Admiralty down to the time of the American entry into the war. Until then Admiralty discussion of convoy reckoned on homeward-bound ships meeting at an ocean rendezvous, on the outskirts of the submarine danger zone, a difficult and dangerous arrangement, and being met there by an escort for shepherding through the U-boat zone.

A lesser argument was that of too many eggs in one basket—that it was not wise to increase the size of the target offered to a submarine, which, set loose in the middle of a convoy, might raise tremendous havoc. It was not appreciated at the Admiralty that the mere fact of ships sailing in company was a *protection*, not a larger and easier target. In practice, convoys did not offer fat, inviting targets. Forced by the convoy escort to keep her distance, the U-boat had difficulty in taking up a favourable position for using her torpedoes. The zigzag course steered by the convoy added to the U-boat's difficulties. Moreover, the ships closed up in a compact body ran less risk of being sighted by a submarine than did ships spread out on a route. Also, the convoy could be diverted by wireless, if a submarine were spotted on its course, in a way which was impossible with single ships, many of which at that time were not fitted with wireless. Another consideration was, as Commander Henderson argued, that if the convoy were adequately

[26] Newbolt, *Naval Operations*, v. 9.

guarded, the U-boat would ordinarily be able to have only a 'browning shot' (a random shot in the hope of hitting one ship in the convoy), which might or might not hit. If it did hit, only a certain percentage of the convoy was lost so far as that U-boat was concerned; whereas in the case of a similar number of ships sailing independently along that track, she would probably account for two or three and perhaps more.

Post-war apologists for the Admiralty admit all this, but they say there was no experience which could have furnished the Admiralty with an answer. Yet, experience there was: the capital ships of the Grand Fleet, which also cruised in close formation with a destroyer screen, never suffered a hit from a submarine, while ramming and sinking two in 1914-15 (*U-15*, by the light cruiser *Birmingham*, 9 August 1914, and *U-29*, by the *Dreadnought*, 18 March 1915). Then there was the experience of the Anglo-Dutch trade, which had been protected by convoy since July 1916. The zigzagging of the ships had rendered U-boat attack more difficult.

Other arguments sometimes heard were the catastrophic consequences of a surface attack on a convoy or of a convoy becoming entangled in a minefield, whereas a single ship might have sailed through safely or, if mined, would have given a warning to those coming after her. The danger from mines was, for instance, one of the considerations that qualified Duff's support of the Longhope conference recommendations of 4 April; and Jellicoe used both arguments in his two books on the U-boat menace. These fears turned out to be grossly exaggerated. The danger from minefields never developed: a total of five ships appeared to have been mined in convoy during the whole war. Also, a convoy sailed undeterred by mines—the minesweeping was synchronized to the convoy's movements—whereas independent ships were either kept out of port or kept inside port when a mine risk was reported. As for surface raiders, apart from two successful attacks by surface forces on the Scandinavian convoy, there was no serious threat from raiders during the convoy period.

Futile strategical conceptions do not entirely explain the Admiralty dragging their feet on convoy. A not unimportant contributory factor was the faulty administration at the Admiralty. They had not at any time during the war made any serious study of the problem of trade protection. The Admiralty had accepted it as a principal responsibility of the Navy *without determining the precise extent of that responsibility.* 'It is as if an insurance company agreed to insure a man's life without troubling to find out his age, occupation or state of health.' Commander Waters sums up one aspect of the situation:

On 4th August 1914, a State War Risks Insurance Scheme was promulgated. There had been no world wide wars for 100 years so that the insurance market had no modern statistics on which to assess war premiums. Moreover ships and cargoes were now individually so costly that it felt unable to underwrite British shipping and cargoes against war risks. The State Insurance Scheme re-insured all cargoes destined for the United Kingdom, and 80% of the insured value of the hulls of British ships provided the ships insured complied with the Admiralty's sailing instructions. Admirable in intent it contravened sound insurance practice by substituting a nominal and flat-rate premium for differential premiums assessed on voyage risk and whether ships sailed under escort or as 'runners'. It thus relieved the insurance market of keeping an actuarial check upon the system of shipping defence operated. Clearly, the safeguard lay in the Admiralty maintaining statistics which would show the relative risk of sailing ships under escort, as transports and supply ships always were, and independently, and consequently which system was the better.

But the Admiralty, being concerned with the protection of shipping routes, and not of merchant ships, did not maintain such statistics. Consequently they were nobody's business and though the War Risks Insurance scheme kept shipping moving at sea [Indeed, the shipowners would not have sailed at the outbreak of war but for the scheme promulgated on 4 August] there was no economic check upon the system of shipping defence employed. In short, the State War Risks Scheme short-circuited the warning system previously operated in war by the Marine Insurance Market.[27]

A related facet of the War Risks Scheme contributed to the delinquency of the Admiralty. As an official study points out:

The confidence inspired by the Scheme also reacted disastrously on the Admiralty. . . . The [U-boat] peril was manifest from the beginning of February 1915, but beyond providing for the patrolling of the inshore lanes of traffic, and arming about one-fourth of the merchant ships, nothing had been foreseen, nothing had been provided for, when two years later the enemy opened his campaign of sinking at sight all vessels trading with this country. The Admiralty had not even taken the

[27] D. W. Waters, 'The Philosophy and Conduct of Maritime War', Part 1. 1815–1918, *Journal of the Royal Naval Scientific Service*, May 1958. This is a restricted journal.

trouble to master the first elements of the problem—the number of sailings to be protected. The result was that we started our anti-submarine work twenty-four months late, and thereby we nearly lost the war.

There are strong grounds for the belief that this delay resulted, in great measure, from the feeling of security created in the minds of both the Admiralty and the country by the War Risk Insurance Scheme. . . . it was false security, as the cash payments made under the Scheme could never take the place of the naval protection which alone could guarantee the arrival of oversea supplies; but the immediate and extra-ordinary success with which the Scheme worked obscured the real nature of the peril with which the country was confronted from the beginning of February 1915.

Both the Scheme from the financial point of view, and the steps taken by the Admiralty from the point of view of protection, were based on the perils of cruiser warfare. Neither the promoters of the Scheme nor the Admiralty had before the war any conception of the risks incident to submarine warfare. So long as the enemy was hampered in that warfare by political considerations the losses could be borne financially by the Scheme, and the necessary volume of supplies could be brought in; but when once the enemy ceased to be restrained by the fear of the neutral States, the Admiralty's system of protection became ridiculously inadequate, and therefore the Scheme became unworkable.[28]

The absence of a true naval staff will partly explain this failure on the part of the Admiralty to know the facts. This was due to the excessive centralization at the Admiralty, where, up to June 1917, the First Sea Lord and the Chief of the War Staff had exclusive control of operations. 'Every paper or signal, however trivial, had to be deferred to them', remarks Admiral Dewar, who served in the Operations and Plans Divisions of the Staff (July 1917– February 1918). He points out:

It was nobody's business in Operations or any other division to plan or think ahead or to investigate such questions [as those pertaining to trade protection] . . . That kind of work was not done because the higher ranks did not delegate authority to do it ['and were themselves too busy to do it', he adds elsewhere]. Instead of confining their atten-tion to important questions of policy and the general direction of affairs, they [the War Staff Divisions] immersed themselves in a flood of routine and current business, much of which could have been decided [by the executive Commands] without reference to the Admiralty. The

[28] Sir Norman Hill *et al.*, *War and Insurance* (London, 1927), pp. 52–3.

human mind can only work efficiently on one thing at a time but they had to switch continually from one subject to another in order to keep pace with the flow of telegrams and papers. Hence, matters requiring thought and discussion had to be evaded or decided with insufficient knowledge of the facts or issues involved. . . .

There is no reasonable doubt that the primary cause of failure to protect shipping was an overcentralized administration at the Admiralty. Congestion at the top and inertia at the bottom prevented investigation of alternative courses of action. The ship was, as it were, running on the rocks because the Captain and Navigator were too busy to lay off the new course. Nor was there any systematic attempt to analyse or evaluate the results of current operations. Valuable information, such as the decisive success of convoy on the Hook-Harwich route, was frequently ignored amongst the mass of material marked to the decisional authorities. It is one thing to read a report and quite another to select and mentally register its important points. The continual perusal of dockets, telegrams and reports, dealing with a wide variety of subjects, acts like a drug. It dulls the perceptive faculties and paralyses power of criticism and selection behind a deceptive façade of hard work.[29]

Behind the ineffectiveness of the Staff lay the lack of a study of war among pre-war officers. Had there been a serious examination of the workings of convoy in history, the objections of the merchant service would not have been an important deterrent to giving convoy a trial; and other criticisms would have been evaluated more accurately.

Under the various circumstances that have been sketched it is not remarkable that the Admiralty made no study to determine the relative merits of convoy and patrol, or if there was really an insufficiency of escort vessels. 'When I first came,' reported Admiral Sims (he had arrived in England on 9 April to determine how

---

[29] The late Admiral Dewar, a Commander at this time, may have been an embittered man in his later years who saw everything through a glass darkly and wrote without a sense of balance, yet he was among the most perceptive thinkers in the Navy of his generation and his writings contain many facts and shrewd insights of great value to the historian. Dewar was Richmond's foremost disciple and much like him: brilliant, cantankerous, stubborn, opinionated, and disdainful of those of small intellectual ability and not as well versed in naval history. He lacked warmth: here he differed from Richmond. Late in life he sadly remarked how he wished he could have been friendlier, but that it was not in his nature. Dewar's failings became finally, and fatally, clear in the *Royal Oak* incident of 1928. He was allowed another command for a few months to qualify him (regulation sea time) for promotion to rear-admiral when he came to the top of the captains' list. Advancement to vice-admiral came in due course, as the custom then was, without further employment. During the Second War he was brought back to serve in the Historical Section of the Naval Staff.

America could best co-operate with the Allies and to keep the Navy Department posted on the naval situation), 'I made enquiries as to the possibilities of convoys for merchant vessels. There were of course, various opinions upon this point but they were not based upon any systematic study. I asked that such a study be made and it has just been completed. I was shown this study the day before yesterday and it appeared to me to be entirely practicable.'[30]

Another reason why Great Britain was allowed to reach the brink of disaster before adopting convoy was that the advocates of convoy were themselves ignorant, unavoidably, of the analytical methods that Professor P. M. S. Blackett, the Admiralty's first Director of Operational Research, successfully applied to similar problems in World War II. Since there was no effective method of tracking a submerged submarine, and since a submarine at periscope depth, and even on the surface, nearly always had the advantage of invisibility over her hunters, it now seems obvious that the chances of destroying the submarine would be greatest either at her base (which was ruled out on strategic grounds) or in the immediate vicinity of her bait, where she would sooner or later have to disclose her presence. If the bait were concentrated in convoys, it could have been proved mathematically that the U-boat's chances of both finding *and* successfully attacking an escorted convoy (whose route could be varied) were greatly reduced. And this was of such primary importance to the safety of shipping as to outweigh all the disadvantages of convoy. Similarly, it could have been proved that a hunting group patrolling an ill-defined area remote from the U-boat's bait could never hope to achieve the results that the same group would expect to obtain in the immediate vicinity of a convoy. But in those days mariners and mathematicians did not keep easy company together!

Finally, problems of organization may have contributed to the delay in adopting convoy. One of the difficulties of running a convoy system was the enormous ramifications of overseas staff as well as expansion of administrative work at Whitehall. Concerning the former, Commander Waters, who studied the matter carefully, in fact found that the independently routed merchant shipping involved a bigger staff than convoy and the world-wide ramifica-

---

[30] Sims to Chief of Bureau of Navigation, U.S.N. (Rear-Admiral L. C. Palmer), 1 May 1917; O.N.I. Register, U.S. Navy Department MSS.

tions. As for the latter consideration, Admiral Dewar has noted: 'A large department overwhelmed with business tends to oppose any extension of its functions. In the case of independent sailings, the Admiralty had merely to issue instructions as to routeing and further responsibility fell on the Master. Convoy, on the other hand, placed much greater responsibilities on the Admiralty. It also meant a great deal of administrative work which the existing organisation could not undertake and which eventually involved the creation of new departments and to some extent the eclipse of those divisions which had opposed the convoy system.'[31]

* * *

It was not only the First Sea Lord, his principal advisers, and shipping and Service opinion. Public opinion generally and important members of the Government were slow to seize upon convoy as the answer to the worsening shipping situation. Archibald Hurd's idea (he was the well-known naval journalist) of a 'radical remedy' (January) was the rapid construction of more merchant vessels. The *Daily Telegraph*'s panacea (22 February) was the energetic pressing on with the policy of arming merchantmen. The *Army and Navy Gazette* (6 January) saw no solution in a regular system of convoy. It referred to 'the inconvenience and delay of a cast-iron system' and warned that 'to concentrate the ships would be to concentrate the risks'. When the onetime Secretary of the Committee of Imperial Defence, Lord Sydenham, wrote to Curzon in February, recommending that the War Cabinet reconsider convoy, Curzon replied (23 February): 'The question of convoys has been considered. You know the drawbacks. (1) The pace of the convoy is that of the lamest duck. (2) We have not enough destroyers.'[32]

2. THE TURNING OF THE TIDE

By April 1917 several factors had combined to weaken the force

[31] Dewar, 'The Defence of Shipping' (*ca.* 1946), i. 13–14; Dewar MSS. 'I have always been convinced myself,' Lord Salter (Director of Ship Requisitioning in 1917) has written to the author (17 May 1968), 'that the principal reason for the delay in the introduction of convoy was that Admiral Jellicoe was very exhausted and very disinclined to take over any further responsibility. To him convoys and their protection would mean a very definite additional responsibility, and one which he did not feel for the loss of dispersed vessels not in convoy.'

[32] Sydenham of Combe, *My Working Life* (London, 1927), p. 349.

of the arguments against convoy. There was, first of all, the experience of the French coal trade. The highly important nature of this trade could scarcely be exaggerated, since the French needed to import at least 1½ million tons of coal a month, mostly from Britain, for the efficient prosecution of the war. Ordinarily, about 800 colliers per month (half of them neutral ships, mainly Norwegian) left England for France. Heavy sinkings in the Channel during the last quarter of 1916, which badly hit the coal trade—in December only 1¼ to 1½ million tons reached France—caused a crisis in this vital trade. Ships loaded with coal were being held up in port (30 to 40 per cent of the days in November and December), and French factories were shutting down for lack of coal.

On 30 December 1916 the French sent a naval officer, Commandant Vandier, to London to explain the precarious position of France and to propose the organization of daily convoys to ensure the safe and speedy passage of colliers at all times. The Admiralty approved the idea in principle and delegated three officers to work out the details with Vandier. What emerged from a conference at the Admiralty (2 January) was 'a modified form of convoy sailing'. There were to be four daily crossings for all steam vessels engaged in the French coal trade. They were to be called 'controlled sailings', because it was considered advisable on account of the number of neutral vessels engaged in the trade to avoid the term 'convoy' as connoting protection. The use of the term, it was feared, might have resulted in the Germans sinking at sight all neutral vessels; even a German threat to do so might have stopped the Scandinavian sailings.

The system came into force on 6 February, and the first convoy sailed on the 10th. There were daily convoys from Penzance, Portland, Weymouth or St. Helens, and Southend. It was not a new departure. From July 1916 a similar system had been operating for ships employed in the Dutch trade, between the Downs and the Hook of Holland (the 'Beef Trip'), under the protection of the Harwich Force. From April 1917, flying boats from Felixstowe were employed to search the route before convoys sailed and to provide air escort to the convoys throughout their passage. The Dutch convoy was an unqualified success. Only three ships were lost to submarines (all prior to the close formation instituted in June 1917—until then the convoys were columns 30 to 40 miles long), although the route was flanked on either side by U-boat bases.

The immunity of the French coal trade to successful attack by submarines after the establishment of the controlled sailings was almost as remarkable. Through April 1917 the U-boats had sunk a mere five of the nearly 2,600 ships sailed in convoy, or a loss rate of 0·19 per cent. For the war, 37,927 ships were convoyed for a loss of a mere 53 or 0·14 per cent. At first the voyage, or as much of it as was possible, according to the time of the year, was carried out at night, the ships leaving the coast shortly before dark protected by two armed trawlers of the Auxiliary Patrol. (The trawlers were adequate, since the ships in the coal trade were mostly slow.) In the spring of 1918 daylight sailings were begun on the five days each side of full moon. These were so successful that regular daylight crossings were started in the summer. Aircraft protection was then instituted. In the summer and autumn of 1918 the escort consisted of one French destroyer and three British trawlers on the Penzance–Brest crossing, and two or three British and French trawlers (alternately) on the Weymouth–Cherbourg and Weymouth–Havre (or St. Helens–Havre) crossings.

The point must be emphasized, however, that the experience with controlled sailings in the French coal trade was valuable, but, for the decision-makers, not conclusive. They were quite different from the working of a regular ocean convoy system. The latter operated in unprotected waters on long routes, whereas the former operated in waters protected by patrols and on short routes, hence a weak escort was sufficient. Indeed, as Duff explained, the convoys were 'only given sufficient escort to give confidence to the Masters, and to act as life-savers in the event of a ship being torpedoed. The safety of the convoy was primarily dependent on the waters through which they sailed being kept clear of S/Ms [by patrols], and on the ease with which a convoy could either be diverted or delayed.'[33] The weakness of the argument is, first, that at the time, on 26 April 1917, Duff admitted that 'the experience we have gained of the unexpected immunity from successful submarine attack on the French Coal Trade' was one of the new factors pointing towards the adoption of a regular convoy system.[34] And there is a basic flaw in Duff's post-war reasoning. The submarines were operating primarily within the 100-fathom line and

[33] From Duff's notes on convoy dictated in about 1929; Duff MSS. (Hereafter cited as 'Duff Notes, 1929'.)
[34] See below, p. 159.

precisely in the waters traversed by the French coal trade convoys, particularly those which went to Brest. The fact that patrols were operating had not the slightest effect upon the security of the convoys. A plot of the shipping losses brings this home unequivocally.

The sensational success of the system of controlled sailings gave the proponents of convoy a powerful new argument. It indicated that even the inadequate protection afforded by armed trawlers minimized submarine attack almost to the vanishing point. The modified convoy system 'did something much more than its own work, for out of it there sprang a strong conviction of the value of convoy which helped to launch a general system of convoy when the United States entered the war'.[35]

The trade between Scandinavia and North Sea ports was also organized on a system of 'protected' or 'controlled' sailings. The heavy losses towards the end of 1916 in Norwegian and Swedish shipping[36] raised the possibility that the Scandinavian neutrals would hold up sailings between Scandinavia and the United Kingdom. This was a serious matter, for not only were Scandinavian imports absolutely essential to Great Britain for the prosecution of the war (metallic ores, wood, nitrates, agricultural produce), but it was just as important to prevent the Germans from benefiting from such trade. The situation forced the Admiralty to institute some form of protection for these vessels. On 15 December they authorized a system of 'protected sailings', between Norway and the Shetland Islands, controlled and administered by the Admiral Commanding the Orkneys and Shetlands, whose armed trawlers bore the brunt of the escort duty. But 'so slowly do the wheels of any huge administration revolve' that it was not until six weeks later that the arrangements went into effect. The first protected sailings to Norway were of individual ships, on 29 January and 10 February. They were escorted through the 'daylight stretch' of 50 miles from the Shetland coast. 'February 24, 1917, may be regarded as a date of no small importance in the history of the war. On it sailed

---

[35] Naval Staff Monograph No. 34 (1933), *Home Waters—Part VIII. From December 1916 to April 1917*, p. 180. The contemporary A.S.D. 'Monthly Report No. 1, May 1917' (1 June 1917) noted: 'The experience gained [through April] provided a strong argument in favour of the general wide adoption of a system of convoy ...'

[36] The greatest number of Norwegian ships sunk in any one month through August 1916 was 13, and for Sweden, 9. In October 1916, Norwegian losses shot up to 56, and Swedish, to 29.

the first convoy from Lerwick [Shetlands] to Bergen.'[37] Seven Norwegian ships and one British were escorted as far as 50 miles east of Lerwick by a destroyer, a whaler, and two armed trawlers. Subsequently, however, in February and March, vessels were escorted singly or in pairs. Westbound traffic was supposed to cross from Bergen at night and be met at daylight 50 miles from Lerwick by an escort of armed trawlers. But for various reasons it was not in effect through March.

It was soon obvious that the system was not working well. By April the loss rate for the Scandinavian trade, running at the rate of 25 per cent for the round voyage, was threatening to end the trade in the near future. The system had practically broken down because of the shortage of trawlers available for escort work and the difficulty of ensuring that neutral merchantmen make their rendezvous at the appointed time. On 30 March the C.-in-C. suggested a conference on the advisability of adopting a convoy system for protecting the Scandinavian traffic. This was approved, and the conference met at Longhope (Orkneys) on 4 April, under the presidency of Sir Frederic Brock, Admiral Commanding Orkneys and Shetlands. Present were Beatty's C.O.S., O. de B. Brock, and representatives of the Trade and Operations Divisions of the War Staff and of all the areas on the East Coast of England and Scotland. The conference unanimously recommended that 'the convoy system be used in preference to the scheme of continuous stream of traffic', and that convoys should consist of a maximum of nine merchant vessels, the escort for which should be no less than two destroyers, one submarine if available, and four to six armed trawlers. The requirements would be 23 to 28 destroyers and 50 to 70 trawlers. It was hoped that 9 destroyers and 53 trawlers could be spared from patrol bases on the East Coast; but the representatives were unable to state for certain whether the necessary vessels could be spared from their respective areas.[38]

Beatty forwarded the conference report to the Admiralty with a strong covering letter of endorsement for the convoy principle in the Scandinavian trade.

[37] Naval Staff Monograph, *Home Waters. December 1916 to April 1917*, p. 182.

[38] The conference report is attached to a covering letter from Admiral Brock to Beatty, 5 April 1917. All the materials cited on this important conference, including the Admiralty minutes on its recommendations, are in a docket in the Admiralty MSS. entitled 'Protection of Traffic Between British and Scandinavian Ports'.

It is necessary to decide the relative urgency of—I. Protecting and patrolling the coast. II. Protecting traffic along the coast.

At first sight it would seem that these two objects are similar and that if the coast is patrolled and protected, traffic should be able to safely proceed along it. Experience has shown, however, that this is not the case; patrols have given little, if any, security to shipping during the war; submarines attack vessels close to the coast and mines are continually being laid off the shore.

Escorts have, however, proved an effectual protection and a system of escorts does, to a large extent, fulfil the conditions of a patrol, the escorting vessels being placed in the best position for meeting and attacking hostile submarines.

It is manifestly impracticable to provide an escort for each individual vessel; the only alternative is to introduce a system of convoys. . . .

It may be expected that the Officers in command at the various Bases will be loath to release Auxiliary Patrol Vessels and Destroyers for the purpose required, working as they do at present in watertight compartments with responsibility only for their particular patrol area. It must, therefore, be for their Lordships to decide whether the present system should continue, or whether resources along the East Coast should be pooled and strong escorts [to include one or two destroyers] provided for regular convoy.[39]

The Longhope recommendation that the Scandinavian trade be placed in convoy met with a lukewarm response from the local senior officers to whom the report was submitted.[40] The Admiralty, too, had misgivings. The D.T.D., Webb, concurred with the proposed scheme, but with an important qualification (12 April): 'The carrying out of this scheme seems to depend entirely upon the necessary patrol vessels being provided without diminishing the local patrols to such an extent that they will be unable to cope with the escorts required for Oilers, Munition Ships, etc., and

---

[39] Jellicoe afterwards denied that Beatty's remarks constituted (as claimed by Newbolt, in *Naval Operations*, iv. 383, and Lloyd George, in his *War Memoirs*, iii. 1158) an approval of a general convoy system, saying that they applied to the Scandinavian trade only. Jellicoe, 'Errors in *Naval Operations*' and *The Submarine Peril*, p. 104n. Strictly speaking, this may be so. Beatty's letter, however, does endorse convoy as a strategical principle. Besides, he had on more than one occasion proposed a convoy system for the whole of the trade to and from Britain. He seems to have made this recommendation to the First Lord but not (in writing, at any rate) to the First Sea Lord. See above, p. 119, and below, p. 158n. Jellicoe could not have been unaware of the C.-in-C.'s advocacy of a general convoy system.

[40] See Newbolt, *Naval Operations*, iv. 15–16. Commented Jellicoe, '. . . probably these misgivings had their effect upon the minds of the heads of Admiralty Departments when they considered the question.' Jellicoe, 'Errors in *Naval Operations*'.

increased minelaying which may be expected.' Duff also concurred with reservations. In a very significant minute (19 April) he was careful to differentiate between his general rejection of a convoy system and his acceptance of it as an exception in the particular case of the Scandinavian trade:

The Scandinavian traffic is not the only trade to be considered, and by concentrating destroyers and trawlers for its protection, the other traffic that is unescorted must suffer to some extent.

The Commander-in-Chief, Grand Fleet, states that patrols have given little, if any, security to shipping during the War. When consideration is given to the immense number of vessels that have navigated round our coasts, and the relatively small number lost by submarine attack, it appears that considerable security has existed and it is thought that the patrols have contributed to this. . . .[41]

It is realised that in at any rate two respects the convoy system is particularly applicable to the Scandinavian Trade; one is the shortness of the night during the summer months, and the other the vessels using this trade being very much of the same speed.

Consequently, if the escorting craft were available, I think it would be well to give the system a trial and accept the want of patrol trawlers for the time. But it seems quite impracticable to find the minimum number of Destroyers required. . .

It is submitted that C. in C. be informed that the principle of convoy for this particular trade route is approved, and patrol trawlers from the areas concerned may be utilised to give the system a trial, but its introduction must depend on the resources of the several Areas concerned being sufficient to provide adequate escorts, as no additional T.B.D.s or Trawlers can be appropriated to this service.

The D.O.D., Rear-Admiral Thomas Jackson, and Oliver agreed that the system should receive a trial (20 April), the latter with serious doubts about its success 'as convoys invite torpedo attack and the available escorts are too few for the number of ships proposed for a convoy.' He disapproved of the conference proposal to attach a submarine to the escort, as it would 'probably result in some fire-eating tramp master ramming her.'

On 21 April, Jellicoe agreed to a trial of the system, with the old pre-war 'River' class destroyers (25.5 knots) from the Humber to be used. On the 24th Admiral Brock was notified that the Longhope

[41] But Duff's faith in patrol had weakened. He had written on 25 March, 'Experience has already shewn that patrolling a route is no effective deterrent to a submarine operating submerged.' Duff's minute on Bayly's memorandum, 'Protection of Sea-Going Trade Leaving and Approaching British Isles.'

proposals of 4 April were approved 'in principle' and were to be given a trial. As worked out, the plan called for the inclusion of any British, Allied, or neutral merchant ships in the convoy, which was supposed never to exceed nine vessels. Twenty destroyers (10 'River' class, 10 30-knotters) and 45 trawlers were detailed for escort duty, out of which number it was estimated that 12 destroyers and at least 36 trawlers would always be acting as escorts. Lerwick was to be the 'central exchange' for all shipping to and from Scandinavia. Outgoing ships proceeded in regular northbound convoys, assembled at Lerwick, and sailed to Norway in daily convoys under a small destroyer escort, with a few armed patrol vessels in company to a certain point. The convoy dispersed on the Norwegian coast, and the destroyers then picked up the westbound convoy at a rendezvous off the Norwegian coast, and were joined by armed patrol vessels at a rendezvous between Norway and the Shetlands. Incoming ships from Norway entered Lerwick and were sent on to East Coast ports in daily southbound convoys, and to the West Coast (Stornoway) twice a week. The first organized convoys sailed from the Humber and Lerwick on 29 April. 'In this trade,' Jellicoe later remarked, as if to under-emphasize the didactic value of the Scandinavian convoys, 'there was a comparatively large number of vessels available for escort duty, and the passage between Norway and the Orkneys [Shetlands] was largely made at night, and once the ships reached British waters they did not need convoy in large numbers, as the total number of ships to be escorted was small and they went to different ports on the East Coast.'[42]

In the first month of the Scandinavian convoys the loss rate was cut 120-fold, to 0·24 per cent, while decreasing port congestion. At first a daily sailing and limited to 6 ships, the convoys gradually increased to between 20 and 50 ships (partly the result of opening out the convoy cycle to a five-day interval to ensure the provision of a support force against enemy surface ships) *without an increase in escort strength and without incurring heavier losses.*

Concurrently with the start of the Scandinavian convoys, convoys were instituted between the Orkneys and the Humber for ships of moderate speed wishing to sail in convoy. These local coastal convoys sailed under the escort of a few armed trawlers. Here, too, there was an extraordinary decline in losses.

[42] Jellicoe, 'Errors in *Naval Operations*'.

There were three decisive factors in the month of April that finally persuaded the Admiralty to give ocean convoy a trial. In chronological order they were: (1) America's entry into the war on 6 April; (2) the unprecedented shipping losses; (3) the revelation towards the end of the month that the ocean escort problem was not nearly so unmanageable as High Admiralty Authority had assumed.

The American declaration of war 'altered the whole situation for three main reasons [Duff stated after the war]: 1st, providing collecting ports for convoys at the most convenient possible ports. 2nd, that in sailing convoys from American ports, the Masters had at least a week of intensive training in handling their ships in convoy before entering the danger zone. 3rd. The assistance given by American destroyers in providing escorts.'[43] In fact, the American entry by itself did not convert the Admiralty to convoy. Thus, three days after that date, they shot off an urgent request to Washington for naval aid. The direction in which the United States could help best was by the provision of the 'vast numbers of small craft' necessary for 'a really vigorous offensive' against the U-boats and protecting merchant ships from their attack. They required 'at least twice as many patrol craft, such as trawlers, sloops, etc., as we have at present, and we require at least another 100 destroyers'.[44] There is not a word in this about convoy needs.

---

[43] Duff Notes, 1929. The third was the most important consideration (by the end of April, 18 American destroyers were *en route* or were preparing to leave for British waters), but Jellicoe (as in his *Morning Post* interview, 21 September 1934) and Duff (particularly in a 1931 memorandum, 'General Remarks on Convoy', Duff MSS.) made much of the first consideration *after the war*—that until the United States was an ally, ports were not available on the American seaboard for the assembly, arming, fuelling, and organization of Atlantic convoys. Since a large proportion of British supplies came from America, dependence on Canadian or British West Indian ports for assembling convoys would have led to delays and difficulties in assembling vessels for North Atlantic convoy that would seriously have reduced the efficiency of the system. To assemble a convoy on the high seas was impracticable, and would court disaster, because of the insuperable difficulties of effecting a rendezvous. The facts are: the greater part of British shipping in the war did not sail from American ports; it was perfectly feasible for ships from the Gulf and southern ports of the United States to assemble at Bermuda or Jamaican ports, and those from the northern ports, at Canadian ports like Halifax—this is what actually happened in World War II, prior to America's entry; and, finally, the Jellicoe-Duff thesis was no argument against placing the non-American trade under convoy. Anyhow, if American neutrality had been so great an obstacle, it is extraordinary that in all his statements to the War Cabinet Jellicoe never once mentioned it. On Duff's views *re* the effect of U.S. entry, see further, below, p. 159.

[44] Jellicoe to British Naval Attaché, Washington, 9 April 1917; U.S. Navy Department MSS.

Nor did Jellicoe's War Cabinet paper of 23 April (see below, pp. 148–9) allude to the practicability of convoy now that the United States was an Ally. The Admiralty were still devoted to fixed routes and patrol.

Of more immediate importance, because underscoring the desperate urgency of trying some fresh method of trade protection, was the steep rise in the curve of tonnage losses, especially during the latter half of the month. Of the total British losses in April through submarine and mine of 545,000 tons, nearly 400,000 were suffered during the 'black fortnight' of 17–30 April. The most alarming statistic showed that British ocean-going vessels (1,600 tons gross and upwards), so vital in the all-important North Atlantic trade, were the principal victims of the holocaust: 120 were lost during April, or over 90 per cent of the British losses. The chance of an ocean-going steamer leaving the United Kingdom and returning safely was but one in four. Especially hard hit were the South Western Approaches (south-west of Ireland) and the western approaches to the English Channel (south-west of Land's End), particularly the former, where British shipping was being sunk with regularity about 200 miles from land. It became known as the 'graveyard of the Atlantic'. These two areas saw an increase in total gross tonnage lost (British, Allied, neutral) over March of 60 per cent: 343,558 tons as against 213,971. Most of the sinkings here were in the open waters of the Atlantic, where permanent patrolling was not possible; but the patrolled routes were also hard hit. The curve of sinkings in the Mediterranean also rose sharply: from a March figure (British, Allied, neutral) of 53,423 tons to 271,657 tons in April, or a 410 per cent increase. The North Sea figure showed a 23 per cent increase (69,527 to 85,331) and the Channel and Bay of Biscay, a decline of 27 per cent (179,918 to 133,231).

'The continuance of this rate of loss [of the Black Fortnight] would have brought disaster upon all the Allied campaigns, and might well have involved an unconditional surrender.'[45] But even at the average of the first three months of the German unrestricted campaign it was obvious that it would soon be impossible to supply both the civil population and the armies in France and elsewhere. Whether through new construction or transfer from foreign flags, the acquisition of new shipping was lagging far behind marine and

[45] J. A. Salter, *Allied Shipping Control* (Oxford, 1921), p. 122.

war losses in these months. At the beginning of the Black Fortnight, the Ministry of Shipping estimated that the reduction in imports for the whole year would be nearly 10½ million tons, or 4½ million more than the Import Restrictions Committee had considered could be achieved through the elimination of non-essentials. A careful analysis of the position by Chiozza Money that took all factors into account reached these lugubrious conclusions: by the end of the year the tonnage available for Britain's export and import service (that is, after making allowance for ships appropriated for war services, etc.) would be reduced from the 8,394,000 tons of 1 January and the then 8,050,000 tons to 4,812,000; the carrying capacity of the 31 December 1917 tonnage would be 2,030,000 tons per month, as against 3,000,000 in January. Since nearly 1½ million tons were needed every month to bring in foodstuffs, this would leave only some 800,000 tons for other imports.[46]

Writing after the war, Jellicoe pointed to the stepped up losses in April as the crucial factor in the introduction of convoy.

Speaking generally, it would seem to me that the Admiralty views on the introduction of the Convoy System might be summed up in a few sentences, such as the following: Until unrestricted submarine warfare was instituted, the losses in the Mercantile Marine from submarine attack were not sufficiently heavy to cause the Admiralty to take upon themselves the very grave responsibility of attempting to introduce the Convoy System, because of its many disadvantages combined with the fear that an insufficiently protected convoy, if seriously attacked by submarines, might involve such heavy losses as to be a real calamity. This view, of course, was very largely influenced, too, by the fact that the provision of a sufficiently numerous force of fast craft for protective duties through the submarine area was a practical impossibility up to April 1917. When, however, towards the end of April 1917 our losses mounted up so seriously, the Admiralty then felt that even very heavy losses in one or two convoys could be accepted without materially adding to our losses under the System of protection then in use, and for that reason, decided to accept the great responsibility of the introduction of the System, first experimentally, and then finally.[47]

At the time Jellicoe made no attempt to minimize the alarming prospect—quite the contrary. On 10 April, the day after Admiral Sims arrived in London, he saw the First Sea Lord. They had

[46] W.C. 125, 23 April 1917, and Appendix II.
[47] Jellicoe, 'Errors in *Naval Operations*'.

known each other for years, a common interest in gunnery having brought them together. Greetings over, Jellicoe handed Sims a memorandum on the British and neutral shipping losses of the last months: 536,000 tons in February, 603,000 in March, and an indicated nearly 900,000 in April. Sims has recorded his impression and Jellicoe's exact words:

It is expressing it mildly to say that I was surprised by this disclosure. I was fairly astounded; for I had never imagined anything so terrible. I expressed my consternation to Admiral Jellicoe.

'Yes,' he said, as quietly as though he were discussing the weather and not the future of the British Empire. 'It is impossible for us to go on with the war if losses like this continue. . . .'

'It looks as though the Germans were winning the war,' I remarked.

'They will win, unless we can stop these losses—and stop them soon,' the Admiral replied.

'Is there no solution for the problem,' I asked.

'Absolutely none that we can see now,' Jellicoe announced. He described the work of the destroyers and other anti-submarine craft, but he showed no confidence that they would be able to control the depredations of the U-boats.[48]

After the war, Jellicoe denied that he had told Sims that there was absolutely no solution for the submarine problem. His real reply, he maintained, was that there was no *immediate* solution: the counter-measures needed time to mature, since some of them necessitated manufacture. 'We certainly were not in the state of panic which has been ascribed to us in certain quarters, but we did want those engaged in war on the Allied side to understand the situation in order that they might realize the value that early naval assistance would bring to the Allied cause.'[49] His denial does not affect the general impression his words had made on Sims; nor, and this is much more significant, did he give any indication that the adoption of the convoy system might offer a solution to the crisis.

Jellicoe's pessimism got worse, if anything. In a paper put before the War Cabinet on 23 April he called their attention to the increasingly heavy shipping losses: 169 ships (British, Allied, neutral) of 406,897 tons (65 ships, 218,094 tons, British) lost to submarines alone in the first eighteen days of the month. 'An even more serious

[48] Sims, *The Victory at Sea*, p. 9.
[49] Jellicoe, *The Submarine Peril*, pp. 70-1, and his press interview, *Morning Post*, 21 September 1934.

feature of the case is the exceedingly heavy losses that have been reported during the last few days': 9 British ships (27,074 tons) in the 24 hours ending noon, 20 April, and 9 more (29,705 tons) in the following 24 hours. 'The continuance of such a rate of loss for even a few days will produce the most serious results.' What did he propose? A multiplication of attack craft. 'Until means can be found *and provided* for a more extended attack on submerged enemy submarines, the only palliative consists in the provision of a sufficient number of small craft to keep them submerged and so cramp their activities.'[50] Here was an admission of the ineffectiveness of the reliance upon fast light craft, especially destroyers, 37 of which had been delivered in the first quarter of the year. Destroyers had only six kills to their credit (through March 1917) in 182 encounters with U-boats since the war began. A U-boat had, therefore, a 23 to 1 chance of survival in an action with a British destroyer. The 70 destroyers in the western area (Queenstown, Plymouth, Portsmouth) had not sunk one U-boat since the unrestricted campaign began. 'Possibly the First Sea Lord was right in thinking that fast light craft were the best answer to the submarines that we possessed; but it was becoming apparent that they were not being used in such a way as to achieve the desired result.'[51]

Although Jellicoe did tell the War Cabinet that day (23 April) that 'the matter [of convoy] was under consideration', it was apparent that no fundamental change in strategy was in the offing, since he expressed doubts about the practicability of convoy even on a limited scale. He mentioned that the trial of the convoy system by the C.-in-C., Grand Fleet, had not been entirely successful: two vessels in separate convoys had already been torpedoed and sunk. 'I am,' he wrote four days after approval of the trial in the North Sea, 'rather afraid the convoy system on East Coast will fail for lack of destroyers, but as you know we are trying it. There are no destroyers at all to carry it out on Western Approaches, but *some day* [italics mine] I may be able to carry it out, and the arrangements for doing so are being prepared. For incoming traffic of course the great difficulty is to collect the convoy, and naturally the difficulty of a convoy keeping station especially at night is very

[50] 'The Submarine Menace and Food Supply' (G.T.-519), 22 April 1917, presented to W.C. 125. The only relatively new element was a call for American assistance in the way of destroyers and patrol craft. On 11 April the United States had promised to dispatch six destroyers in the near future, with more to come.
[51] Newbolt, *Naval Operations*, iv. 380.

great indeed. In fact most merchant captains say it is *impossible*. I have interviewed a large number on this point.'[52] The First Sea Lord had the support of the Operations and Trade Divisions of the War Staff, which, 'immersed in the daily round of work regarded it with little favour. (Trade Division favoured defensive armament for merchant ships and dispersion of routes. It was evidently not prepared to initiate the organisation that a convoy system required.) The war had outrun them . . .'[53]

A startling discovery by Commander R. G. H. Henderson early in April served as the catalytic agent. In his capacity as head of the organization for the controlled sailings in the French coal trade, Henderson was in regular contact with the Ministry of Shipping. From Norman Leslie there he received information that he had been unable to get from various Admiralty departments: the exact number of merchantmen entering and clearing United Kingdom ports weekly in the ocean trades. His object was to ascertain the true size of the escort problem in a system of ocean convoy. The Admiralty had always argued that the number of cruisers and light craft that would be needed to protect the enormous fleet of ocean-going steamers trading in and out of British ports rendered a convoy system utterly impracticable. Henderson now discovered that the return (supplied by the Customs authorities) that accompanied the Admiralty's published weekly statistics on British shipping losses gave a totally false picture. It showed the number of merchant vessels *of all nationalities* of over 100 tons net that had entered or left United Kingdom ports during a week as some 5,000 in all. These figures, Henderson realized, had no relation whatever to the volume of ocean-going trade, because they included small coastal craft and cross-Channel steamers (some of which were counted several times in the weekly return, since they made repeated calls) arriving from or leaving for another coastal port. The meaningful figure was the number of ocean-going steamers (1,600 gross tons—about 1,000 tons net—and upwards) arriving and leaving every week: 120 to 140 of each. Henderson saw light. An ocean convoy system was not nearly the gigantic task that the Admiralty's figures indicated. The approximately twenty arrivals

[52] Jellicoe to Admiral Sir Frederick Hamilton, C.-in-C., Coast of Scotland, 25 April 1917; Hamilton MSS.

[53] Naval Staff Monograph, *The Naval Staff of the Admiralty: Its Work and Development* (1926), p. 76. The Naval Historical Branch of the Ministry of Defence appears to have the one copy extant.

and twenty departures per day did not pose an insurmountable convoy escort problem; 300-odd arrivals and 300-odd departures *did*.

The Ministry of Shipping, Lloyd George, Admiral Dewar, and others have claimed that the key argument of the anti-convoy party, the insufficiency of escorts, was largely due to their bemusing themselves with these inflated entry and clearance statistics.[54] It was obviously out of the question to provide escorts for thousands of ships, to say nothing of the magnitude of the administrative task that would have been involved in such a giant-sized convoy system. Were the Admiralty deceived by their own statistics? They had given out the 2,500 figure in order to make the announced losses appear less serious than they actually were. That is, they were intended to keep up everybody's morale, more especially that of the neutrals, by disguising the actual rate of ocean shipping losses, as well as to mislead the Germans as to the success of the U-boat offensive. As Carson told the onetime First Lord Reginald Mc-Kenna, who had raised a question about the return: 'The reason why total figures are given for sailings and arrivals is that, as you know, the German submarine campaign throughout February succeeding in frightening neutrals into keeping their ships in port, and we are particularly anxious not to advertise this fact more than we could help.'[55] An officer who was in a position to know is clear that the return 'was essentially propaganda. It was, in fact, similar to our casualty lists and bulletins, and like these it told no untruths, but not necessarily the whole truth.' At the same time the writer vouches 'from personal experience that he never heard any officer who had the least responsibility for these questions make the slightest reference to the form, except to state the losses, or give any indication that he was making use of it to form an opinion

---

[54] Thus, Lloyd George writes: 'The blunder on which their policy was based was an arithmetical mix-up which would not have been perpetrated by an ordinary clerk in a shipping office. It nevertheless bewildered the Sea Lords and drove them out of their course for months. . . . The Admiralty never examined their grotesque figures. On these calculations they were right in concluding that it would be quite impossible to furnish escorts for convoying the merchant shipping that entered and left our ports, as its volume, according to their fantastic estimate, far exceeded anything the Navy could deal with.' *War Memoirs*, iii. 1146–7. And see Ministry of Shipping, *The System of Convoy for Merchant Shipping in 1917 and 1918* (1919), p. 1; copies in Captain Stephen Roskill's and Lord Salter's possession. Norman Leslie was the author of this publication.

[55] Carson to McKenna, 27 March 1917; Carson MSS. (Belfast).

when dealing with these questions'.[56] Although none of the Admiralty authorities could have been so ignorant as to reckon escort requirements in terms of the weekly return furnished by the Customs, they were, nevertheless, guilty in that they had made no attempt to ascertain even the approximate number of ships that would need escort, and had apparently assumed that the number was very large, if well below the figure of 5,000. They did not learn until the end of April that no more than 280 vessels a week would require ocean convoy.

It was certain as April neared its end that only an immediate change in Admiralty policy could save the day. The situation was the gravest that had arisen since the German sweep into France in the early weeks of the war. Salvation was to come from Duff and the Anti-Submarine Division of the Staff, which was having second thoughts on the subject of ocean convoy. Or was the Allied Saviour the British Prime Minister?

3. LLOYD GEORGE'S INTERVENTION

The Prime Minister possessed to an extraordinary degree the attributes lacking in Asquith: imagination or fertility of resource, initiative, drive, and an unusual capacity for work (when exhausted, he was able to revive himself with short snatches of sleep), as well as a gift for galvanizing those with whom he came in contact (Northcliffe called him a 'vitalizer') and for getting to the root of a problem. He also had great charm of manner, fiery eloquence, and unlimited self-confidence. One particular facet of Lloyd George's methods was productive of much that was invaluable, but which at the same time engendered much friction and bitter resentment at the Admiralty. He was, as his son, the second Earl Lloyd George, reminds us, 'no respecter of procedure, of seniority, of tradition'.

---

[56] Captain Bertram H. Smith, 'Lloyd George and Earl Jellicoe: the Facts of the Matter', *British Legion Journal*, February 1935. During this period Smith was in the Trade and Mercantile Movements Division of the Admiralty War Staff. It ought to be pointed out that the Admiralty figures had the effect of minimizing the critically dangerous loss rate: 40 ocean-going ships lost in one week (the week ending 22 April) as against 5,206 arrivals and sailings did not look nearly as disastrous as the same 40 sunk as against 280 arrivals and departures of ocean-going ships. Thus, Carson and the figures that he gave to the House of Commons on 13 February: 'Twelve thousand ships [vessels over 100 tons net] in and out [of United Kingdom ports] in eighteen days [the first eighteen of February] does not look anything like a paralysing effect or a sweeping of the seas.'

Of this side of the Prime Minister Hankey comments on 'what was really his main fount of knowledge—sucking the brains of the best men he could get on every subject. This was a continuous process. At breakfast, lunch, dinner, and between meals, whenever opportunity offered, Lloyd George was engaged in picking up knowledge from every sort and kind of person, in fact, from anyone who had knowledge to impart—and especially knowledge bearing directly or indirectly on the war.'[57] Or as Lloyd George himself wrote: 'When I meet men possessing special knowledge and experience on any subject, it has been my habit through life to question them on the theme they know and like best. The information I thus acquire leaves a deeper and more inerasable impression on my mind than what is communicated to me in any other way. . . . freedom of access to independent information is quite compatible with order and due respect for the hierarchy, if that liberty is tactfully and judiciously exercised by the Minister and wisely acquiesced in by the service. There must be no appearance of flouting the men at the top. On the other hand, they must not make it impossible to act without forcing an open disregard of their authority.'[58]

Beatty, who had hailed Lloyd George's appointment, for 'he is the one man of that rotten crowd [of politicians] who has his heart in winning this war, whatever other blemishes he has',[59] frankly admired his searching, probing ways. After one visit by the Prime Minister to the Grand Fleet, Beatty remarked, 'There is no doubt he is a wonderful man with a mass of energy and will allow nothing to stand in his way when he wants to find out something.'[60] The Admirals at Whitehall were not so enchanted with the Prime Minister's method, of which they were quite aware, of secretly eliciting information from young naval officers and asking their advice.

One of the Prime Minister's young informants was Lieutenant-Commander J. M. Kenworthy (afterwards 10th Baron Strabolgi), to whom he owed 'much . . . for making me acquainted at this critical stage with the views of the younger officers in the Navy'.[61] Kenworthy was at this time serving in the 3rd Battle Squadron, which was stationed at the Nore. Although he was in the Navy

[57] Hankey, *The Supreme Command*, ii. 576.
[58] Lloyd George, *War Memoirs*, iii. 1172.
[59] Beatty to Lady Beatty, 7 December 1916; Beatty MSS.
[60] Beatty to Lady Beatty [1917]; Beatty MSS.
[61] Lloyd George, *War Memoirs*, iii. 1173.

only a few years and did nothing of note, he played a role in the spring of 1917 by keeping the Prime Minister *au courant* with opinion among the younger officers in the Fleet.

Another of Lloyd George's informants was Herbert Richmond, Captain of the pre-dreadnought *Commonwealth* (3rd B.S.) and from the end of April of the dreadnought *Conqueror* (2nd B.S., Grand Fleet). Richmond seemed to have 'everything', including charm and brilliance. He was a good executive officer when a commander, a good captain, a talented man with many more gifts than his contemporaries. He had studied war all his life (he won renown after the war as a naval historian) and was recognized as a man with a fine brain. He was, indeed, often far ahead of his time, as in his advanced ideas regarding naval education and the organization of the Naval Staff (as the Admiralty War Staff was renamed in May 1917), enthusiasm for combined operations, advocacy of magnetic mines and strategic bombers, and the use of torpedo planes to attack an enemy fleet in harbour. When he was brought to the Admiralty early in 1918, the First Sea Lord, Wemyss, warned him that he was regarded as 'dangerous' and 'full of wildcat schemes'. His really deadly failings were his intolerance of those with differing views and disdain for those not equally grounded in naval history. He was so intolerant that even Wemyss, who was the easiest person in the world for any junior officer to get on with, found him too difficult.

The key figure among Lloyd George's naval informants was strategically situated right on the Admiralty War Staff—the leader of a band of young convoy-minded officers: Commander Reginald Henderson, of the A.S.D. Here was a brilliant, persuasive, and imaginative officer, with a great certitude in his own judgement and with new ideas always bubbling in him. (He eventually became, not long before the Second War, Third Sea Lord and Controller of the Navy, dying really from overwork—he could not spare himself.) Henderson was responsible for the organization of the controlled sailings in the French coal trade, whose experience converted him to a firm belief that ocean convoys were practicable. In all the long discussions which preceded the convoy system, he was the moving spirit. It is not too much to call him the chief architect of the convoy system, though his principal ally, Norman Leslie, the liaison official between the Ministry of Shipping and the Admiralty, and the Head of the Ministry's Convoy Section from April, deserves nearly as much credit. Leslie, in Lord Salter's opinion, 'was competent, patriotic, devoted, and industrious, with good judgement in the practical making and implementing of merchant shipping policy under war conditions'. His particular service was in convincing the Admiralty, eventually, that the merchantmen would in fact soon keep station if given a chance, and in overcoming the obsession of most naval officers that they would be incapable of doing so.

Henderson worked behind the back of his Chief, Admiral Duff, in urging the adoption of convoy on the Prime Minister. Duff knew that somebody in the Admiralty was disloyal, but he had no idea who it was until much later. By the strictest code of the Navy, or for that matter of departmental procedure anywhere in the Government, Henderson's methods were of course indefensible; but they can be justified in the desperate circumstances of the time and the discipline which then prevailed at the Admiralty, so different from that of the civilian departments, where juniors were expected to express differing views and the reasons for them.

Persuaded as he was in the early months of 1917 that the directing heads of the Admiralty were lacking in energy and resourcefulness, Lloyd George used Henderson's views and those of other junior officers, and of Maclay and his people, who distrusted the Admiralty's trade-protection thinking and methods, to cross-examine and otherwise needle the Admiralty chiefs. He was, furthermore, increasingly out of patience with the pessimism which in his view strongly coloured the opinions of Jellicoe and Carson.

Hankey played an important role in converting the Prime Minister to convoy and to doing something about it. 'Every morning,' writes the then Secretary of the War Cabinet, 'I used to find on my office table the list of sinkings for the last twenty-four hours. ... For the first and only time in the war I suffered from sleepless nights.'[62] On 11 February Hankey had 'a brainwave on the subject of anti-submarine warfare': convoy was the only effective answer to the U-boat. That night, after getting an expression of interest from the Prime Minister, he prepared a memorandum which argued the case for a system of organized convoys with great cogency and was in effect a forceful critique of the position of the Admiralty. 'Perhaps the best commentary on the convoy system,' it concluded, 'is that it is invariably adopted for our main fleet,

[62] Hankey, *The Supreme Command*, ii. 640.

and for our transports.'[63] There was a two-hour breakfast discussion at 10 Downing Street (13 February) of Hankey's 'peccant document', following a reading of it. Present were Lloyd George, Hankey, Carson, Jellicoe, and Duff. The Admiralty spokesmen

resisted a good deal . . . The objections that were raised were very formidable: if a submarine did locate a convoy it would get a big bag; the value of speed would be lost owing to the need of the convoy going the speed of the slowest ship; zigzagging would be impossible to ships in convoy; cargo ships would never be able to keep station; great confusion would arise in the event of a fog; and, most formidable of all, there were not enough cruisers and destroyers to supply the necessary escorts. I did my best, with such tact as I could muster, to meet every point. But it was a case of *Athanasius contra mundum*. Beyond a point I could not pit my amateur views against theirs on technical issues. Nevertheless I remained unshaken in my own conviction that convoy was the only answer to the submarine attack on merchant ships, and, what was infinitely more important, Lloyd George was of the same opinion, and I have no doubt that from that moment his mind was made up.[64]

Jellicoe was not shaken in his opinion (he later recorded that he did 'not personally recollect this discussion, so that it could not have left much impression on my mind').[65] Yet something had

---

[63] The memorandum is quoted *in extenso* in Newbolt, *Naval Operations*, v. 10–14. There is reason to believe that the memorandum was based on material supplied by Henderson.

[64] Diary, 13 February 1917; Hankey, *The Supreme Command*, ii. 647.

[65] Jellicoe, *The Submarine Peril*, p. 112. Jellicoe registered a strenuous protest not only against Newbolt's account of the conference, but of his quoting Hankey's paper. 'I recollect having breakfast once with Mr. Lloyd George, but cannot say what took place. Certainly I never saw any report of what was supposed to have taken place, and I protest emphatically against history being based on such evidence as notes taken but never submitted to those present, to say whether they were correct.' And the paper ought not to be included, as 'I have always understood from the historian that he will only make use of official documents in writing the official history . . .' Newbolt's rejoinder was that 'The history is compiled from official documents, but it would be out of the question to take no account of other evidence when it is authentic evidence and is not overborne by documents. . . . In any case the objection to the inclusion of Sir Maurice Hankey's Memorandum cannot be sustained. This document was prepared by the Prime Minister's order to express his view as head of the War Cabinet: it was read in his presence and at his request to a conference of members of the War Cabinet: it was filed in the official archives and was in its consequences one of the important official acts of the war. Lord Jellicoe has forgotten that its inclusion in the text of the history was due to the suggestion made to the Historian by himself and Admiral Duff in person, that all the documents relating to the introduction of the convoy system should be printed in full, in order that they

been gained. Carson demonstrated his open-mindedness at the 13 February meeting by promising to seek the convoy views of a representative delegation of merchant-ship captains, and to be guided by the results of the controlled sailings in the French coal trade and the Scandinavian trade, which had recently begun. Obviously, the second promise would need time to fulfil. The conference with the sea captains was duly called (23 February),[66] and it produced the expected result: a unanimous disapproval of convoys, which opinion was transmitted to the War Cabinet. I should point out that Carson did not agree with the Admiralty position on convoy. Almost from the start he was in favour of giving the system a trial; but in line with his announced policy of backing his naval advisers and giving them a free hand, he would not press his case.

The Prime Minister was convinced that the Admiralty could save the situation if they would but use the convoy system. Yet six weeks were to pass before he took action. Hankey attributes the delay to his preoccupation with military affairs (the great Nivelle offensive on the Western Front was being prepared), his desire to avoid 'a spectacle of internal disunion' on the eve of the first meetings of the Imperial War Cabinet, and his inability to meet the Admiralty argument about the insufficiency of escort craft. I would add Jellicoe's very high professional reputation and the fact that the issue was a purely technical one, and, finally, that Lloyd George was also at loggerheads with Robertson. Could he have fought the C.I.G.S. and First Sea Lord simultaneously—and survived? Meanwhile, the Prime Minister gathered ammunition from Henderson and other junior officers. With the critical loss rate, Henderson's revelation may have been the crucial factor in stirring Lloyd George to action. At a War Cabinet on 23 April the Prime Minister 'referred to the possibility of adopting the convoy system, which, he said, was favoured by Admiral Beatty and by Admiral

---

might speak for themselves, instead of being epitomised by the Historian.' Jellicoe denied that the document was official. 'Its filing in the archives of the War Cabinet does not make it official so far as the Admiralty was concerned. The paper was never referred officially to the Admiralty and was only read after breakfast apparently to some of us who were invited to breakfast with Mr. Lloyd George.' Jellicoe, 'Errors in *Naval Operations*'. Let it be said here that the convoy chapters in Newbolt's final draft were greatly softened down as a result of the many alterations suggested by Jellicoe and Duff, who were supported by Manisty (on whom more elsewhere).
[66] See above, pp. 126–7.

Sims'.[67] Jellicoe's report at this War Cabinet that the matter was under consideration finally exhausted Lloyd George's patience with the Admiralty. Very soon after the War Cabinet of 23 April he made up his mind that if the patient was about to expire under the existing treatment, nothing could be lost by trying a different

[67] W.C. 124. Beatty had endorsed the convoy system at a meeting with the Prime Minister and the First Lord at Rosyth on 14 April. Newbolt's factual reporting— that the Prime Minister 'quoted the [pro-convoy] views of Admirals Beatty and Sims' (*Naval Operations*, v. 17)—disturbed Jellicoe mightily. Beatty 'never expressed any views on the subject of Atlantic convoy. He dealt only with Scandinavian convoy. It is incorrect and most misleading to insinuate that he had expressed himself as favouring a general convoy system. As for Admiral Sims, he had had no opportunity of studying the question. He had only been in the country for a fortnight and knew nothing about the escorting craft that were available, or the various difficulties connected with convoys. It seems to me in the highest degree absurd to quote the views of Admiral Sims as if they could possibly at that period have been of value.' He later added: 'Sims had not at that time [April 1917] suggested convoy to me, and I saw him daily.' One can only sympathize with the harassed Newbolt when he replied in his minute: 'Neither Admiral is here "quoted": what the Historian states is that the Prime Minister "quoted" the views of Admirals Beatty and Sims. The authority for this is the War Cabinet Minute, which was shown to Lord Jellicoe in our conference of January 12, 1928. It should be noted that the Historian does not state what the views of the two admirals were.' Jellicoe, 'Errors in *Naval Operations*'. For Beatty's attitude, see above, p. 119. As regards Sims, Lloyd George may have read too much into the Admiral's report to his Government on 19 April, wherein he challenged the prevalent Admiralty view that it was impracticable for merchant vessels to proceed in formation. With a little experience, Sims thought, merchantmen could safely and sufficiently well steam in open formations'. This was by itself hardly an endorsement of a convoy system. Elsewhere in the same report Sims observed, approvingly, that the real obstacle to the adoption of convoy was 'simply that the necessary vessels are not available . . .' Sims, *The Victory at Sea*, p. 379. Lloyd George, who must have seen the whole report, quotes only the part about steaming in formation. *War Memoirs*, iii. 1161. Sims's authorized biographer also gives the Admiral more credit than he would seem to deserve. 'Sims, in one of his first talks with Jellicoe, "suggested that merchant ships would have to be convoyed *eventually* [italics mine] in fleets", but the suggestion was not received with approval. . . . For three weeks after his arrival he labored to persuade the senior officers at the Admiralty that the convoy was not only possible but practical.' Elting E. Morison, *Admiral Sims and the Modern American Navy* (Boston, 1942), pp. 347–8. (And see Sims, *The Victory at Sea*, pp. 111, 113.) I find nothing in Sims's dispatches during April that would bear this out. To be sure, he claimed in a letter of 3 July to 'have been devoted to this convoy system ever since the first week I got here in London.' But this should be juxtaposed with the 'eventually' reference above and Jellicoe's flat contradiction quoted above. He did repeatedly advocate (with the backing of the Ambassador in London, W. H. Page) to the U.S. Navy Department that they send out every available destroyer and as many patrol boats as possible. His biographer has counted thirty-two such messages during the three months May–July. But at first neither Sims nor the Navy Department was thinking beyond the needs of the patrol system. From May, more especially from June, that is, after the Admiralty had definitely accepted convoy but before a full scheme was in operation, the system had a no more vigorous and persistent advocate than Sims.

remedy, however risky. He decided, he tells us, to force convoy upon the Admirals. On 25 April he secured War Cabinet approval for an exceptional measure—a personal visit on the 30th to the Admiralty 'and there take peremptory action on the question of convoy'.[68] The War Cabinet minutes are less precise: 'The Prime Minister should visit the Admiralty with a view to investigating all the means at present in use in regard to anti-submarine warfare.'[69] The Admiralty were informed that day of the coming visit. On the next day, 26 April, Jellicoe told the Imperial War Cabinet that, 'as the convoy system required an elaborate organisation and a large number of destroyers, the Admiralty had not yet been able to adopt it'. He talked about introducing an Atlantic convoy system when the necessary cruisers and destroyers could be provided.[70]

On that same day Duff submitted an important memorandum to the First Sea Lord:

It seems to me evident that the time has arrived when we must be ready to introduce a comprehensive scheme of convoy at any moment.

The sudden and large increase in our daily losses in Merchant Ships [The two days alone prior to this minute had seen 17 British ships of 62,000 tons lost], together with the experience we have gained of the unexpected immunity from successful submarine attack in the case of the French Coal Trade, afford sufficient reason for believing that we can accept the many disadvantages of large convoys with the certainty of a great reduction in our present losses.

Further, the United States having come into the War eliminates some of the apparently insuperable difficulties to a comprehensive scheme of convoy.[71]

[68] Lloyd George, *War Memoirs*, iii. 1162.

[69] W.C. 126. Lloyd George's report to the War Cabinet on his visit listed 'the question of convoy' as one of the twelve subjects investigated.

[70] I.W.C. 12.

[71] Duff had in mind here (to quote from Newbolt's draft) that it was 'calculated to gradually ease the situation in regard to the provision of escorts'. Jellicoe, however, stated that he was 'certain that Admiral Duff had in mind also two other points, viz., the provision of escorting cruisers outside the submarine danger zone, and the most important question of assembly ports for the convoys'. Though without doubt true, this does not invalidate Newbolt's interpretation of the aspect of America's entry that was uppermost in Duff's mind at the time. Indeed, on 12 January 1928 Jellicoe himself had assured Newbolt 'emphatically', as the latter noted, 'that the shortage of escorts was the principal difficulty and that the situation in that respect was changed by the entry of the U.S.A. Admiral Duff was present and concurred.' But the Historian removed the offending words in his final draft, and he also jettisoned a substitute wording that Jellicoe understood he had agreed to accept: '. . . the entry of the U.S.A. into the War which would greatly ease the situation by

The number of vessels roughly estimated in the attached paper as the minimum necessary for escort work is large, but the necessity of further safeguarding our food supply is becoming vital.

Duff's attached outline proposal called for the convoy of all vessels, British, Allied, and neutral, bound for the North and South Atlantic from the United Kingdom, but excluding the fast vessels (15 knots and above). Ocean convoy escort requirements were estimated at 45 warships or armed merchant vessels, with 45 destroyers needed to meet the convoys at the danger zone (about 20° W.) and escort them to a port of refuge.[72]

Oliver concurred (27 April) 'to work out the scheme, as until this is done it is not possible to judge how far it will be practicable'. Jellicoe's laconic minute (27 April) read: 'Approve'. Orders went out almost immediately for a trial convoy from Gibraltar. In other words, the Admiralty had virtually made the plunge—they were willing to extend the Channel and North Sea experiments to the Atlantic—three days before Lloyd George's celebrated descent on the Admiralty (30 April). 'The Admiralty had not yet definitely decided that the convoy system should be adopted,' Jellicoe informed Sims on 30 April, 'but there was every intention of giving it a thorough and fair trial.'[73]

A postwar debate raged over this point: Had the Admiralty accepted ocean convoy 'spontaneously and on its merits' or only as the result of the Prime Minister's impending unorthodox visit? Was that visit, in other words, the decisive agent in the conversion of the Admiralty, or was it merely anti-climactic? Winston Churchill, Captain Roskill, Admiral Dewar, the historian A. J. P. Taylor, and many others state what has become the standard interpretation. In Churchill's words: 'The menace implied in this

---

converting a neutral into an ally, with the consequent advantages of giving us Ports of Assembly for convoys, as well as escorting cruisers, escorting destroyers, and numerous other facilities which a neutral could not give.' Jellicoe, 'Errors in *Naval Operations*'.

[72] Technical History Monograph, *The Atlantic Convoy System, 1917–1918*, pp. 10–11. Since 20 to 30 of the approximately 279 destroyers then in Home waters could be detached immediately for convoy duties, and by the end of April 18 American destroyers were coming or preparing to come, there would shortly be enough to start a convoy system. But the figure usually mentioned by the Admiralty as the minimum needed to start the system was 70, and Duff before long increased his estimate to 72.

[73] Sims, *The Victory at Sea*, p. 114.

procedure was unmistakable. No greater shock could be administered to a responsible department or military profession. The naval authorities realized that it was a case of "act or go".'[74] The originator and principal authority of this school of thought is Lloyd George himself, who wrote in 1934:

> It was clear that the Admiralty did not intend to take any effective steps in the direction of convoying. After first discussing the matter with Sir Edward Carson, I informed the Cabinet that I had decided to visit the Admiralty and there take peremptory action on the question of convoys. Arrangements were made accordingly with the Board that I should attend a meeting to investigate with them all the means at present in use in regard to anti-submarine warfare. I stipulated for the right to send for any officers, whatever their rank, from whom I desired information.
>
> Apparently the prospect of being overruled in their own sanctuary galvanised the Admiralty into a fresh inquisition, and by way of anticipating the inevitable they further examined the plans and figures which Commander Henderson had prepared in consultation with Mr. Norman Leslie of the Ministry of Shipping. They then for the first time began to realise the fact which had been ignored by them since August, 1914, that the figures upon which they had based their strategy were ludicrous, and that therefore protection for a convoy system was within the compass of their resources.
>
> Accordingly, when I arrived at the Admiralty I found the Board in a chastened mood. We discussed the whole matter in detail. We agreed to conclusions which I thus reported to the Cabinet. . . .[75]

Lloyd George, then, takes credit for the introduction of the convoy system. That the visit itself was anti-climactic there is no doubt. Lloyd George may have come to the Admiralty on 30 April in order to tell the Board to 'act or go', but, as Hankey says, the Prime Minister 'found that his task was greatly simplified'. The Admiralty were now agreed to institute an ocean convoy system, at least on a trial basis. But this is a long way from confirming that the Prime Minister's projected visit had in fact forced the hands of the Admiralty by putting the fear of God into them. The charge led to a stinging rebuke from Carson of the 'little popinjay', who had [in *War Memoirs*, iii] told 'the biggest lie ever was told'.[76] 'The

---

[74] Churchill, *Thoughts and Adventures* (London, 1932), p. 136.
[75] Lloyd George, *War Memoirs*, iii. 1162–3. The minute to the War Cabinet is quoted below.
[76] Carson's interview in the *Morning Post*, 24 September 1934.

monstrous charge we are asked to believe,' Duff asserted, 'is that on a threat of "act or go" the naval chiefs turned a complete somersault in order to retain their positions.'[77]

The first suggestion I heard that Lloyd George's visit to the Admiralty was primarily in connection with the Convoy Organisation, was when the [Newbolt] chapter on Convoy came under discussion. My impression was that he came to look into Admiralty Organisation generally; in fact, I recall you telling me that I must be ready to answer, and I understood the outcome of his visit to be that Oliver and I became members of the Board . . . There is no foundation for the belief that his visit was in any way the cause of my suggestion that the time had arrived for starting Convoy. It must be obvious that if Ll. G. came with the intention of forcing Convoy on an unwilling Admiralty, he would have dealt with you not the Director of a Division of the War Staff (A.L.D.) [Duff]. My minute of 25th [26th] April had no connection whatever with Ll. G.'s visit. It was the direct result of

(1) The serious and progressive loss of ships weekly.
(2) The assured prospect [with America's entry] of additional naval forces becoming available as the organisation developed.

These two factors changed the situation and warranted the introduction of convoy without delay. Had the losses remained stationary, the risk would not in my opinion have been justified until the measures in course of development had been brought into use. I have no doubt there are many Downing Street candidates for the credit of Mercantile Convoy—Lloyd George, Hankey, Clement Jones [Assistant Secretary of the War Cabinet], etc. but it is very easy to be wise after the event and one hears no mention of Downing Street follies, such as Sea-Lions on which we were forced to waste time and energy.[78]

[77] Duff Notes, 1929.
[78] Draft of a Duff to Jellicoe letter (August 1928); Duff MSS. Jellicoe's position comes out best in his response to Newbolt's original draft, which contained Lloyd George's position. In an interview with the Official Historian Jellicoe 'discovered what is really in his mind on the subject. He told me quite frankly that in his view, it was the expressed intention of the Prime Minister to visit the Admiralty (about April 25th) that caused you [Duff] to recommend the trial of the Convoy in your minute of about April 25th [26th]. In fact, that it was due to Ll. G. that we started it. I told him that . . . I felt certain that it was the heavy daily losses at that time that led to the change, and that I recollected your coming to me in the evening of one of those days and saying that the losses were so heavy that you considered we should try Convoy, as even a bad disaster to a trial convoy would not be worse than the losses we were suffering.' Jellicoe to Duff, 13 August 1928; Duff MSS. In Volume v of *Naval Operations*, which finally appeared in 1931, Newbolt had changed his stance. There is no mention of any direct connection between Lloyd George's coming visit to the Admiralty and the decision to give convoy a trial, which decision is praised as 'one of the most important of the war'. *Ibid.*, p. 20.

I see no reason whatever to doubt the truth of Duff's statement. It was his minute of 26 April, *not* Lloyd George's intervention, that was decisive in converting the First Sea Lord to a trial of the convoy system. And this minute was prompted, *not* by the news of the Prime Minister's coming visit to the Admiralty, but by the two factors mentioned in the document above, and by a third, Henderson's figures on arrivals and departures in the ocean trades, which Duff received about this time. Duff's minute of the 26th mentions the first two (as well as the influence of the French coal trade), and Lloyd George's minute for the War Cabinet on his discussions at the Admiralty on the 30th adds the third as well, along with another consideration:

I was gratified to learn from Admiral Duff that he had completely altered his view in regard to the adoption of a system of convoy, and I gather that the First Sea Lord shared his views, at any rate, to the extent of an experiment. Admiral Duff is not enamoured with the system, but a number of circumstances have combined to bring him to the view which I believe most of my colleagues share, that, at any rate, an experiment in this direction should be made. One of these reasons is that now that the United States of America have entered the War, he thinks it should be possible to find escorts which were formerly impracticable. Another is that experience has shown that he cannot rely on merchant ships to find salvation from the submarines by zigzagging and dousing their lights, and he therefore estimates these factors as a means of protection to a single ship, lower than he formerly did. Moreover, as the result of an investigation in concert with a representative of the Shipping Controller, he finds that the number of ships for which convoy will have to be supplied is more manageable than he had thought. Further, the losses which he last reported to me on the subject were not, in his opinion, sufficient to justify the adoption of this experiment, which he warned me might involve a great disaster. Now, however, he calculates that he could afford to lose three ships out of every convoy without being worse off than at present, and he therefore thinks the experiment justifiable. Finally, a very experienced merchant Captain, the Commodore of the White Star Line, whom he had consulted on this question, and who had hitherto been [a] pronounced opponent of the system of convoy had, after seeing the Admiralty scheme, come round to the view that it is very desirable to adopt it. . . .

As the views of the Admiralty are now in complete accord with the views of the War Cabinet on this question, and as convoys have just come into operation on some routes and are being organised in others, further comment is unnecessary.[79]

As for the Prime Minister's visit itself, it was an all-day affair, during which he saw Carson, Jellicoe, Duff, Webb, Captain H. W. Grant, Assistant Director of the Operations Division, and W. H. Gard, the Assistant Director of Naval Construction. The visit had few, if any, of the forceful and unpleasant overtones the popular account would have us believe. Thus, a Lloyd George biographer writes of how the P.M. 'invaded' the Admiralty and 'dragged forth the truth'. He 'demanded to see any officers who could produce the figures of weekly traffic in and out of British ports. At once, a real check-up was set on foot.'[80] I can find no confirmation of any 'demand' to see the statisticians forthwith, and of how they explained their method of computing the phenomenal figure of 2,500 weekly entries and 2,500 clearances. The Prime Minister had received the true facts from Henderson some time before. Lord Beaverbrook tells us (on Lloyd George's authority?) that the Prime Minister 'seated himself in the First Lord's chair. This was possibly an unprecedented action. It was well within the powers and competence of the Prime Minister; yet there may be no parallels in our history. For one afternoon the Prime Minister took over the full reins of Government from the head of a major department of state.'[81] Very dramatic, but, alas, of doubtful veracity! Here again Hankey's testimony is unimpeachable. The Prime Minister, Curzon, and he 'spent the whole day there very pleasantly, lunching with Jellicoe and his wife and four little girls—Lloyd George having a great flirtation with a little girl of three.'[82]

Lloyd George's minute for the War Cabinet expressed 'much regret that some time must elapse before convoy can be in full working order and I consider that the Admiralty ought to press on with the matter as rapidly as possible'. This statement contained the seed for a renewal of the guerrilla warfare between the politicians and the admirals, since the Prime Minister was not at all convinced that the Admiralty's death-bed repentance was sincere.

[79] 'Note by the Prime Minister of His Conference at the Admiralty, April 30th, 1917' (G.T.-604), written by Hankey immediately after the conference.

[80] Frank Owen, *Tempestuous Journey: Lloyd George, His Life and Times* (London, 1954), p. 360.

[81] Beaverbrook, *Men and Power, 1917–1918*, p. 155.

[82] Diary, 30 April 1917; *The Supreme Command*, ii. 650. Nor did Jellicoe or Duff afterwards recall the least unpleasantness on that occasion.

Trouble was also brewing over Lloyd George's conviction that the Fleet was too defensive-minded in its strategy. Immediately, however, he decided to do something about the Board of Admiralty. His visit to the Admiralty was an anti-climax so far as convoy was concerned, yet it had significant results in another direction. The Prime Minister's report to the War Cabinet was, in its main thrust, very critical of the Admiralty, whose faulty organization was seen to be at the bottom of all that was wrong with the naval side of the war. For this point of view, Lloyd George had much support in the press and the Service.

*　　*　　*

This extract from a 14 February 1933 letter written by Sir Norman Leslie to Lord Maclay (as the wartime Shipping Controller then was) is full of interest.[83]

... when Henderson came along he [Salter] recommended me to you to act as his opposite number. . . . I suppose Salter had learnt that I knew something about ships; anyhow he threw me at Henderson like a bone to a dog, and very indignant I, because I was quite satisfied with my work and did not know what Henderson was after.

When I found out what this extraordinary young man had in mind I caught fire with enthusiasm at once and worked out my side of it eagerly. We spent all day in each other's company, and so far as I can remember at this distance of time, after he had been convinced by our figures that the numbers were manageable, the only qualms he had were due to the fears expressed about station keeping. I flung myself at this with gusto. Was it likely that the breed of seamen who in Nelson's day could navigate in convoys under sail were going to start ramming each other with steamers the speed of which could be controlled by turning a handle? Did he appreciate that the tramp skipper had to go to sea in any weather, and that sometimes his ship was in ballast drawing 14 or 15 feet; sometimes loaded down to her marks with a cargo of ore threatening to lurch her funnel overboard; sometimes with a full cargo of oats almost as crank as an india rubber ball? Was a man in charge of a ship like that, with one eye on his coal consumption and the other on his

[83] The original is with the Leslie MSS. in the custody of his daughter, Miss Cecil Mary Leslie. I have used the copy in Captain Stephen Roskill's papers. Apropos of Leslie's arguments about station keeping, there is Lord Hurcomb's crude remark of that time (he was in the Ministry of Shipping) that 'if you give the skipper of a ship loaded with iron ore a choice between going to the bottom in two or three minutes and keeping station, *he* won't be in any doubt'. Lord Hurcomb's letter to the author, 5 August 1968.

cancelling date, and with a total crew of some forty men, less of a sailor than a watch keeping Naval Officer with five or six hundred men to do his bidding in a ship fitted with every known gadget and practically always of the same draft? Have preliminary classes for them, I urged, with blackboard lectures given by sensible officers who will not treat them de haut en bas and they will keep station as well as any officer in the navy. To his objection that a body of ship masters had already been consulted and had not shared my opinion I replied that the proposition had either not been understood by them or had been so put as to elicit the answer that was desired. I used similar arguments with Admiral Duff and the event proved that I was correct.

The question of delay could be largely met by common sense in loading the ships for particular convoy dates and was in its essence not very different from the conduct of an ordinary business running a regular line. With goodwill and intelligence on the part of those responsible for loading and discharging the steamers there should be no more delay than is incurred in making up the goods trains for a railway. Indeed the resemblance between our convoy system and that of a railway company often struck me, and when our through Mediterranean convoy was started it seemed natural to call it the Port Said Express. From that time on Henderson and I were rarely out of each other's company. When he was not in my room at the Ministry of Shipping I was in his room or in Admiral Duff's room at the Admiralty, and as you know we had a private direct telephone between us.

VII

The Aftermath of 30 April

(May 1917 – July 1917)

You should hear how men up here speak of Whitehall! It's refreshing, I assure you, after these years of adulation to find that men's eyes are at last being opened to the humbugs who have governed us.

CAPTAIN H. W. RICHMOND to Commander K. G. B. Dewar, 9 May 1917.

. . . neither Admiral Jellicoe nor Admiral Duff really believed in the principle of convoys, though they were willing to assent to a cautious trial of this expedient. They had been convinced against their will and at heart remained of the same opinion still.

LLOYD GEORGE, *War Memoirs.*

1. REORGANIZATION OF THE ADMIRALTY

PARALLEL to the growing restiveness over the failure of the Admiralty to solve the U-boat problem was that over the seeming lack of an offensive naval strategy. Once more, in the spring, a public debate flared up over the correct employment of the Fleet.[1] Two schools of thought were again revealed, each with its naval and civilian spokesmen. Basically, the problem boiled down to the proper aim of naval strategy. The 'victory' or (to its opponents) 'sea heresy' school held that Britain was not asserting that naval supremacy in the North Sea which the numbers and the superior capabilities of British ships and seamen should be making possible. Securing Britain's communications was not enough. It was retired Admiral Sir Reginald Custance who initiated the controversy with a letter in *The Times* of 7 May. His contention was that the 'directing naval minds' were deeply imbued with the unsound and dangerous doctrine, one with pre-war roots, that success in a war at sea could be achieved without battle, and that destruction of the enemy's fleet was an object secondary to the controlling of his sea communications. The correct doctrine, as employed by

[1] See *From the Dreadnought to Scapa Flow*, iii. 263–8, for the similar controversy in 1916.

the great leaders of the past, Custance asserted, was that the first object of naval warfare was to force the enemy to fight and to destroy his fleet. 'Unfortunately our plans appear to have been based on a different principle.' He linked his argument to the U-boat problem, which would disappear if the High Seas Fleet were crushed. 'If the massed fleet is destroyed the action of the submarine is weakened, since its exit is impeded by the small surface craft and submarines of the victor, which are then free to pass in to gun range in the enemy's waters with mines, nets, and every new device.'

Custance's most powerful support came from the former First Lord, Winston Churchill, who insisted with a force and eloquence all his own on the tremendous importance of an aggressive policy for the Navy.[2] After having once (September 1914) talked of digging the German ships out 'like rats', then reversing this position in the *London Magazine* (October 1916), where he had declared that it did not matter whether they fought the Germans at sea or not,[3] he now pronounced a directly opposite view. He deplored the fact that Britain's great fleets were 'relegated to the role of "keeping the ring" '. A way must be found to gratify the wish of every sailor in the Navy to 'get at them'. Instead of directing their policy to answering that problem, the Admiralty 'have had for at least two years the avowed acceptance, and even proclamation of the opposite principle, "wait about till they come out"; and the problem of "how to get at them", which is essentially a problem of mechanical preparation for a supreme act of naval aggression, has been entirely laid aside. . . . is all this accumulation of deadly war energy to wait idly on the off-chance of the German Fleet emerging from its harbour to fight a battle until peace, perhaps an unsatisfactory peace, is declared?' How could a way be found? Churchill pointed to the 'immense surpluses' of old ships. He did not spell out the kind of offensive in which he would use these obsolete and obsolescent pre-dreadnoughts, but one gathers that he wanted to send in the older capital ships against the enemy's naval bases, blast a way into these strongholds, and destroy every ship found inside. That such a 'digging out' operation was foredoomed to failure had not entered his mind. Forcing the Dardanelles would have been child's play in com-

---

[2] 'The Real Need of the British Navy', *Sunday Pictorial*, 24 June 1917.
[3] See *From the Dreadnought to Scapa Flow*, ii. 48, iii. 263.

parison to an attack on such fortified places as Wilhelmshaven and Kiel.

Into the mêlée leaped the so-called defensive school, represented by the onetime First Lord of the Admiralty, Lord George Hamilton, the well-known journalists Leyland, Bywater, Hislam, Hurd, and Fiennes, the historian Pollard, and the two most influential Service journals, the *Army and Navy Gazette* and *Naval and Military Record*. Their riposte (mainly in *The Times* during May) was that the conditions essential to the success of an offensive strategy were lacking. The power of the defence in the shape of submarines, destroyers, forts, long-range guns, elaborate minefields in the Bight, and aircraft had so enormously increased in proportion to offensive power that to attempt to force an action upon a fleet so protected was to risk almost certain disaster for the attacking force. And how could the High Seas Fleet be destroyed, when it clung to shelter and persistently refused to put to sea? The crucial point made was that the control of communications, that is, the British blockade, had achieved even more conspicuous results than the blockades maintained in Nelson's time. As Fiennes put it, 'The action of the Navy since the beginning of the War has, of course, been in essence offensive. If a man's house be picketed so that the butcher and the baker cannot call; so that he cannot catch his train to the office or send his dirty linen to the wash, it is impossible not to regard him as the victim of offensive action.'[4]

The conflict between the two schools of opinion naturally remained unresolved. Actually, both gave offensive action the first place, but the doctrine that the enemy's fleet must be destroyed at all hazards did not meet with general acceptance in the Navy. Beatty was furious with Custance for suggesting that the Navy was not doing its best or as much as they ought.

I see old Custance has again returned to the Press. The nebulous old fool, always destructive criticism, never constructive. It is so cheap and nasty. He now says, 'The controlling mind is imbued with the one idea that the safety of our ships is more important than the destruction of the Enemy.' Perhaps he refers to the Admiralty, but I and not the Admiralty am the controlling mind of the Grand Fleet, and I am not aware that my actions during the War have been such as to permit him to make such an appalling statement. . . . he has roused a

---

[4] Gerard Fiennes, 'Conditions of a Naval Offensive', *Nineteenth Century and After*, August 1917.

considerable feeling of resentment in the Fleet. . . . I should like to pull his nose.[5]

Sturdee wrote to Custance twice, telling him that he was quite wrong, and that the Fleet was profoundly disgusted that a flag officer should write as he had. The King asked Sturdee if Custance was really mad, as he wrote such nonsense![6] Richmond found Custance's letter

maddening. . . . He talks sometimes such sheer nonsense that I am bewildered by him. He infers that if the H.S.F. had been destroyed we would have maintained a close blockade. He must either be ignorant of the number of bolt holes on the Frisian coast, or of the potentialities of the modern submarine. If we are unable with a flotilla at Dover, mines, and other contrivances . . . to maintain a bar to straits 20 odd miles across, how in the world can we maintain one on the length from Emden to Sylt? He talks as if a naval victory involved the destruction—the entire destruction—of the enemy's fleet. Such a victory has never occurred in History and is far more improbable today. . . . Does C. imagine that our naval victory would be so complete as to destroy the whole flotilla & light cruiser force, every battle cruiser & battleship? If not, how in the name of common sense can a thin line of blockade be held. He makes me utterly sick.[7]

Richmond held no brief for the Admiralty; but the gravamen of his complaint was different. He was the intellectual leader of a group of junior officers, the 'Young Turks' of the Grand Fleet, among them, Dewar, Drax, and Kenworthy, who engaged the sympathy of a number of senior officers like Beatty, Tyrwhitt, Keyes, and Reginald Hall, also Hankey. On the central point the Young Turks and the 'sea heresy' school were in agreement: the Admiralty were not doing enough with the Fleet: defensive ideas

[5] Beatty to Lady Beatty, 10 May 1917; Beatty MSS. Of Churchill's article he wrote: 'It is disgusting that a man who has been a Cabinet Minister and First Lord of the Admiralty should be allowed to write articles in a rag of a paper belittling the officers and the Great Service of which he was once the head. It is of course useless to expect a man such as he to do anything but intrigue, and he has evidently made use of or is attempting to make use of a certain feeling that has been put about by others, that the Navy ought to be doing more, to make capital for himself and assist his intrigues to try and push himself into office. . . . [But] there will always be dirty dogs who endeavour to make capital out of the difficulties of others.' Beatty to Lady Beatty, 3 July 1917; Beatty MSS.
[6] Madden to Jellicoe, 26 June 1917; Jellicoe MSS.
[7] Richmond to Dewar, 12 May 1917; Dewar MSS. Dewar did not like Custance's arguments any better than did Richmond.

governed their strategy. As Dewar once stated their case, 'The general preference for the Navy for passive defence varied by spasmodic and discursive attack is the natural instinct of those who have never thought about war. I think it was someone in the *Naval Review* pointed out that the first instinct of a man who finds his pocket being picked is to catch hold of his watch whereas the correct policy is to smite the thief heavily between the eyes.'[8] In Richmond's opinion, 'Folk by a crude reading of Mahan, have absorbed the idea that all naval war consists in a battle of Armageddon.' He would take no more risks with the Grand Fleet than would Jellicoe and Beatty. 'The destruction of the German Fleet is a means to an end and not an end in itself. If in endeavouring to destroy the German Fleet we run risks which may prejudice our success in the greater object of the destruction of Germany, those risks are too great. . . . Take no risks with the G.F. The whole operations all over the world depend upon it.'[9] Galling to Richmond was the absence at the Admiralty of any 'glimmering of the value of continuous minor offensives'. 'They have no idea beyond the G.F.'[10] Sending a swarm of British submarines into the Baltic to disrupt Germany's trade was one offensive measure recommended by the Young Turks. The favourite was Richmond's scheme for combined operations on the coast of Syria to assist the campaigns in Egypt and Palestine by drawing away Turkish troops. And such diversions would draw submarines to the coast and away from the attack on trade. In the late spring and summer Richmond pressed these ideas on the Admiralty through Beatty with results to be noted elsewhere.

By the beginning of May the hubbub in the press was focusing on one point. The Navy was not to blame, whether for the failure to afford shipping complete security against U-boat attack or for the defensive strategy; it was the organization of the Board of Admiralty that was at fault. All forces of discontent, inside and outside the Service, could unite on this issue. Even journals and persons who were not criticizing Jellicoe's ability or his capacity to

[8] Dewar to Richmond, 6 January 1917; Dewar MSS.

[9] Richmond to Captain Plunkett-Ernle-Erle-Drax (H.M.S. *Blanche*, attached to the 5th B.S.) and Lieutenant W. S. Chalmers (on Beatty's staff), 29 August 1916; *Portrait of an Admiral*, p. 219.

[10] Richmond's views were coloured by his antipathy to Jellicoe. This stemmed in part from the latter's refusal to bring him into the Naval Staff, for which Richmond thought, and rightly, he had special qualifications.

fill the position of First Sea Lord agreed that there must be a reform at the Admiralty that would free the Sea Lords for thinking.
'The present Board,' explained the *Daily Mail* (30 April), 'is a
collection of heads of departments, all so fully occupied with
departmental work that they have no time for the hard thinking
that is required in war.' Several times in the next days the *Daily
Mail* returned to the theme that the Board of Admiralty was
mainly a Supply Board, not the Board of Strategy which it ought
to be. Each of the Sea Lords was wrapped up in his own departmental concerns. The work of supply should have a different
organization.

Criticism in the Grand Fleet went further. At a conference with
the First Lord, the Prime Minister, and the Naval Secretary at
Rosyth, 14–15 April, Beatty stressed the absence of a genuine
staff system at the Admiralty. There was 'no planning body' there,
'no executive authority by which rapid decisions are obtained and
instant action given'. The remedy lay in a thorough reorganization of the Staff system.[11] A visit to the Admiralty on 17–18 April
strengthened his feelings about the general inefficiency of the
Admiralty. 'The impression left on my mind after two days at the
Admiralty was that there seemed to be a lack of concrete ideas and
principles, that they were meeting troubles as they came, they were
not foreseen, and cut and dried plans based on sound principles
were lacking. . . . I know the Admiralty dislike intensely receiving
suggestions, which makes them receive them in an antagonistic
spirit; and, if they do adopt them, do so in a modified form which
accepts the principle, but spoils the working by a lack of thorough-
ness which ruins the whole thing.'[12] The situation had become so
desperate—the 'mediocre crowd' at the Admiralty were 'failing
with ignominy'—that Beatty could see no salvation in any reorganization of the Admiralty. 'Nothing but a clean sweep would
be of any value.' He had no intention of leaving the Grand Fleet
'to clean up the mess for them', because he still considered the
Grand Fleet to be 'the end of all things . . . if the G.F. came to an
untimely end, we may as well put up the shutters and we are
finished as a Great Power.' He was afraid that those who went to
the Admiralty in any reorganization would be no improvement

---

[11] From Beatty's notes for the conference; Naval Staff Monograph, *Home Waters.
December 1916 to April 1917*, p. 369.
[12] Beatty to Carson, 30 April 1917; Chalmers, *Beatty*, pp. 447–8.

upon those they replaced. 'Jellicoe is absolutely incapable of selecting good men, because he dislikes men of character who have independent views of their own. It is a fatal mistake and is insurmountable.' For a moment he had thought of Churchill as the only possible saviour of the country, but he finally (10 May) came down on the side of Fisher: 'He is a man—unscrupulous but still a man, which is more than anybody at the Admiralty is.' Carson he found 'disappointing and will not take a strong line'.[13]

Few officers in the Grand Fleet had a good word for the régime at Whitehall. Thus, O. de B. Brock, Beatty's Chief of Staff, talked of the 'apathetic way in which things were done up there in Whitehall, their opposition to every suggestion'.[14] This, too, is a refrain in Richmond's diary and correspondence of the period. Commander Henderson, of Duff's organization, stated that 'it took *days* for any proposal to get through the barbed wire of the various departments—the string of minutes put on by everybody, the eventual emasculation of the proposal at the hand of the several authorities, and finally its death at those of the Head Executioner. The Admiralty won't use convoy, haven't got mines, won't make attacks or diversions to force the enemy to do what we want. . . . Tom Jackson [D.O.D.] is universally execrated as the source of all this inertia and opposition.'[15] Richmond pushed his strong view that the Board of Admiralty had too much to do: the First Sea Lord was too concerned with 'inconsequent little matters', and the Junior Sea Lords, as heads of large administrative departments, were too immersed in their work to be able to take any efficient part in the conduct of the war. The Board should be reconstituted and 'a real Board—the Supreme Board' (First Sea Lord as Chief of the Staff, Oliver, Duff, and either Vice-Admiral Sir Montague Browning, C.-in-C., North America and West Indies, or Vice-Admiral Sir Rosslyn Wemyss, C.-in-C., East Indies) set up for operations, and, because wholly free from administration, able to anticipate what the enemy might do and to think out in advance broad lines of strategy.[16] Something of this sort did finally emerge.

[13] Beatty to Lady Beatty, 3, 8, 10, 13 May 1917; Beatty MSS.
[14] Richmond's diary, 30 April 1917; *Portrait of an Admiral*, p. 246.
[15] Diary, 4 May 1917; *ibid.*, p. 247.
[16] Richmond's paper of 17 February 1917 (sent to the Prime Minister) and letter to Admiral Sir William Henderson, 26 March 1917; *ibid.* pp. 233–5, 239–41.

One of the subjects that Lloyd George investigated during his visit to the Admiralty on 30 April was 'the organization of the Admiralty and more particularly of the War Staff, in connection with Anti-Submarine warfare'. The revelation of weaknesses in the naval war machine led to a reorganization of the Admiralty which was announced by Carson in the House of Commons on 14 May. The impetus for it had come from the Prime Minister and Hankey, and Service and public opinion generally, *not* from the Admiralty, as Jellicoe would have us believe.[17]

The immediate *raison d'être* of Lloyd George's intervention in the administrative set-up at Whitehall was the necessity of a reorganization of the Admiralty War Staff to free the First Sea Lord from *matériel* concerns, so that he could concentrate on the larger issues relating to the war at sea. The other side of the coin was the need 'to develop and utilize to the best advantage the whole of the shipbuilding resources of the country' and to remedy the apparent inability of the Admiralty to provide sufficient A/S craft and weapons. A reorganization scheme was approved by the War Cabinet on 2 May. Regarding the first, as the Prime Minister saw it, the situation 'clearly called' for the appointment of 'someone of energy and ability' to superintend the whole of the shipbuilding resources of the country (mercantile as well as naval, to solve the problem of conflicting claims to *matériel* and labour, with the mercantile passing out of the province of the Ministry of Shipping). As for the second object, needed was an organization parallel to the Ministry of Munitions *vis-à-vis* the Army. Both responsibilities would be delegated to one man.

Lloyd George wanted, and got, Sir Eric Geddes for the new post. He was given the ancient, now revived, title of Controller (it had latterly become a mere sub-title of the Third Sea Lord, but became extinct in 1912), with a seat on the Board of Admiralty. It was the first time the incumbent was a civilian. Lionel Halsey (promoted to rear-admiral in April), who relieved Rear-Admiral F. C. T. Tudor as Third Sea Lord, was to help Geddes. (Tudor returned to sea, as C.-in-C., China, after five years at Whitehall.) Halsey's primary job was responsibility for naval design and equipment; Geddes's, for production. (Halsey was chosen, thought Beatty, 'because he is a complaisant individual without much character or independent ideas'.) His place as Fourth Sea Lord

[17] Jellicoe, *The Crisis of the Naval War*, p. 11.

was taken by Rear-Admiral H. D. Tothill, 'a worthy officer without high qualifications', in Beatty's estimation.

Geddes was a 41-year-old Scotsman who sang Scotch songs with gusto—a big, strong-faced man. He was a masterful person. 'Force, energy, and decision shine from his features.' Sims described him as 'a man after Roosevelt's heart—big, athletic, energetic, with a genius for reaching the kernel of a question and of getting things done.' ('Roosevelt' was no doubt Franklin D., then Assistant Secretary of the United States Navy.) A railway engineer by training, Geddes had done a magnificent job in organizing the Army's railway transport in France as Director-General of Military Railways. ('Transport is my religion', he once told Lord Riddell.)

Aware of his ignorance about naval supplies, Geddes 'loathed' the idea of going to the Admiralty, and had accepted only on Lloyd George's insistence and after Jellicoe had assured him of his support. Jellicoe, though not Carson, had needed some persuasion, but he accepted the situation with grace and even with optimism. 'I expect [a] great increase in rapidity of production from the change. Geddes is a superman, an excellent fellow and has the complete whiphand of L.G. . ... I am very sanguine of the result of the change.'[18] Jellicoe found Geddes to be a great help to the Admiralty. 'He gets things done', the First Sea Lord remarked a month after Geddes's arrival. Nevertheless, one gets the impression that the Admiralty resented the implication in Geddes's appointment that the Admiralty had failed to meet the great responsibility with which they were charged and were worried over what the appointment portended. After a visit to the Admiralty and a long interview with Jellicoe, Tyrwhitt noted, 'I think they are all very much worried by the new régime.'[19]

The Admirals did not take kindly to a civilian Controller—a *Vice-Admiral* at that (the temporary rank of Honorary Vice-Admiral) and one with the temerity to wear his naval uniform! No civilian had ever before entered the Royal Navy in such a high position, and the last instances of a landsman being appointed an admiral were the great Blake and George Monk in the seventeenth century. Tyrwhitt found it 'strange that a private person can suddenly be transformed into a real live admiral by the stroke of a

[18] Jellicoe to Beatty, 10 May 1917; Beatty MSS.
[19] Tyrwhitt to his wife, 21 May 1917; Tyrwhitt MSS.

pen!' Geddes had received flag rank at his own insistence. 'He had discovered by bitter experience in France what it meant for an un-uniformed functionary to order about men in uniform. That is why he had been given the rank of a [Major-]General, for obedience to his orders then became automatic.'[20] Lord Esher thought it was right out of Gilbert and Sullivan: 'Geddes—a general to-day, and an admiral to-morrow.' Actually, since Geddes continued his Army connexion for a few months, he enjoyed the 'amphibious distinction of being at once both a General and an Admiral—an unprecedented attainment for a civilian.' At the Admiralty he was known as 'Goddis'!

Geddes did not enhance his popularity at the Admiralty when he brought a host of railway officials and other civilians to help him. Oliver sardonically comments: 'They were in everybody's way learning their job.'[21] Geddes managed in his seven weeks as Controller to speed up mercantile shipbuilding. Not a desk-bound administrator, he became a familiar figure in many shipyards, with his hands stuffed deep into the pockets of his uniform tunic and his cap rather down over one eye à la Beatty.

In addition to freeing the First Sea Lord from matériel problems and to strengthening the shipbuilding and production departments

---

[20] Lloyd George, War Memoirs, iii. 1234. The Geddes family version is that Jellicoe had 'insisted that the Controller must be a naval officer. Ll. G. countered by creating Eric a Vice-Admiral.' Baron Geddes, The Forging of a Family (London, 1952), p. 241.

[21] Oliver MSS. Lloyd George in his 30 April report to the War Cabinet had recommended the formation of a Statistical Department in order that the Admiralty's statistics, especially regarding mercantile losses from submarines, be 'tabulated and co-ordinated more completely than appears to be the case at present'. On 28 May Lieutenant-Colonel Beharrell, a North-Eastern Railway man, came to the Admiralty from the War Office as Director of Statistics. This determined and down-to-earth Yorkshireman, of strong jaw and Napoleonic head, was an excellent choice. He was clear-headed, tactful, and kindly, and had an extraordinary ability with figures. Yet Oliver found Geddes's statisticians particularly trying. 'Railways work by statistics, but they are not altogether applicable to the R.N. in war time. Sir George Beharrell [knighted in 1919] arrived at the head of a mob of some hundred people to make up statistics and graphs and he used to bother me frequently for material to work on. To get peace and to keep him away and occupy him and his staff, my staff used to make up data mixed with weather conditions and the phases of the moon which kept them occupied. In a few months wonderful graphs arrived but you cannot run war like a railway; you must look ahead, not back.' Ibid. Beharrell's statistics showed for the first time quantitatively what was happening in the submarine war. Oliver's inability to see that foresight must be based on sound knowledge of the past is very illuminating, and it goes a long way towards explaining why the Admiralty were so dilatory in adopting and extending the convoy system.

of the Admiralty, there was an important reorganization of the Staff system. The crux of the matter, as Lloyd George had discovered on 30 April, was the 'over-centralization'. This was a survival from the Fisher–A. K. Wilson era of the monolithic 'great man' who alone held all the secrets and gave all the orders—a system that was utterly unsuited to the growing complexity of warfare. Lloyd George's proposed reorganization had the object of freeing the First Sea Lord and the heads of the Staff of as much administrative responsibility as possible to free them for concentration on the naval conduct of the war. Stated in its simplest terms, the reorganization, as finally worked out, involved Jellicoe becoming in name what he had been in fact, Chief of the Naval Staff (C.N.S.). ('C.O.S.', which is what Oliver had been since November 1914, disappeared from the Navy List.) 'The adoption of the title of Chief of the Naval Staff by the First Sea Lord necessarily made the functions of the Staff executive instead of advisory' (Jellicoe). Oliver and Duff were to be his two assistants, both joining the Board as additional Sea Lords with the titles, respectively, of Deputy Chief of the Naval Staff (D.C.N.S.) and Assistant Chief of the Naval Staff (A.C.N.S.). Oliver superintended the work of the Operations, Mobilization, and Intelligence Divisions, and the newly formed Signal Section, of the Staff. (The last-named became a Division in August.) Duff supervised the Trade, A/S, and (the newly formed) Minesweeping Divisions, the Convoy Section, and, when organized later in the summer, the Mercantile Movements Division (assembly, movements, and protection of convoys), into which the Convoy Section was incorporated. Briefly, Oliver was responsible for operations against the German surface craft; Duff, for trade protection and A/S warfare. The three officers, Jellicoe, Oliver, and Duff, had always worked in close co-operation, and, with altered titles, they would continue to do so. The difference now was that the Naval Staff had the executive authority; the D.C.N.S. and A.C.N.S. could act with Board authority. This was supposed to mean a speed-up of business and a reduction of the immense administrative burdens on the First Sea Lord. It did not quite work out that way, however, as Jellicoe did not take advantage of the fact that the D.C.N.S. and A.C.N.S. were now Members of the Board. Nor did Oliver surrender his centralizing proclivities.

The larger significance of the reorganization has yet to be

mentioned. Prior to the changes announced by Carson, naval operations were directed by the First Sea Lord and a War Staff Group
(First Lord, First Sea Lord, C.O.S., the Secretary, the Naval
Secretary, and A. K. Wilson), assisted by the War Staff, while
matériel and supply were in the hands of the Sea Lords, from the
Second to the Fifth, and the Civil Lords. As a result of the reform,
operations were to be directed by the First Sea Lord with the
D.C.N.S. and A.C.N.S., while those responsible for supply were
reinforced by a Controller. In effect, the Admirals were relieved
of the burden of business management; the work of supplying the
Fleet with stores, victuals, fuel, and shell would henceforth be concentrated in civilian hands—the Controller, who, however, would
work through a largely naval staff (4th and 5th Sea Lords, D.N.O.,
etc.). The naval men would now only have to say what they
wanted, and the business men would provide it. In other words,
the new department under Geddes served pretty much the same
function as had the old Navy Board. Until 1832 the military side
of the Navy was directed by an Admiralty Board, and the *matériel*
(or supply) side by a Navy Board. To sum up, under the reform of
May 1917 the Admiralty organization reverted to a modified form
of the pre-1832 system. It was divided more distinctly into two
sides, Operations and Administration, restoring what had been lost
in the 1832 reforms, when the First Lord, Sir James Graham, had
merged the two Boards into a single board on the plea of economy
and efficiency. The effect had been, as Captain A. C. Dewar
has written, that 'the Admiralty congratulated itself on swallowing
up the Navy Board, but the work of the Navy Board swallowed
up the real functions of the Admiralty. The successors of
St. Vincent became slaves of the lamp of administration and
supply.'

As part of the upheaval at the Admiralty, the D.O.D., Jackson,
left the Admiralty. (In July he was appointed to the command of
the Egypt and Red Sea Division of the Mediterranean Squadron.)
He was succeeded by Rear-Admiral G. P. W. Hope, a gifted
officer who never asserted himself, yet inspired confidence. One
of the very best of Beatty's Captains (commanding the battleship
St. Vincent) took over Duff's work as D.A.S.D. He was the charming, very human, and very capable W. W. Fisher ('Tall Agrippa').
Possessed of a restless and original brain, Fisher was already a
marked man in the Navy. As his biographer observes, 'Fisher

brought to his new task qualities which could not be equalled. He had more than two years' experience of war at sea, technical knowledge of a high order, first-rate organizing ability, remarkable power of inspiring enthusiasm, a very alert mind, and a capacity for working very long hours without disturbing his own temper.'[22] He was, Lord Fisher (no relation) wrote to him, '*Absolutely the right man in the right place.*' And so he proved to be. 'Few men,' said L. S. Amery (1937), 'did more to win the war.'

Public opinion, as reflected in the press, almost unanimously welcomed the organizational changes, which were hailed as fundamental and long overdue. At the Admiralty there was doubt and apprehension. 'These changes looked well on paper,' wrote the Secretary afterwards, 'and no doubt gave the impression that the Admiralty would now show striking results, but in fact they meant little. No further extraordinary exertions were required to maintain the material strength of the Fleet and the measures for meeting the submarine menace were scarcely affected by them. Many of the changes were unwelcome to the Naval Lords, and undoubtedly a great deal was forced upon Sir E. Carson from outside the Admiralty.'[23] To Tyrwhitt and Richmond the Admiralty changes were mere 'eyewash'.[24] The latter and his cohorts wanted new blood at the Admiralty, beginning with replacements for Jellicoe (Wemyss was their candidate) and Oliver; a true reorganization of the Admiralty 'on fighting lines, giving wider power to the Lords, greater freedom to the First Sea Lord, to enable him to evolve the grand strategy & opening up channels of thought to the officers, who require encouragement only to propose schemes of every kind for the employment of every element of the Navy'.[25] The reconstruction of the Admiralty left Beatty 'cold'. 'The same as before, but with new labels and Tothill instead of Tudor, but it seems to please the Critics, which is apparently all that is desired. It is not the system that is wrong, but those that run it.'[26] The document that follows gives us the Beatty position in full.

[22] Admiral Sir William James, *Admiral Sir William Fisher* (London, 1943), p. 72. See further, *From the Dreadnought to Scapa Flow*, ii. 16.
[23] W. Graham Greene, 'Sir Edward Carson at the Admiralty', 1930; Carson MSS.
[24] Tyrwhitt to his wife, 17 May 1917, Tyrwhitt MSS.; Richmond to Dewar, 12 May 1917, Dewar MSS.
[25] Diary, 5 June 1917; *Portrait of an Admiral*, pp. 256–7.
[26] Beatty to Tyrwhitt (May 1917); Tyrwhitt MSS.

ADMIRALTY ORGANIZATION

(a) The lack of a staff system—no planning body, no executive authority—by which rapid decisions are obtained and instant action given.

(b) Lack of sympathy shown amounts to a positive dislike to receiving ideas and proposals. Result—no progress is made. Thought is discouraged.

Every proposal for offensive action has been systematically shelved, or so picked to pieces and sent back for correction, that time—the most decisive factor—has been lost.

Every objection has been found to new proposals; they were never encouraged. The Motor Boat attack on Wilhelmshaven was put back every time it was brought forward.

Schemes for blocking Zeebrugge were sent back for more complete details—no help was given to certain officers who had extensive schemes.

Schemes for diversionary attacks have been turned down.

Concrete examples:

(i) The Heligoland Barrage—proposed by the C.-in-C. to be carried out on a vast scale for which a corresponding preparation was required.

Admiralty reply pointing out all the difficulties. The principle was finally adopted after delay, but deplorably executed, small fields being laid in driblets as opposed to the idea of large fields in one operation. Consequence—fouling of areas and easing the task of enemy minelayers [minesweepers?].

(ii) The more offensive use of our submarines hitherto tied to the coast—proposed by the C.-in-C. early in the year.

Every conceivable objection raised but after much delay (letters taking as long as six weeks to answer) the policy was adopted in principle.

(iii) Introduction of the convoy system. Considered on being suggested, impracticable. Now at length being generally introduced, but matters of detail which one way or another should be settled in 7 days are taking as many weeks due to the want of executive action and authority.

(c) The remedy lies in a thorough reorganization of the staff system at the Admiralty and the introduction of a personnel capable of running such a system. The officers responsible for the higher direction must not only be freed from administrative detail, but their training must be such that they will be content to leave the detail and deal with broad conceptions and ideas.

(d) The Second Sea Lord must be the right-hand man of the Chief of Staff, definitely responsible for the conduct of a certain branch of the war, and ready to fill the place of the Chief of the Staff should the latter be absent from the Admiralty. The Second Sea Lord should be placed under the D.M.D. [Director of the Mobilisation Division. This sentence is presumably an inversion: the D.M.D. should be under the Second Sea Lord.]

Other Directors of Operations over certain branches of the war will be required, the whole working under the First Lord and Chief of the Staff who should not himself undertake the conduct of any particular branch.

Under the various Directors subordinate staffs would be required.

(e) The nucleus of a staff organization exists. The personnel to carry it out are required. This is the crux of the problem.

The recent reorganization at the Admiralty only affected the supply departments. It attempted also to introduce the staff system on the operation system but actually achieved nothing, the personnel question not being faced, the line of least resistance being taken by calling the same people by other names.[27]

The Historical Section of the Naval Staff took a kindlier view: 'It is not possible to tabulate the results of this reorganization [of the Staff]; they belong to the sphere of "immeasurables", but it is permissible to think that they were not small, and the impetus given by the Naval Staff exercised a very considerable influence on the war against the submarine.'[28]

2. CONVOY PROBLEMS

During May and June the shipping situation looked almost as menacing as in the darkest days of April. The sharp drop in losses during May (about a third below the April figures) was not maintained in June. The figures in the latter month were 15 per cent above those for May, if still not so bad as April. The U-boats accounted for nearly all losses in the two months.

British Shipping Losses
(gross tonnage, with number of ships in parentheses)

	By Mines	By Surface Craft	By Aircraft	By Submarines	Total
May	28,114 (14)	819 (1)	2,784 (1)	320,572 (106)	352,289 (122)
June	19,256 (4)	3,947 (1)	3,718 (1)	391,004 (116)	417,925 (122)

[27] 'Notes for Conference' (July 1917), probably for a conference with Jellicoe on or about 19 July; Bellairs MSS.

[28] Naval Staff Monograph No. 35 (1939), *Home Waters—Part IX. 1st May, 1917, to 31st July, 1917*, p. 116.

Britain's Allies suffered tonnage losses during these two months of 102,960 and 126,171. In the same period the neutrals lost 137,957 and 139,229. The grand totals, British, Allied, and neutral, were:

	By Submarines	By All Forms of Enemy Action
May	549,987 (264)	593,206 (287)
June	631,895 (272)	683,325 (290)

The substantial decrease in losses in May was most marked in the South Western Approaches and to the westward—over 50 per cent—and in the Mediterranean. This big drop in May 'must be attributed partly to the increase in submarines sunk (seven [in Home Waters] in May as compared with three in April), and partly to increased vigilance and greater energy in attack, and partly perhaps to a stricter attention to routeing instructions, induced by the heavy losses of April'.[29] In June the sinkings rose nearly 50 per cent in the south-west and west. Only in the Mediterranean was there a marked reduction in sinkings, of 27 per cent.

*   *   *

The drop in the Mediterranean was probably the outcome of the Allied naval conference that had met at Corfu (headquarters of the French fleet), 28 April–1 May, to see what could be done to protect shipping more efficiently. (During these four days, as if to justify the conference, U-boats sank 14 merchant vessels of 27,000 tons.) The principal recommendations were: (1) Merchant shipping would make use of coastal patrol routes and neutral territorial waters as far as possible, and navigate only by night when submarines were operating in the neighbourhood. (2) There was a compromise between the French-favoured fixed patrolled routes and the British-favoured dispersal of ships on unpatrolled routes. The former method was to be operative only when coastal routes could be used, the latter, when vessels had to cross the open sea, as between Malta and Alexandria—but with important ships (not more than three in a convoy) to be escorted through their voyage. (3) A fixed net barrage would be erected across the Straits of

[29] Naval Staff Monograph, *Home Waters. May 1917 to July 1917*, p. 87. The actual number of U-boats sunk in April was 2; in May, 7, of which one was sunk in the Mediterranean.

Otranto. (4) The need of centralizing Allied direction was finally recognized. A central authority would be established at Malta with responsibility for all arrangements affecting routes, escorts, and patrols in the Mediterranean.

The Allied naval authorities approved the recommendations of the Conference, and the measures subsequently taken under the first two heads above seem to have been quickly effective.[30] Technical officers were sent out to report on the feasibility of a fixed barrage in the Straits of Otranto. The Allied Naval Conference meeting in Paris, 24–27 July, decided not to proceed with it, since it could not be protected adequately by surface craft. The Italian Admiral stated definitely that he could not allocate any destroyers for this service on account of the danger of a meeting between the Italian and Austrian Fleets. He dared not risk a single destroyer. The fourth recommendation (above) created some difficulty, as both France and Britain wanted the supreme control of the new organization. Mutual concessions were made at the Paris Naval Conference: a British vice-admiral would be appointed C.-in-C. of the British naval forces in the Mediterranean and head of the organization at Malta, with the task of framing the general principles that would guide the control, escort, and navigation of mercantile traffic in the Mediterranean. But in order that there should be no doubt about the French C.-in-C.'s supreme authority in disposing of all the patrol forces in the conduct of operations, the British Admiral was to fly his flag ashore

Vice-Admiral Sir Rosslyn Wemyss, C.-in-C., East Indies, was appointed to the Mediterranean command on 20 June. This command, which St. Vincent said should be filled by an officer of grandeur, had been Wemyss's life's ambition. Alas, he never assumed the post, becoming Second Sea Lord instead. On 26 August Vice-Admiral Sir Somerset Gough-Calthorpe took up the Mediterranean appointment. This meant the reintroduction of a British C.-in-C., Mediterranean, an appointment that had lapsed when Admiral Milne had returned to England following the *Goeben* fiasco in August 1914. As for Gough-Calthorpe, an officer who served on his staff provides this thumb-nail sketch: He 'was not sufficiently sure of himself—he temporized and waited. . . .

---

[30] The number of British ships sunk in the Mediterranean, except for a setback in August, steadily declined up to October 1917: April, 32; May, 25; June, 17; July, 8; August, 13; September, 7.

He has been described as ninety per cent wisdom and ten per cent initiative.'[31]

In the meantime, on 22 May, Rear-Admiral George Ballard, S.N.O. Malta, had started small convoys of three or four ships, escorted by a few armed trawlers, between Malta and Alexandria in both directions. These convoys were a success: only two of the 275 vessels escorted from 22 May to 16 July were sunk. This preliminary system was a promising start; but 'that it was practicable to form convoys of more than three or four ships in the Mediterranean', states a post-war report, 'did not at the time occur to the minds of many Allied officers.'

*   *   *

The cold figures of shipping losses in May and June do not reveal the full gravity of the situation. The tonnage under repair increased sharply. The figure of 131,000 tons of British shipping (steamers of 1,600 tons gross and upwards) undergoing serious repairs on 31 January had shot up to 262,000 at the end of April, and was 454,000 at the end of June. 'This could not go on. Excluding ships completing or under repair, and allowing on the one hand for war and marine losses, and on the other for all gains by new construction or transfer, the available ocean-going shipping had been reduced, since February 1st, by more than one-tenth, giving an annual rate of depletion of about 25 per cent. At this rate the margin of safety would soon disappear beyond all possibility of recovery by accelerated construction or economy in employment. The question of protection had become an overmastering preoccupation before which all other problems paled.'[32]

The Shipping Controller was full of gloom and foreboding. Papers prepared by him in June showed plainly that by 1 December, assuming a monthly rate of loss of about 300,000 tons of British shipping, there would not be enough tonnage left to bring in necessities.[33] Maclay's statisticians presented the Shipping Control Committee with these figures (27 June): on the average, over the previous three-and-a-half months, 20 ocean-going ships had been lost each week, though latterly they had been above that

[31] The Naval Memoirs of Admiral J. H. Godfrey (privately printed, 1964–6, 7 vols. in 10), ii. 99.
[32] Fayle, Seaborne Trade, iii. 132.
[33] Jellicoe to Beatty, 30 June 1917; Beatty MSS.

figure. For direct war requirements, ships available for overseas imports numbered 1,300 at the outside. At the rate of 20 losses a week, 1,040 ships would be lost in one year; at 25: 1,300; at 30: 1,560. New tonnage in the next twelve months would not, from indications, exceed 300 ships. 'The conclusion to which all this points,' said the Controller, 'is that by some means or other equilibrium *must* be brought about between losses and gains, and that with the least possible delay.' They would reach the 'irreducible minimum' of monthly imports, 1,900,000 tons, if losses continued at their present rate, in January or February 1918. 'Since to balance a loss of 20 large ships a week an output of at least 4,500,000 gross tons, at home or abroad, would be required it is clear that at the best the task before us is a stupendous one. Of course decreased loss from more effective protection has the same effect as increased building but the task is so stupendous that it will call for all we can do and at once either by increased building, increased protection or decreased consumption to accomplish it.'[34]

Beatty was pessimistic. 'It seems to me that the Admiralty are riding for a fall and it will be a heavy one. The submarine menace is no more in hand to-day than it was three months ago!!! They might flood the Admiralty with civilians and soldiers, but it will serve no purpose unless the heads change their views and adopt the strongest measures.' By the 'strongest measures' he undoubtedly meant the adoption of a comprehensive and regular convoy system. A few weeks later: 'They are sinking masses of our ships, and our futile Admiralty seem incapable of preventing them or of arranging any scheme for deflecting the traffic from the zone where they are so active. The situation is very serious . . .'[35]

In a Glasgow speech on 29 June the Prime Minister informed the country that the losses, heavy as they were, were hundreds of thousands of tons below the Admiralty forecast, and that they were beginning to 'get at the enemy' and were 'likely' to destroy more and more of his submarines. He was whistling in the dark. For the quarter ending 30 June 1917, there had been 325 encounters with U-boats in Home waters, out of which a preliminary

[34] Maclay to Lloyd George, 27 June 1917; Lloyd George MSS. By 'increased protection' he had in mind 'the drastic application of the Atlantic policy', that is, convoy. Maclay to Lloyd George, 18 June 1917; Lloyd George MSS.
[35] Beatty to Lady Beatty, 4, 29 June 1917; Beatty MSS.

classification of kills (1 July) gave only 6 'certainties' and 13 'probables'.[36] The actual figure was 11 (one of them credited to the French), as compared with 10 in the first quarter: January—2; February—4; March—4; April—2; May—7; June—2.

But what of the convoy system in this period? The matter had apparently been settled at the end of April. On 27 April Duff had submitted detailed proposals for a trial ocean convoy from Gibraltar. They were accepted at once, and the next day the Admiralty informed the S.N.O. Gibraltar that the convoy should sail in about ten days' time. On 10 May a convoy of 17 merchant vessels (6½ knots average speed) left Gibraltar, escorted through the danger zone as far as 11° W. by three armed yachts, and with two Q-ships as ocean escorts. They were met on 18 May outside the submarine danger zone (some 200 miles from the English Channel) by eight destroyers from Devonport, supplemented by an air escort (a flying-boat from the Scillies) on reaching the Western Approaches. As the convoy approached the Scillies, the five ships for West Coast ports were detached and escorted by two of the destroyers as far as the Smalls, where the ships dispersed (20 May), while, on the same day, the 11 vessels for East Coast ports were brought into Plymouth by the remaining six destroyers. They sailed that evening, with drifters providing further escort to the Downs, where they arrived safely on 22 May, and from where they sailed to their ports of destination. The experiment was a 100 per cent success. Not a ship had been lost, no U-boats were sighted, station-keeping was quite good, and the convoy made the voyage two days shorter than would have been the case had the vessels come home independently on the various devious routes which were then prescribed. Several of the masters were interviewed, and they were unanimous in their opinion that the convoy system was a practicable proposition from the merchant service point of view. They all emphasized the sense of security afforded to both the crews and themselves and stated that they had enjoyed more sleep than they had had for months. The experience showed Jellicoe that 'the system was at least practicable'.[37] This is an under-statement. But no further convoys were sailed from Gib-

---

[36] A.S.D., 'Monthly Report No. 2, June 1917', 1 July 1917. The figure for kills was revised a month later to show 9 'known' kills (including one in the Mediterranean) and 7 'probables'. 'Monthly Report No. 3, July 1917', 1 August 1917.
[37] Jellicoe, *The Crisis of the Naval War*, p. 117.

raltar until 26 July—a two months' delay, of which the Ministry of Shipping was afterwards highly critical. 'Had the convoy system then been put in force immediately on all the routes, as was strongly urged, before the enemy had any inkling of it, there is every ground for saying, from the subsequent success attending convoys, that the losses of the next two months would only have been a fraction of the ships which were sunk before the system was started on the grand scale, by which time the enemy had begun to realize what was being attempted.'[38]

There were two other important convoy developments during May. On about 1 May the Admiralty accepted in principle a comprehensive scheme of convoy for the Atlantic trade. On 3 May they asked if the Navy Department would send a convoy of 16 to 20 British or Allied vessels (under 12 knots seagoing speed) under the escort of the group of American destroyers that was about to sail for Queenstown. The U.S. Navy was not keen on convoy. Although willing to assist the Admiralty in carrying out an experimental convoy in the North Atlantic, the American naval authorities, reported the British Naval Attaché in Washington, were 'very strongly' opposed to this scheme, Admiral Benson, the Chief of Naval Operations, particularly so. 'The Navy Department does not consider it advisable to attempt the character of convoy outlined. In large groups of ships under convoy, fog, gales, inexperience of personnel, and general tension on merchant vessels make the hazards of the attempt great and the probability of a scattering of the convoy very strong.' The Navy Department suggested sending instead, experimentally, small convoys—groups of four vessels, each group convoyed by two destroyers.[39] The Admiralty at first agreed, then, on 22 May, decided against this. In the event, an experimental North Atlantic homeward-bound convoy of 12 ships (speed, 9 knots) sailed from Hampton Roads, Virginia, on 24 May. Two slow steamers were forced to drop out—one of them was torpedoed and sunk, the other made it to port. The convoy was escorted by the British cruiser *Roxburgh* (Captain F. A. Whitehead), and, on arrival in the danger zone, 6 June, by eight destroyers. (Aircraft and trawlers also played a role in the danger zone.) South of Ireland the six West Coast ships were detached

[38] Ministry of Shipping, *The System of Convoy for Merchant Shipping in 1917 and 1918*, p. 4.
[39] Cable and letter by Commodore Guy Gaunt to Admiralty, 5 May 1917; Technical History Monograph, *The Atlantic Convoy System, 1917–1918*, p. 4.

with a destroyer escort for the Smalls, while the four East Coast ships made for Portland. By 10 June all the ships in the convoy had arrived safely at their destinations. Despite fog and heavy weather, Whitehead was able to report to the First Sea Lord that the station-keeping was excellent and that he was prepared to escort as many as 30 vessels. Four other convoys left Hampton Roads in June: on the 4th, 12th, 19th, 25th, with 12, 11, 18, and 20 ships, respectively. None was lost, though one ship was torpedoed.

Meanwhile, on 15 May, a conference at the Admiralty had decided on the appointment of an Atlantic Trade Convoy Committee of officers to draw up a complete organization for a regular ocean trades convoy system. Chosen on 17 May were four Naval Staff officers and a representative of the Ministry of Shipping. The Committee presented their report on 6 June, by which time they had before them the successful experience of the first two ocean convoys. They proposed the establishment of a system of regular inward-bound and outward-bound Atlantic Ocean convoys (arranged in cycles of eight days) with cruisers serving as ocean escort and a destroyer escort responsible for bringing in, or taking out, the convoy from or to a rendezvous 300 to 400 miles from Britain. A total of 52 cruisers or 'armed escort ships' would be needed for ocean escort, as well as 84 destroyers or similar craft. The report was concurred in by Duff and Jellicoe (11, 14 June). The latter's minute praised the Committee's recommendations, 'which are sound and well thought out. Propose to put them into force as the situation develops and the necessary vessels for escort and convoy duty become available.' Carson approved (15 June). Despite the Committee's recommendations and the success of the first convoys, nothing was done immediately to institute the regular system recommended by the Committee beyond notifying the departments concerned on 25 June that the Admiralty had 'approved generally' of the Committee's recommendations, which would 'be put into force as the necessary vessels for escort and convoy duty became available',[40] and instituting on the same day the necessary machinery for introducing and building up the system with the establishment of a Convoy Section of the Trade Division of the Naval Staff. Nothing was done to make available the naval forces needed.

It was only slowly that convoy was extended. A complete system

[40] *Ibid.*, p. 17.

was not in operation until the end of the year, which story I leave for a later chapter. This was the situation at the end of June: regular homeward-bound convoys had not been started. There had been only the experimental Gibraltar convoy of May and the five North Atlantic homeward-bound convoys of May–June. Outward trade was still unconvoyed, as was the whole of the South Atlantic and Mediterranean trade. The Admiralty no longer objected to convoy in principle and were prepared to see a fair trial made. But their hearts were not in it. They regarded convoy as the last shot in their lockers, were sceptical of its success, and had a lingering preference for a trade protection system based on patrolling. Besides, it was argued against an extension of convoy that they could not provide escorts yet for a large proportion of the Atlantic trade. As a consequence of this attitude, Jellicoe and Duff were reluctant to institute a general convoy system and made no extraordinary efforts to speed up its development. They had, to be sure, approved of the four additional North Atlantic convoys in June. The deciding factor here was the need to give protection to oilers from North America.[41] The situation as regards naval oil fuel stocks was critical, owing to the increasing consumption of oil fuel and to the heavy losses incurred in April. At the beginning of June there was only a little under three months' supply, which was considered to be the absolute minimum compatible with safety.

Manisty, who headed the Convoy Section of the Naval Staff, wrote after the war that Jellicoe 'did not seem confident as to the success of the system, but he believed it to be the only chance, and he was prepared to take the responsibility of the decision, and to support the scheme to the full, as he did'. There is contemporary evidence of the mood of the directing heads at this time. At a War Cabinet meeting on 13 July the Prime Minister instructed the Admiralty to examine the possibility of a redistribution of destroyer flotillas in Home waters in order to increase the number of destroyers available for convoy work. Jellicoe's paper the next day showed that not one of the 218 modern and 76 old destroyers in Home waters, all engaged in important work (trade protection, screening the Grand Fleet against submarine attack, Dover Straits patrol), could safely be withdrawn for convoy work.[42] Writing no

41 *Ibid.*, p. 22.
42 'Destroyer Situation' (G.T.-1408).

doubt of the Admiralty conference on 15 May, Duff had this to say:

After a pretty thorough investigation of the question of Convoy generally, I reported that to introduce the system generally we should require 52 Cruisers for ocean escort, and 75 T.B.D.s for dangerous zone escort. To provide this force, great sacrifices in other directions (which will not be faced) would have to be made, and all the resources of the U.S. roped in. I further pointed out that a partial system would be folly, *as it would eat up all our meagre patrol-force of T.B.D.s and leave the Trade routes unprotected.* However, the system is regarded by the Cabinet as likely to prove our salvation, and *we are being forced into giving it a partial trial.* . . . The whole question is further complicated by the necessity of keeping troopship escort going, as well.[43]

Nearly six weeks later we find Duff still not completely sold on a regular system of ocean convoy. 'The system is to be extended as rapidly as our resources will admit. . . . Where they [the escorts] are to come from, Heaven only knows; but a recent visit to the War Council [Cabinet] showed me very clearly that they look on Convoy as the only salvation to a very critical position, and great pressure will be brought to extend the system at once. Outward convoy cannot at present be tackled, except in the case of Oilers, where the necessity is vital and immediate action essential. We have not yet fully considered the problem, but in my opinion, an outward convoy a week from Plymouth or Falmouth must be arranged very soon.' And, most revealing of all, a month later: 'The success, up to date, of the Atlantic Convoy, has led to what I consider a very optimistic view being taken of this method of protecting Merchant Ships. What the Authorities will not recognise is, that the slow speed of the convoy lays it particularly open to attack, and even one S/m getting to close quarters may result in the loss of two or three ships.'[44] Duff was in the end, as we shall see, able to find the needed ocean escorts and escort craft to develop the system.

The scepticism of the U.S. Navy was undoubtedly a partial explanation of the Admiralty's go-slow attitude. They were not prepared to co-operate with the British in instituting a regular system of Atlantic convoy and preferred that armed American

[43] Duff to Admiral Sir Alexander Bethell (C.-in-C., Plymouth), 17 May 1917; Duff MSS. Italics mine.
[44] Duff to Bethell, 26 June, 21 July 1917; Duff MSS.

ships sail independently. The crux of the matter, though, as summed up by Jellicoe, was that 'Even by mid-July, *by which time we had been reinforced by 18 U.S. destroyers and no doubt by some of our own vessels by that time completed,* even so we were only able to provide anti-submarine escorts for 4 homeward-bound convoys every eight days from New York, Sydney [Cape Breton], and Hampton Roads. . . . And only 21 [ocean] escort ships were available by July as against the requirement of 52 stated by the Convoy Committee.'[45] The basic difficulty here was that as late as June the Admiralty were still greatly overestimating the number of weekly sailings of ocean-going merchantmen for which escort would be needed and, despite the experience of Harwich, East Coast, and cross-Channel convoys, the size of the escort that was required for each convoy. And, of course, there was the unwillingness to strip further the Grand Fleet and other services of their small craft.

Although the approach route system and patrol and hunting tactics were, patently, not ensuring the safety of trade, the Admiralty retained their faith in these outmoded methods, if with shrinking forces. By June, as the convoy system began to expand, the only destroyers and P-boats with the special task of hunting U-boats were the Irish Sea hunting flotilla and a few based on Queenstown, Devonport, and Milford Haven. A special hunting operation was mounted: from 15 to 24 June a large force of destroyers and submarines (about one-half of the destroyer strength of the Grand Fleet) was concentrated in zones about the north of Scotland, distributed over the known incoming routes of the U-boats, in an attempt to catch as many of them as possible. 'The results achieved', according to the Official Historian, 'only gave additional proof of the extraordinary difficulty of intercepting submarines, even when their routes were known. The outcome was that submarines were sighted sixty-one times by our forces on patrol, and attacked on twelve occasions. None of the attacks caused loss or damage, or affected submarine activities in the approach routes further south. . . . The Admiralty, whilst admitting that the operation was disappointing in its results, agreed that it ought

[45] Jellicoe, 'Errors in *Naval Operations*'. Jellicoe's figure of U.S. destroyers was badly off. The first six had arrived at Queenstown on 4 May, twelve more in May, ten in June, and another nine in July, for a total of 28 by the end of June and 37 by the end of July—of the 66 on the Navy list when the war started. However, no American cruisers were assigned to convoy duty until the first week in July, although Sims had asked for them at least seven times.

to be repeated as soon as possible in order to give it a fair trial.'[46]

If evidence is still needed to demonstrate the lack of enthusiasm for the general adoption of convoy at this time, we have this testimony from Dewar, who was attached to the Operations Division in May to prepare 'a weekly appreciation of the naval situation generally, and of the developments of the submarine campaign in particular', for the First Sea Lord and the War Cabinet. (This had resulted from one of the Prime Minister's recommendations of 30 April to the War Cabinet.) 'Remarks favourable to it [convoy] were deleted from the Weekly Appreciation and the suggestion [July 1917] that outward-bound ships should be placed under convoy as quickly as possible was crossed out, with a note in the margin to say that "these ships were being sunk because patrols had been withdrawn to provide escorts for the homeward convoys". Not only was this statement incorrect, but it showed a simple faith in the system of patrolled routes along which our ships had been shepherded like sheep to the slaughter.'[47]

In the Prime Minister's view, the Admiralty were dragging their feet. 'The High Admirals had at last been persuaded by the "Convoyers" not perhaps to take action, but to try action. But there was a reluctance and a tardiness in their movements. They acted as men whose doubts were by no means removed, and who therefore proceed with excessive caution and with an ill-concealed expectation that their forebodings will be justified by the experience. . . . these disappointing successes [Gibraltar, North Atlantic] simply irritated the Admirals into sullen recalcitrance.'[48]

The slow and reluctant co-operation of the Admiralty in extending the convoy system was a major reason for the Prime Minister's complete loss of faith in his First Sea Lord. There were other reasons.

3. CARSON'S DISMISSAL

One result of the Prime Minister's celebrated visit to the Admiralty was, Lord Beaverbrook informs us, a 'severe blow' to Carson's prestige. 'Lloyd George had staged a deliberate encounter with the Naval High Command, and had emerged triumphant. But he had lost faith in Carson, Jellicoe and even his Board of

[46] Newbolt, *Naval Operations*, v. 55.
[47] K. G. B. Dewar, *The Navy from Within* (London, 1939), p. 217.
[48] Lloyd George, *War Memoirs*, iii. 1164–7.

Admiralty.'[49] His particular target was Jellicoe, whom he wished to replace with an officer of an optimistic outlook, fresh ideas, and more vigour—a professional head of the Navy who had a greater faith in convoy, would pursue the A/S war with more energy and resourcefulness, and who would look more kindly upon the possibility of offensive action by the Fleet.

Lloyd George found Jellicoe singularly unimpressive, which was perfectly natural. The two men were poles apart in temperament: one, eloquent, passionate, optimistic, ruthless; the other, rather silent and reserved, pessimistic, incapable of ruthlessness. 'In the eyes of the Ministers who exercised the Supreme Control,' says Hankey, 'his worst defect was his apparent pessimism', and he adds: 'I sometimes wondered whether his pessimism was not assumed in order to induce the politicians to make a still greater naval effort.'[50] There was nothing 'assumed' about it. The U-boat threat had brought to the fore the strain of latent pessimism that was a part of Jellicoe's make-up. His pessimism is referred to by many of his contemporaries. King George V, Beatty, Lord Fisher, Churchill, Sir William Robertson (C.I.G.S.), Lloyd George, Haig, and Repington, as well as Hankey, all mention it. Although traces of it were visible from the commencement of the war, the trait became more noticeable after Jellicoe went to Whitehall, and particularly in the spring of 1917. Thus, Robertson: 'The situation at sea . . . has never been so bad as at present, and Jellicoe almost daily announces it to be hopeless.'[51] And Beatty: 'Even the King [who was visiting the Grand Fleet] says that J.J. is too pessimistic and conservative.'[52] Fundamentally, it was Jellicoe's thorough pessimism about the war at sea, as well as his supposed reluctance to introduce, then to expand, convoy, that turned the Prime Minister against him. Carson was aware of Jellicoe's increasing despondency, and tried to get him to take occasional rest periods as a cure. It was the convoy factor that was decisive with Lloyd George. When Jellicoe agreed to proceed with convoy, it was, the Prime Minister believed, with a pessimism and lack of enthusiasm that convinced him that the Admiral must go.

There was a third factor. Reinforced in his thinking by the

[49] Beaverbrook, *Men and Power*, pp. 155–6.
[50] Hankey, *The Supreme Command*, ii. 656.
[51] Robertson to Haig, 26 April 1917; Robert Blake (ed.), *The Private Papers of Sir Douglas Haig, 1914–1919* (London, 1952), p. 221.
[52] Beatty to Lady Beatty, 24 June 1917; Beatty MSS.

strategic ideas of the Young Turks in the Fleet, Lloyd George made the charge that the First Sea Lord was not sufficiently alert to the possibilities of a more aggressive strategy by an overwhelming fleet. There was, as he put it, an 'atmosphere of crouching nervousness' at the Admiralty because of their 'lively apprehension' of the enemy's submarines. He was attracted to the possibility of more offensive operations in the Bight. Especially could he not understand why something was not done to destroy or neutralize the Flanders harbours which were used as enemy submarine and destroyer bases. He thought it was possible to find physical means of absolutely sealing up the exits from the bases. Sims's point of view was without question identical to that of the Admiralty. When Lloyd George expressed this opinion to him (17 April), Sims pointed out that nets, mines, and obstructions were no solution. That such methods 'inherently involve the added necessity of continuous protection and maintenance by our own Naval forces is seldom understood and appreciated. I finally convinced the Prime Minister of the fallacy of such propositions by describing the situations into which we would be led: namely, that in order to maintain our obstructions we would have to match the forces the enemy brought against them until finally the majority if not all of our forces would be forced into dangerous areas where they would be subject to continual torpedo and other attack, in fact in a position most favorable to the enemy.' The frequent heavy weather was a serious added difficulty, as the heaviest anchors used for nets, mines, and obstructions were swept away in a few hours. Moorings would not hold; they chafed through. 'The [English] Channel is not now, and never has been, completely sealed against submarine egress, let alone the vaster areas of escape to the north. Submarines have gone under mine-fields, and have succeeded in unknown ways in evading and cutting through nets and obstructions.'[53] Later in the spring the Prime Minister turned to a fresh tack. Why could the Fleet not turn its great guns on the Flanders harbours? We will be returning to this disagreement in a moment.

Jellicoe did not conceal his impatience with the Prime Minister's views on naval strategy. When he heard that Lloyd George was going to Rosyth, he reminded Beatty

[53] Sims to Josephus Daniels (Secretary of the U.S. Navy), 19 April 1917; Sims, *The Victory at Sea*, pp. 381-2.

what an impressionable man he is and how apt to fly off at a tangent. One has to be cautious in talking to him. He is a hopeless optimist and told me seriously the other day that he knew for a fact we could feed the population even if *all* our supplies from abroad were cut off!! He gets figures from any source and believes them if they suit his views. It is a continual fight to prevent more side shows being started. He is at present mad on one in Palestine, fed from the sea, and it is hopeless to get him to realise that every ship sent there means a drain on the Navy for protection.[54]

Lloyd George's eloquent persistence on behalf of a more aggressive use of the Fleet could not move Jellicoe. 'The caution of knowledge opposed itself to the valour of ignorance', as Ian Colvin says. The only naval measures deemed possible by the Naval Staff were long-range bombardments and mining operations. The very heavy German coast-defence batteries made most accurate shooting, and naval bombardments had consequently to be at long range and then only in fine weather with good visibility. But Lloyd George, like Winston Churchill in 1914–15, thought he knew better than the experts.

In one direction the Prime Minister did have a small measure of success. He had the idea of an 'offensive' section of the Staff. (Richmond, Hankey, and Dewar strongly influenced him in this matter.) His investigations on 30 April had proved to his satisfaction that the weakest point in the Admiralty organization was the lack of a thinking division—one charged with the investigation and preparation of large plans. The pressure of work in the Operations Division, which dealt with the actual conduct of current operations, left it little time to initiate plans for offensive operations. This Lloyd George held to be an important reason, apart from the inherently defensive strategy of the Admiralty, why no offensive naval operations were being undertaken from time to time. The Prime Minister and the War Cabinet made Carson aware that they were not happy with the situation.

Carson, too, felt that the Navy could be doing more, even if it involved risks. He, therefore, asked Beatty to consider using some of his forces 'in trying to prevent ingress and egress of submarines. . . . The sinking of ships goes on without abatement, and I have no doubt risks will have to be taken if we are to get at the root of the

[54] Jellicoe to Beatty, 12 April 1917; Beatty MSS.

evil—I mean of course well considered plans . . .'[55] Though not prepared to force his ideas on the Admirals, he did make this proposal to Jellicoe: 'Without entering into the question as to how far such criticism [public and official] is justified, *if at all*, it is clear to my mind that we ought to be in a position to silence it by being able to state positively that the possibility of taking the offensive at sea is continuously under review by the Naval Staff, and that Staff plans worked out in detail are constantly being put forward and considered.' He proposed that a special section be formed under the D.O.D. whose sole duty would be the examination and preparation of plans for offensive operations.[56] Jellicoe did not care much for the idea. He confided to the C.-in-C.: 'The six-monthly agitation for a "vigorous naval offensive" is beginning and the First Lord has been got hold of by the agitators and wants me to start a special staff to consider offensive operations *only*. This means that I shall get in any wild schemes produced for employing the Grand Fleet in southern waters. . . . I shall have to spend time which I can't afford in checking these schemes. If you can rub in to the First Lord the objections to risking the GF in such operations, you will help me. I don't think he needs much convincing.'[57] He had no powerful objections to a planning section as such; it would at any rate lessen criticism of Admiralty methods 'due to a want of knowledge of the circumstances'. He was not, however, prepared to see Richmond (who, he must have known, was no great admirer of his, and was, in any case, full of ideas for joint operations for which he had no use) head the new section, which is what the Prime Minister seemed to want. (Robertson, who was impressed with Richmond's reputation as 'a first-class naval officer who seems to have a General Staff mind', urged upon the Prime Minister, 26 May, that Richmond would be of far greater use on the Naval Staff than in a ship.) Jellicoe also put his foot down on the functions of the new section.

. . . there appears to be some misconception as to whose business it should be to initiate offensive operations. The proper officers for this duty are the senior officers of the War Staff, including myself, the D.C.N.S. and the Director of Operations. Obviously our experience fits us better for this purpose than the experience of more junior officers.

[55] Carson to Beatty, 20 June 1917; Admiralty MSS.
[56] Carson to Jellicoe, 7 June 1917; Admiralty MSS.
[57] Jellicoe to Beatty, 8 June 1917; Beatty MSS.

. . . Further, it is only by having a considerable knowledge of current operations that it is possible to say what vessels are available for carrying out any special offensive. The working out of *details of a plan* is of course another matter and is one for the proposed staff. . . . At the same time I would remark that I have been considering possible offensives ever since the commencement of the war, and I am fairly certain that there is no feasible operation the possibility of which has not been considered a great many times.[58]

On 16 July a Planning Section of the Operations Division was started. Its sole duty was to plan; it was not to initiate (to the grievous disappointment of the Young Turks). Captain Dudley Pound (formerly Captain of H.M.S. *Colossus*, 4th B.S.), a protégé of the onetime First Sea Lord, Admiral Sir Henry Jackson, became its head. Though himself a future wartime First Sea Lord (1939–1943), and more staff-minded than most officers of his time, Pound was not an ideal choice. He was a man of imposing physique, great mental capacity, good judgement, and simplicity of character, imperturbable, grim (but he often unbent), with a clear and logical mind, extraordinary power of concentration, and an enormous capacity for both work and play (he needed little sleep). At the same time he was too rigid, too methodical, too much a master of detail; and the evidence, though conflicting, would indicate that, like so many of his contemporaries, he was a supreme centralizer who did not know how to employ assistants. The whole of his staff consisted of himself, Dewar, Halliday (a marine officer), Kenworthy, and another officer, the latter two only for a special task the First Sea Lord gave the section on 31 July. 'Section 16 was the Cinderella of the Naval Staff', Dewar says. (Dewar continued with his weekly appreciation, doing both jobs until relieved on 15 August of the responsibility for the appreciation by Lieutenant-Colonel Beharrell, assisted by Captain T. C. Crease.)

The Prime Minister was 'hot for getting rid of Jellicoe', Hankey noted on 3 July after a visit to the Prime Minister. Yet he had to move slowly and with extreme caution. The Fleet as a whole, to say nothing of the general public, had not lost faith in Jellicoe, despite the impressions Lloyd George had carried away from his most recent visit to the Grand Fleet at the end of June. Even Beatty, for all his criticisms of his onetime Chief, had to admit to Carson that Jellicoe was the best possible man to be First Sea

[58] Jellicoe to Carson, 9 June 1917; Admiralty MSS.

Lord.[59] He tried to bolster Jellicoe's morale by advising him not 'to be worried by what the intriguers set themselves to do. And you must stick at all costs to your intention of not volunteering to go, that would be Fatal. Do not be goaded into any step of that kind no matter what the Press or anybody else says. History is only repeating itself and never did anybody occupy a Big Position but sooner or later somebody wanted to turn him out and nowadays the Press is the medium which is used for the purpose. But if you ignore entirely their insinuations and manoeuvrings you are in a very strong position. . . . Keep yourself fit and damn the Papers and the Critics.'[60]

Jellicoe was under no illusion as to the danger in which he stood.

I fancy there is a scheme afoot to get rid of me. The way they are doing it is to say that I am too pessimistic. This is because I point out the necessity for concentration of forces on the SM menace and the great danger of not being able to feed the Country. . . . I expect it will be done by first discrediting me in the Press . . . I've seen signs of it already. Of course, putting aside one's duty to the Country, I should be delighted to go, and have done with all politicians, but if I am of use here, in the opinion of the Navy, I certainly should not volunteer to go. I am not conceited, nor ambitious in the least, but I believe I *am* of some use here because I have both sea and office experience.[61]

Jellicoe's future largely depended on the First Lord's support. Carson would not hear of Jellicoe's removal and never wavered in his loyalty to him. He had great respect for the Admiral and liked and trusted him, which feelings were reciprocated by Jellicoe. The Admiral was, in Carson's opinion,

the best man at his job that I met with in the whole course of the War— for knowledge, calmness, straightness, and the confidence he inspired in his officers. . . . Mr. Lloyd George, indeed, was so rude to Admiral Jellicoe that the First Sea Lord came to me several times and pressed me to accept his resignation. 'As the Prime Minister had obviously no

[59] Carson's press interview; *Morning Post*, 24 September 1934.
[60] Beatty to Jellicoe, 2 June 1917; Jellicoe MSS. And a few weeks later (27 June): 'What we want now is closer communion between you and I and between us we can knock out any hair [*sic*] brained schemes. I will come down and see you if necessary but we must collaborate. There can be no question of any difference of opinion between us. I feel that when we meet and talk things over we always agree and we must present a broad and firm front to those gentlemen with wild cat schemes.' Jellicoe MSS.
[61] Jellicoe to Beatty, 30 June 1917; Beatty MSS.

confidence in him,' he argued, 'it would be better if the Government got someone in whom they trusted.' 'My dear Admiral,' I said, 'Who is your Ministerial chief?' and he replied, 'Why you, sir.' So I said, 'Have you ever found that I lacked confidence in you?' And he was good enough to reply that there were the happiest relations between us. 'Then, my dear Admiral,' I said, 'let me say to you what I should say to the youngest officer in the Service—"Carry on." '[62]

Since Carson refused to be the Prime Minister's hatchet man, some time late in April or in May Lloyd George decided to replace him. In Beaverbrook's words, 'the shield that sheltered Jellicoe must be thrust aside'. Quite apart from this consideration, Lloyd George was determined to get rid of the First Lord 'in the interests of Sir Edward Carson himself. His own exasperation at the obstacles thrown in the path of effective action was visibly telling on his strength. Someone was needed at the head of the Admiralty with a greater reserve of vitality, with more resource and greater mastery of detail.'[63] Also, somebody 'who was accustomed to force his will on his subordinates'. He had to move warily, as the First Lord had powerful friends in Parliament and the press, and he could be a terrible nuisance to the Government on the Opposition Bench.

The Service, getting wind of what was afoot, rallied behind Carson. Admiral Lord Beresford and Admiral of the Fleet Sir Hedworth Meux spoke out strongly in May, the latter telling a Liverpool audience (2 May): 'In Sir Edward Carson we have got what the Navy considers the right man. I hope you will not allow these [press] attacks . . . to drive him out of office.' Carson's friends were convinced that much of the bitter criticism of the Admiralty was inspired by his position as the leader of the Ulster Unionists, the alleged idea being to force Carson's resignation by discrediting the Admiralty.

Field-Marshal Sir Douglas Haig, the C.-in-C., played a key role in driving Carson out. He had a poor opinion of him as an administrator and felt that he was out of place as First Lord of the Admiralty. As for Jellicoe, initially Haig had 'liked very much what I saw of Jellicoe though I should not look on him as a man of great power or decision of character'.[64] After several meetings with the Admiral in the spring of 1917, his opinion of him soured.

[62] Carson's press interview; *Morning Post*, 24 September 1934.
[63] Lloyd George, *War Memoirs*, iii. 1176.
[64] Diary, 15 December 1916; Blake, *Haig*, p. 186.

199

'. . . I am afraid he does not impress me—Indeed, he strikes me as being an old woman!' In the same letter, Geddes 'ought really to be put in Carson's place as the latter is worn out'.[65] Haig had, in Lloyd George's words, 'great admiration for Jellicoe's knowledge as a technical sailor, but he thought him much too rigid, narrow and conservative in his ideas'.[66] Haig, furthermore, was alarmed over the inability of the Admiralty to do anything effective about the submarines. At the end of June, Haig launched what Beaver-brook describes as 'a well-organized, thoroughly considered and widespread campaign' to drive both Carson and Jellicoe from the Admiralty. It began with a conversation at the Admiralty with Geddes on 20 June that strengthened the Field-Marshal's distrust of the Naval High Command. He found the Controller full of charges and anything but loyal to his colleagues and superiors. Geddes was 'most anxious about the state of affairs at the Ad-miralty. The first Lord (Carson) has recently married, is very tired, and leaves everything to a number of incompetent sailors! Jellicoe, he says, is feeble to a degree and vacillating. Only one Admiral (Halsey) is fit for his post.'[67] Haig promised to arrange meetings with the King and the Prime Minister at which Geddes could explain the state of affairs at the Admiralty. That same day Jellicoe was guilty of a first-class gaffe that played directly into the hands of his enemies. The incident has to do with the impending Battle of Third Ypres. We must go back a way.

Ever since January 1915 the Admiralty had been interested in regaining the Belgian coast ports which were the bases of the Flanders submarines. Nothing had come of General Sir John French's plan to eject the enemy from Zeebrugge and Ostend through an amphibious operation.[68] At various times the Ad-miralty had tried to interest the Army in reviving the project or doing it alone. They received little encouragement, although desultory discussions were periodically carried on between the naval and military staffs. Thus, the First Sea Lord wrote at the end of 1915 (in a letter that reflects the cordiality of Admiralty-War Office relations): 'We are trying to get the Military to ad-vance along the Belgian coast and to try to take Ostend, from

[65] Haig to Lady Haig, 7 May 1917; *ibid.*, pp. 229–30.
[66] Lloyd George, *War Memoirs*, iii. 1176.
[67] Diary, 20 June 1917; Blake, *Haig*, p. 240. Lord Fisher was describing Carson at about this time as 'a tired, indolent, elderly lawyer, totally unfit for his position'.
[68] See *From the Dreadnought to Scapa Flow*, ii. 197–8.

PLATE V

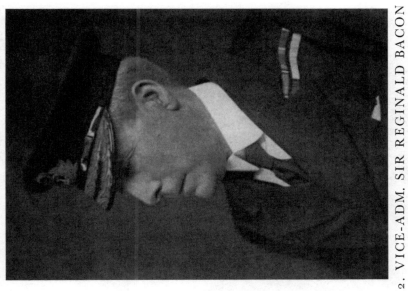

2. VICE-ADM. SIR REGINALD BACON
Commanding Dover Patrol, April 1915–
December 1917

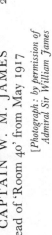

[Photograph: by permission of Miss D. C. Bacon]

1. CAPTAIN W. M. JAMES
Head of 'Room 40' from May 1917

[Photograph: by permission of
Admiral Sir William James]

PLATE VI

GROUP ON BOARD H.M.S. *QUEEN ELIZABETH*

Left to right: Rear-Admiral W. E. Goodenough; unknown; Beatty; the King of the Belgians; Vice-Admiral Sir John de Robeck, Commanding 2nd Battle Squadron; the Queen of the Belgians; Rear-Admiral Richard F. Phillimore, Commanding 1st Battle Cruiser Squadron; unknown; Rear-Admiral Sir O. de B. Brock

[Photograph: Imperial War Museum

which we can bombard Zeebrugge, but they are apathetic and it is a French job, and they I fear won't help us in any way. It is quite extraordinary to see that the Military seem to expect the Navy to be at their beck and call, and do exactly what they want, without any attempt at reciprocation.'[69] When the U-boat threat was intensified in the autumn of 1916, and the Germans staged their Zeebrugge-based destroyer raids into the Channel, the Admiralty pressed the matter once more, being convinced that these menaces could be 'practically eliminated' only by the destruction or capture of the enemy's naval bases on the Belgian coast. 'It would release an enormous number of small craft for work in other areas, making the English Channel immune from destroyer attack and raids, and give us in turn an advanced destroyer base which would be useful in protecting the Dutch trade.'[70] The First Lord, Balfour, followed this up with a memorandum for the War Committee that stressed the impossibility of isolating Ostend and Zeebrugge from the German bases that supplied them, via inland waterways and by 'creeping along the Dutch coast', with submarines, destroyers, mines, torpedoes, and guns. Bombardments by monitors and aircraft had impaired their efficiency as naval bases but had not destroyed them. Only a joint operation could achieve this by driving the Germans from the Belgian coast.[71]

On 21 November 1916 the War Committee went on record as favouring, 'if practicable', military action designed to occupy Ostend and Zeebrugge, or at least to render those ports useless as destroyer and submarine bases. 'There is no operation of war to which the Committee would attach greater importance . . .' A high-level conference at the War Office (Robertson, Haig, ackson, Oliver, Bacon) on 23 November agreed on the value of the operation, and on 1 December the C.I.G.S. informed the French C.-in-C., Marshal Joffre, that the British Government 'desire that the occupation of Ostend and Zeebrugge should form one of the objectives of the campaign next year'. Joffre approved the plan in principle. It was agreed that the main British effort on the Western Front in 1917 would be made in Flanders, with the primary object of countering the U-boat danger. The details of

---

[69] Jackson to Jellicoe, 21 November 1915; Jellicoe MSS.
[70] 'Combined Strategy in Connection with Submarines' (G.-97), by the First Sea Lord (H. B. Jackson) and C.O.S. (Oliver), 16 November 1916.
[71] 'The Navy, the Army, and the Belgian Coast', 19 November 1916; Asquith MSS.

the plan were worked out in the succeeding months. The First Sea Lord reminded the War Cabinet of the Navy's special interest in the forthcoming campaign:

The occupation and fortification of Zeebrugge and Ostend by the Germans has greatly added to the difficulties of the Navy. These ports, on which a large number of submarines and destroyers are based, are a constant menace to our cross-channel communications and to our south-eastern coasts. Their fortifications are very strong and they are quite invulnerable to purely naval attack. The canal system of Belgium makes it possible for the destroyers and submarines when not in use to be kept well inland at Bruges, where no form of attack, except air raids, can possibly reach them. Any further advance of the German armies along the North Coast of France would be *fatal* to our cross-channel communications.[72]

On 8 June 1917 the Prime Minister set up a Committee on War Policy under his own chairmanship, with Curzon, Milner, and Smuts (who had just become a member of the War Cabinet) as members. (Bonar Law was 'virtually a member', says Hankey, who was the Committee Secretary.) Whereas the War Cabinet settled 'immediate day-to-day problems', the new Committee would review war strategy as a whole. Its first task was to consider Haig's proposal for a major British offensive against the German lines in Flanders, designed, at a minimum, to clear the whole Belgian coast and roll back the German right flank. When the Committee pressed the Admiralty as to whether the Navy alone could not destroy Ostend and Zeebrugge as U-boat and destroyer bases with an intensive bombardment, thereby simplifying the military problem, Jellicoe scotched this idea. It was, he pointed out, impossible to destroy these harbours by a naval bombardment that was dependent on aerial spotting and had necessarily to be carried out by the monitors at ranges of 12 to 14 miles. A bombardment would only damage ships in harbour and destroy workshops and floating docks. The War Cabinet had recently suggested that battleships be used. But this was 'an operation which I am sure that no responsible naval officer would recommend, and it is, indeed, hardly practicable. The vicinity and approaches to these two ports have been heavily mined both by the Germans and ourselves and a great deal of minesweeping would be necessary

[72] Admiralty paper for the Imperial War Cabinet, 'A General Review of the Naval Situation' (G.T.-277), 24 March 1917.

before heavy ships could be brought into the neighbourhood, and even then the depth of water would not permit their getting in sight of their objective.'[73] Jellicoe's firm position did not enhance his popularity with the politicians. 'I have got myself much disliked by the Prime Minister and others because I have urged the necessity for this operation and *not* a purely naval bombardment, or rather & it, and have pointed out that a naval bombardment alone will never turn the Hun out of Zeebrugge and Ostend.'[74]

In a separate paper for the War Cabinet on 18 June, Jellicoe had commented on the profound importance of the capture and occupation of Ostend and Zeebrugge. He made his position even clearer two days later with a gloomy statement on the prospects of crushing the U-boat peril so long as the enemy had the use of the Belgian bases. Haig tells the story:

A most serious and startling situation was disclosed to-day. At to-day's Conference [of the War Policy Committee], Admiral Jellicoe, as

[73] Jellicoe's memorandum, 'Attacking Ostend and Zeebrugge', 18 June 1917; Jellicoe MSS. Attached was a Bacon memorandum in support of the Admiralty position. (Bacon always believed that engaging batteries was unprofitable, and that the only justification of a bombardment of Zeebrugge was the possibility of damaging the lock gates. They measured a mere 90 feet by 30 feet, so constituting a poor target, as a bombardment by three 15-inch monitors on 12 May proved; there were no hits on the locks. Bacon estimated 'the mathematical chance of hitting a lock-gate at Zeebrugge from a bombarding distance, assuming absolutely accurate aiming, was once every sixty-seven rounds'. The actual chances of hitting from a moving platform—a ship at sea—were 'considerably less'. Bacon, *The Dover Patrol*, i. 112. The bombardment of 12 May and one of Ostend on 5 June, also by monitors, inflicted damage without appreciably hampering German operations from these bases.) The Prime Minister had already been rebuffed by the C.-in-C. when he tried to win Beatty's support for a purely naval bombardment, whether of the Belgian coast ports or Heligoland, Borkum, or Sylt. (This was on about 1 June, during a visit to the Grand Fleet.) It was a futile policy, Beatty had assured him. And to Jellicoe on 2 June: 'It is quite amazing the false ideas that are held by some as to the power of a ship's artillery. . . . But I think he was relieved to find that the opinions of the Sea Officers and the Admiralty were the same, and we were in line.' Jellicoe MSS. The First Sea Lord also received support from Corbett, who was then with the Historical Section of the otherwise defunct (for the duration) Committee of Imperial Defence. He confirmed Jellicoe's impression that 'the use of a fleet by itself to bombard coast defences with the object of forcing the enemy fleet to sea or of destroying it inside the defences has seldom, if ever, been attempted. Against an effective fleet and effective defences it has certainly never been undertaken with success. . . . Our own practice may I think be summarized thus: A main fleet has never been used by itself to attack main bases or the fleet they contained, but it has been occasionally used to cover such attacks by specially prepared vessels. Nor am I aware of any real departure from this principle by the fleet of any other Power.' Corbett to the D.N.I., Hall (who had made the query at Jellicoe's request), 16 July 1917; Admiralty MSS.
[74] Jellicoe to Beatty, 30 June 1917; Beatty MSS.

First Sea Lord, stated that owing to the great shortage of shipping due to German submarines, it would be impossible for Great Britain to continue the war in 1918. This was a bombshell for the Cabinet and all present. A full enquiry is to be made as to the real facts on which this opinion of the Naval Authorities is based. No one present shared Jellicoe's view, and all seemed satisfied that the food reserves in Great Britain are adequate. Jellicoe's words were, 'There is no good discussing plans for next Spring—We cannot go on.'[75]

Lloyd George challenged 'this startling and reckless declaration', but he could not shake the First Sea Lord. After the meeting, the Admiral told Smuts that he had, if anything, underestimated the case. Jellicoe did his cause no good by this 'bombshell'. 'This example of Jellicoe's pessimism,' wrote Hankey, 'which had already caused annoyance owing to its effect on [General] Pershing and the Americans generally, caused great irritation.'[76] Jellicoe's opinion was a firm conviction, not a spur-of-the-moment effusion. In the following weeks he returned to the theme of the imperative necessity of clearing the Belgian coast. 'I say that if we wait till next year we may never get the chance and we must get the north coast of Belgium before the winter sets in.'[77]

War Policy Committee discussions on Haig's plan, which had begun on 19 June, when Haig had explained his plan in detail, continued over the next month. It was not until 25 July, six days before the British offensive was due to start, that the War Cabinet definitely approved the Flanders offensive—on Lloyd George's part, with reluctance and grave misgivings. Jellicoe's views may have tipped the balance, for they had made a considerable impression upon most of the Committee.

The Navy's share in the campaign was to be the landing of a division of Rawlinson's 4th Army, with a large number of tanks and some artillery, from monitors early in August. The tanks and guns would be landed over specially designed pontoons, each of which would be pushed on to the beach, broadside-on, by two monitors abreast of one another. The landing would be effected on the Belgian coast near Westende, so as to turn the enemy's flank and drive them out of Ostend, Zeebrugge, and Bruges. The signal for this operation would be given when the British Army had

[75] Diary, 20 June 1917; Blake, *Haig*, pp. 240–1.
[76] Diary, 30 June 1917; Hankey, *The Supreme Command*, ii. 654.
[77] Jellicoe to Beatty, 10 July 1917; Beatty MSS.

reached Roulers—between 4 and 8 August was the date given to Beatty. Beatty was dubious about the Navy's role. 'Presumably the Navy is not required to do more than convoy the 24,000 men and Tanks to the Beach. The only protection provided by them will be that of a smoke screen—always a doubtful factor. And the Military engage to overcome by intense artillery fire all opposition to the Landing. This sounds a very optimistic view and until one knows more not a very possible one. If the Land Artillery can do so much it is difficult to understand why it is necessary to land a flanking party such a very short distance behind Enemy trenches but no doubt all this will become clear when we have the Plans.'[78] De Robeck (Commanding 2nd B.S.) also, with his vast experience at Gallipoli in 1915, was, Madden reported, 'most decided that a successful landing was impossible'.[79] These fears did not materialize. Jellicoe did not think the coast operation would bring out the High Seas Fleet: the Germans were more likely to send out some light cruisers and destroyers, therefore they should consider reinforcing Tyrwhitt.[80] It, too, was an academic question. Since Haig's advance never got as far as Roulers, the Navy played no role in Third Ypres (or Passchendaele, as the battle is commonly known). Haig called off the joint operation on 23 September.

Was clearing the Belgian coast vital to the offensive against the U-boats? Captain Roskill has shown that the Flanders flotillas were accounting for very nearly a third of the mercantile sinkings (February–May 1917), and the High Seas Fleet flotillas (which generally operated from Kiel and Wilhelmshaven), slightly over two-thirds, but that the capture of the Flanders bases would in fact not have materially affected the U-boat campaign. Had the Army seriously threatened Ostend and Zeebrugge, the Germans would in all probability have shifted the two flotillas eastwards to Kiel and Wilhelmshaven. 'This would have reduced their effectiveness somewhat, especially in attacking our Channel shipping, but it is difficult to believe that their accomplishments would have fallen very appreciably. . . . The U-boat campaign should not have been allowed to exert the influence that it undoubtedly did exert on the land operations in Flanders . . .'[81]

[78] Beatty to Jellicoe, 13 July 1917; Jellicoe MSS.
[79] Madden to Jellicoe, 13 July 1917; Jellicoe MSS.
[80] Jellicoe to Beatty, 4 July 1917; Beatty MSS.
[81] Roskill, 'The U-boat Campaign of 1917 and Third Ypres', *Royal United Service Institution Journal*, October 1959. Roskill's case is even stronger than he states, since his

Roskill goes too far when he suggests elsewhere that Haig's persistence in continuing into the autumn what Lloyd George afterwards called 'one of the blackest horrors of history' was determined in part by Jellicoe's 'ominous forecast' about losing the war if the Flanders bases were not captured.[82] Jellicoe's strong support of the campaign on naval grounds, and his lugubrious forecasts of what would happen if the enemy were not cleared from the Belgian coast, was a major factor in the Army's decision to launch the Flanders campaign and in Lloyd George's refusal to overrule the Generals. (Petain's confidential revelations of the mutinous state of the French Army and his insistence that the British must maintain maximum pressure on the enemy was at least as important a factor in Haig's decision as Jellicoe's anxieties.) But as the battle continued, it was dominated more and more by its own internal impulses, and the original objectives (Ostend, Zeebrugge, Roulers) were lost to view. The crux of the matter, as John Terraine has written, was that: 'Fundamentally, the Flanders campaign had two objectives: to clear the Belgian coast, and thereby remove the menace of the German U-boat bases at Ostend and Zeebrugge, to which the Admiralty attached such undue importance; to capture or dominate by artillery the railway center of Roulers, on which the whole German position in western Flanders largely depended. . . . But Roulers lies northeast of Ypres; Ostend lies due north. The axes of these projected advances pulled away from each other; only immense force, or a correspondingly weakened enemy, could make the pursuit of both at the same time feasible.'[83]

We must return to our main theme. On 25 June, Haig saw Lloyd George, Curzon, Balfour, and Asquith, separately, preaching to all the sermon that the very unsatisfactory state of affairs at the Admiralty was a serious matter calling for quick action.[84] The

---

calculations leave out the Mediterranean losses. The Flanders boats accounted for no more than 24.5 per cent of all shipping losses in February–May 1917. As a matter of interest: Mediterranean, 22 per cent, High Seas Fleet U-boats, 52.5 per cent, Baltic and Black Sea, 1 per cent.

[82] Roskill, *The Strategy of Sea Power* (London, 1962), p. 132. He is not alone. Keyes afterwards told Richmond that 'the Passchendaele offensive had to be kept going because J. said that unless the Army captured Ostend and Zeebrugge, we could not continue the war . . .' Diary, 1 July 1919; *Portrait of an Admiral*, p. 353.

[83] Terraine, *The Great War, 1914–1918: a Pictorial History* (New York, 1965), pp. 305–6.

[84] This may have been the occasion of which Lloyd George speaks in his *War Memoirs* (iii. 1176): 'A conversation I had with Sir Douglas Haig in the early summer of 1917 finally decided me.'

next day there was a celebrated breakfast party at 10 Downing Street. Present were Lloyd George, Haig, Milner, and Geddes. The Admiralty and its inefficiency was the subject of discussion. Geddes repeated what he had told Haig on 20 June. The upshot is described by Haig. 'The proposal [by Lloyd George] to put Robertson in Carson's place was considered, replacing Jellicoe and two or three other "numbskulls" now on the Board, etc. . . . L.G. said he was firmly decided to take immediate action to improve matters, but was uncertain as to what was the best decision to take at present.'[85] Robertson, approached that day by Haig, refused to consider going to the Admiralty on the ground that he would have to become a politician! This was just as well. The C.I.G.S. had sound judgement and was a veritable work horse, but he was unimaginative and understood little about politics.

On 28 June Haig returned to France. Lord Beaverbrook speculates on the 'real motives' of Haig's 'intrigues' in London. 'It may have been that he was moved by genuine anxiety. . . . Or again, it is possible that he may have been interested mainly in diverting the lightning from striking at himself, for the dismissal of Haig had been a principal objective of Lloyd George for many months.'[86] It is my guess that it was the former, with the shared alarm over Jellicoe's views drawing the Prime Minister and the Field-Marshal into a temporary alliance, despite their differences over military strategy.

It was Milner (well described by L. S. Amery as 'the acknowledged mainstay of the War Cabinet') who came up (26 June) with a simple and diplomatic solution to the Carson problem: Geddes to become First Lord and Carson to be booted up to the War Cabinet. 'The Prime Minister seized on the Milner Plan. It brought wonderful relief and a magnificent escape from the perils of political strife with Carson.'[87] Curzon and Bonar Law threw their support to Lloyd George, as did Maclay in a forceful letter of 28 June on Admiralty maladministration. '. . . private meetings are being held of shipmasters and others, to consider the position and there is a danger that unless something is done in connection with the Admiralty, we shall have these men refusing to go to sea. Statistics prove that what are called the areas of concentration as

---

[85] Diary, 26 June 1917; Blake, *Haig*, p. 242.
[86] Beaverbrook, *Men and Power*, p. 166.
[87] *Ibid.*, p. 169.

now managed, have become veritable death traps for our Mercantile Marine and our men are realising this. . . . The confidence of our Mercantile Marine in the Admiralty has been frittered away and does not now exist.' Maclay sent a copy of the letter to Bonar Law with a covering note: 'Changes are wanted right from the top downwards, and the position should be faced.'[88]

Lloyd George still hesitated, undecided as to Carson's successor, though leaning towards Geddes. For a few days at the end of June he was strongly inclined to Hankey, who, with support from Milner, talked him out of it. Hankey protested his unfitness for the post, and Milner convinced the Prime Minister that Hankey was 'practically irreplaceable' as Secretary of the War Cabinet.[89] By 3 July Lloyd George was definitely for Geddes, and on the 5th he informed the King of the contemplated change. 'He seriously contemplates making *changes at the Admiralty*. When he visited the Grand Fleet last week he gathered that there was dissatisfaction with the Admiralty: the Government are of the same opinion. Sir John Jellicoe is too pessimistic: if things do not go quite right he "is apt to get 'cold feet': grouses: says the war can't go on many months more etc. etc." . . . He is inclined to put Sir E. Carson into the War Cabinet. . . . the man he had in his mind [to succeed Carson] was Sir Eric Geddes.'[90] The King raised no objections.

On 6 July Lloyd George made the plunge: through a letter by messenger late that night, he invited Carson to join the War Cabinet. 'We need your insight, courage and judgment.' (Also, as he had told the King, Carson's speech-making talents were needed. Few members of the Government were able to attract public audiences.) Carson's response was cool. The vacillating Prime Minister retreated (7 July) and told him he could remain at the Admiralty, if he preferred. Finally, there was Milner's catalytic letter of 16 July, insisting that the matter was urgent and there must be no further delay in announcing the changes, as 'the longer we wait, the more likely is it that something will get out, and then the papers will begin gossiping and criticising and the

[88] *Ibid.*, p. 170.
[89] Diary, 30 June, 3 July 1917; Hankey, *The Supreme Command*, ii. 654–5.
[90] Stamfordham's memorandum for the King of his conversation that afternoon with the Prime Minister, 5 July 1917; Windsor MSS. The italics represent the King's underscoring.

whole thing will be blown upon.'[91] The next day the changes in the Government were announced in the press: Carson to the War Cabinet, Geddes to the Admiralty, Churchill to the Ministry of Munitions, and certain other changes. Geddes was sworn in as First Lord on 20 July.

Geddes was 'fully aware of the sacrificial lamb technique, and was most unwilling to accept political office. Ll.G. insisted . . .'[92] Carson was not happy with the change in his position. He was 'rather sick about it', thought one Minister, who 'gathered that he had not discussed it beforehand with L.G. to the same extent as I had and that this apparently needless abruptness was rather a blow to him'.[93] But his patriotism triumphed over his deeply wounded feelings. Carson's transfer to the War Cabinet at a time when, it was said, his work at the Admiralty was beginning to bear fruit, was regarded by the Conservative press and the Navy as a very real loss to the country. He had established himself in the confidence and the trust of both the Admiralty and the Navy. 'I weep', Tyrwhitt wrote, 'to think that Carson has gone. . . . I think he was the best 1st Lord we've had for years and knew a great deal more than people thought.'[94] The Liberal press, on the other hand, was glad to see him go—a 'new guidance or stimulus' was required to meet the submarine problem.

Carson's tenure of office as First Lord had been the shortest since that of the Marquess of Ripon (February–August 1886). Notwithstanding the exceptional difficulties with which he had to contend during these few months, and the fact that he never had a reasonable chance to show his administrative talents, he often told his wife in later years that, with all the anxieties, his time at the Admiralty was one of the happiest of his life.

With Carson out of the Admiralty, what future did Jellicoe have? The answer would come from Geddes, and it would be determined largely by the status of the war at sea in the weeks and months to come.

[91] Lloyd George MSS.
[92] Geddes, *The Forging of a Family*, p. 242.
[93] Diary, 17 July 1917; Christopher Addison, *Four and a Half Years* (London, 1934, 2 vols), ii. 411.
[94] Tyrwhitt to Keyes, 20 July 1917; Keyes MSS.

PART II

Ebbing of the Tide:
the Jellicoe–Geddes Period
July 1917 – December 1917

VIII

A Revolution at the Admiralty

(July 1917 – October 1917)

As First Lord of the Admiralty, Geddes' overriding vitality was soon felt in every branch of activity. Difficulties and hesitancies disappeared in every direction. There was a quickening in action all round. The convoy system at last had a fair chance. . . . The attack on the submarine was developed. . . . Best of all, there was real drive put into all these operations.

LLOYD GEORGE, *War Memoirs.*

[Geddes] is of course profoundly ignorant of the Navy though good at a railway!

JELLICOE to a friend, 29 December 1917.

I. THE GEDDES RÉGIME

GEDDES OFFICIALLY succeeded Carson on 20 July 1917. Although he was new to ministerial office, his remarkable ability, enormous energy, initiative, resourcefulness, courage, talent for administration, and experience in many fields were well known, and the nation welcomed his appointment. Businessmen, incidentally, were by no means rare birds as civilian heads of the Admiralty. Lords Cawdor and Goschen, Lord George Hamilton, and W. H. Smith were evidence of that.

The Navy was not exactly enthusiastic over Geddes's appointment. It wondered whether he had not been put in as an unconscious 'warming-pan' for Churchill—a frightening prospect! The Service press hoped that Geddes would quit 'masquerading' as an admiral (he did revert to mufti) and not be tempted to form 'crude and uninstructed opinions on matters of strategy and tactics' and otherwise interfere with the Naval Staff. The Service was, nevertheless, prepared to give the new First Lord the benefit of the doubt, particularly after his promise to his constituents not to interfere with strategy. (Geddes was adopted by Cambridge University so that he could have a place in Parliament from which to answer questions and expound naval policy.) Thus, Rear-Admiral Evan-Thomas wrote to his sister-in-law: 'We have made the great Enrico Geddes now First Lord of the Admiralty—the other day assistant manager of a Railway—a bullet-headed sort of a cove who anyway looks you straight in the face which is more than those confounded Politicians will do. So perhaps he will suit us quite well.'[1] Even those officers who disliked or distrusted Geddes as First Lord did not question his ability or driving power.

Geddes, we learn on good authority, was astonished 'at the lack of any method of conducting Board meetings—the vagueness, the lack of preparation, & the absence of minutes, the amateurishness of the whole concern'.[2] For this reason, among others, the strong man kicked up a tempest during his first months. 'Geddes took a long time to settle down', Hankey recalls. 'It was not a post that he took to rapidly and at first he was inclined to be impatient, restless and suspicious of outside interference. . . .'[3] Oliver found the commotion disturbing. 'We have been upside down here ever since the North-Eastern Railway took over the management, but manage to worry along somehow doing our jobs.'[4] Beatty, on the other hand, heard there was 'a different atmosphere at the Admiralty now. Everything is much more alive and even J. R. J. [Jellicoe] is more cheerful and not so pessimistic.'[5]

Geddes acquired a high level of naval expertise in a hurry. According to Sims, 'In a short time he had acquired a knowledge of the naval situation which enabled him to preside over an international naval council with a very complete grasp of all the problems which were presented. I have heard the great naval specialists who attended say that, had they not known the real fact, they

[1] Evan-Thomas to Mrs. Thomas Barnard, 26 July 1917; Evan-Thomas MSS.
[2] Richmond's diary, 16 August 1917; *Portrait of an Admiral*, p. 267. Richmond's informant was his father-in-law, Sir Hugh Bell, who as a director of the North-Eastern Railway knew Geddes intimately. Geddes transformed the casual system. Meetings were now held at regular intervals, preceded in good time by an agenda and a précis of information on the matters due for discussion. Minutes were kept, decisions were made by vote, recorded by the Secretary, and circulated by him for action to the departments affected.
[3] Hankey, *The Supreme Command*, ii. 655. It could not have improved Geddes's temper that, in the midst of all the initial tribulations, he had to beat down a suggestion from Lady Londonderry that the light cruiser *Cavendish*, soon to be launched, have her name changed to that of her distinguished ancestor, *Castlereagh*. He also found himself involved in the sticky problem of passages for women to and from India.
[4] From the Oliver MSS.; James, *A Great Seaman*, p. 189.
[5] Beatty to Lady Beatty, 26 September 1917; Beatty MSS.

would hardly have suspected that Sir Eric was not a naval man.'[6]

Sir Alan Anderson, for years one of the heads of the Orient Line, took Geddes's place as Controller. Geddes assigned responsibility for the administration of the business relating to the *matériel* of the Navy to the Controller for 'design and production', and to the Third Sea Lord, Halsey, for 'requirements of design'. This was only the first of the important personnel and organizational changes made at the Admiralty at this time.

Sir W. Graham Greene had been Permanent Secretary of the Admiralty since 1911. In Beatty's words, he was 'one of those half dead men'. The then Secretary to the Civil Lord sums him up as 'a dry old stick, a bachelor, devoted to the office, experienced, prudent and precise'.[7] He was a tireless worker (he often remained at the Admiralty until 2 a.m.) who had performed his duties without fanfare. Sir Vincent Baddeley, who served under Graham Greene, considered him 'one of the ablest civil servants of his generation'. Lloyd George, however, had no confidence in him. He had never seen Graham Greene, but he was strongly influenced in the matter by Hankey. Graham Greene was dragging his feet over executing the recommendations for Admiralty reorganization in the Lloyd George–Hankey paper of 30 April. Hankey was incensed and protested violently to the Prime Minister. The *Daily Mail* (2 May), undoubtedly inspired by Downing Street, found a 'grave flaw' in the Admiralty organization which was 'prejudicial to our chances of success in grappling with the German submarines'. This was the presence on the Board of Graham Greene, who 'holds in his hands all the strings of the Admiralty, and . . . exercises more actual power than any of the Sea Lords, including probably the First Sea Lord himself . . . the enervating influence of the secretariat.' This was going too far. The charge (repeated on 5 May) was nonsense and revealed an abysmal ignorance of the workings of the Admiralty. The Secretary was a member of the Board (though not a *full* member, that is, a Lord Commissioner, until 31 October 1921), but he filled that position largely so that he might keep in touch with proceedings and see that its decisions

---

[6] Sims, *The Victory at Sea*, p. 259. Archibald Hurd flatly contradicts this judgement. 'He was a man after Lloyd George's heart—cheerful, confident, always in a hurry to produce results. No men more ignorant of naval affairs were ever associated together than the Prime Minister and Geddes.' Hurd, *Who Goes There?* (London, 1942), p. 139.

[7] Mr. Norman Macleod's letter to the author, 26 March 1966.

were carried out. Otherwise his job was to co-ordinate the work of the departments, to act as adviser on administrative matters, and to regulate the civil side of the administration. Graham Greene had performed these duties ably. As for the alleged connexion between him and the submarine menace, this hardly calls for comment. No matter. For some time the Prime Minister had been asking Carson to dismiss Graham Greene. Having full confidence in him, Carson had refused to do the Prime Minister's bidding. The new First Lord, who had no use for Graham Greene, put up no fight, and now, at the end of July, he asked the Secretary for his resignation. He gave no reason. There was general satisfaction with the announcement that Sir Oswyn Murray would succeed Graham Greene on 7 August. (Churchill welcomed the opportunity to add the latter to his staff as Secretary.)

Murray had been associated with the Admiralty for 20 years, following a brilliant career at Oxford (firsts in 'Mods', 'Greats', and Jurisprudence at Exeter), since 1911 as Assistant Secretary. He remained Secretary until his death in 1936. Those in a position to know believe that he was probably the ablest Secretary of the Admiralty in modern times—'conscientious, painstaking, efficient and absolutely reliable . . . He never showed himself keen to push himself forward . . . In administration I believe he showed himself firm, conciliatory and impartial.'[8] What first impressed Norman Macleod was 'his ability to find solutions to the most complicated and difficult administrative problems . . . Murray displayed what the Greeks called *epieikeia*, sweet reasonableness, which never failed to carry conviction whether he was giving evidence before a Royal Commission or taking part in a Committee meeting . . . It was extraordinarily difficult to find good reasons for differing from him.'

Graham Greene's departure presaged his own fate, thought Jellicoe. 'It will not be long before I too am retired,' he told Graham Greene in August.[9] A more positive harbinger was Burney's retirement. On 17 July Lloyd George summoned Jellicoe to 10 Downing Street and informed him that the Second Sea Lord, Burney, and the D.C.N.S., Oliver, must go. Jellicoe recommended

---

[8] Graham Greene in a memorandum on Murray, 21 December 1937; Graham Greene MSS.

[9] Ian Colvin, *The Life of Lord Carson* (London, 1932–6, 3 vols., vol. i by Edward Marjoribanks), iii. 275.

PLATE VII

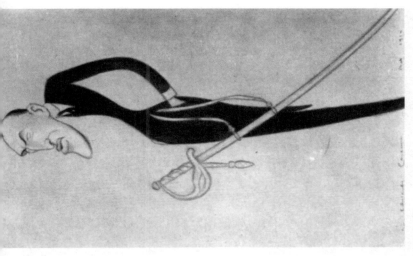

SIR EDWARD CARSON
First Lord of the Admiralty, December 1916–July 1917

1. Photograph at Admiralty House :
by permission of the Ministry of Defence

2. Caricature by Max Beerbohm :
National Portrait Gallery

PLATE VIII

SIR ERIC GEDDES

Controller of the Admiralty, May–July 1917, First Lord of the
Admiralty from July 1917.

[*Painting by James McNalty : by permission of Sir Reay Geddes*

Burney's retention but was not prepared to force the issue. Oliver was another matter. He had been Jellicoe's principal assistant on the Naval Staff and, having been there since the fourth month of the war, was intimately acquainted with the work. If Oliver left the Board, he, Jellicoe, would have to consider his own position.

The Prime Minister [recounts Jellicoe] thereupon remarked that I was bound by the same rules as any midshipman and must do as I was told. But I informed him that there was no Board in existence owing to the change of 1st Lord and that I should certainly consider myself free to decline an invitation to join the New Board were Sir H. Oliver omitted. A prolonged discussion took place but I refused to alter my decision. Sir Eric Geddes argued with me at some length after the meeting broke up, but failed to shake me. I eventually said that I was going up to the Grand Fleet the next day on business and would consult Sir D. Beatty and Sir C. Madden on the subject of my retention of office or otherwise. This I did. Both these officers urged me most strongly to remain at the Admiralty . . . whatever happened in regard to Sir H. Oliver.[10]

On his return to the Admiralty, Jellicoe once more tried to keep Burney on the Board, because, he claimed, he possessed greater sea experience than any other flag officer, as well as good judgement, attributes essential in a Second Sea Lord, who was responsible for naval operations in the First Sea Lord's absence. He was also thoroughly qualified to carry out his ordinary duties, which dealt with fleet personnel. As regards Oliver, Jellicoe reiterated his position. Oliver's 'intimate knowledge of the whole course of the war . . . is an invaluable asset. It enables him to forecast the meaning and probable effect of any move on the part of the enemy. I have rarely known him to err in any forecast that he has made . . . and his continued close association with the War Office staff is very useful in all matters relating to troop movements and other military business. . . . I should view with the very greatest apprehension his removal from his present position. It would certainly be most detrimental to the naval conduct of the war and, by throwing upon me the large amount of detail work of which his experience enables me at present to be relieved, would prevent me from devoting sufficient attention to the larger questions involved.'[11]

[10] Jellicoe's autobiographical notes. The Prime Minister's objections to Oliver's remaining at the Admiralty 'were based upon the personal dislike conceived by the Prime Minister for Sir H. Oliver. The latter stated his ideas too bluntly and plainly before the War Council [War Cabinet] to suit Mr. Lloyd George.' *Ibid.*
[11] Jellicoe to Lloyd George, 28 July 1917; *ibid.*

The incident was closed with a compromise. Oliver was permitted to stop and Burney was relieved by Vice-Admiral Sir Rosslyn Wemyss on 7 August. Jellicoe had not been able to prevent the sacking of his old and reliable friend, Burney, although he 'deeply regretted' it and was 'very sorry' about him. 'It is a great blow to anyone's pride to be moved without any reason being assigned and he feels it greatly.'[12] Burney was sacked because of the widely held belief that he was worn out and had become an obstructionist, and that such a person, who acted for the First Sea Lord when the latter was absent, was a positive danger. Not a single flag officer afloat supported Burney.[13] The affair marked the beginning of a distinct coolness in the relations between Jellicoe and Geddes.

2. FURTHER REORGANIZATION

Lloyd George had not dared to force Jellicoe's resignation on an issue, the Burney-Oliver affair, that would have brought the wrath of the Fleet upon his head. Geddes had, furthermore, accepted his position on the understanding that Jellicoe should not be relieved immediately. 'Geddes knew', says Lloyd George, 'that Jellicoe had the confidence of the senior officers in the Navy, and that it would therefore be a distinct advantage to secure his co-operation if that were at all possible. He promised to tell me without delay if he found that he could not work with or through him. It was not long before he discovered that the proper co-ordination and full efficiency of the Admiralty were being seriously handicapped by personal factors, among which was the lack of sympathetic confidence between Admiral Beatty . . . and Admiral Jellicoe . . . After consultation with me, Geddes decided to bring in a Deputy First Sea Lord, to facilitate co-operation between the Grand Fleet, the Harwich Force, and the Admiralty.'[14] This was one aspect of the major overhaul of the organization of the Board of Admiralty in September and October.

The substance of an important memorandum of 10 September over the First Lord's signature, but which represented a com-

[12] Jellicoe to Beatty, 4 August 1917; Beatty MSS. Jellicoe's recommendation of Burney for a baronetcy was turned down; he did achieve this honour in 1921.
[13] Madden to Jellicoe, 7 August 1917, on Geddes's authority; Jellicoe MSS. Burney eventually (13 October) was appointed C.-in-C., Coast of Scotland (Rosyth).
[14] Lloyd George, *War Memoirs*, iii. 1177–8.

promise between Geddes's proposals and Jellicoe's ideas, was as follows:

. . . when the Board is a large one dealing with a wide range of subjects of great complexity and diversity, it can only satisfactorily function as a Board on a limited number of important matters of principle.

It cannot to-day so function on operational instructions . . . issued in its name at all hours of the day and night . . . In fact in the present war at any rate the Board of Admiralty has never so functioned, and in my opinion cannot do so. The position is unsatisfactory, however, to me as First Lord, to the Board as a whole, to the First Sea Lord who is Chief of the Naval Staff, and to his Deputy and Assistant, who in the name of the Board deal with operational matters by telegraph continuously without any possibility of consultation with their colleagues. . . . It is in my opinion desirable that the duties and responsibilities of the Naval Staff and of the Board as a whole should be more clearly defined . . . [My scheme] has the result of strengthening the Board's control by delegation and definition, and has also the effect of regularising the position and responsibilities of the Chief of the Naval Staff. In other words, the steps proposed would make the theoretical collective responsibility of the Board . . . more of a reality in respect of matters of principle, whilst relieving it as far as possible of a fictitious responsibility in respect of detailed executive orders. . . . [The position of the Second Sea Lord was unsatisfactory.] Although not in intimate touch with operations from day to day it is his duty, by virtue of his personal seniority, as also by tradition, to relieve the First Sea Lord and take charge of operations in his absence . . . It cannot in my opinion be a satisfactory arrangement for the Second Sea Lord to take control of operational matters possibly for one night only when he is not in close touch with them in his work. . . . The Naval Staff engaged in War plans have admittedly not expanded as they would have liked to do and should have done. . . . [The remedies follow.]

In the first place, I propose that day to day operational and executive orders should be issued in the name of the Chief of the Naval Staff more or less as is the case with C.I.G.S. to-day. . . . I also propose that the Second Sea Lord should in future be, both in name and in fact, the Deputy First Sea Lord . . .

In the next place, it is proposed to group the Members of the Board into two recognised Committees:—

(1) The *Operations Committee*, consisting of—First Sea Lord and Chief of the Naval Staff, Deputy First Sea Lord, Deputy Chief of Naval Staff, Assistant Chief of Naval Staff, and Fifth Sea Lord, as necessary; and (2) The *Maintenance Committee*, consisting of—Second Sea Lord, Third Sea Lord, Fourth Sea Lord, Controller, Civil Lord

[a second Civil Lord was added in January 1918], Financial Secretary, with Fifth Sea Lord attending as necessary. [The Deputy First Sea Lord was later added to represent the Operations Committee.] The First Lord would be ex officio Chairman of both Committees. . . .

Further, it was proposed to add to the Naval Staff a Plans Division to deal with the 'consideration and preparation of strategic plans and questions of policy for Operations Committee' and with the 'consideration of and proposals for use of new weapons and *matériel*.' (See below.) A new division under a Director of Training was to deal with principles of training of all officers and ratings in combatant and staff duties, complements and establishments, staff duties, training and organization and the compilation of manuals and text books. A new division under a Director of Mercantile Movements would take over all work of convoy, escort, and routeing.

By these reforms it was hoped:

(1) To ensure that matters of great importance and high policy be referred to the Board collectively.

(2) To decentralise the business coming to the Board by utilising the Operations or Maintenance Committees of the Board as a sieve before matters come to the Board.

(3) To strengthen and improve the Naval Staff side of the Admiralty, and to provide for skilled and untrammelled consideration of War problems.

(4) To define and fix responsibility for naval operations orders, and regularise and limit the present procedure which permits unlimited power to be exercised without the authority of the Board as a whole, or of any constituted section thereof.

(5) To do so without in any way limiting or abrogating the responsibility to the Crown and Parliament of the First Lord.[15]

The various proposals received Cabinet approval and were implemented in the course of the following weeks.

The division of the Admiralty organization into two sides was Jellicoe's particular contribution to the reorganization. He defined the duties of the Operations Committee as follows: 'It will deal with the questions of naval strategy, operation of policy, and other subjects connected with the provision, equipment, efficiency, organisation, and utilisation of the Navy as a fighting force.' It

---

[15] Geddes, 'Memorandum on Admiralty Organisation' (G.T.-2003).

met once or twice a month, and in practice was concerned more with problems of *matériel*. The function of the Maintenance Committee was 'to deal with questions affecting the provision of personnel, matériel, and important supplies, the carrying out of works and other subjects connected with the efficient maintenance of the Fleet in accordance with the wishes of the Operations Committee'. When the subjects dealt with by the Committees were of great importance, they were to be referred to the whole Board of Admiralty, either by the First Lord or by the decision of the Committee concerned.

The titles of the Sea Lords were expanded to indicate their respective sphere of responsibility: Second Sea Lord and Chief of Naval Personnel; Third Sea Lord and Chief of Naval Matériel; Fourth Sea Lord and Chief of Supplies and Transport; Fifth Sea Lord and Chief of Naval Air Service.

One feature in the reorganization, the institution of the Plans Division, put a great strain on Jellicoe's relations with Geddes. As we have seen, Jellicoe had established a Plans Section of the Operations Division of the Naval Staff. When Geddes proposed to convert this section into a division of the Staff, separate and distinct from the Operations Division, Jellicoe 'objected very strongly to this, pointing out that the plans could not be made independently of the Director of the Operations Division, as the Plans Section would not be conversant with the daily movements of the Fleet, and would have an insufficient knowledge of vessels which were available for various operations and that the proposed arrangement would inevitably lead to much confusion. I saw that it was useless to press my objections to the point of resignation, and therefore gave in, intending that the Director of Plans, although nominally independent of the Director of Operations, should work in the closest collaboration.'[16] Worse followed when Geddes appointed Keyes (Rear-Admiral 4th Battle Squadron, Grand Fleet, since June) as Director of Plans on Wemyss's strong recommendation. Through 'some misunderstanding', Keyes was appointed without Jellicoe's approval. To this Jellicoe 'took some exception as I considered him quite unfitted by temperament and brain power for the post, although I knew of course his other sterling qualities, but the appointment had been made and I agreed to let it stand. The organisation never worked well and I

[16] Jellicoe's autobiographical notes.

found that my work was increased by the necessity for constantly dealing with two people.'[17]

Finally, to give effect to a key recommendation in the Geddes report, an important innovation was introduced in an Order in Council of 23 October. The First Sea Lord in his capacity of Chief of Naval Staff was hereafter to be responsible to the First Lord for the issue of executive orders to the Fleet dealing with war operations and ship movements, which orders should be issued in his own name. 'The responsibility for these orders is not Board responsibility unless the question at issue is referred to the Board, as unless operation orders result from Board decision, the responsibility of issuing them remains, under Order in Council, on the shoulders of the Chief of Naval Staff and of the First Lord. The procedure [for holding weekly Board meetings] is, however, designed to ensure that important operational matters shall be brought before the full Board whenever the circumstances admit of this.'[18] In other words, there was no collective responsibility of the Board in regard to operations except when such matters were put before the Board. The Order in Council clarified a point that had in Churchill's time at the Admiralty been responsible for much confusion and bitterness.[19]

What was the broader significance of the changes? Completing what had been started in May 1917, the reorganization 'was intended to decentralise work, to organise it into groups of divisions

---

[17] *Ibid.* It was at the end of September (though not formally until mid-October) that the Plans Section of the Operations Division was expanded and instituted as a Division of the Naval Staff. It was concerned with strategic plans as distinct from day-to day operations, which were the province of the D.O.D. There were two sections, each under an Assistant Director: Section A, under Captain Dudley Pound, for plans of operation, and Section B, under Captain Cyril Fuller, for determining the quantity, and arranging for the provision, of the *matériel* to carry out plans. Rejoiced Richmond: 'It is something to be thankful for that in spite of the opposition o several Boards and the Staff, a planning branch has at last been formed. 39 months! and only by means of pressure of 2 civilian First Lords!' Richmond to Dewar, 12 December 1917; Dewar MSS. Richmond revised his opinion a month later, when he discovered from Beatty that Plans Division was mainly wrapped up in *matériel* work. 'Instead of its being a real planning division, it appears to be a division which considers proposals for employment of inventions. . . . It all looks to me like beginning at the wrong end of the stick. No one says what we *want to do* & asks for staff which will do it. It is *all* started from the matériel end, not the strategic.' Diary, 17 January 1918; *Portrait of an Admiral*, pp. 295–6.

[18] Quoted in Sir Oswyn A. R. Murray, 'The Admiralty. X. The Naval Staff', *Mariner's Mirror*, July 1939.

[19] See *From the Dreadnought to Scapa Flow*, ii. 225–8, 268–72, 302–6.

closely associated with one another and to give the Naval Staff executive authority on a definite constitutional basis in order to enable it to cope with the multiplicity and complexity of its work'.[20]

It was at this time that Wemyss, pursuant to the memorandum of 10 September, was elevated to Deputy First Sea Lord and given Staff duties (this was strictly Geddes's idea) in addition to the usual responsibility for personnel that devolved on the Second Sea Lord. When Wemyss realized that the twin burdens were too much for one man, and that the Second Sea Lord could not possibly find the time to study Staff matters, he prevailed on the First Lord to allow him to handle Staff work exclusively as a Deputy First Sea Lord, with another officer to be appointed Second Sea Lord. On 27 September Wemyss relinquished the duties of Second Sea Lord in favour of Vice-Admiral Sir H. Leopold Heath, a sound officer, if not one of original ideas. (He had 'a pumpkin on his shoulders' rather than a head, thought Richmond, who got to know him well in 1918.) The fact that Wemyss happened to be senior to Heath facilitated the smooth working of the new arrangement by which the Second Sea Lord was divorced from operational duties. Wemyss's duties were confined to Staff work; this included the supervision of the work of the Plans Division.

Beatty was pleased with Wemyss's new appointment. 'He seems to have a fairly good grasp of the various situations and has good sound common sense to assist him in making his decisions, and we are agreed on all the most important questions and I consequently feel more hopeful for the future. But there is no doubt that things have been mis-managed to an appalling extent in the past.'[21] Jellicoe's supporters were suspicious, believing that the appointment was part of a scheme to oust Jellicoe. Madden had warned him of the introduction of 'a fifth wheel'. Jellicoe, too, regarded the Deputy First Sea Lord as a kind of fifth wheel of the coach. He saw no necessity for the position, because, as Chief of the Naval Staff, he already had a Deputy and an Assistant. 'The introduction of a Deputy First Sea Lord was only agreed to by me as the result of my conversations with Beatty and Madden. The idea emanated from Sir Eric Geddes who saw in this appointment a way of overcoming the Prime Minister's objections to Sir H.

[20] Naval Staff Monograph, *The Naval Staff of the Admiralty*, p. 89.
[21] Beatty to Lady Beatty, 10 October 1917; Beatty MSS.

Oliver remaining at the Admiralty. . . . The intention was that in my absence Admiral Wemyss could represent me at the War Council instead of Sir H. Oliver.'[22] He refused to shift any of his responsibilities to Wemyss. The latter complained to Jellicoe in December that he was 'merely giving an extra opinion on dockets which could well be dispensed with'.[23]

The fears of the Jellicoeites were not without foundation. Geddes 'remained rather restless; the real trouble was that both he and Lloyd George were still dissatisfied with the First Sea Lord'.[24] Why should this have been the case? Certain factors and incidents worked to discredit severely the theory of sea power for which Jellicoe was understood in many quarters to stand. These were (1) the apparent failure to meet the submarine campaign; (2) the continued defensive strategy of the Admiralty; (3) the tragic story of the two Scandinavian convoys within a few weeks of each other; (4) the unsatisfactory result of the 17 November action in the Heligoland Bight; and (5) the continued porousness of the Dover Straits. Season these ingredients with personality factors and a vociferous press agitation, and the result was Jellicoe's dismissal at the end of the year.

---

[22] Jellicoe's autobiographical notes.
[23] Lady Wester Wemyss, *The Life and Letters of Lord Wester Wemyss* (London, 1935), p. 364. 'When I joined the Board, I found that the First Sea Lord was not taking advantage of the fact that his Deputy and Assistant Chiefs of the Naval Staff were Members of the Board, and the latter, so far as their day to day work was concerned, were hardly more than Directors of Divisions, and I myself, as Deputy First Sea Lord, was not saddled with that responsibility which alone justified my appointment: I more than once talked to Lord Jellicoe on the subject, but he did not share my view, and considered that in spite of his three Deputies being Members of the Board, he alone was responsible for the issue of orders, etc. No argument that I could use enabled me to shake his ruling in this matter, and the consequence was an overloading of the machine in one direction which became wellnigh unbearable, and prevented him from considering other subjects than day to day operations.' Wemyss's memorandum of 28 May 1919; Wemyss MSS.
[24] Hankey, *The Supreme Command*, ii. 655.

IX

Offensive Schemes

(July 1917 – December 1917)

The whole atmosphere of the Admiralty in the autumn of 1917 was discouraging. Any forward move, any kind of offensive operation, had to be forced through in face of the fiercest resistance. The joke used to be that it was a 'jolly old war' and the longer it went on 'the better'.

LIEUTENANT-COMMANDER J. M. KENWORTHY
(then with the Plans Division), *Sailors, Statesmen—and Others.*

These various plans for offensive operations in 1917 have been mentioned in order to make it clear that every possible avenue through which the forces of the enemy could be rendered immobile or destroyed was considered in full detail.

If none of them were adopted it was because, after detailed consideration, they were found to be either impossible of achievement or that the attempt to carry them out might endanger our surface command of the sea.

JELLICOE, *The Submarine Peril.*

I. MINING AND OTHER SCHEMES

PARTLY AS a result of the dissatisfaction with the status of the A/S campaign, there was no dearth of offensive schemes emanating from the Admiralty (especially the new Plans Division) and the Grand Fleet in the latter months of 1917. The Admiralty judged none of those involving the Grand Fleet as practicable, mainly because they involved seeking out the enemy in his own waters. It was regarded as more than probable that an attempt to force an action would be abortive and would merely result in the loss of a few ships from mines. If a fight did result, damaged British ships would stand a poor chance of getting away, whereas the German ships would have a good one. Also, the mere existence of the Grand Fleet and its known preparedness for action sufficed to achieve the main strategical object of a battle fleet, viz., to secure and maintain the surface command of the sea. An aggressive mining campaign was another matter.

The minelaying campaign, an attempt to destroy the enemy submarines before they reached the large open spaces of the sea, had been neither very impressive nor apparently very successful in the first half of 1917: two U-boats were destroyed, one in the Heligoland Bight and one east of Dover. By July, however, as Jellicoe kept strengthening the minefields in the Bight as rapidly as the delivery of mines permitted, they were beginning to constitute a real danger to the U-boats. From mid-August minelaying in the Bight, as well as in the Dover Straits, by surface and submarine minelayers became one of the chief A/S measures. The principles adopted were to mine just outside neutral territorial waters in positions where it was believed that U-boats left and entered these waters, and to lay mines across the suspected tracks of enemy submarines.

Over 20,000 mines were laid in the Dover Straits and the Bight in the second half of 1917. Altogether, 15,686 mines in seventy-six minefields were laid in the Bight alone during 1917, as compared with: 1914, nil; 1915, 4,538 in nine minefields; 1916, 1,782 in seventeen minefields. Six U-boats were accounted for in the Bight between 31 August and the end of the year. The improved (German-type) mines, which were being delivered in large numbers from September, the simultaneous large increase in the number of minelayers (as through the fitting of light cruisers and destroyers to serve as minelayers when required), and the high quality of the information gathered by N.I.D., explain these successes as well as those elsewhere, particularly in the waters off Zeebrugge and along the U-boat transit routes to the west. All told, mines accounted for 22 U-boats during 1917 in Home waters (including one lost on German mines)—all but three in the latter half of the year. The total number of U-boats destroyed by mines (including German) in all theatres during 1917 was 26, or double the total for the period through 1916, and 40 per cent of the 65 submarines accounted for by the Allies through all means during 1917. (The figure includes stranded boats.) With the increase in the difficulties of movement in the Bight, from April 1917 the homeward-bound U-boats began to be deflected through the Kattegat, and by the end of 1917, outgoing boats were often using that channel.

A serious obstacle to a consistently effective mining of the Bight could not be overcome: enemy minesweepers persisted in sweeping channels, which were marked and buoyed, through the minefields. (This was not possible in the Straits of Dover, which, moreover, could be closely patrolled.) From early in 1917 until the end of the war the contest between the British minelayers and the German minesweepers in the Bight was a feature of the naval activity in the North Sea. Gradually, from the winter of 1917–18, the minelayers got the upper hand and the British rate of laying mines began to surpass the German rate of sweeping them up.

A more ambitious mining policy came to the fore during 1917: the scheme of laying a mine barrier from the Orkneys to Norway, a distance of some 250 miles, to prevent the 'North about' egress of German submarines from the North Sea. The idea (originally suggested by Admiral Bacon in 1916) was intriguing. The U-boats would be confined to the North Sea (except for those hazarding the Channel route), since the barrage would be too far to the north to be interfered with by the German minesweepers. The number of mines required, as well as the lack of minelayers, seemingly put this solution beyond the realm of the practicable in 1917. When Sims discussed such a project with the Admiralty, he was told: 'If we haven't mines enough to build a successful barrage across the Straits of Dover, which is only 20 miles wide, how can we construct a barrage across the North Sea, which is 230?'[1] The vast expanse of water to be mined and the great depth of the water (360 to 960 feet) called for a special type of mine as well as a huge quantity. The existing mines, which could be fired only by contact, would not do. A new mine had to be invented, then manufactured in immense quantities.

The Americans had had a particular fondness for this scheme ever since they entered the war. Lord Northcliffe, on an official mission in the United States, in reporting current American naval opinion declared: 'Our alleged inactivity in dealing with the submarines hampers our work as much as the question of Ireland.' American naval observers included among 'possible policies to end or lessen losses' a barrage of continuous mine-nets to block the northern exit of the North Sea, or, alternatively, a continuous wall of mines at either end of the North Sea.[2]

[1] Sims, *The Victory at Sea*, p. 32.
[2] Northcliffe's telegram to Lloyd George, 5 July 1917; U. S. Navy Department MSS. At this time President Wilson was expressing himself as 'greatly surprised at the failure of the British Admiralty to use Great Britain's great Naval superiority in an effective way. In the presence of the present submarine emergency, they are helpless to the point of panic. Every plan we suggest they reject for some reason of prudence. In my view, this is not a time for prudence but for boldness even at the cost of great losses.' Wilson's cable to Sims, 4 July 1917; Morison, *Admiral Sims and the Modern American Navy*, p. 358.

The Admiralty began to undergo a change of heart towards the end of the summer, after the Planning Section of the Naval Staff had stated that the barrage was technically feasible. Jellicoe put the project before an Allied naval conference that met in London on 4–5 September. The conference endorsed it, provided it was not undertaken 'until an adequate supply of mines of a satisfactory type was assured'. Jellicoe was not carried away, making no bones about the fact that it would take a long time to get the needed mines: at least 100,000 was his figure.[3] On 2 November, after the Americans were able to guarantee the mass production of new-type mines that could do the job, the two Governments agreed to proceed. The new 'antenna' mine could be laid at any depth. From it a long thin copper cable projected up to within a few feet of the surface and was kept in position by a small metal buoy. A submarine making contact with any portion of an antenna produced an electric current which caused the mine to explode. One line of antenna mines could do the work of perhaps five contact-mine lines. That, at any rate, was the theory.

The position of the Admiralty and of the Grand Fleet was that mining would at best furnish only an impediment to the U-boats; it could not be a complete solution, since mines were but a temporary obstacle. Other offensive schemes engaged the minds of many at the Admiralty and in the Grand Fleet—schemes whose object was to break the stalemate at sea as well as to end the submarine menace. The basic idea was that the immobilization or destruction of the High Seas Fleet in their bases, whether through bombardment or blocking the principal German ports in the Bight, would solve the submarine problem as well, since the High Seas Fleet was the bulwark behind which the U-boats were able to wage their campaign. Their co-operation made possible the work of the minesweepers. If the fleet were destroyed, or even seriously weakened, British mining would render all approaches to the German bases impassable, or the defensive minefields would be forced and the Bight overrun by British warships.

There was a resurrection of 1914–15 plans to capture and hold one or more islands in the Bight (Heligoland, Borkum, and Sylt were those most commonly mentioned) as a forward base for aircraft and small craft, with older battleships (protected against mine and torpedo by a 'bulge') in support. This force would

[3] 'Report of Naval Conference of Powers United against Germany'; Admiralty MSS.

establish a close blockade of the enemy's bases. The idea was that offensive operations by the British small craft would compel the Germans to use many of the U-boats to reinforce their flotillas rather than to employ them in trade warfare. The larger purpose, however, was to force a decisive action between the two battle fleets, as the High Seas Fleet would be expected to come out to support counter-attacks on the blockading ships. If the German heavy ships did not come out, the British advance force would gradually whittle down the strength of the German lighter craft and be able to mine close in to the German bases without serious interference. Thus, the U-boats would be penned in.

Churchill, who as First Lord had been the most ardent supporter of such projects, forwarded to the Admiralty late in July proposals for offensive operations in the Heligoland Bight whose end product would be the capture of Borkum, Sylt, and Heligoland as oversea bases. The plan in each case was spelled out. His object, as summed up by the Director of the Planning Section (it was not yet a Division), was 'to find a means of fighting and compelling the enemy to fight, and so to cow his Naval forces and thus to establish a far greater control of all sea approaches to his harbours', with presumably 'the ultimate object of sealing the enemy's ports to prevent the egress of the submarines'. What Churchill was calling for was, in effect, a resumption of the policy of close and aggressive blockade which had been adopted in former wars and lay at the heart of his strategic schemes in the first six months of the war. The Churchillian venture into higher naval strategy evoked no interest at the Admiralty.[4]

Jellicoe has clearly stated the Admiralty's objections to island-capturing proposals, which originated outside the Admiralty but were examined by the Naval Staff. Mining close inshore would run into the obstacle that since 'mines of the design then in existence could not be laid in water of a less depth than six fathoms, whereas a submarine could pass out, even at low tide, in water of a depth of three or four fathoms, a passage out would therefore always be left'. Concerning the islands, Heligoland, if captured, would be subject to constant air and naval attack 'unless our own inshore squadron was able to remain in sufficient proximity to prevent this. There were considerable difficulties in the way of carrying

---

[4] The résumé of Churchill's paper by Pound, with his own remarks, is in an August 1917 paper in the Admiralty MSS.

out such a policy.' Borkum would be very difficult to capture; if taken, the anchorages would be subject to intense air attack and bombardment from long-range guns on the mainland. The same disadvantages applied to Sylt. Even if they succeeded in sealing the German North Sea bases,

it would only reduce the submarine menace and not abolish it, as the enemy would then use Kiel as a point of departure for the boats. This would, of course, increase the length of their passage to their fields of operation, but would not deny their exit. It did not appear possible to seal the Baltic exits, unless we could maintain a blockading force in the Sound and Great Belt. Such a force could only be maintained if we had disposed of the High Sea Fleet; or, alternatively, by the use of a base in the Kattegat, where we could keep a fleet capable of dealing with any force which might be sent against our blockading ships.

Other difficulties included a shortage of small craft required for a close blockade and the unwillingness of the United States and French Navies to lend Britain the battleships needed to form the inshore squadron.[5] These arguments were turned against a still more ambitious scheme that came to the fore in mid-summer. (See next section.)

A scheme favoured by Lloyd George and Churchill was the destruction of the German naval bases by naval bombardment alone. This was what President Wilson had in mind when he stated in a speech (August 1917): 'We are hunting hornets all over the farm and letting the nest alone. None of us knows how to go to the nest and crush it, and yet I despair of hunting for hornets all over the sea when I know where the nest is.'[6] Responsible authorities at the Admiralty held that a naval bombardment alone was impracticable and dangerous. The bases were protected by powerful, well-concealed guns which out-ranged the guns on the largest warships and were stationary, whereas the latter would be moving. In Sims's figure, 'For our ships to go up against such emplacements would be like putting a blind prize fighter up against an antagonist who can see and who has arms twice as long as his

[5] Jellicoe, *The Submarine Peril*, pp. 63–6. On the earlier history of the proposals to capture a German island, see *From the Dreadnought to Scapa Flow*, ii. 178–97.

[6] Morison, *Admiral Sims and the Modern American Navy*, p. 361. Sims sent Captain Pratt (Office of Naval Operations, Navy Department) a cutting from the *London Magazine*, Percival Hislam's 'Digging Out Tactics', with the hope that he would read it 'prayerfully, and circulate it where you think the information is most needed'. Sims to Pratt, 28 July 1917; U.S. Navy Dept. MSS.

enemy's.' Beatty asked of Lloyd George's advocacy of a Heligoland bombardment, '. . . what sacrifices are we to go to to achieve a result which can only be justified by the effect it will have on the war? Who is going to hold it afterwards and what provision will be made to protect it? Some very large questions to which it is necessary to have complete answers.'[7]

2. A BLOCKING OPERATION

On all sides in British and American naval circles it was being suggested (and indeed had been since the spring) that the obvious way to deal with the U-boats was to prevent them from getting to sea, that is, as in the case of hornets, to stop the holes—close the German river mouths and exits of the Baltic by mines and other measures, so as to keep the U-boats in and prevent those at sea from returning to their base.

Aware that the American representatives at the forthcoming Allied naval conference in London would 'press strongly for some offensive or blocking measure in German waters,' on 31 July the First Sea Lord asked the Planning Section of the Operations Division 'to consider whether the only real remedy to the S/M menace, viz. blocking the submarines in port, is really feasible, although no doubt very costly'. For this purpose the Planning Section was constituted as a committee, with the onetime First Sea Lord, Sir Henry Jackson (then serving as Admiral President at Greenwich), as Chairman. Jellicoe made no attempt to conceal that his object was 'purely negative—to prove the impossibility of doing anything. . . . they had to produce something to shew that the matter had been considered . . .'[8] He had asked for a detailed plan and on 18 August it was submitted.[9]

It was a scheme of vast magnitude for blocking all the exits from which the German submarines could issue—the Elbe, Jade, Weser, and Ems—and closing the exits from the Baltic as well. (The principal harbours were the Jade and Elbe, since the U-boat building and repair yards lay up these rivers.) The efficient blocking in, that is, the containment, of the enemy's heavy ships was the

[7] Beatty to Carson, 18 July 1917; Colvin, *Carson*, iii. 271.
[8] Richmond's diary, 25 August 1917, reporting what Beatty had been told by Jellicoe during the latter's visit to the Grand Fleet, 24 August; *Portrait of an Admiral*, p. 269.
[9] 'Blocking the German Harbours to Effectually Prevent the Exit of Their Submarines to the Sea'; Admiralty MSS.

essential preliminary to the blockade of the U-boats, since it was impossible to maintain an effectual blockade of the rivers against the U-boats unless the High Seas Fleet could be prevented from interfering. This meant, in the first instance, blocking the exits from the Jade and the Weser. Should this be effected, German ships in the Baltic and other ports would be isolated from the main fleet at Wilhelmshaven. Next in importance was the blocking of the exit from the Elbe, which would be equivalent to closing the Kiel Canal, as far as the North Sea was concerned. As a precaution, the Ems, which was of less importance, would be heavily mined at the beginning of the operation. The blocking operation would take the form of sinking concrete-filled old warships (merchant ships could not be spared for the purpose) across the entrance to the rivers. To make this operation practicable, they must first capture and hold the strongly fortified islands of Wangeroog (whose heavy batteries commanded the projected blocklines in the main channels of the Jade) and Heligoland (whose heavy guns, with those on Wangeroog, 'may be counted on to leave little or no blind area in which our vessels could manœuvre free from gunfire, though at long range, between the two islands'). Heligoland would be used as a temporary war base for the British covering fleet until the completion of the blocking. Heligoland must come first, as the attack on Wangeroog was not held feasible so long as Heligoland remained in German hands.

It was expected that a 'determined attack' on Heligoland would draw out the High Seas Fleet and that a naval engagement would follow. This raised the old bugaboo of having to meet the German Fleet in their own waters.

The avoidance of a Fleet Action in the German Bight has rightly been considered by us a sound policy, as such an action would give the Enemy many advantages, especially if, when the Fleets met at sea, the German tactics enticed our fleet into the Bight. These advantages would be reduced to some extent if our fleet were first to arrive on the scene, and drew them out from their inner waters, engaging them from seaward whilst their manœuvring was restricted in the intricate channels of the exits from the River. When both fleets were in the open, the danger from mines and submarines would not be very different for the two Fleets, though probably never in our favour, even though our Mine protecting devices [paravanes] recently fitted have greatly reduced the risk from the mines which may be passed over by our heavy vessels.

Risks would remain and heavy losses must be expected in such an encounter, but the present comparative strength of the two opposing fleets is so much in our favour, that we could afford more losses than the Germans in Capital Ships before our strength was reduced to a dangerous margin, though probably the main operation of blocking the ports would have to be abandoned.

However, it is not seen how the exit of German submarines to sea can be stopped by blocking their Rivers and Channels without running this risk in the operation outlined above, and detailed consideration of the work involved [does] not show it to be impractical for other reasons.

With the main channels of the rivers blocked, how were they to prevent the U-boats getting out of harbour? After discarding solid obstructions (concrete blocks) and a combination of these and mines, the Committee decided that, given the length of the line to be blocked and the depth of the water, the only practicable scheme was a barrier of mines alone. Since a line of mines could not be maintained in the shallow estuaries in the face of the shore batteries, the plan was to lay down three lines of mines between Wangeroog and Heligoland, and between Heligoland and Pellworm (mouth of the Eider). 21,000 mines would be needed for a total length of 43 miles. It would be necessary to hold Heligoland and Wangeroog. If the latter were not held, the enemy could easily keep a channel open close inshore of that island. Borkum and Juist would need to be captured before the channels of the Ems could be blocked with mines, but this phase of the operation would be left till the last.

'So far as the submarine campaign is concerned it would be hardly worthwhile blocking the German North Sea ports if the Baltic exits were left open.' As for the best method of closing them (the Belts and Sound), 'Owing to the large areas involved in the Belts and to the depth of water at the northern end of the Sound, it would not be possible to use sunken ships, and mines [7,500 'H' mines] would therefore have to be used. . . . The possibility of maintaining the block of the Baltic exits will depend on the power of the Allies to maintain, in the vicinity, a force superior to that which the Germans may bring against us.' Kalo Bay, at the upper end of Aarhus Bay, with its fine anchorage and narrow entrance which could be easily protected against submarines, would make an excellent base—if the Danes would permit this.

The report did not make a recommendation. It merely described a plan in great detail, discussed the problems, and concluded: 'With favourable weather and good luck, the whole of the operations might be completed in 10 days. . . .' Jackson, at any rate, regarded the scheme as too risky. This is evident in his introduction to the Committee's report:

It must also be considered what may be the result if our efforts fail, and the early attacks on these fortresses result in the loss of a large percentage of our 'Capital' Ships and of our Destroyers, and that with British determination we doggedly continue the attempt till our Fleet is reduced to equality or even inferiority to that of our Enemy. The Initiative, with surface vessels, would then, more than ever, be in their hands. It may be that they, in their turn, would retaliate by blocking our fleet in at Rosyth, and thus be left for a time, free to use their Command of all Seas in the full sense of the word. There would soon be Raiders on our Commerce in all Waters in addition to the Submarines. Invasion would also be a practicability.

The risks of failure must therefore be carefully balanced against the chances of success. . . .

A careful study of the German Fortress guns in and round the Bight, leads one to the conclusion that the Germans have so arranged them as to give the maximum support possible to their Fleet, in the event of it being called on to defend its bases in the Bight, which, without this mobile defence, is one of the best sheltered spots in Europe for keeping out an unwelcome intruder.[10]

Jellicoe and the Naval Staff deemed the scheme impracticable for these reasons: (1) The soldiers would not consider taking Heligoland unless the Navy would guarantee to put down, and maintain so long as required, a barrage a short distance from the top of the cliff. The Navy would not consider maintaining within howitzer range of the island the vessels needed for such a barrage. (2) The soldiers thought they could take Wangeroog, but did not think it could be held because of its proximity to the mainland. (3) It was impracticable under heavy fire to place the blockships

[10] Even Dewar, who on 19 July had written to Bellairs (intended for Beatty's eye) that they could 'effectively throttle the submarine menace at its source', had to admit the operation was impracticable, though for different reasons. 'On going more thoroughly into the question of a naval offensive, I have come to the conclusion that the blocking of the rivers, which necessarily include the capture of Heligoland and Wangeroog, is impracticable. I do not say it is impossible but I don't think we have the capacity to carry it out. The Admiralty and Staff are the weak links in the chain. The alternative is to establish a mine barrage across the North Sea.' Dewar to Richmond, 12 September 1917; Dewar MSS.

with the necessary degree of accuracy. (4) The line of blockships was broken by sand banks over which submarines normally could not pass even at high water, but it would be possible for the Germans to dredge a channel through the sand round the end of the blockline.[11] (5) 'For these operations,' Jellicoe wrote, 'it was clear that we should require the assistance of our Allies, both in regard to the provision of ships for sinking in the German rivers, and for the operations leading up to this work. When the scheme was explained to the representatives of the United States, France, and Italy, they stated that they could not provide the necessary ships.'[12] (6) The Baltic exits 'would still remain available for enemy use, as they could not be blocked without violating Danish and Swedish neutrality'.[13] The *coup de grâce* to the suggested close offensive in German waters came with the statement by the U.S. Navy Department (late October or November) that it was impracticable, in which view the Operations Committee of the Admiralty concurred (20 November).

In response to Jellicoe's request that he consider 'whether the only real remedy to the Submarine Menace, viz. blocking the submarines in Port, is really feasible', Beatty had Madden investigate. Madden's conclusion (7 August) was that blocking the deep-water exits of the Ems, Jade, Weser, and Elbe by block ships was impracticable, as was the erection of a barrage of mines and nets, which depended on the co-operation of all the neighbouring neutral countries. The last remark highlights the most obvious defect of all the blockading proposals: there was no real force behind them. The enemy was not going to be blocked in his harbours by minefields unless they were closely covered by a fleet more powerful than their own, and it would be making a gift of many destroyers, etc. to the enemy to attempt to do so. By the end

---

[11] To this point in the paragraph a summary of the Admiralty objections as given in Keyes to Churchill, 1 December 1926; Keyes MSS.

[12] Jellicoe, *The Submarine Peril*, p. 68. Forty old battleships (of which Britain would supply 18) and 43 old cruisers (Britain would supply 13) would be needed to block the German harbours, the Admiralty estimated. The Allied naval conference in London of early September accepted the plan in principle; the Allies agreed to let the Admiralty know in due course what contribution in old warships they were prepared to make. That was as far as they went. The Allies could have found the ships; but they doubted the wisdom of using the cruisers, given their vital importance to an expanded convoy system, and had even more serious doubts about the feasibility of the project.

[13] *Ibid.*

of September, the blocking operation was as good as dead. But this was not before Beatty had played an ace up his sleeve.

3. A NAVAL AIR OFFENSIVE

Beatty appreciated how seriously the U-boat threat to shipping worked against a Grand Fleet, or indeed any naval, offensive strategy. 'It is not necessary,' he wrote, 'to recapitulate the many points which necessitate the absolute suppression of the submarine, but it will do no harm to mention that the principal are: To enable American co-operation to be more powerful and certain (without which the French cannot be expected to continue the War after this next spring). The development of a strong naval offensive in the Adriatic. The co-operation of naval forces with military forces on the coast of Palestine. In fact wherever you look, naval offensive action which might be of value is interfered with by the Sub-marine Menace. The Economic and Industrial situation of all the Allied Powers is such that the Military Policy is jeopardised and reduced in efficiency by it.'[14] The most effective A/S policy was to

[14] Beatty to Geddes, 25 September 1917; Admiralty MSS. On the references to Pales-tine and the Adriatic, see above, p. 171. For months Richmond, with his *idée fixe* that the Mediterranean was an area where they could do more, had been pressing for a joint operation on the Syrian coast. A few thousand troops there would be able to tie down many times more that number of Turks—100,000 perhaps. British troops were available and the War Office appeared to be interested. Beatty had pushed this scheme but without success. The Admiralty objection was that sub-marines made the operation impossible. As for the Adriatic, Beatty was attracted to Richmond's idea of a long-range naval bombardment of Pola and a large-scale bombing attack (better still, Allied combined operations to capture the base), the destruction of the Whitehead works at Fiume, and the mining of Cattaro and Pola. These operations, if successful, would go very far towards crushing the U-boat campaign in the Mediterranean as well as lessening Austrian pressure in northern Italy by drawing troops to the Adriatic coast. The Admiralty evinced no interest in these offensive possibilities in the Mediterranean, which only drove Richmond wild. With special reference to Pola, which was for him 'the centre of the problem': '. . . a counter offensive from the sea at Pola is not so unutterably impossible as the timid British school of strategists would have us believe. . . . Surely there is someone at the Admiralty with courage to propose such an attempt. Most men fear ridicule, I am afraid. They are appalling moral cowards.' Richmond to Dewar (late Novem-ber 1917) Dewar MSS. He further relieved his feelings with blistering entries in his diary. 'All this talk of Armageddon in the North Sea has bewildered our strategists. . . . we seem again to be affected with this terror, this belief that an overwhelmingly strong High Seas Fleet is going to come out & crush us. Why should we think this? And should we be so weakened by such a detachment as to render our position here precarious? Ships are built to be used, not to be laid up in cotton wool against some future event.' Diary, 12 December 1917; *Portrait of an Admiral*, p. 286.

block the exits of German harbours to the passage of submarines. All measures of blocking were effective only if the enemy were unable to remove the blocks. So long as they had a naval force in the Bight superior to any which the British could permanently maintain there to prevent the removal of the obstacles, the British were unable effectively to limit the operations of the U-boats.

Beatty was anxious to exploit the potentialities of the torpedo-carrying aircraft, for, in his view, the key to a successful blocking operation lay in a bold use of naval air power: sustained large-scale attacks against enemy naval bases. 'Besides being one of the few ways in which offensive action against the German Fleet is possible, it is one of the few ways in which our command of the sea can be turned to active account against the enemy.'[15] He had the strong support at the Admiralty of the Director of Air Services (Fifth Sea Lord), who emphasized the 'enormous advantages' of torpedo-carrying aeroplanes 'if gone into in a wholesale manner. ... At the close of an engagement, in the failing light, an attack delivered by, say, 24 such craft approaching from the East, would be very effective and would be hard to counter. An attack at dawn on ships at anchor in Cuxhaven, Schillig Roads, or other enemy bases could hardly fail to have results.'[16] Strongly influenced by the ideas of Richmond and Flight-Commander Rutland ('Rutland of Jutland'), Beatty put forward a plan to immobilize the High Seas Fleet by a massive surprise attack with torpedo-carrying planes, which would be transported by carriers to within striking distance of the German bases. In addition to the torpedo planes, flying boats would take part. Since they had a radius of action of 600 miles, they could be independent of carriers and could fly from the English coast. He raised this possibility at a meeting with the First Sea Lord and the D.O.D. (Hope) in the *Queen Elizabeth* on 24 August. 'An attack at dawn by torpedo planes on a very large scale, accompanied by aircraft of the larger type [flying boats] carrying 230-lb. bombs to attack lesser craft and dockyards would be most difficult to repel. If by such an attack the heavy ships of the Fleet could be sufficiently damaged to prevent them

---

[15] Beatty to Admiralty, 7 October 1917; Admiralty MSS.

[16] Paine's minute of 30 August 1917; Admiralty MSS. Pound, in a minute of 14 September, endorsed Beatty's ideas. 'The torpedo carrying aeroplane will soon become a most formidable weapon in a fleet action; it will be the one weapon which will be able to deal satisfactorily with "turning away" tactics by the enemy.' Admiralty MSS.

from taking part in local operations, then the question of blocking would form the next step in the programme.'[17] At the same meeting Jellicoe and Hope questioned the capability of the torpedo plane: it was still in the far future, such planes would have to come within 15 feet of the sea to discharge their torpedoes, they could never be certain of finding the High Seas Fleet together in the Schillig Roads, and no *matériel* was then available for the operation. Oliver affirmed that the C.-in-C.'s proposal was 'far beyond the *matériel* which can be obtained'.[18]

Beatty met this objection by stating that the Air Ministry (really the Air Board, which was in fact a ministry) had been established (December 1916) on the clear understanding that the naval and military requirements were first met. 'The trouble hitherto had been that there was no definite policy with regard to the Naval requirements in the air; the Navy had never stated what they wanted. . . . The C.-in-C. therefore urged that air requirements with regard to any contemplated air offensive should be got out forthwith; that the high importance of an operation having for its ultimate object the immobilizing of the High Sea Fleet should be clearly stated, and he had very little doubt that every effort would be made [by the Air Ministry] to provide the necessary material.'[19]

Beatty returned in October to the project of an air offensive against the German naval bases, now stressing a larger consideration. 'A sustained air offensive on the scale proposed would impose

---

[17] 'Additional Notes on the Naval Offensive', a paper prepared by Richmond for Beatty and shown to Jellicoe on 24 August; *Portrait of an Admiral*, p. 268. Aware that Richmond's name 'stinks at the Admiralty', the C.-in-C. told Jellicoe the paper was the work of a Grand Fleet committee! The details of the air attack were worked out in a separate paper by Rutland and Richmond, both of whom held the strong opinion that torpedo planes *were* a satisfactory weapon. 'Considerations of an Attack by Torpedo Planes on the High Sea Fleet'; Admiralty MSS. Beatty forwarded it to the Admiralty with his endorsement (11 September): 'Every endeavour should be made to be ready for operations by the Spring of 1918.' The plan called for 121 torpedo planes of the new type (90 m.p.h., 3$\frac{1}{2}$-to-4 hour radius of action), which could be transported to within an hour's flying time of Wilhelmshaven in eight suitable merchant ships of 16 to 20 knots. The latter would be fitted with blisters and paravanes for protection against submarines and mines, and fitted to carry and to launch torpedo planes. (Space for the storage of torpedo-carrying aeroplanes was not available in existing carriers.) An escort of destroyers would accompany the carriers. The planes would attack in waves of forty.

[18] 'Notes of Conference Held on Board H.M.S. *Queen Elizabeth* on Friday, the 24th August, 1917', and Oliver's minute, 19 September 1917; Admiralty MSS.

[19] Bellairs, 'Notes on Conference with Captain Pound, 23rd Sept. 1917'; Bellairs MSS. Repeated almost verbatim in Beatty to Geddes, 25 September 1917; Admiralty MSS.

upon the enemy the necessity for active measures of defence. Attempts to attack the carriers and their covering forces might well lead to actions of increasing magnitude, involving their heavy ships, thus affording opportunities which have hitherto been denied to us. It is submitted, therefore, that comprehensive plans may be prepared by the Naval Staff in readiness to be put into execution as soon as the necessary carriers, aircraft, torpedoes and bombs are available.'[20] He hammered away on his plan at a conference with Wemyss on 10 October. The latter was in agreement on the necessity of an air offensive at the earliest possible moment, but he was forced to throw cold water on the crux of the proposal, the provision of carriers. Only the *Argus*, which was capable of carrying twenty torpedo planes, could be ready by the spring of 1918. The situation was more promising as regards machines: 100 torpedo planes, under construction, would be ready by the spring, and 100 of the day 'bombers' being prepared for the offensive on the Western Front in 1918 could probably be diverted to the Navy if this course were pressed on the War Cabinet. In short, the Navy would only be able to mount a spring air offensive on a comparatively small scale. The possibilities in 1919 were another matter and were being fully considered by the Naval Staff, Air Ministry, and War Cabinet.[21]

The official reply to Beatty first dwelt on the merchant vessels in his plan. 'The overall dimensions of this type of [torpedo] aeroplane, even when folded, are considerable, and very large ships would be required to accommodate such a number with adequate

[20] Beatty to Admiralty, 7 October 1917; Admiralty MSS.
[21] 'Conference between Commander-in-Chief, Grand Fleet, and Deputy First Sea Lord Held on 10th October, 1917'; Bellairs MSS. The Admiralty were at this time pushing an air offensive scheme of their own, one which was blocked by an insufficiency of suitable machines and carriers. At the first meeting of the Air Raids Committee of the War Cabinet, 1 October, Jellicoe submitted a paper entitled 'Offensive Bombing Operations from Seaplane Carriers'. The idea was to bomb Bremen, with its eight or ten submarine slips. No attack should be made with fewer than 30 machines, but it would be spring before a sufficient number would be available for this and various other projects the Admiralty had in view without diverting seaplanes from their useful A/S work round the coast. Moreover, only the seaplane carriers *Furious* and *Campania* had long flying decks capable of sending off bombing machines (to undertake bombing operations from carriers from which seaplanes had to be hoisted out was too uncertain in the weather conditions of the North Sea), and they could carry between them the paltry total of 11 machines and thirty-three 112-lb. bombs. (There were no aeroplanes capable of carrying bombs which folded to the dimensions necessary for stowage on board the two seaplane carriers.) Nothing came of the scheme. Cab. 27/9; P.R.O.

facilities for flying from the deck. In fact, it is uncertain whether eight such ships could be found, and, in any case, the withdrawal of shipping space in ships of this speed cannot be contemplated at the present time. Furthermore, a very large amount of dockyard work would be involved in reconstructing and adapting the vessels for the end in view, while the labour facilities are already seriously constricted by production of new ships of all classes, and repair work to vessels damaged by torpedo.' Moreover, the torpedo carried by the 'Cuckoo' was 'a weapon of short range and small offensive power; and attacks of this nature against the enemy's capital ships have yet to be practised and developed, and are a very uncertain quantity.' The Admiralty did not accept the proposition that, 'under existing circumstances, the air presents the greatest facilities for conducting an offensive against the enemy's vessels and bases,' but 'the possibilities of developing such an offensive in the future are being fully considered.' Beatty's C.O.S. had to admit that the Admiralty had made out 'a strong case. The torpedo airplane is not sufficiently developed to warrant the construction of eight large ships urgently needed for other work.'[22] For the remainder of the year little was heard of a naval air offensive.

*   *   *

Having explored the various plans for offensive operations to defeat the U-boats and found them to be 'either impossible of achievement or that the attempt to carry them out might endanger our surface command of the sea,'[23] the decision-makers at the Admiralty had by the end of 1917 concluded that the main functions of the Fleet must remain essentially defensive: to control British and Allied trade communications, defend the country from invasion, ensure the transport of reinforcements to France, safeguard the passage of the American Army, keep the enemy from breaking out, by means of mine barrages, and carry on an active offensive against the U-boats by means of the concentration of patrol craft and kite balloon forces, and by ensuring to the utmost with the naval forces available the efficiency of the barrages. There was no scope for adventures anywhere, the Baltic included.

[22] Admiralty to Beatty, 20 October 1917, and O. de B. Brock's minute; Admiralty MSS.
[23] Jellicoe, *The Submarine Peril*, p. 69.

4. A BALTIC OFFENSIVE

Lord Fisher had had the idea early in the war of sowing the North Sea with mines and then transferring the Grand Fleet to the Baltic; but, as Jellicoe afterwards summarized the difficulties, 'We had not a hundredth part of the mines necessary for such a scheme, and in any case, passages can always be swept through an undefended minefield. Before the fleet could pass the Belts it was necessary that the adjacent shores could be held by us. The idea was not seriously put forward.'[24] Baltic offensive ideas kept cropping up, however, even if they found no favour at the Admiralty after Fisher's departure, nor in the War Committee of the Cabinet. Balfour when First Lord had found it necessary to repudiate such schemes.

Such a campaign has a great attraction for some people whose opinion is not to be lightly dismissed; but I doubt whether it would be approved by any sailor with war experience. The ordinary approach to the Baltic (the Sound), is too shallow to permit any of our large ships to go through. Every approach without exception is heavily mined at the southern or German end; all are within easy reach of the great arsenal of Kiel; and it would be quite impossible to force a way through without serious loss. The effort would be more costly than the naval attempt on the Dardanelles—and there is no military prize comparable to Constantinople to reward our efforts if we succeeded.[25]

Less ambitious Baltic operations received careful Admiralty consideration in the autumn of 1917 as a means of relieving Russia of German naval pressure and, if it came to this, of ensuring against the German acquisition of any part of the Russian Baltic Fleet. At first the Admiralty had expected that nothing but good would come of the March Revolution: the rejuvenation of the Russian Navy, etc. These hopes had been quickly dashed as gloomy reports began to arrive of the chaotic state of the Baltic Fleet—of the murder and imprisonment of officers, and other evidence of a breakdown of discipline. An early Admiralty War Staff appreciation of the situation pointed to the

urgent importance that law and order should be again established in the Baltic Fleet without delay, or the results, once the Baltic is clear of

[24] Jellicoe, 'A Reply to Criticism', n.d.; Jellicoe MSS. And see *From the Dreadnought to Scapa Flow*, ii. 191–6.
[25] Balfour's memorandum for the War Committee, 'Report on Recent Naval Affairs. October 1916' (G.-86), 14 October 1916.

ice, may well be disastrous not only to Russia, but to our cause in general. . . . The fall of Riga and a landing in Finland are both possible, and even probable, without the immediate co-operation of all arms of the Navy. It is a difficult, by no means impossible, task for the Germans to break through the minefield closing the Gulf of Finland, in which case the Russian Fleet in their present state of disorganisation would be at the enemy's mercy, and it is not improbable that a number of capital ships would surrender and be used against us.[26]

This estimate prompted Jellicoe (with War Cabinet approval) to have the Government telegraph the Russian authorities, pointing out the imperative need to get their Fleet organized and prepared to proceed with minelaying when the ice broke. He was afraid they would not be ready. To help the Russians, he asked Beatty (12 April) occasionally to send a battle or battle-cruiser squadron down towards Horns Reef between the third week in April and the middle of May, that is, during the ice-breaking season, so as to keep the High Seas Fleet on the North Sea side. Beatty did send the battle cruisers to a position off the Little Fisher Bank (the area westward of Jutland Bank) at the end of April—as a cover for a minelaying operation, but also no doubt to meet Jellicoe's request.

The immediate cause for anxiety disappeared in the spring, after the Russians had relaid the minefields in the Gulf of Finland, and made a pretty good job of it, notwithstanding the lack of discipline in the Baltic Fleet. The situation became serious in October, when a German army occupied the Island of Oesel at the mouth of the Gulf of Riga. This brought the Germans within practical striking distance of the important Russian naval base of Reval, in the Gulf of Finland, and even of the Russian capital itself, Petrograd (the Leningrad of today) (Chart 1A). The Germans had virtually complete control of the Gulf of Riga before the month was over. A Naval Staff appreciation for the War Cabinet summarized the position:

The Russians have lost their outpost bases except Hangö and Hapsal and will be compelled either to give fight or remain behind minefields and batteries either at Reval or Helsingfors. Should the former place fall, a retirement to Cronstadt would be forced on them. They would then be situated in some form similar to the German Fleet in the Heligoland Bight, with this difference, that the German coast batteries are

[26] Admiralty War Staff paper for the War Cabinet, 'The Effect of the Russian Revolution on the Situation in the Baltic' (G.T.-351), 1 April 1917.

very good and *we* do not hold an advanced base on their coast; whilst the Russian coast batteries are very poor and the Germans will have an important advance base in Russian territory. On the other hand, it is possible that the German main operations in this direction have ceased for the winter, and it is understood that they are relieving part of their land forces, leaving garrisons only in the Islands, and the more power-ful ships of their Fleet are being replaced by battleships and cruisers of older type, though the naval forces remaining will be numerically the same as before.[27]

The Russian Provisional Government expressed the hope that with nearly two-thirds of the whole German Fleet (including 12–16 battleships) in the Baltic, it might be possible for the British Fleet to seize this favourable occasion to take the offensive. The Prime Minister, Kerensky, was aware that an attempt to force the Baltic would be a dangerous operation, but 'in view of great interests at stake risk was worth running for appearance of British Fleet in Baltic would at once effect radical change in situation in this country'.[28]

Some time in the early autumn of 1917 Jellicoe had instructed the Plans Division to study the prospects of passing a fleet into the Baltic to relieve German naval pressure on the Russians. Had the report been favourable, he planned to have Roger Keyes com-mand the force. The Plans Division, however, did not consider the operation a practicable one so far as using heavy ships was con-cerned. Jellicoe was in full accord with the report. He afterwards stated the case against Baltic operations:

The principal reason was that prolonged *occupation* of the Baltic was not practicable unless the High Sea Fleet was first put out of action, or unless the Elbe was blocked, and a sufficiently strong force sent to the Baltic to reinforce the Russian fleet, and to hold the Great Belt against the High Sea Fleet. An immense amount of mine-sweeping would be required and the ships guarding the Belts would be subject to heavy air and submarine attack by day and in narrow water, and to destroyer attack at night.

A *raid* into the Baltic, carried out with a view to bringing the High Sea Fleet out to face action in that sea, although practicable, was an

[27] 'German Operations in the Gulf of Riga' (G.T.-2420), 26 October 1917.
[28] Sir George Buchanan (British Ambassador in Petrograd) to Foreign Office, 17 October 1917; Admiralty MSS. Actually, as Jellicoe informed the Russian Naval Attaché, only a small part of the German Fleet, with not more than a quarter of their battleships, was in the Baltic.

operation involving the use of a fleet both in the Baltic and in the North Sea, since, in the absence of our fleet in the Baltic, the High Sea Fleet might, instead of facing us in the Baltic, emerge into the North Sea, cut off our communications with France and generally obtain control of our waters.

There was the alternative of endeavouring to force a passage through the Sound into the Baltic for submarines. This would have probably involved a loss of several destroyers, and in view of the conditions in Russia at the time, it was not considered desirable to send even submarines into the Baltic.[29]

All that the Admiralty would do to assist the Russians was to have several squadrons cruising in the North Sea with a view to attracting the attention of the German Navy. When the Russian Naval Attaché pressed for stronger action—'an energetic demonstration in the narrows of the two Belts . . . [to] compel the German Fleet to return to the North Sea'—all Jellicoe would do was to extend the demonstration into the narrows late in October. A force of destroyers and submarines, supported by light cruisers (with the battle cruisers and 2nd Battle Squadron in support, though well behind), steamed into the central part of the Kattegat and sank the German auxiliary cruiser *Maria* and about ten fishing vessels. The demonstration was too weak to influence German strategy in the Baltic.

It is difficult to see how the British could have done very much more. Even putting to one side all other considerations, as Rear-Admiral Victor Stanley, the Head of the Naval Mission to Russia, told the Chief of the Russian Naval General Staff, were the British Fleet to enter the Baltic, the German Fleet would probably retire to the Kiel Canal at once and block the British exit from the Baltic by sinking a few ships. The British force would thus be caught in a trap.[30]

---

[29] Jellicoe, *The Submarine Peril*, pp. 68–9, which is in effect a résumé of the Plans Division paper, 'Operations in the Baltic', 21 October 1917 (Admiralty MSS). Cf. Kenworthy's account in *Sailors, Statesmen—and Others: an Autobiography* (London, 1933), pp. 128–34, which has the Plans Division strongly favouring a Baltic expedition, and being frustrated by the British and French politicians. They were ' "fed up" with Kerensky and his Government and would not risk a ship to help them. Keyes was as disgusted as I was. . . . We both felt like weeping. This was the worst blunder, the greatest betrayal of the whole war.' This account may well be fanciful. At any rate, it does not jibe with the contents of the Plans Division paper of 21 October.

[30] Buchanan to Foreign Office (telegram), 23 October 1917; Admiralty MSS.

With the Bolshevik *coup d'état* on 7 November and the likelihood of Russia pulling out of the war, there appeared to be a distinct danger of the Baltic Fleet falling into German possession. This was a matter of profound concern to the Admiralty. To prevent the four dreadnoughts in particular from falling into enemy hands, there was talk of dispatching the six old British submarines that were operating in the Baltic into Kronstadt harbour to torpedo the Russian battleships. One flaw in this plan was that the Germans would before long succeed in raising the sunken ships in the shallow and smooth water of the harbour and use the dockyard facilities to ready them for action. Eventually, on 23 November, the War Cabinet[31] approved this action proposed by the Admiralty: (1) to destroy the British submarines in the Baltic; (2) to encourage the escape of the Russian destroyers from the Baltic; (3) 'to encourage, so far as may be feasible, the destruction of other vessels in the Russian Baltic fleet [meaning the four dreadnoughts above all], by Russians, who remain loyal to the cause of the allies . . .' Finally, 'the Admiralty were authorised to sanction any expenditure required by their representatives in Russia in the furtherance of the above objects', meaning, of course, bribery.

To the British public, to say nothing of the Fleet, the unwillingness of the Admiralty to do anything substantial to help a mortally wounded ally made little strategic sense and was shameful into the bargain. It was not impressed with Geddes's statement in the Commons (1 November) that if the fleet had forced the entrance to the Baltic—a difficult operation—it would have been 'an act of madness', having regard to the certainty that the Germans would have retorted by occupying and fortifying the Danish islands commanding the Sound and the Belts, and would have caught the fleet in a trap. 'Our fleet in the Baltic, if it got through, would soon wither to impotence with its vital communications cut.' No responsible officer, Geddes asserted, would support such an enterprise.

As the year came to an end, it was obvious that Germany no longer had any reason to maintain a considerable proportion of her Navy in the Baltic—the Russian menace no longer existed—and therefore could, for the first time in the war, concentrate her naval strength in the North Sea 'at her selected moment'. The prospect, all the more threatening because the Germans might acquire at least part of the Russian Baltic Fleet, was one of the factors that

[31] W.C. 281A.

led to a re-evaluation of British naval strategy at the highest levels early in the New Year.

5. THE NORTHERN NEUTRALS IN NAVAL STRATEGY

Relations with the neutrals continued strained. The Allied objectives—to secure from neutrals those raw materials on which they were largely dependent, and to prevent such raw materials going into Germany—conflicted with the natural desire of the neutrals to make as much money as they possibly could. A blockade against Holland and the Scandinavian countries would soon have brought them to their knees, though certain vitally important articles would be lost to the Allies, such as Norwegian iron ore and fish, also their large mercantile marine, on which the British largely depended for the carrying of coal and supplies to themselves and their Allies. British policy had therefore been to secure favourable commercial treaties with these countries, under which a certain percentage of their key exports went to Britain, and to secure the enforcement of the treaties through the 'Black List' and the curtailing of bunkering facilities. The latter was an important lever, since the Northern neutrals drew their supplies from overseas, and their ships had therefore to be bunkered during long voyages.

Certain organs of the British press were vociferous in their demands that the blockade of Germany, the most powerful weapon in the Allied arsenal, must be tightened. The blockade was 'still leaking grievously', charged the *Daily Mail* (20 March 1917). 'Food in enormous quantities is reaching the enemy. . . . Food is no longer imported directly into Germany, it is true. But we permit neutral ships to carry fertilisers and fattening stuffs, which are the raw materials of food, to neutral countries, such as Holland and Denmark, where they are properly worked up into food and sent to the Germans.' The fault, as the *Daily Mail* in particular saw it, lay in the Foreign Office control of blockade policy—'the curse of Foreign Office interference'. That responsibility should forthwith be transferred to the Admiralty, which could be trusted to stop the yawning holes. This problem was, of course, no longer serious, once the United States joined the Allies.

A by-product of the blockade of Germany, and an extremely important factor in British defence calculations from the autumn of 1916, was the concern of the Admiralty and the War Office that the pressure of the blockade might force the enemy to invade the Jutland peninsula of Denmark and carry off food supplies and livestock. Or Germany might invade because she suspected Denmark would join the Allies and therefore wished to occupy Jutland in order to keep Allied forces out. What help could Britain give the Danes in either contingency? the Government wondered. A joint Staff appreciation in October 1916 admitted that, for naval reasons, no assistance was possible. 'The route to be followed by transports proceeding to Denmark passes within 200 miles of the German principal base, from which the German fleet can emerge at full strength at any time it may select. The British fleet would have to be kept constantly at sea to protect the line of communications, and at a strength superior to that of the whole German navy. The enemy may be expected to make full use of his submarines . . . to attack our covering fleet and transports, and we should incur heavy losses from submarine attack without necessarily being given any opportunity of making a corresponding attack upon the enemy.'[32] A War Cabinet committee which examined the position of the Northern neutral countries in the summer of 1917 concluded, as regards Denmark, that Britain was not in a position to give either military or naval assistance to that country.[33] Thereafter one hears little of the Danish problem.

There was a similar problem as regards Holland. She was a neutral country and of more use to Britain as such than as an ally. They got a lot of food, also information about Germany, from her. The Dutch often overlooked British ships going inside territorial waters, 'and when they did protest,' says Oliver, 'the Dutch Naval

[32] 'The Military Situation in Denmark', 11 October 1916, over the signature of Robertson, the C.I.G.S.; Admiralty MSS. Oliver was afraid, moreover, that on however small a scale an expedition to Denmark began, it would 'increase and swell, similarly to the Dardanelles expedition, and a few months after its inception it would have reached similar dimensions'. Also, their existing overseas commitments made it impossible to meet the naval or mercantile requirements, 'and to undertake another large expedition would produce such a drain on our resources as to render stagnation and failure inevitable in the other theatres of oversea operations'. Oliver's basic argument, however, was: 'As long as the war is going favourably, if slowly, nothing should be risked which might enable Germany to redress the balance at sea.' Oliver's memorandum, 'Denmark', 2 October 1916; Admiralty MSS. Oliver's views about Denmark have a general application to all the projects of this kind that were discussed in 1916–18. The First Sea Lord, Jackson, stressed the tonnage factor, which was the 'determining' one. Minute of 2 October 1916; Admiralty MSS.

[33] Bellairs, 'Notes on the Report of the Committee . . .' (of the War Cabinet which examined the position vis-à-vis the Northern Neutrals), 8 September 1917; Bellairs MSS.

Attaché used to come to me and it was fixed up amicably.'[34] The Admiralty view was, therefore, to leave the Dutch alone. In general that was the position of the Government, despite attempts made by Lord Robert Cecil, Chairman of the Restriction of Enemy Supplies Committee, to get the War Cabinet to take drastic steps against the Dutch. It would be a different matter if the Dutch were forced to join the Germans or if, as was feared, the Germans intended to violate Dutch neutrality with the object of seizing the mouths of the Scheldt. This would mean (besides the loss of food for Britain) the control of the Dutch coast, additional bases for submarines and destroyers, and would increase the risk of invasion and interruption of Britain's cross-Channel communications with France. Whenever a German move into Holland seemed probable, accordingly, as in the spring of 1916, the two Staffs had to decide what measures would be required to block the enemy, who would brush aside any purely Dutch resistance.

In the summer of 1917 indications again pointed to an enemy advance into Holland. This expectation was based on the anticipated success of the Flanders operation—the Third Battle of Ypres. If the enemy were driven out of Zeebrugge, it was highly probable (or so Beatty and the naval and military planners at Whitehall believed) that they would attempt to seize the Scheldt and establish a base there for their submarines. A fresh joint Staff appreciation saw no great military advantages in Holland joining the Allies (the drain on resources, etc.), but drew up a plan for the seizure and occupation of Walcheren, should the occasion arise, with the object of denying the enemy the use of the Scheldt. The operation was, they considered, possible if Holland were not hostile: a mixed brigade, supported by sufficient naval force off the island, would be sufficient. If the Dutch were hostile, the only practical operation would be to attempt to drive the enemy from the Kadzand area, thereby denying them the West Scheldt.[35]

Beatty thought that it would be 'nothing short of disastrous' if Holland joined the Central Powers. On the other hand, if she joined the Allies, the naval and air advantages would be 'immense'. He saw interesting possibilities in the Dutch situation for accomplishing the two supreme objectives of the Fleet: bringing the High Seas Fleet to action and defeating 'the supreme menace

[34] Oliver MSS.
[35] 'The Closure of the West Scheldt', 8 August 1917; Admiralty MSS.

under which we suffer', namely, the U-boats. He urged that plans be prepared and forces made ready to seize Holland proper, if there were 'any decided indications' that the Dutch intended to join the enemy, or to assist the Dutch if they joined the Allies. His ultimate goal was the establishment of a powerful air and naval base in Holland. 'Continuous offensive operations [by light craft in the Heligoland Bight and by aircraft which would bomb Essen, Hamburg, etc.] could be carried out which might eventually lead to movement of German heavy ships. The German Command would be disturbed, a withdrawal of submarines for defence purposes would result, and the naval initiative would pass to the Allies.'[36]

The C.-in-C. received qualified support in Whitehall. The General Staff were reluctant to commit sizeable forces even in a friendly Holland (the superiority of enemy communications was one consideration), and were not prepared to do much more than to make feints of landing. The Foreign Office stipulated that on no account should the neutrality of Holland be infringed—she would resist it—until the Germans had actually crossed into Holland. This, in the opinion of both the C.-in-C. and the Plans Division, ruined the chances of seizing Walcheren, for it was inevitable that their forces could not arrive until too late. 'The C.-in-C. pointed out [to Pound] that it was essential we should anticipate the enemy, and that the whole efforts of the Foreign Office with Naval and Military co-operation should be to bring Holland in prior to the Germans moving across the border, and to ensure that our forces arrived beforehand. From information supplied from official sources he felt that this was not impossible provided we abandoned the policy of pin-pricks and treated Holland in as generous a manner as possible as regards the supply of coal etc.'[37] He was even more outspoken two days later.

If we are sufficiently strong and sufficiently determined the Dutch are much more likely to come in with us than go against us . . . we must be prepared to anticipate any move on the part of the Enemy to the Schelde . . . I gather that the Foreign Office view is that on no account should we move until the Enemy has crossed into Holland. This delay would be fatal. . . . This provides an instance of the Foreign Office

[36] 'Appreciation of the Situation Regarding the Question of the Entry of Holland into the War', 7 August 1917; Admiralty MSS.
[37] 'Notes on Conference with Captain Pound', 23 September, 1917; Bellairs MSS.

dictating Military Policy which is obviously wrong. I gather further
that any Force we should employ would be a small Force. Again, this
is wrong. It must be strong and well supported, so strong that it may
cause the enemy to move a large naval force to interfere with it. It
should be protected by a strong British Naval Force, possibly the
Grand Fleet, to the northward. To sum up it is essential that we should
anticipate the Enemy and be prepared for a move into Holland *with
adequate forces*. Such a move might develop into an operation on a
grand scale requiring strong naval support. Obviously we should not
move unless we are forced to do so by the necessity of forestalling the
Enemy.[38]

Beatty was prepared to turn the screws on Holland. He pointed
out to the First Lord that the danger was a German move and the
Dutch not resisting but pleading *force majeure*. 'He emphasised that
a strong foreign policy must meet this and we must not be content
to allow naval and military considerations to be dictated by
diplomatic considerations with the consequence that we should
wait to act until too late. Holland should be informed that if she
does not resist Germany and join the Allies as soon as Germany
moves, then it is the intention of the Allies to seize the Dutch
colonies and establish themselves at the naval base of the Helder
[Willemsoord] (with the object of carrying out an air and naval
offensive on important German positions) or consider the feasibility of obtaining a base in the Frisian Islands, Terschelling or
Ameland.'[39]

Late in October, complying with instructions from the War
Cabinet, the Plans Division worked out plans to send a small combined force (principally naval: monitors and gunboats) to Walcheren
in the event of a German violation of Holland with the object of
seizing the Scheldt. Events in November 'rendered this question
of no further immediate interest', and the Admiralty so notified
the War Cabinet on 3 December. 'Reliable information' had been
received that the Dutch had sent large numbers of troops into
Walcheren. For the Admiralty this was sufficient indication that
'so long as Holland does not join the Central Powers she would
also oppose an occupation of the Island by the enemy. Under these
circumstances, it seems hardly necessary to proceed further with

[38] Beatty to Geddes, 25 September 1917; Admiralty MSS.
[39] 'Conference between Commander-in-Chief, Grand Fleet, and Deputy First Sea
Lord Held on 10th October, 1917'; Bellairs MSS.

the preparations . . .'[40] There was the additional consideration that, with the failure of the Flanders campaign to dislodge the enemy from Zeebrugge, they were much less likely to try to seize the Scheldt.

Norway had presented a special problem since the autumn of 1916. Her decision (occasioned by the U-boat destruction of Norwegian shipping) to prohibit the passage of belligerent submarines through her territorial waters (15 October 1916) evoked a strong German protest. The Foreign Office opined that if Norway were forced to come to terms with Germany, the direct and immediate effect on Britain would be 'almost incalculable', as through the stoppage of British supplies of Norwegian and Swedish iron and steel, nitrates, zinc, aluminium, and other products the Ministry of Munitions considered vital, and the loss of the considerable Norwegian tonnage chartered to carry coal to France and otherwise engaged in Allied trade. The conclusion was that it was clearly to the Allied interest that Norway should not capitulate, even if it meant war.[41] Having an exaggerated idea of what the Grand Fleet could do, the Foreign Office assumed that British sea power could in that event protect Norway from invasion. The War Staff pointed out there was no base in southern Norway capable of accommodating a fleet superior to the High Seas Fleet; the absence of capital ships would weaken the Grand Fleet; and 'there would always be a great risk of their being cut off by a superior force before they could receive support'.[42] The Admiralty reconsidered their position in the light of the great naval strategic advantages Germany would gain by bending Norway to her will. The plan was now (December), in case the Germans declared war on Norway, to base a squadron (light forces) at Kristiansand to intercept merchant shipping or to attack the enemy's forces when possible. Germany held her hand; she had no desire to extend the war.

Beatty added a fresh element to the Norwegian situation soon after becoming C.-in-C. Disturbed by the escape of the raider *Wolf* into the Atlantic on 30 November, he remonstrated with the Admiralty (15 December) that he could not intercept either

[40] Memorandum by Geddes, 'The Position in Holland' (G.T.-2847).
[41] Sir Eyre Crowe's (Assistant Under-Secretary of State for Foreign Affairs) memorandum for the War Committee, 29 October 1916; Admiralty MSS.
[42] Admiralty War Staff paper, 'Norway', 28 October 1916; Admiralty MSS.

raiders or contraband unless the fleet were permitted to enter Norwegian territorial waters for search purposes. He was prepared to see Norway thrown into the war by the adoption of such a policy; the situation would be advantageous to Britain whether Norway became an enemy or sided with the Allies. He expressed himself frankly to the new Foreign Secretary on the same day:

I put this to you. Germany wages war ruthlessly, acknowledges no laws. . . . Results, Neutrals are afraid of her. And she works her will. For us they care nothing, and are so afraid of Germany that they won't help us to help them. The blind adherence to international laws . . . prevents us from winning the war and is helping us to lose it. The Enemy can pass out raiders to any extent; can pass in contraband in large quantities, and so prolong the contest, by using the protection of neutral waters. They have announced their intention of continuing the War to the knife, greater ruthlessness, further violations of the laws of nations, while we continue to wage war in a spirit of benevolence.

Surely, we should either in consequence assert our intention of visiting and searching vessels in Territorial Waters . . . or do it without asserting it. We don't injure Norway beyond possibly their amour propre, and what is that compared to the vast material damage they are suffering daily from Germany. Is it not now time that we took the gloves off? . . .

Consider this. A German supply ship for replenishing German submarines is chased on the Norwegian coast and takes refuge in her waters and is thereby protected by the country whose merchant ships she is assisting to destroy. Surely when International Law makes such possible it is time it was altered or abolished. I hope you will excuse this tirade, but!![43]

The escape of the *Seeadler* a few days later emphasized the hindrance to effective operations imposed by the strict observance of territorial waters.

The Admiralty agreed with Beatty that, as a neutral state which had been treated ruthlessly by Germany, Norway might well close her waters to German vessels, and as she was too timid or weak to do it herself, the British were morally justified in doing it for her. But the policy of infringing Norway's territorial rights was regarded as impracticable, owing to the bad effect that might be produced on other neutrals, particularly Sweden and the United States. This would probably cause a cessation of certain supplies

[43] Beatty to Balfour, 15 December 1916; Admiralty MSS.

for which they were dependent on Norway, and cut off supplies from Sweden. This was the line the War Cabinet took on 29 January 1917. In view of the danger to British interests which would be involved in any general violation of territorial waters, for example in Spain or Sweden, 'It would not be in our interests to take the initiative by any violation of Norwegian neutrality.'[44]

At the same time the War Cabinet and the Service ministries did not lose sight of the problem of what action would be taken to assist Norway if Germany forced her into the war. The matter was under regular consideration through most of 1917, as Germany's arbitrary actions against Norway (the capture of a Norwegian ship by a U-boat and of Danish ships with meat for Norway, etc.) seemed likely at various critical moments to propel Norway into war, despite her great reluctance to adopt this course. It was not expected that Norway would enter voluntarily, since she was supposed to be in great fear of Germany, particularly as regards aerial attack, but that she would be forced into war by Germany. The Admiralty War Staff and the General Staff were averse to Norway's entry into the war as an ally. Her naval and military resources were not sufficient for her own defence, hence an extra strain would be put on the Allied forces. The Services doubted Britain's ability to protect Norway against air raids or to seize a naval base if Norway resisted.

By September 1917 the Admiralty had begun to undergo a change of heart, caused by 'the lapse of time and the progress of enemy submarine warfare'. On 3 September the First Sea Lord intimated to the War Cabinet 'that the time might come, but had not yet arrived, when the establishment of a naval base in Norway might be of great advantage from the point of view of an active offence against enemy submarines.'[45] He was mindful, as he informed the War Cabinet on 7 September, that Norway's joining the Allies would necessitate the appropriation of tonnage to maintain British forces in Norwegian bases and the diversion of many small craft from convoy escort work and the protection of the western trade routes to Norwegian waters in order to protect the occupied bases.[46] In the autumn the Naval Staff worked out plans for the immediate occupation of Kristiansand as an advanced base

[44] W.C. 47.
[45] W.C. 227.
[46] W.C. 229.

for a Grand Fleet detached squadron, if it became necessary to assist Norway. This would be worth doing, in the Navy's judgement, for a number of reasons: (1) the temptation to the Germans to attack the squadron's lines of communications might lead eventually to a general action between the Grand Fleet and the High Seas Fleet; (2) it would deny this port to the German Fleet, while providing a base for operating against the U-boats in the Skagerrak; (3) it would more easily open up to attack U-boats and raiders attempting to pass through Norwegian territorial waters; (4) the squadron would be well placed to attack the German transports and lines of communication, if the enemy attempted a landing, the most likely place for which was Frederikshald Fjord, near the Kristiania (now Oslo) Fjord. Such action might succeed in drawing out the High Seas Fleet.[47]

From the point of view of the Grand Fleet and the Admiralty, the unimaginative policy of the Government towards the Northern neutrals, Holland and Norway in particular, nullified a strategy that offered possibilities of seizing the naval initiative, strengthening trade defences, and perhaps even enticing the High Seas Fleet out. The frustrations of the Grand Fleet were only intensified. In defence of the politicians, it must be said that they had the imagination to see that Beatty's ideas were likely to get Britain into a mess: his desire for another battle, though laudable and an important factor in morale, might well lead to unsound strategy when straining for conditions to bring one about.

*   *   *

The feeling of frustration among Grand Fleet officers mounted throughout 1917 until by the end of the year there was almost a revolutionary atmosphere at Scapa and Rosyth. Offensively-minded officers like Richmond and Drax, supported at the Admiralty by Wemyss, Keyes, Dewar, and others, were desperately unhappy over the absence of an 'offensive spirit' in Whitehall. Richmond caustically referred to those in authority at the Admiralty as 'ignorant pretenders' who threw away opportunities, and Dewar believed that it was 'the most incompetent administration which it is possible to imagine'. 'No doubt Providence will save us,' Drax wrote to Beatty's Secretary, 'We need hardly hope

[47] 'The Situation Regarding the Northern Neutral Countries', 14 September 1917; Admiralty MSS.

that the Admiralty will.' His plea was that Beatty 'take the responsibility of recommending (or demanding) the selection of those men who alone can save the situation'.[48]

It is easy to sympathize with the restlessness of the Young Turks: standing on the defensive generated little joy. There was little virtue in offensive-mindedness when it leads only to impracticable proposals like an attempt to block the German ports or a Baltic sortie. (Such operations were, to be sure, not pushed by the more enlightened Young Turks.) Combined operations in the Adriatic and Eastern Mediterranean and a more aggressive use of aircraft, on the other hand, were more promising uses of the Fleet and deserved fuller consideration than they received in high quarters. So far as the naval air offensive was concerned, the root trouble went back to 1915. Two years were lost before the Navy built a true aircraft carrier. It can be argued that, had the Admiralty gone all out for carriers in 1915, the torpedo attack on the High Seas Fleet for which Beatty pressed in 1917–18, might have been practicable by 1918. A sympathetic Board in the first years of the war (I especially have in mind the Balfour-Jackson Board of 1915–16) would have made much difference; yet the early technical difficulties, which were great, would have remained.

A NOTE ON MINELAYING IN THE BIGHT

David Woodward concludes from his study of the pertinent volumes in the German official histories: 'The value of the British minelaying effort in the Bight has tended to be minimized, at least in the period before the new and efficient H2 mines came into service in September 1917, but the German account makes it clear that from the beginning the British mines were reckoned a great danger. Their overall effectiveness is shown by the fact that during 1917–18 the Germans lost 28 destroyers and torpedo boats, about 70 minesweepers and armed trawlers, and at least four U-boats in the Bight minesweeping operations.'[49]

[48] Drax to Paymaster Frank T. Spickernell, 11 August 1917; copy in Richmond MSS. Spickernell told Drax that 'there is no possible remedy unless David Beatty goes to the Admiralty as First Sea Lord: then all will be well'. Drax to Richmond, 16 August 1917; Richmond MSS. For Drax Beatty was most needed where he was. Richmond was not so sure. In Beatty 'we have the makings of a real statesman. The question of whether he should not be at Whitehall intrudes itself more than ever upon me.' Diary, 22 September 1917; *Portrait of an Admiral*, p. 274.

[49] Woodward, 'The High Seas Fleet—1917–18', *Royal United Service Institution Journal*, August 1968.

X

The Convoy System in Operation

(July 1917 – December 1917)

> The shipping situation in 6–9 months may have reached the limit below which it is not permissible to go and yet be able to feed, munition, and store allied countries with absolute essentials.
>
> JELLICOE's minute for the D.O.D., 31 July 1917.

> The [U-boat campaign] is the Biggest Thing we are up against and is going to cause us to win or lose the War. Our Armies will be useless if they [the U-boats] really get the upper hand of us.
>
> BEATTY to Jellicoe, 22 July 1917.

> The greatest Allied triumph of 1917 was the gradual beating off of the submarine attack. This was the real decision of the War, for the sea front turned out to be the decisive flank in the gigantic battlefield.
>
> LLOYD GEORGE, *War Memoirs*.

1. EXTENSION OF OCEAN CONVOY

BY EARLY July, Geddes (then still Controller) had worked out his mercantile shipbuilding programme. His goal was a yearly output for British yards of 3,100,000 tons, which target involved a doubling of the production rate of the last peacetime year, 1913. Geddes knew this could not be realized before 1919. His expectation was a total output for 1917 of 1,566,000 tons (1,190,000 tons, June–December, and the 376,000 tons completed through May), or 30 per cent above the Shipping Controller's estimate. The actual mercantile tonnage completed in British yards during 1917 was 1,163,000 tons gross. The 2,300,000 tons estimated for 1918 had to be lowered to 1,800,000 in November 1917, after it became clear that steel and labour shortages (among other factors) had made the original figure for 1918 unrealistic. The revised figure represented little more than two-thirds of the losses in ocean-going steamers, at the average rate of the September–November losses. 'Thus,' as Fayle sums up the matter, 'so far from making good the havoc wrought in 1917, there would still be a cumulative deficit. The prospect of an eventual output at the rate of 3,000,000 tons a year was cheering in relation to the recovery of the mercantile marine after the war; but it was evident the war might be won or lost before its effect could be felt. The reduction in the prospective programme was the more serious inasmuch as all hope of making good the deficit by oversea purchase had been finally extinguished.'[1]

Jellicoe continued his strenuous efforts to reduce the Army's shipping requirements. On 9 October 1917 he reiterated his position in a paper for the War Cabinet: the secondary military operations in the Near East, which absorbed so many merchant vessels, with small craft to protect them, were denuding Britain of the ships needed for importing essential supplies for herself and the Allies, and causing heavy losses because of the insufficient number of vessels for the protection of that shipping. He agreed with the C.I.G.S., Robertson, though for a different reason, that there should be a concentration of military forces on the Western Front, with the armies in the Eastern theatre adopting a defensive strategy. Such a policy would do more than assist the Navy greatly in the A/S campaign: it would render possible greater assistance to the Americans in the transport and convoy of their troops to France, give Britain the tonnage to keep up their own essential imports, and enable them to help their Allies in the provision of coal and wheat, so as to tide them over the winter.[2]

Various expedients, such as the concentration of traffic upon the shorter North American route (Chiozza Money's plan) and drastic curbs on imports, had helped to conserve tonnage. 'These measures', Newbolt says, 'had . . . given us a breathing space; but it was quite obvious that such expedients could only operate for a certain time; the excess of losses over replacements must, in the end, swallow up the tonnage saved by these special measures and then the breathing space would end in national asphyxiation.'[3] Only the convoy system promised to be able to effect a sharp and permanent reduction in the shipping loss rate.

We have seen that the first experimental ocean convoys had sailed in May, from Gibraltar on the 10th and Hampton Roads on

[1] Fayle, *Seaborne Trade*, iii. 213.
[2] 'Future Naval Policy' (G.T.-2250), 9 October 1917.
[3] *Naval Operations*, v. 128.

the 24th, that four more had left Hampton Roads in June, that the pioneers of convoy were confident that an expansion of the system would defeat the U-boats, and that, as late as June, High Authority were not absolutely convinced that the answer lay in a system of convoy. An important factor in the expansion of convoy in July was the change in the American attitude. Sims's untiring efforts on behalf of an extension of convoy, along with the complete success of the first convoys (the 71 ships of the five convoys that had crossed the Atlantic in June had all arrived safely), finally converted the Navy Department to a belief in the system. 'It would seem suicidal,' Sims pleaded with the Secretary of the Navy, 'if the convoy system as proposed by the British Admiralty is not put into immediate operation and applied to all merchant vessels thus forcing submarines to encounter anti-submarine craft in order to attack shipping.'[4] A strong letter of 29 June to the Secretary of the Navy asserted the blunt truth that 'If the shipping losses continue as they have during the past four months, it is submitted that the Allies will be forced to dire straits indeed, if they will not actually be forced into an unsatisfactory peace.'[5] But the game had been won, as he admitted three days later. 'I have been putting it to our Navy Department as strongly as I know how . . . and not until yesterday was there any reply on the subject. . . . I am happy to see that our Government has now expressed its willingness to help out with the convoy.'[6]

In July a North Atlantic Homeward Convoy System was put into effect by regular convoys (running alternately to East and West Coast ports) from Hampton Roads, beginning on 2 July; from Sydney, Cape Breton (for ships from Canadian ports), beginning on 10 July (Halifax was added in August); and from New York (for ships from U.S. Atlantic ports north of Philadelphia), beginning on 14 July. The Hampton Roads convoy ran every four days, the others, every eight days. Thirteen homeward-bound mercantile convoys sailed across the Atlantic in July (some arriving early in August). Of the 245 ships convoyed, which included 46 oilers, only one was torpedoed and sunk (off Tory Island on 6 August), representing a loss of 0·41 per cent in numbers and 0.38 per cent in tonnage.

[4] Sims to Daniels, 20 June 1917; U.S. Navy Dept. MSS.
[5] Sims, *The Victory at Sea*, pp. 387–90.
[6] Sims to Captain William V. Pratt, 2 July 1917; U.S. Navy Dept. MSS.

Although a regular North Atlantic homeward convoy was in operation by the middle of July, no convoy arrangements had been made for the Mediterranean or the South Atlantic trade, and, despite the Convoy Committee's recommendation of homeward and outward convoys from the start, *all outward-bound ships continued to be sailed independently.* The decisive consideration that led to the further extension of the convoy system was the continuing heavy shipping losses. The last reserves of ocean-carrying power were fast being used up, Sir Norman Hill warned the War Cabinet early in July. (He was the Chairman of the Port and Transit Executive Committee, which was the supreme authority over ports and harbours.) At a series of conferences between the War Cabinet, Admiralty, and Ministry of Shipping officials, and representatives of the shipowners (12, 13, 20 July), the last-named predicted a complete breakdown in ocean shipping unless the losses in the approach areas could be swiftly reduced. As a result of these meetings the Admiralty were now prepared to risk the employment of smaller destroyer escorts than they had deemed safe, as well as to experiment with trawler escorts for the slow ships (mainly ore ships homeward-bound from the Mediterranean). It was the readier to do so because by various devices the number of escort craft was beginning to increase substantially, and an intensified destroyer-building programme was about to get under way. (It provided for the construction of an additional 110 by the end of 1918; 45 additional sloops and 60 large trawlers of good speed were also in the programme.)

Most pressing was the problem of the outward-bound trade, as it was evident by the middle of August that the U-boats were shifting their attack from homeward-bound to outward-bound ships. 'At first the danger to homeward-bound vessels had been considerably greater, because they converged and were more easily found, because they were not in possession of the latest submarine information and because they were loaded and therefore more valuable than outward vessels which were often in ballast. In April, for example, the risk attaching to the homeward-bound vessel was more than twice as heavy as that of the outward-bound one, but by August the proportion was reversed.'[7] The U-boats naturally preferred attacking the unescorted ships; but it is also

[7] Salter, *Allied Shipping Control*, p. 126. At the end of April the proportion sunk had been 7 per cent outward bound and 18 per cent homeward bound.

true that the organized homeward-bound convoys were not so easy to find.

With the U-boats sinking almost exclusively outward-bound shipping by August, and convoy a proven success, Duff pressed on the First Sea Lord the need to institute an outward-bound ocean system immediately. He had a particular reason. 'My main reason for hurrying on with the outward convoy, was in order to give as many ships as possible experience of sailing in Convoy before the bad weather sets in.'[8] Jellicoe was no longer going slow on convoy; from the latter part of July he was doing everything possible to extend and strengthen the system. Thus, we find him, apologetically yet firmly, drawing on the 2nd Cruiser Squadron for three cruisers, explaining to the C.-in-C., 'I know that you realise the vital importance of the complete introduction of the convoy system . . .'[9] The decision to institute regular outward Atlantic convoys was taken on 11 August and the first one sailed two days later. With the forces at their disposal this extension of convoy was made possible only by adopting a Convoy Committee proposal that the outbound convoys be dispersed when through the danger zone and the destroyer escort be used to bring in a homeward convoy. (See below, pp. 268–9.) By this date, Gibraltar homeward convoys had begun. (The first regular one sailed on 26 July.) By mid-October, because of losses in the Gibraltar approaches, through slow ($7\frac{1}{2}$-knot) outward convoys for the whole passage to Gibraltar had also been started.

Ocean convoy continued to justify itself. Only three ships were torpedoed (one was saved) in July–August out of the nearly 600 convoyed homewards. Six others were lost after becoming separated from the convoy. Of the approximately 200 ships in outward convoys, only three were lost. These encouraging results facilitated a further extension of the system to the South Atlantic, where U-boats had begun to work, and with good results, in the focal Azores-Canaries area. The convoys ran from Sierra Leone (faster ships) and Dakar (slower ships), the first one sailing from the former on 22 September, and from the latter on 11 August. By the end of September, 83 ocean convoys had been brought in; of their 1,306 merchant ships, 1,288 had arrived safely and a mere 18 had been lost, of which eight had been sunk when out of convoy.

[8] Duff to Bethell, 26 August 1917; Duff MSS.
[9] Jellicoe to Beatty, 4 August 1917; Beatty MSS.

During this period only two ships of the 789 sailed in 55 outward convoys were sunk. Newbolt regards September as the turning point.

Meanwhile, the situation was highly unsatisfactory in the Mediterranean, where a general convoy system was not operating yet, whether for the through or inter-Mediterranean trade. (There had been a restricted system since May between Malta and Port Said.) The shipping losses were not the most serious factor in the situation. These had declined from 56 ships in April to 36 in May, and 20 in August; but this reduction was achieved mainly by holding up sailings. 'Night sailings from port to port on the North African Coast, similar procedure on the coast of Italy waiting for escort, which had no appointed time to arrive or to start, occupied a prodigious time. It was a common thing for a vessel to wait eight or ten days at Port Said, and cases were known where Italian ships bound for Italy had been detained at that port for three or even four weeks for this reason. From Gibraltar to Port Said about 30 to 32 days was a common passage.'[10]

Wemyss and Gough-Calthorpe, C.-in-C., Mediterranean, from August, advocated the trial of an inter-Mediterranean system. The shortage of escort craft made this impossible, Jellicoe stated at an Admiralty meeting on 14 August, though he told Calthorpe to go ahead and report what could be done after he had investigated the matter on the spot. The Allied Naval Conference in London early in September recommended that a general system of convoy be adopted in the Mediterranean so far as resources permitted. Maclay pressed hard, in a letter to Geddes on 11 September, for the development of convoy in the Mediterranean in view of 'the remarkably satisfactory experience of convoys'. Soon afterwards the Admiralty finally made the plunge. Local convoys were started for part of the trade in October, and through convoys in October–November, to and from Port Said. The first through outward convoy left the United Kingdom on 3 October, and the first homeward-bound through convoy sailed from Port Said on 16 November.

Local Mediterranean convoys, escorting and routeing, were controlled from Malta by Rear-Admiral J. A. Fergusson as British Admiral of Patrols. (The Admiralty controlled the through-Mediterranean convoys.) Fergusson, a good officer without much personality, did not have his heart in the job. Commodore G. H.

[10] Ministry of Shipping, *The System of Convoys for Merchant Shipping in 1917 and 1918*, p. 24·

Baird, who succeeded him in April 1918 (the appointment was then retitled Director of Shipping Movements, Mediterranean), was an exceptionally able man.

Gough-Calthorpe was no great believer in convoy. It was 'at the best, a deterrent, and not a reliable safeguard', and he anticipated that 'the measure of protection afforded by this system is bound to become less as the enemy gains in skill and experience, and that the true solution is to be found in an increased and increasing offensive which should, in time, enable us to dispense, altogether, with the need for these methods of defence'.[11] Even as he wrote, the convoy system was proving itself. Only nine of the 381 ships (about 40 per cent of the Mediterranean traffic) sailed in convoy during November were lost—a vast improvement over the previous situation. This was not all. Since March 1916, the Far Eastern trade (shipping east of 100° E.) had been compelled to use the long Cape of Good Hope route till, in April 1917, even the Bombay and Karachi ships had to travel that way. This had reduced losses, but at the cost of a serious reduction in carrying power. Mediterranean convoy allowed the reopening of the Suez route for this shipping. The gain in time for the India ships alone was represented by the ability of 90 ships to carry the cargoes for which 130 ships had been needed, thus releasing 40 ships for work elsewhere.

To the intense disappointment of the British, the escort craft in Mediterranean convoys were mostly their own. The Chief of the French Naval Staff had agreed to pool all the French escort and patrol craft with the British. 'This consummation, however, was never arrived at, and though certain convoys were protected by mixed escorts of French and British ships, it cannot be said that the British Commander-in-Chief through the French Flag Officer at Malta ever had direct control over any of the French antisubmarine craft.' The Italians preferred to go it alone altogether. They 'made no disguise as to their reluctance to pool their antisubmarine craft with our own. They made no promises, and right through to the end of the war consistently refused to bring any of their vessels under the central direction, or to assist in the protection of Allied convoys except to an almost negligible extent on one or two particular convoy routes. They confined practically all their

[11] Gough-Calthorpe to Admiralty, 28 November 1917; paper No. 69, 'Convoy Policy and Results in Mediterranean, 1917–18', Barley-Waters MSS.

endeavours to the protection of traffic along their coastal routes.' 'This is the more extraordinary when it is remembered how vital to her interests was the safeguarding of a continuous stream of ships bearing coal and grain to her shores.'[12] Mediterranean naval strategy was always bedevilled by national and personal antagonisms, by political and prestige considerations, and by the political desire of the Italian Government to have its light forces readily available to protect Adriatic coastal towns against Austrian raids.

The ocean convoy system was in full swing by November 1917, except for coastal traffic (not to be confused with coasting trade: see below, p. 281), where there were only the Scandinavian convoys and partial convoy on the East Coast. The Convoy Committee's recommendation for an interlocking coastal convoy system, with the ocean convoy assembly and dispersal ports as close to the main ports (when not identical) as was possible, was ignored and was never instituted.

When the convoy system was fully working, there were always, on the average, sixteen homeward convoys at sea, of which three were in the Home Submarine Danger Zone (Western Approaches, Irish Sea, or English Channel), under destroyer escort. There was an average of seven outward convoys at sea, of which four to five were in the Home Danger Zone. It is worth emphasizing that the convoy system protected *neutral* as well as British and Allied shipping—not one of its lesser advantages.

2. ORGANIZATION

A central organization known as the Convoy Section of the Trade Division of the Naval Staff had been set up at the Admiralty on 25 June to manage the convoy system. It had a staff of ten (later increased to 15), housed in the lower rooms of Admiralty House and headed by Fleet Paymaster H. W. E. Manisty (formerly of the Trade Division of the War Staff) as 'Organizing Manager of Convoys'. As an independent section, it was responsible directly to the A.C.N.S., Duff (through his Naval Assistant, Commander Henderson). When the Section was incorporated into the new Mercantile Movements Division of the Naval Staff in September 1917, it was directly responsible to the Director of Mercantile Movements (Captain F. A. Whitehead), who was

[12] Naval Staff Monograph, *Mediterranean Staff Papers Relating to Naval Operations from August 1917 to December 1918* (1920), pp. 4–5, 56.

under the A.C.N.S. The institution of the Convoy Section removed the conduct of convoys from the Trade and Operations Divisions, and placed it under a unified control working closely with N.I.D. and with the Convoy Section of the Ministry of Shipping (headed by Norman Leslie). The latter controlled the employment, destination, cargo, and bunkering of all ships requiring escort. The Convoy Section allocated escorts and controlled the movements of convoyed ships from their ports of assembly to their destinations, assigning their routes, directing their passage, and giving orders for dispersal to avoid the dangerous areas.

An extremely important part of the Convoy organization was the Chart Room, which was in the capable hands of Commander J. W. Carrington. It was responsible for the routeing of convoys, it plotted their position and that of U-boats, and could take immediate action to divert a convoy from areas where U-boats had been reported, something that could not often be done with ships sailing independently. On the whole of the west wall of 'X' room (a spacious drawing-room on the ground floor of Admiralty House looking west over Horseguards Parade) was spread a large Home Waters convoy chart (6 by 9 feet), on which was plotted every report of an enemy submarine. Positions of 'Today' were marked with red flags, 'Yesterday' with blue flags, and 'Day before yesterday', with grey flags. This chart

may be regarded as the focus of the convoy system. . . . It is permissible to give a picture of its working. Midnight at the Admiralty. The Atlantic, Homeward Convoy passing through rendezvous H. is due and has been picked up 200 miles from Cape Clear. Down the pneumatic tube from Room 40 comes a cylinder rattling noisily into the wire basket—a directional perhaps from *U.65* and an intercepted signal from *U.69*. They are quickly plotted and their positions lie only a few miles off the thread of thin red silk marking the track of the incoming convoy. There is a rapid consultation. Rear-Admiral Duff or Captain W. W. Fisher may come down. Commander Reginald Henderson or Paymaster Commander H. W. Manisty may look in. But in any case action is taken rapidly. A message goes out within a quarter of an hour to the Commodore of the convoy. He has received it by 1 a.m. and the whole convoy has been swung off its course. At dawn when the two submarines rise to the surface the convoy is many miles away.[13]

13 Naval Staff Monograph, *The Naval Staff of the Admiralty*, pp. 80–1. The last sentence cannot have been written by a submarine officer! Submarines spent their nights on the surface, charging their batteries, and *dived at dawn*.

One innovation, scarcely noticed at the time, proved to be an important help in the A/S campaign of 1917–18. This was the extended use of intelligence derived from intercepts of the German wireless signals by 'Room 40', the secret intelligence or deciphering section of the Naval Staff.[14] Concerning its important role, the officer who headed it at the time (under the D.N.I.) writes:

We kept a careful watch on all the movements of the High Sea Fleet. The submarines talked a lot when they were at sea, and the interesting thing is that it was we who made them talk. We were continually laying mines at the end of the swept channels out of Wilhelmshaven and Brünsbuttel. Every submarine returning from the Atlantic made a wireless signal reporting the tonnage she had sunk and the position she would be at a time and date at the end of a swept channel, so that she could be met by minesweepers or told to arrive at some other position. If they did not report their arrival, they might blunder into a minefield. Then when we laid that mine barrage from North of Scotland to Norway [1918], they reported on their outward journey when they had safely passed it. To concentrate for an attack in the Atlantic necessitated quite a lot of signals, and with our numerous stations round the coast, including the Shetlands and Ireland [about forty wireless stations, direction-finding and intercepting], we were able to fix them by bearings—and usually read their signals. We had our bad periods when the Germans brought in a new signal book, but we had great luck picking up a book from a crashed Zeppelin and a sunken submarine, so these blank periods did not last long. Our men were brilliant at reconstructing a signal book, but it was a slow process, as the Germans never used the groups in the book but always encyphered them. The cypher the Germans used was the Playfair type—squared paper with numbered columns, writing the groups down and reading them across. If we had the book, the job was to find the key word which gave the order for numbering the columns.

But what was even more important than warning the Anti-Submarine Division when submarines would be expected on the trade routes and when they had left and when they returned was that the submarines often used wireless when in the Atlantic. The method of attack they

[14] For the genesis of Room 40, see *From the Dreadnought to Scapa Flow*, i. 132–3. Room 40 was manned mostly by Germanists, brilliant academics like Waterhouse of Dublin, Sandbach of Birmingham, Bullough and Bruford of Cambridge, and Willoughby of Sheffield. It was by no means confined to academics. At one pole was Lord Lytton, subsequently Viceroy of India; at the other, E. Molyneux, the well-known fashion designer; and in between were noted personalities like Desmond MacCarthy, who achieved literary fame, and F. C. Tiarks, the banker, who was also a first-class German scholar.

developed was concentrated attack on one convoy by several U-boats, but to do this they had to interchange signals. These were picked up by D.F. [direction finding] and intercepting stations and we were able to warn the Anti-Submarine Division, who ordered the convoys to avoid the area by a large alteration of course. Several valuable convoys escaped attack by avoiding these concentrations of submarines. Geddes was so pleased with the safe arrival of these convoys that he sent for me and R. G. H. Henderson (Duff's Assistant) and told us that we had been promoted to Captain [October 1917]. Promotions were made half-yearly and this immediate promotion of two Commanders was I think a unique occurrence.

I think it is true to say that without the Room 40 information the defeat of the submarines would have been far more difficult and more prolonged.[15]

Well into 1917, however, there was an almost complete water-tight division between the Holy of Holies and the intelligence sections of N.I.D. Room 40 was not open to the officers of Section 14 of N.I.D., the German Section, which dealt with information on the German Navy—its organization, squadrons, coasts and harbours, and ships and officers—nor to E.1 Section of N.I.D., the Enemy Submarines Section, which kept track of U-boat movements and kept the histories of the boats.

Co-operation with the German Section would have been enormously useful to Room 40, and Room 40 could have supplied the German Section with priceless information, but they were not allowed to work in conjunction. . . . The case of E.1 Section was precisely similar. . . . All reports [from British and neutral sources] of ships attacked and reports of sighting and attacking German submarines came to E.1, and were duly plotted and recorded there. Room 40, on the other hand, obtained its information from German sources, and knew nothing of British reports. It took in the submarines' signals and knew their

[15] Extracts from two letters from Admiral Sir William James to the author, 19 December 1962, 22 May 1965. 'The Germans, aware that we were reading their signals, changed their signal book from time to time and eventually changed the cypher every 24 hours. They also changed the code word for Playfair type cypher used by the submarines. But the cryptographers had accumulated so much knowledge of the German wireless and traffic and customs that they seldom failed to solve the cypher by noon each day and the submarine cypher within a few days.' Admiral James, 'Room 40', *University of Edinburgh Journal*, Spring 1965. By 'concentrated attack on one convoy by several U-boats' (penultimate paragraph of the long quotation above) Admiral James does not mean a tactical concentration ('wolf-pack' tactics) as in World War II. What he means is that the Germans concentrated their efforts, once a convoy was located, in bringing it under attack from successive submarines within whose reach it might pass.

identity and time of departure. E.1 followed their track across the ocean so far as British reports could give it, but the two sections were not allowed to work in conjunction.[16]

Room 40 behaved as it did not from perversity, but out of fear of compromising the secrecy of its information and methods. (Yet this special intelligence on the U-boats was passed on to the French Naval Staff, which plotted it on charts which were issued to the French commands). The result, nevertheless, was a severe handicap to any comprehensive study of U-boat movements.

In May 1917 Room 40 at last came under the direction of the brilliant D.N.I., Reginald Hall, who made it a section (25A) of the Intelligence Division under Commander W. M. James.[17] Hall, when the news of the destruction of an enemy submarine reached N.I.D., would invariably turn to one of his young assistants, Leonard Willoughby (Lieutenant, R.N.V.R.), with: 'Willoughby, go and fetch the rum!'

An immediate result of this more wholesome state of affairs was that all the secret intelligence derived by Room 40 from intercepts was made available to the Convoy Section of the Naval Staff and was plotted on the convoy charts in X room of Admiralty House. 'For the first time one could see the latest information as to enemy submarines side by side with the track of a convoy, and as the Commodore's ship was always equipped with wireless, it was possible to at once divert a convoy from a dangerous area.'[18] In September the Room 40 material was also made available to Sections 14 and E.1 of N.I.D. The latter section (renumbered 25B at about this time) worked in the same room in close association with the Charting Section, 'following up the track of each submarine and "vetting" every report in the light of previous reports from sea and the cumulative knowledge of the section.'

[16] Naval Staff Monograph, *Naval Staff Appreciation of Jutland* (1922), pp. 132–3. A footnote adds: 'The prohibition was a real and not a nominal one. The only channel of communication was through the Director of the Intelligence Division himself, which was a very different thing from the sections coalescing. This policy of secrecy was accepted quite as a matter of course, the enormous handicap it offered to staff work being apparently ignored.'

[17] James is known to the Navy by the nickname 'Bubbles', because as a boy he had sat for his grandfather Millais's portrait which Pears the soapmakers later purchased and, with the addition of a piece of soap and 'Pears' printed across it, used as an advertisement of their product. The advertisements were plastered up all over England well into this century.

[18] Naval Staff Monograph, *Home Waters, May 1917–July 1917*, p. 159.

Fleet Paymaster E. W. C. Thring, who headed up E.1, had by 1917 become a crack specialist on the U-boats. 'Le brave Thring', the French called him.

> By hard work and persistence [a co-worker of his writes] he amassed a huge amount of information which proved later to be of untold value, and in time he developed what I can only call an uncanny 'feel' for what the enemy was doing. From a chart of plotted sinkings he would say, 'That . . . and that . . . and that are the work of Submarine U-: she will have so and so many torpedoes and so and so much fuel left.' The various Captains acquired recognized characteristics in his mind (I kept a gallery of their photographs with notes on their careers for him) and his forecasts were of uncanny accuracy. A lot of his information came from Room 40, but there was a good deal more to it than that.[19]

A naval control staff was appointed at each port of assembly at home and abroad for the local organization of the convoy and for the issue of sailing orders and confidential instructions to the masters. As regards the convoy itself, each one had its Commodore, who was either a naval officer or an experienced merchant master, who hoisted his broad pennant in one of the merchant ships and was responsible for the navigation and general control of the convoy, while the Senior Officer, Escort, was responsible for its protection.

Homeward convoys dispersed off the North Channel, if 'Northabout' Ireland; if 'Southabout', they dispersed off the Smalls (for Irish Sea and Bristol Channel ports) and off St. Catherine's Point (for Channel and East Coast ports). The convoy assembly ports for outward-bound ships were all on the West Coast: Buncrana (soon changed to Lamlash), Queenstown (Milford Haven replaced it early in 1918), Devonport, and Falmouth. Ships proceeded to them independently. Liverpool was added in March 1918, and Southend in June 1918.

Whereas the homeward Atlantic convoys sailed in convoy throughout the entire voyage (the escort was ordinarily a single cruiser, since the Atlantic was clear of powerful enemy surface craft), outward convoys had a destroyer escort only through the Home submarine danger zone. (The limits of A/S escort were between longitude 12° W. and 17° W.) The escort left at dusk (the merchant ships then dispersing, that is, sailing on independently)

[19] Mrs. Mary T. Carrington's letter to the author, 21 May 1965.

and steamed the intervening distance (60 to 100 miles) during the night to meet a homeward convoy at dawn. The escorting vessels from the start exhibited conspicuous skill in meeting the convoy at the rendezvous at the scheduled time. The destroyer escorts were doing double duty, as there were never suitable craft available for separate escorts for outward and homeward convoys. The officers and men, as well as their ships, were under a severe strain.

Outward Gibraltar convoys remained in company under an anti-raider escort (Q-ships) and were met off Cape St. Vincent by an A/S escort (sloops, torpedo boats, and armed yachts) from Gibraltar which had previously escorted a homeward Gibraltar convoy clear of the Straits. The homeward convoy from Gibraltar had a Q-ship ocean escort and was shepherded through the Home danger zone by trawlers and a destroyer or two. In the case of a through-Mediterranean convoy (United Kingdom–Port Said), after the destroyer escort parted company, it was unescorted until it met its new escort to the westward of Cape Spartel. After that it had an escort until arrival at Port Said. The escort in the Mediterranean consisted of a destroyer, 2 sloops, and 4 trawlers, but the trawlers were discontinued after the first convoy because they were too slow.

'One of the most extraordinary aberrations of maritime strategists of the late 19th and early 20th centuries,' Commander Waters has written, 'was the irrational conviction that the greater the number of ships in a convoy the greater was the risk to the ships in convoy.'[20] Duff and Henderson had quickly perceived the fallacy of that doctrine, the former remarking: 'It would appear that the larger the convoy passing through any given danger zone, provided it is moderately protected, the less the loss to the Merchant Service; that is for instance, were it feasible to escort the entire volume of trade which normally enters the United Kingdom per diem in one large group, the submarines as now working would be limited to one attack, which, with a destroyer escort, would result in negligible losses compared with those now being experienced.'[21] This view was not generally held at the Admiralty, and when the convoy system was introduced, the

[20] Thus: 'It is evident that the larger the number of ships forming a convoy, the greater the chance of a submarine being enabled to attack successfully, and the greater the difficulty of the escort in preventing such an attack.' Admiralty War Staff, 'Remarks on Submarine Warfare', January 1917.
[21] Duff to Jellicoe, 26 April 1917.

policy was to sail small convoys—small by the standards of previous wars.

The size of the first trial convoy from Hampton Roads was limited to 12 ships; by the end of June, 20 was the limit. In September the limiting size of convoys was laid down at 26 ships; Admiralty approval was needed for larger ones. It was found necessary later to raise the limit to 36, with special Admiralty approval needed for larger ones, since, from September, all ships unless too slow (7 or 8 knots) or with a speed approaching 20 knots, were included in convoy. In practice, 20 to 25 was usual. The largest convoy (HN73, which sailed New York on 18 June 1918) consisted of 47 ships. 'Destroyer Escorts' for the Submarine Danger Zone (destroyers or other suitable vessels—P-boats, sloops, or trawlers) became fixed at: over 22 ships in convoy: 8 escorts; 16–22: 7; under 16: 6. On account of life-saving requirements, troop convoys (which, initially, were a separate organization) were limited to 14 ships and provided with a considerably larger destroyer escort. Since there were not sufficient destroyers or P-boats available for all convoys, escorts composed of two destroyers or two sloops and about eight to ten trawlers escorted the outward and homeward Gibraltar convoys and homeward Dakar convoys in the Home Submarine Danger Zone. These were slow 7 to 7¼-knot convoys. The trawlers rendered good service with slow convoys, only one meeting with a mishap, and she disappeared at sea. They proved ideal craft for life-saving. Significantly, these slow convoys with a composite escort suffered no greater losses than did the fast ones which were protected by destroyers alone.

From the beginnings of ocean convoy, air escort and support was an integral part of the system. Within the limits of their endurance (up to 100 miles from shore), and weather conditions permitting, flying boats, aeroplanes, and especially airships were employed to patrol ahead of ocean convoys and to provide close escort. In addition, air escort was provided for the French Coal Trade convoys, the convoys on their way through the North Channel (between Northern Ireland and Scotland), the traffic between Larne and Stranraer, and the cross-Channel transports on the Folkestone–Boulogne route. Non-rigid airships did the bulk of the patrolling and escort work. They had this important advantage over heavier-than-air craft in escort work: they were able to keep station with a convoy. It used to be said, when an airship joined a convoy, that 'everyone else could go to sleep'. As the Official Air Historian records:

> The airship, slow in speed and in manœuvre, could seldom hope to destroy a submarine. [In fact, they destroyed none during the war.] The U-boat commander usually had time, once he sighted an airship, to make an unhurried dive out of harm's way. But this is not to say that the airship was not feared. She could, and would, call up surface craft to attack with depth-charges, and she might be able to follow the track of the U-boat below the water, either by direct observation or through a trail of oil. The submarine could only be brought to the surface again with caution. If she reappeared and found the airship, or surface ship, within striking distance of her, she had to face certain attack and possible destruction. The airships, in fact, were treated by the U-boat commanders with the respect paid to the policeman by the law-breaker and were given a wide berth. Not by 'doing', but by 'being' they saved many vessels. Submarines, time after time, were forced to dive to escape detection, and the consequent reduction of their speed below the surface, more often than not, made it impossible for them to get into position to deliver an attack.[22]

Of the hundreds of convoys in 1917 with aircraft escort, only one was successfully attacked; one ship was lost.

At first the use of aircraft in the convoy system was sketchy. In July 1917 it was planned to double the size of the air services. This was not found practicable, although on 1 January 1918, 291 seaplanes and flying boats, 23 aeroplanes, and about 100 airships were engaged in A/S duties in Home waters. It was not until the summer of 1918 that the use of aircraft became highly developed.

Kite balloons towed by convoy escorts were used in inshore waters as an aid to submarine hunting. Since, as in the case of their work with the Fleet, the balloons might call a U-boat's attention to the presence and course of the convoy, they were used mostly with destroyers for independent submarine hunting.

3. PROBLEMS

The 'insuperable' obstacles to the successful working of an ocean convoy system which had been stressed by naval opinion failed to materialize. Merchant ships did experience some difficulty in keeping station in convoy. (The cruising formation of convoys was in columns of no more than five ships, with the columns six to eight,

[22] Jones, *The War in the Air*, iv. 60–1.

later four to five, cables apart, and the ships in the column three, later two, cables apart.) But their skill was sufficient to enable them to keep together and to zigzag in formation. New signalling equipment, engine-room telegraphs, and officers and crew trained in station-keeping and A/S methods further minimized the difficulty. Not that sailing a ship in convoy was ever a picnic. The atmosphere and the perils of a convoy are described in a minor classic of the sea:

Steaming in formation at night without lights adds to our 'grey heires'. The menace of collision is ever present. Frequently, in the darkness, we have no guide-ship in plain sight to regulate our progress. The adjustments of speed, that in the daytime kept us moderately well in station, cannot be made. It is best to turn steadily to the average revolutions of a former period, and keep a good look-out for the broken water of a sister ship. On occasion there is the exciting medley of encountering a convoy bound the opposite way. In the confusion of wide dispersal and independent alterations of course to avert collisions, there is latitude for the most extraordinary situations. An incident in the Mediterranean deserves imperishable record: 'We left Malta, going east, and that night it was inky dark and we ran clean through a westbound convoy. How there wasn't an accident, God only knows. We had to go full astern to clear one ship. She afterwards sidled up alongside of us and steamed east for an hour and a half. Then she hailed us through a megaphone: "Steamer ahoy! Hallo! Where are you bound to?" "Salonika," we said. "God Almighty," he says. "I'm bound to Gibraltar. Where the hell's *my* convoy?" '[23]

It was an incidental advantage that the Atlantic homeward-bound convoys had the opportunity to receive practice in station-keeping before entering the danger zone—at least an hour a day for a week to ten days. The bad or inadequate station-keeping often experienced at the beginning of each voyage had time to develop into proficiency during this period.

Another disproved objection to convoy was the 'too many eggs in one basket' theory. 'Although nearly twenty convoys had been attacked [by the end of September], in no instance, even when the attack was successful, had such wholesale havoc been wrought as the opponents of convoy had anticipated; generally only one ship was sunk; in no instance had a formed convoy lost more than two vessels.'[24]

[23] David W. Bone, *Merchantmen-at-Arms* (London, 1919), pp. 182–3.
[24] Newbolt, *Naval Operations*, v. 141.

Another, and perhaps the chief difficulty throughout, was the loss of time involved in collecting a convoy at an assembly port and reducing all its vessels to the speed of its slowest member. (Initially, there was the difficulty of ships unable to maintain the convoy speed: the convoy would consequently be late at the escort rendezvous or an escorting ship would have to be detached to look after the 'slowcoaches'.) These shortcomings were largely overcome after the convoy system had become properly organized. The remedies for the first were (1) to make the loading port the assembly port, and (2) using a direct route to the dispersal point and the unloading port, and not having to 'call for orders' at Queenstown or Falmouth. The remedies for the second were (1) the organization of convoys of various speeds and (2) of fleets of ships of equal speed; (3) the use of a direct route—no diversion; and (4) a continuous cycle—no suspension of sailing. Moreover, the provision of regular sailings helped to solve the congestion problem at the ports.

By mid-September 1917, homeward convoys had been reorganized on a speed/destination basis. Slow, medium, and fast convoys were being run. Slow ($8\frac{1}{4}$ to 10-knot ships) and medium (10 to $12\frac{1}{2}$-knot ships) convoys in the North Atlantic system ran alternately for East and West Coast ports; the fastest (above $12\frac{1}{2}$-knot ships) ran for the West Coast ports only. The South Atlantic convoys were slow (below 10 knots) from Dakar, and fast (above 10 knots) from Sierra Leone, and split in the Western Approaches into East and West Coast portions. The Gibraltar homeward convoys contained 7- to 11-knot ships, and sailed alternately for East and West Coast ports.

The provision of ocean escorts, for the protection of convoys against raiders, gave no trouble. They were procured by breaking up the 2nd Cruiser Squadron, fitting a number of merchantmen for escort duty (these cargo-carrying 'commissioned escort steamers' were armed with three or four 6-inch guns), and drawing on the cruisers of the North American–West Indies Squadron and the armed merchant cruisers of the 10th Cruiser Squadron (the Northern Patrol). The drafts on the latter two were made possible by America's entry into the war. The 10th Cruiser Squadron, to the westward of the Shetlands and the Faeroes, had been intercepting contraband cargoes from a neutral America which might have found their way to the enemy. Most of the trade entering the

Northern neutrals came from the United States. With the United States as an ally, the 10th Cruiser Squadron's principal *raison d'être* disappeared. Its main purpose now was to intercept enemy surface raiders, a role in which it had never been very successful. On 29 November 1917 the much weakened squadron was finally abolished and its 17 armed trawlers put to work on A/S operations and convoy escort duties. (Thereafter the maintenance of the North Sea cordon depended on Grand Fleet light forces and, even more, on the restriction of enemy trade through the system of embargoes and the agreements with neutral shipowners.) The Official Historian of the trade warfare wrote the squadron's epitaph: 'So came to no inglorious end the 10th Cruiser Squadron. . . . The squadron with its crews of merchant seamen had earned the gratitude of the nation.' These valiant ships (the squadron had never exceeded 25 armed merchant cruisers and 18 armed trawlers) and men had done their job well in the 'eternal fog and gale' of northern waters, first under Admiral de Chair, then under Admiral Tupper. (The climatic description, from Keble Chatterton, has helped to establish what is a myth. The weather in these waters is, in fact, variable.) They could look back on this record of the 'biggest of all blockades that the world has ever experienced': ships intercepted, 8,905; ships sent into port under armed guard, 1,816; fishing craft boarded, 4,520.

Ocean escort for the New York convoy was usually provided by the U.S. Navy (light cruisers); for the Gibraltar convoy, a Q-ship or an American coastguard gunboat was ordinarily regarded as sufficient. In 1918, North Atlantic convoys were often strengthened by an American battleship or armoured cruiser.

More troublesome than ocean escorts was the provision of destroyer escorts for the Submarine Danger Zone. Towards the end of 1917 Jellicoe was giving serious consideration to laying up a large part of the Grand Fleet and maintaining an 'Active Force' consisting of the Battle Cruiser Force and a single battle squadron. He would use the 17 destroyers and 4 flotilla leaders (that is, about one flotilla) so freed for anti-submarine work presumably as convoy escorts rather than in patrol work. The arrival of the American Fleet in European waters (November 1917) had reduced the risks of such a policy. Beatty would have none of it: the Grand Fleet must be kept as strong as possible. No decision had been reached when Jellicoe left the Admiralty.

Already, however, the destroyer escort problem was being solved, as slowly but surely the requisite number of craft were obtained: from the United States[25] and from other services (Portsmouth, Dover, and the Grand Fleet), to say nothing of merchant ships armed with 6-inch guns. In July 1917, 91 A/S escorts were available for ocean convoys: 64 destroyers, 11 sloops, 16 P-boats; in November 1917, 170: 102–24–44; in April 1918, 195: 115–35–45; in September 1918, 150: 116–16–18. The small initial American contribution was enough to help tip the balance of the scale in favour of convoy. Asked afterwards what difference the arrival of the first American ships at Queenstown made to his command, Admiral Bayly, C.-inC., Coast of Ireland, replied: 'All the difference.'

Before their arrival we had to protect the incoming trade bound for the Channel and Irish Sea with thirteen coal-burning sloops, a few trawlers, and an occasional destroyer sent for a short time. They had not only to protect the trade, but now and then had to be taken off patrol to escort some specially valuable ship to the mouth of the Channel, where the sloop was relieved by a destroyer from Devonport, or to Liverpool. Also they could not be kept going like oil-burning destroyers, as it took them one day of their time off to coal, and in bad weather longer. So that when the convoy system was at last introduced it would have been quite impossible for the sloops to carry it out.[26]

Great Britain provided destroyers for 70 per cent of all convoys, and cruisers for 61 per cent; the United States, 27 per cent and 35 per cent, respectively; France, 3 per cent and 4 per cent, respectively.[27]

An important incidental advantage of convoy was the new sense of security that it gave to the masters and men. If a ship was hit, the presence of others ensured a considerable saving of life. Furthermore, rescue tugs when available accompanied the outbound convoys through the danger zone and met homebound ones. Then,

---

[25] Twenty-eight were working with the Royal Navy at the end of June 1917, and 37 by the end of July. At the end of the war the Americans had 68 destroyers in European waters: 24 at Queenstown, 38 at Brest, and 6 at Gibraltar. The United States could not do better because her destroyer escorts were needed for the increased flow of traffic between her shores and France. Of course, another naval advantage gained from the American entry was that the British were able now to make all the arrangements for the North Atlantic convoys at the American end.

[26] Bayly, *Pull Together!*, p. 242.

[27] Dreyer, *The Sea Heritage*, p. 221.

too, the chances of saving a torpedoed ship were better than ever, because the attacking submarine was prevented by the escort from delivering the *coup de grâce* with another torpedo or by gunfire.[28]

An officer, writing from 'an inside knowledge of the North Atlantic convoys', makes the interesting point that 'during practically the whole period of the convoy system, luck of the weather was as much upon our side as it had generally, in the past, been upon the side of Germany. Never had the summer routes been so free from ice, whilst the fogs, just thick enough to permit the regular sailing of the convoys, were amply sufficient to nullify the activities of any lurking submarines.'

The crucial point is that the convoy system quickly justified itself through the actual results.

4. RESULTS

The total number of operational U-boats reached its wartime peak, 139, in September. The number of U-boats at sea in the last eight months of 1917 never exceeded the October daily average of 56: 47 in May, 55 in June, 41 in July, 46 in August, 55 in September, 39 in November, and 48 in December.[29] The use of large ocean-cruising submarines posed a new threat. Most of these 'U-cruisers' (*U-151* through *U-157*) displaced 1,870 tons when submerged and 1,510 tons in surface trim, could carry eighteen torpedoes, and were armed with two 5·9-inch and, in some cases, two 3·4-inch guns. They demonstrated their extraordinary endurance in the 105-day maiden war cruise of *U-155* in the Atlantic (24 May–4 September 1917), during which she covered 10,220 miles, only 620 of which were run submerged. The total bag was nearly 52,000 tons gross of British, Allied, and neutral shipping (10 steamers, 7 sailing vessels). The U-cruisers

had an awe-inspring aspect—nothing less than a new type of diving *Möwe*. They pushed the boundary of the U-boat campaign right down to the north-west coast of Africa; so it became necessary to extend the convoy areas to counter this new menace. . . . Grandiloquently dubbed by the Germans 'U-cruisers', [they] merited no such ornate rating.

[28] See further, below, p. 280, n. 34.
[29] This was considerably more than the contemporary estimate: August, 23–30; September, 44; October, 40–42; November, 20–26; December, 23–30. Jellicoe, *The Submarine Peril*, pp. 47–50. The total number of boats in commission varied between 164 and 172 (monthly averages) between July and December 1917.

None the less, these large boats gave the Allies a foretaste of what commerce-raiding might be like were it waged by 'oceanic' submarines of two, three, and four thousand tons displacement. Had the so-called U-cruisers of the 1917 and 1918 programmes ever come to sea in large numbers, the area of depredations might have extended in 1919 to the St. Lawrence, the United States coast, and perhaps even to the Cape, the Caribbean, and the Plate.[30]

In June merchant shipping losses had reached their second highest peak: British losses of 417,925 tons (122 ships) and Allied losses of 126,171 (79) for a total of 544,096 tons (201). Compare these figures with those of the rest of the year:

British Shipping Losses

	By Mines	By Surface Craft	By Submarines	Total
July	44,927 (11)	—	319,931 (88)	364,858 (99)
August	17,651 (6)	1,608 (1)	310,551 (84)	329,810 (91)
September	22,335 (9)	—	173,437 (68)	196,212 (78)*
October	13,324 (6)	1,159 (1)	261,649 (79)	276,132 (86)
November	18,754 (8)	—	154,806 (56)	173,560 (64)
December	23,608 (8)	2,284 (1)	227,195 (76)	253,087 (85)

*Includes one ship of 440 tons sunk by aircraft.

Britain's Allies suffered these tonnage losses in the same period:

July	111,683 (72)
August	128,489 (63)
September	119,086 (64)
October	127,932 (53)
November	87,646 (42)
December	86,981 (46)

The grand totals, British, Allied, and neutral, were:

	By Submarines	By All Forms of Enemy Action
July	492,320 (210)	546,911 (227)
August	489,806 (178)	511,317 (188)
September	315,907 (149)	345,239 (160)
October	429,147 (150)	458,496 (169)
November	259,521 (113)	292,682 (128)
December	353,083 (149)	394,115 (168)

[30] Gibson and Prendergast, *The German Submarine War*, p. 218. Nine of these U-cruisers became operational during the war, two were built but did not become operational, and 38 were building or projected when the war ended.

The July and August losses, though lower than they had been, were disquieting, but the rate of loss diminished significantly after August. The September figure of British tonnage destroyed was 40 per cent below the August figure and only about one-half the monthly average of the unrestricted campaign through August. The total losses (British, Allied, neutral) in September were a third less than in August and nearly one-half the monthly average of February–August. Even the October increase in British shipping losses was not alarming: half of the 80,000-ton increase was in the Mediterranean (27,000 tons lost in September, 68,000 in October), where homeward convoys had not yet been instituted. At that, the 276,000 tons lost were considerably less than for any previous month of the unrestricted campaign. The last-quarter British sinkings—702,779 (235)—were little more than half the peak figure of the second quarter: 1,315,496 (413). Clearly, the most critical stage was past, even if shipping losses continued to exceed replacements.

The extraordinary reduction of shipping losses was *not* due to the wholesale destruction of U-boats, as was popularly imagined at the time, although the intensification of the A/S measures already in force, particularly in mining, did increase the destruction rate to the point where the sinkings of U-boats in the last four months of 1917 equalled the German construction rate:

U-boat losses with number of boats commissioned given in parentheses

July	7	(11)
August	5	(12)
September	10	(8)
October	6	(13)
November	8	(5)
December	8	(6)

Spindler emphasizes that *in relation to the number of 'active' or operational boats* the loss of U-boats during 1917, taken as a whole, was no higher than the losses in the previous years—that it was greater only for the last six months of 1917, when 44 of the 65 losses during the year occurred.[31]

[31] *Der Handelskrieg mit U-Booten*, iv. 507–8. His figures of U-boat losses calculated as a percentage of *Frontboote* are—1914: 4·0; 1915: 4·6; 1916: 2·7; 1917: 4·3 for the year and 5·7 for the second half of the year. The year 1916, he says, has to be left out of these calculations because of the fact that during a considerable part of the year the U-boats were not used in trade warfare in the waters around Britain: the fewer losses corresponded to the reduced activity.

It was neither mines nor any of the other older forms of A/S warfare that explain the dramatic drop in shipping losses. The graph of sinkings fell in almost direct proportion to the increasing number of ships under convoy. By the end of October 1917 it was apparent that the convoy system was a success—that an effective reply to the U-boats had been found, even if the merchant tonnage loss rate was still uncomfortably high. The percentage of losses to sailings provided the confirmation. Ninety-nine homeward convoys had been brought in, comprising 1,502 steamers. Only 10 vessels (0·66 per cent) had been torpedoed while in contact with the convoy. If we include 14 other ships sunk after being separated from their convoy (by bad weather or the disobedience of their masters), the percentage was still a mere 1·57. Through October 1917, 77 outward convoys, with 1,052 ships, had sustained a percentage loss of only 0·57. Thus, the round voyage loss rate in convoy was 1·23 per cent, or one-twentieth of that of the Black Fortnight of April (when ships were being lost at the rate of one in four voyages) and one-sixteenth of that of the whole of April. By the end of the year the last doubts about the efficacy of convoy had been removed.

By this date the Admiralty were in a position to evaluate the results of convoy. In September the Statistics Department, which Geddes had set up when he was Controller, began to turn out figures and charts. Oliver ridiculed this activity:

> We have been upside down here ever since the North Eastern Railway [i.e., Geddes and Beharrell] took over the management, but manage to worry along somehow doing our jobs. Geddes is mad about statistics and has forty people always making graphs and issuing balance sheets full of percentages, etc. Unfortunately worrying about what happened last month does not help the present or the future and wastes a great deal of time. It may be well enough in a Life Assurance business or a railway. We do not get anything done quicker now than this time last year and most things a good deal slower but there is more made of them on paper.[32]

But without the kinds of material produced by the Statistics Department an efficient convoy system would probably not have been possible.

On 15 January 1918 the Director of Statistics at the Admiralty issued a 'General Review' of the U-boat campaign and the results of the A/S measures from the commencement of unrestricted

[32] James, *A Great Seaman*, pp. 159–60. See above, p. 176, n. 21.

warfare to the end of 1917.[33] The figures related to British shipping (except where otherwise stated) of 500 tons gross and above. These are the more important facts that were brought out:

Attacks by U-boats. The 138 attacks on British shipping in February 1917, with the loss of 65 ships, had risen in April to 217 and 124, respectively. The figures had declined to 145 and 74 in July, which reduction had continued until December, when attacks rose to 126 and losses to 67 (from the November low of 43). The average monthly attacks in the six months February–July, 170, had been reduced by 35 per cent in the last five months of the year, August–December, to an average of 111 a month.[34] Of greater significance was:

Losses by U-boat attack. There was an average monthly loss of 85 ships in the first period (February–July) and of 60 in the second (August–December), or a reduction of 30 per cent.

Losses in Areas and Trades. Whereas in Home waters the average reduction per month in the second period as compared with the first was 25 ships (44 losses as against 69), in foreign waters it was only 4 ships (24 v. 28). The statistics also showed that the reduction in Home waters had occurred almost exclusively in the Atlantic traffic in the Western Approaches: the 'Scilly-Fastnet-Tory Triangle'. The monthly losses here in the second period represented a 90 per cent reduction on the previous six months' average (a monthly average of 3 v. 30). 'There could be but one explanation,' Waters and Barley fairly conclude, 'namely, the adoption of convoy for ocean shipping.'

Losses—Distance from Land. The distribution of losses was as follows:

[33] 'Losses of British Merchant Tonnage. General Review: February–December, 1917'; Admiralty MSS. There is a convenient summary and commentary in the Waters-Barley MSS. on which I have relied: No. 74, 'Review of Shipping Situation and Effects of Convoy on U-boat Operations, February–December 1917'. Much of the raw material is also to be found in a Statistical Section document, 'Records, Merchant Vessel Losses, 1917–1918', in the Naval Historical Branch.

[34] Another significant change produced by the convoy system (as well as by the rapid progress in fitting merchant ships with defensive armament, 90 per cent of the vessels under the British flag being so armed by the end of 1917 as compared with 56 per cent in April) was the virtual disappearance of 'sunk by gunfire', which had accounted for a large proportion of the merchant ships lost prior to August 1917. In April 1917, 30 per cent of the attacks were by gunfire, which figure had dropped to 6 per cent by January 1918. There was but one instance of a U-boat attacking a convoy by gunfire. On that occasion the only escort was a small armed merchant cruiser that must have been indistinguishable from the rest of the convoy.

	Under 10 Miles from Land	10–50 Miles	Over 50 Miles	Total
February–July	74 (20%)	91 (25%)	200 (55%)	365
August–December	110 (58%)	65 (34%)	17 (8%)	192

In other words, before the convoy system was in full operation, the U-boats had worked far out to sea, especially off the south-west coast of Ireland and south-west of the Scillies. They sank vessels as far as 300 miles out in the Atlantic. The ocean convoy system gave the U-boats fewer attractive targets, causing them, by October, to abandon the Western Approaches and to come inshore to the Irish Sea and the English Channel. Here (except for the French coal trade in the Channel) shipping continued to be sailed independently along the patrolled lanes. Whereas few British ships were lost in the open sea (more than 50 miles out to sea) in the last months of 1917, as compared with the heavy losses in pre-convoy days, losses in coastal waters were serious in the latter part of the year, and on a rising curve, with many ships being sunk in the south of Ireland, off the Yorkshire coast, and off Start Point, the Lizard, and Land's End. In other words, convoy was forcing the U-boats to tackle the weakest link in the shipping defence organization, the unescorted ships in coastal waters (and in the Mediterranean, prior to the start of the convoy system there). Here, too, they might hope to find ships which had been dispersed from a convoy or were proceeding to a port of assembly.[35]

[35] 'This meant in effect that tonnage being sunk was no longer for the most part large steamers homeward bound with cargoes, but smaller vessels in the coasting trade, and steamers bound round the coast in ballast to load at Cardiff and elsewhere, with a certain number of ships on their way to an assembly port for outward convoy.' Technical History Monograph, *The Atlantic Convoy System, 1917–1918*, p. 31. The average size of ships sunk in the four months preceding the adoption of ocean convoy, April to July, was 5,084 tons gross. In the four months September–December 1917 this had fallen to 4,342 tons. The process was continuous, so that in September 1918 the average size was only 2,827 tons. This was a direct result of the convoy system, which reduced size as well as the number of the U-boats' victims. The drastic reduction in the number of ships torpedoed in the open sea had a humanitarian effect. 'The result from the point of view of life-saving was enormous. It meant that a crew, even when their ship was torpedoed and they had to take to their boats, were rarely more than 10 or 20 miles from the land, and probably had a coastal patrol boat to their assistance in less than half an hour. This was a very different ordeal from that which had to be faced in the first six months of 1917, when the ships were sunk 200 and 300 miles from the land, and when a large proportion of those who managed to get into their boats died of exposure before they were rescued or reached land.' *Ibid.*, p. 32.

281

There was a paradox in the situation, as Barley and Waters have pointed out. 'It must remain a curious and indeed painful reflection that ocean convoy having been found to be the efficient antidote to U-boats operating in the Atlantic and Western Approaches against our ocean going ships, and to U-boats operating against the cross-Channel trade and the Scandinavian trade, the same antidote was not promptly applied to the U-boat inshore activities which immediately ensued. But instead of observing the principle of concentration of force implicit in convoy the principle of dispersion of A/S force was adhered to for inshore operations.'[36]

Losses—Convoy. Of the 26,404 British and foreign vessels sailing in organized convoy to the end of 1917 only 147, or 0·55 per cent, had been lost. The breakdown shows:

	Sailings		
	Homeward	*Outward*	*Total*
Atlantic Trades	2,445	2,039	4,484
Through Mediterranean	19	62	81
Scandinavia-Lerwick, Humber			6,155
French Coal Trade (Cross Channel)			15,684
Total all Convoys			26,404
Mediterranean Local Convoys (From the Monthly A/S Division Report of Dec. 1917)			902

	Losses			Loss Rates		
	Homeward	*Outward*	*Total*	*H.*	*O.*	*T.*
Atlantic Trades	26	12	38	1·06	0·59	0·85
Through Mediterranean	3	3	6	15·79	4·84	7·41
Scandinavia-Lerwick, Humber			74			1·20
French Coal Trade (Cross Channel)			29			0·18
Total all Convoys			147			0·55
Mediterranean Local Convoys (From the Monthly A/S Division Report of Dec. 1917)			17			1·90

[36] Paper No. 49, 'U-boat and Anti-Submarine Warfare, First World War, 1914–1918'; Barley-Waters MSS.

British Merchant Vessels 500 GRT and above in U.K. Overseas Trades sunk before joining convoy, within 3 days of dispersal from convoy, and 'lost' from convoy

Area	Before Journey	After Dispersal	Straggling	Total	
Scandinavia, East Coast, and North Sea	2	3	1	6	15%
English Channel	7	3	2	12	30%
Bristol Channel and Irish Sea	4	5	2	11	27.5%
Western Approaches	—	1	3	4	10%
Other areas	—	5	2	7	17.5%
Total	13	17	10	40	100%
	32.5%	42.5%	25%		100%

Stragglers, then, constituted but a quarter of these losses, whereas one-third occurred before joining convoy and over 40 per cent occurred after dispersal from convoy. Nearly one-third of the losses occurred in the English Channel, the very area where, as convoy losses showed, the U-boats could be expected to attack ships out of convoy most. Similarly, the Irish Sea and Bristol Channel losses showed that it was in United Kingdom coastal waters that most losses could be expected. (This was confirmed by the statistics of losses related to distance from land.) Yet it was in these waters there were the fewest or no convoys. The implication should have been indisputable—to develop convoy in coastal waters.

Another set of statistics pointed to the same inescapable conclusion: see the table *The Proportion of Losses in Convoys and Independent Sailings* printed on page 284. These figures reveal that although 88 per cent of the overseas shipping was in convoy by December 1917, the loss rate of the 12 per cent sailed independently in that month was over four times that of ships in convoy, and that when 20 per cent of the overseas ships had been sailed independently (September), their loss rate had been seventeen times that of ships in convoy. It also showed that the loss rate for convoyed ships had remained consistently low, in the order of 1 per cent, and this was despite the fact that the U-boats were operating predominantly in coastal waters, where diversionary routeing was virtually or totally impracticable. In all the U.K. overseas sailings in the four months 0·75 per cent of those sailed in convoy were lost, compared with 5·7 per cent of those sailing

The Proportion of Losses in Convoys and Independent Sailings

Trade		September Sailed	Sunk	October Sailed	Sunk	November Sailed	Sunk	December Sailed	Sunk	Total Sailed	Sunk
America Gibraltar Dakar	Convoyed	766	0·52%	722	0·78%	750	0·40%	715	1·26%	3,003	0·7%
	Independent	86	8·14%	66	12·12%	62	1·61%	88	5·68%	302	7·0%
Independent : Convoy Loss Rate		1:15.5		1:15.5		1:4		1:4.5		1:10	
All U.K. Overseas Trades	Convoyed	1,038	0·38%	1,036	0·77%	1,047	0·76%	1,011	1·10%	4,132	0·75%
	Independent	261	6·51%	158	9·49%	150	1·33%	142	5·00%	711	5·70%
Independent: Convoy Loss Rate		1:17		1:12.5		1:1.7		1:4.5		1:7.6	

independently. In short, by 1918, sinkings in Home waters and the Atlantic were confined almost entirely to independent shipping in the Channel, Irish Sea, and off the North-east Coast.

It is evident that the convoy system was mainly responsible for the spectacular reduction in shipping losses, not other means and methods such as intensified mining, depth-charge production, arming of merchantmen, or A/S patrols. Spindler agrees. 'The decisive success of the convoy system becomes evident through these figures': the convoy statistics through December 1917.[37] Convoys made targets harder to find, since the merchant vessels were concentrated. (This argument had been overlooked by the convoy party, which had stressed the protection afforded by the escort and by group manœuvring.) 'The visibility circle of a dozen or twenty ships in a convoy formation was very much smaller than the collective circles of the same number of ships sailing independently, and the actual chance of any given submarine sighting the group was much less than the chance of her sighting one or more of the ships, if they were brought in along various routes and at various times.'[38] The Admiralty, moreover, could divert the course of the convoy by wireless from any dangerous area. 'One of the assets of the ocean convoy system was that it provided intelligence of U-boat dispositions and movements. It forced the U-boats to spend long periods searching for targets, and to communicate with one another and their Headquarters in attempts to locate convoys. We were able to exploit this by prompt evasive routeing and reinforcement of threatened convoys—in a word, to counter, for the

---

[37] *Der Handelskrieg mit U-Booten*, iv. 510. One scholar (Mancur Olson, Jr., *The Economics of Wartime Shortage*, Chapel Hill, North Carolina, 1963) has maintained that convoy was not decisive—that the economic measures the British had already taken, such as the increase in agricultural production, the control of food consumption, and the substitution of supplies from North America for those normally imported from more remote areas, were by themselves defeating the U-boat campaign. Without underestimating the importance of these economic counter-measures, I do not see how the British could have held out beyond 1917, had the shipping losses continued at the spring rate. And this they would have done but for the introduction of a general convoy system.

[38] Newbolt, *Naval Operations*, v. 141. The war diary of *U-94* (Lieutenant-Commander Saalwächter, who was a senior Admiral in World War II) for August 1917 has this revealing entry: 'The convoys, with their strong and efficient escorts making an attack extremely difficult, are in my view quite capable of drastically reducing shipping losses. The chances of sighting a convoy of 7 ships is less than that of sighting 7 independent ships. In the case of a convoy it is mostly possible to fire on only one ship. For any ship torpedoed in convoy, the chance of immediate help is a factor of considerable importance to morale.' Spindler, *Der Handelskrieg mit U-Booten*, iv. 224.

first time, force with force, and before harm had been done to threatened ships.'[39] If a U-boat did sight a convoy, unless she happened to be on a bearing from which she could attack, she would have great difficulty in getting into proper position without being sighted. If the U-boat was sighted, she was liable to instant attack by the warship escort, or the convoy could render itself immune by altering course. 'Details from British sources of the success of the convoy system', Spindler writes, 'were confirmed from reports submitted by the C.O.s of the U-boats returning from patrol. The U-boats' chances of pressing home a successful attack on a merchant ship were much reduced.'[40]

Simultaneously, the situation as regards mines was gradually improving. The equipment of all the larger classes of ships, naval and mercantile, with paravane mine-protection gear, rendered those ships largely immune from the risk of damage by moored mine. The expansion of the minesweeping force was an important factor. By the end of 1917, the regular sweeping force numbered 726 vessels. The number of mines swept up during 1917 was double that of 1916: roughly, 4,000 as against 2,000. The anti-mining campaign was helped by the great losses inflicted on the German submarine minelayers in the latter part of 1917: 18 of the 44 German U-boat losses in that period. This will, incidentally, help to explain the decrease in mines swept up—from a monthly average of 397 in February–July 1917 to 284 in August 1917– December 1918. Fifty-five British vessels were sunk by mine during the six months February to July 1917, and 34 during the five months August to December.

German minelaying continued to the end, and new types of mines and principles of minelayings (such as the practice of submarine minelayers following British sweepers and laying a fresh

---

[39] Waters, 'The Philosophy and Conduct of Maritime War', Part 1, 1815–1918, *Journal of the Royal Naval Scientific Service*, May 1958.
[40] *Der Handelskrieg mit U-Booten*, iv. 511. He adds: 'Only an increase in the number of war-front boats could have brought about a balance. But in spite of the efforts made, it was impossible to bring more new boats to the war front than were being lost. . . . It was inevitable that the effective protection given to enemy shipping should lead to a drop in the U-boat successes.' *Ibid.* Admiral Gladisch, too, acknowledges the great success of the convoy system. 'Trial convoys and those which later ran regularly were entirely successful. The convoy system turned out to be the most important expedient in the war against the U-boat danger; it was extremely difficult for the U-boats to locate targets compressed into a confined area, and it was almost impossible to attack protected convoys with gunfire.' *Der Krieg in der Nordsee*, vii. 11.

minefield in the area that had just been swept) constantly required new methods of minesweeping. But the mine was no longer a serious factor in mercantile losses, especially British, during the last year of the war. A mere 10 British ships, of less than 20,000 tons, were sunk by mines in the first ten months of 1918. Contrast this with the 97 ships, of 255,100 tons, lost to mines in the first ten months of 1917.

A military decision in the war was unquestionably dependent in the first instance upon the submarine campaign. And here the high hopes of the German Government and Naval Staff had been shattered. They were dismayed to realize that the unrestricted campaign, which was supposed to force Britain to sue for peace in six months (and the German public had been so informed), that is, by 1 August, had failed in its primary objective, and this even before the convoy system was in full operation. 'Admiral Holtzendorff's widely-ventilated five-months pledge indeed proved a devastating time-bomb for German morale . . . creating extreme tension on the U-boat front and apathy in the submarine construction program, while sowing the seeds of profound popular disillusionment when the astronomical Allied shipping losses of 1917 failed to produce a British collapse.'[41] In July, Erzberger, a leading member of the Centre Party, attacked the Government in the Reichstag for having misled the nation with its rosy forecasts. His speeches, which accurately reflected the growing feeling of unrest over the war in general and the disappointment over the results of the U-boat campaign in particular, resulted in the moving of a motion for peace in the Reichstag (19 July). The indecisive U-boat campaign may have been a factor in the disorders that broke out in the High Seas Fleet in July and August 1917, and which became known to the British. (The direct causes of the disorders were grievances over rations and harsh discipline, together with the dull and monotonous patrolling just offshore that followed the discontinuation of genuine offensive sorties.) Long before the winter of 1917, the Army High Command had lost their faith in the U-boat and decided that the war must be won on land.

[41] Philip K. Lundeberg, 'The German Naval Critique of the U-Boat Campaign, 1915–1918', *Military Affairs*, Fall 1963. This article is a mine of information from the German documentary sources, or rather the published ones, and in its way the most authoritative summary available of the U-boat campaign.

As more of the U-boats were being sunk, with diminishing merchant tonnage destruction, 'the morale of the crews was beginning to show signs of deterioration—leave was overstayed, and sickness feigned. Faults arising from inexperience had to be overlooked by the officers, and deference had to be shown to old and experienced hands, because such men were getting more scarce every month and their goodwill had to be cultivated. Shorter and shorter became the periods of refit and overhaul.'[42]

During the autumn of 1917 it became obvious to the Admiralty that the shipping situation was no longer desperate. Geddes announced to the London Naval Conference in September that 'the convoy system has undoubtedly been a success'. Jellicoe said the same thing. Indeed, for the first time he was optimistic. In a paper for the War Cabinet (9 October) he intimated that after the spring of 1918 the U-boat menace should be 'well in hand'. Throughout the autumn the predominant note in official public references to the U-boats and the shipping situation was one of cautious optimism. This was the tone of the First Lord's speeches in the House of Commons.

Geddes was never able to establish rapport with the House of Commons. Addison remarked, 'He somehow has not the instinct of managing it.' Geddes's maiden speech, on 1 November, was proof of that. He was content to read his speech, and in a somewhat monotonous if clear tone, 'like a company managing-director at a shareholders' meeting'. But the facts that he presented and the lessons he drew from them kept his large audience interested and attentive for an hour and twenty minutes. His most important statement was: 'In September 90 per cent of the total vessels sailing in all Atlantic trade were convoyed, and since the convoy system was started—and it has been criticised in some quarters—the total percentage of loss per convoyed vessel passed through the danger zone is 0·5 per cent, or 1 in 200.' He also made the point that the shipping losses might still be serious, yet they seemed to have got over the worst period. There had been a huge increase in output of merchant tonnage in 1917; the output for the first nine months showed a 123 per cent increase on the same period of 1916. The First Lord was heartily cheered on resuming his seat and Asquith congratulated him on having made 'one of the most lucid and comprehensive statements on naval adminis-

[42] Gibson and Prendergast, *The German Submarine War*, pp. 204–5.

tration and policy' he had ever listened to. The First Lord's statement was free from vulgar boasting and silly optimism about the
end of the war. On the contrary, he calmly asked the country to
prepare for 'a long war'. Yet the speech was, taken as a whole,
optimistic. His businesslike statement in the Commons on 13
December admitted that they were not yet destroying German
submarines as fast as the Germans were building them. The curves
of losses and of construction were approaching each other, but
there was still a gap. It was, nevertheless, clear from the speech
that the submarine threat, if not yet mastered, was being held, the
downward tendency of British and Allied shipping losses being
still in progress and the upward trend in shipbuilding and in
destruction of U-boats continuing satisfactorily.[43]

Lloyd George admitted after the war that 'Germany's supreme
effort to blockade Britain had practically failed by the end of 1917
owing to the growing success of our efforts to protect our shipping,
to the increase in our output of new ships, to the better use we
were making of our shipping, and to the plans we had put through
for adding to the yield of our own soil. The Allied losses were still
heavy, but by the end of 1917 we knew that the German effort to
blockade us would not succeed.'[44] Lloyd George was being wise
after the event. It was not at all obvious to him at the time, any
more than it was to the press or to the Navy at large, that the
power of the U-boat for mischief had been severely curtailed.
Thus, in October, Beatty vented on 'the Great Geddes' his disappointment that the U-boat threat was still not under control.
'I do not see anything can improve the situation unless the Enemy
will come along and conveniently wipe out the Admiralty all
together . . .'[45] Sims reported at this time: 'There are many indications at hand to indicate that the crisis of the campaign is past,
but the fact cannot be escaped that losses still continue greater
than construction and there are many serious problems facing the
Allies before it can safely be assumed that we are winning the war
as far as the submarine campaign is concerned.' And at the end of
the year: 'Speaking generally of the [submarine campaign] it must

[43] Privately, the First Lord was even more confident. He told Lord Riddell, the press
lord, that he was convinced that the U-boat menace would be overcome during 1918.
Diary, 14 December 1917; *Lord Riddell's War Diary, 1914–1918* (London, 1933),
p. 299.
[44] Lloyd George, *War Memoirs*, iii, 1195.
[45] Beatty to Lady Beatty, 5 October 1917; Beatty MSS.

be recognized that the situation is still very serious if not critical.'[46]

Why was there no general awareness that the back of the U-boat campaign had been, or at the worst was being, broken? Losses, as indicated, remained high. Moreover, a great many naval officers, and not only naval officers, did not appreciate the proven efficacy of convoy. For one thing, they still regarded it as a 'defensive' measure, which was almost a pejorative term. So brilliant an officer and student of history as Richmond could say: 'Cruising and convoy are valuable defensive measures, but inadequate protection, as they always were in the past against vessels far easier to suppress than submarines.'[47] Dewar, clever as he was, wrote: 'The defensive method of dealing with submarine attack on trade can be written down as a comparative failure, for the enemy submarine promises to bring the war to an unsuccessful ending in the not far distant future. Convoys, mining, hydrophones, etc., may temporarily reduce the process of attrition. . . .'[48] Churchill, in his naval strategy paper of July (above, p. 229), included convoy among 'purely defensive Naval measures'. The Admiralty did nothing to correct this inaccurate appraisal of convoy. In June 1917 the Anti-Submarine Division included convoy for merchant shipping under the category of 'purely "defensive" measures'.

Jellicoe informed the London Naval Conference that the convoy system 'may be regarded as a successful defensive measure against submarine attack', and he left the impression that Admiralty policy was still based on 'offensive' methods. Indeed, even after the convoy system was in full working order, the Admiralty continued to hunt submarines with hunting flotillas in the Irish Sea and North Western Approaches, and later, in 1918, in the North Sea to

---

[46] Sims to Daniels, 17 October, 31 December 1917; U.S. Navy Dept. MSS.

[47] Richmond to Dewar, 22 August 1917; Dewar MSS.

[48] Dewar's paper for Beatty, 'A Naval Offensive Against Germany', 20 September 1917; Bellairs MSS. What Dewar pressed for during the whole of his time in the Plans Division was the destruction of more U-boats through the use of Grand Fleet destroyers, submarines, and light craft 'for patrolling minefields and hunting submarines in certain limited areas in the northern and middle parts of the North Sea, through which we knew they [were] passing . . . the proposal simply amounted to using the Navy proper to hunt the submarine, instead of leaving it to trawlers and drifters, which had neither the necessary speed, armament, training, nor organisation.' This strategy was predicated on the belief that the Grand Fleet at this stage of the war had for its main function the support of its light craft employed in A/S operations. But the Admiralty would do nothing to reduce the instant readiness of the Grand Fleet to fight the High Seas Fleet or deal with a raid or invasion attempt. Dewar to Churchill, 1 November 1926; Dewar MSS.

waylay U-boats on passage north of Scotland. Newbolt explains this state of affairs: 'In so far as the system achieved its success by evading contact with the enemy, it withdrew the destroyers and sloops employed as escorts from opportunities of offensive action. Their counter-offensive, when a convoy was attacked, had again and again been successful in avoiding or minimising loss to the vessels under their charge; but although escorting destroyers claimed on several occasions to have sunk or damaged the enemy, the destruction of no German submarine could yet be definitely traced to the activities of ships engaged in convoy.'[49] In short, the success of the convoy system was equated with the number of U-boat kills for which it was directly responsible. Judged by this criterion, the convoy system was not functioning too well. We know today, however, that in the first six months of the developing convoy system, July–December 1917, though only a fraction of the resources were devoted to convoy as compared with patrol, *convoy escorts destroyed as many U-boats as did patrols*: four; six, if we include U-boats sunk by escorts to single ships.[50]

Naval circles, moreover, felt that the convoy efficiency would not be maintained in the approaching months. First, the fog and heavy weather in the winter would increase the difficulty of handling ships in convoys (while impairing enemy activity). Indeed, there was 'a growing feeling' that it might be necessary to revert to the patrol system temporarily during January and February.[51] In the second place, the Germans were expected to make a vigorous reply to the convoy system by sending one or more battle cruisers, accompanied by a large and fast liner fitted as a collier, out on the Atlantic trade routes to co-operate with the new submarine cruisers in smashing the Atlantic convoys. The escape of raiders during the winter months, when there were over twenty hours of darkness in northern waters, could not be prevented. The Admiralty, which had always expected that the Germans might try this (in 1914, for example, they had detached a battle cruiser

---

[49] *Naval Operations*, v. 142, with special reference to the convoy system through September 1917.

[50] Historical Section, Admiralty, *The Defeat of the Enemy Attack on Shipping, 1939–1945* (1957, 2 vols., of which the second, 1B, consists of plans and tables), 1B, Plan 4, as revised in Lieutenant-Commander D. W. Waters's letter to the author, 5 June 1968. Waters and Barley were the authors of this restricted publication. On the 'escorts to ships' reference, see above, p. 118.

[51] Sims to Daniels, 19 December 1917; U.S. Navy Dept. MSS.

to protect the Canadian troop convoy) took this possibility extra seriously from the latter part of August. The time such a force could operate on the trade routes was considerable: six to eight weeks, apart from any supplies captured in prizes, was the estimate. The successful attack by German light cruisers on a Norwegian convoy in October showed what a few raiders might accomplish if loosed on the high seas.[52]

To sum up, as the year approached its end, there was no general awareness, in the country, the Navy, or the Government, that the most effective possible antidote to the U-boat menace had been found and that the menace was at last being contained. Shipping losses remained high and convoy did not appear to be the complete answer. The overshadowing need, in the public view, was for more shipping; therein lay the country's salvation. For example, *The Times* (14 December) endorsed the First Lord's plea (Commons, 13 December) for ' "ships, and more ships, and still more ships".
. . . The country has scoffed at the submarines too long, and Ministers have too often treated the menace lightly. It is real, *it increases in magnitude* [italics supplied], but it can and will be defeated if we all pull together.'

[52] The Operations Division of the Staff proposed that they base four Japanese battle cruisers on Portland with the function of preventing the exit of any raiders through the Channel or to hunt them down if they broke out northabout, and that they have battleships in readiness to escort convoys, one dreadnought with each convoy. Oliver saw an advantage in employing the Japanese battle cruisers as proposed; the other recommendation was not practicable. 'The few convoys which could be escorted by using the few Dreadnought Battleships which could be spared by the Allies would not be worth the trouble. It would be best to disperse the trade at once so that the enemy vessels would have to steam about to find it or else operate near focal points; if they did the latter it would be easier for the Allies to find them and bring them to action.' Operations Division, 'Possible German Operation to Defeat the Convoy System', 5 September 1917, and Oliver's minute, 17 September; Admiralty MSS. We have seen (above, pp. 43–4) that the Government opened negotiations with Tokyo with a view to having the Japanese sell them two battle cruisers, or, as second best, to attach them to the Grand Fleet, partly as a measure of preparedness against high seas raiding during the coming winter. As Oliver had foreseen, the Japanese showed no willingness to co-operate.

XI

Home Waters: A Tale of Woe

(October 1917 – December 1917)

The failure in the North Sea [17 October convoy incident]. . . . in many respects is one of the most disquieting incidents for a long time past. It is, we believe, the first occasion on which a convoy, protected by warships, has been attacked and destroyed. . . . it would be false to say that the country feels the same confidence in the administration of the Navy that it does in the capacity and spirit of the Navy itself. On the contrary, there is and has long been a deep and widespread disquiet in this respect.

DAILY NEWS, 23 October 1917.

I am depressed at the raids on the convoys [17 October, 12 December]. It is a pity, but it is easier to raid than to protect them.

COMMODORE SIR REGINALD TYRWHITT to his sister, Frances Tyrwhitt,

14 December 1917.

1. THE INCIDENT OF 17 OCTOBER
(*Chart 4*)

TWO EVENTS in the autumn of 1917 gave rise to considerable criticism of Admiralty methods, not unmixed with some genuine apprehensiveness as to whether the Navy was efficiently fulfilling its many functions. The Scandinavian convoys had been a decided success; yet they had inherent dangers not to be found in the Atlantic or Mediterranean convoys:

(a) They had to sail through an area in which they were liable to attack by enemy surface-craft in force.
(b) Their Port of Assembly for the homeward voyage was in a neutral country.
(c) They were largely composed of neutral ships.
(d) Owing to the presence of neutral ships and the fact that the ships traded to ports in close proximity to the enemy, it was impracticable to ensure secrecy as regards the general method of procedure.

(e) Their passage was short and was practically in the Danger Zone for the whole voyage.[1]

The advent of bad weather late in September (practically uninterrupted through the rest of the year) opened up opportunities for the Germans. Reports, mainly from U-boats, had strengthened the impression that a heavy convoy traffic had developed between the Shetlands and Norway, somewhere along the line of Lerwick-Bergen. Scheer decided to make a surprise raid with surface craft against this traffic. The strategic aim was to help the U-boat campaign by causing the British to strengthen the protection of the Scandinavian trade. Working in the German favour was the possession of bases on the flank of the convoy route, which allowed them to arrive undetected at the eastern end of the route. Chosen for the task were the light cruisers *Brummer* and *Bremse*. They were particularly well-suited to this operation in view of their high speed (34 knots), radius of action, and resemblance to British cruisers.

On 17 October, when about 65 miles east of Lerwick, a westbound Scandinavian convoy of 12 vessels (2 British, 1 Belgian, 9 Scandinavian), protected against submarines by the destroyers *Mary Rose* (in command) and *Strongbow*, and two armed trawlers, was attacked repeatedly by the *Brummer* and *Bremse*. The raiders sank the destroyers and with merciless brutality the bulk of the convoy itself (the nine neutrals with a total tonnage of 10,248), and then escaped unscathed.[2] Of the ship's company of the *Strongbow* four officers and 41 men were saved; two officers and eight men were the only survivors of the *Mary Rose*. Her Captain had gone down. The destroyers had put up a splendid fight against

---

[1] Technical History Monograph TH 8 (1919), *Scandinavian and East Coast Convoy Systems, 1917–1918*, p. 4.

[2] Newbolt is very severe on the Germans. 'Throughout the attack the Germans displayed a severity which is hard to distinguish from downright cruelty. They gave the neutral masters and crews no chance to lower their boats and get away, but poured their broadsides into them without warning, as though they had been armed enemies. . . . In the case of the destroyers the enemy's conduct was even worse; for to their everlasting discredit fire was opened and maintained upon the *Strongbow*'s survivors.' *Naval Operations*, v. 155. The German rebuttal to the latter charge is worth noting: 'Some of *Strongbow*'s crew, who had taken to the lifeboat, and others who had leapt into the water, became additional victims of the gunfire, possibly from shots falling short; it stands to reason that there was no intention whatsoever of firing on them. The statement in the British Official History, that defenceless survivors from the *Strongbow* were deliberately fired on, cannot be refuted strongly enough.' *Der Krieg in der Nordsee*, vii. 47.

their superior foes despite the inevitability of defeat, so enabling three of the merchantmen to escape. In brief, it was a gallant, but disastrous, action.

What had gone wrong? Several things; excessive secrecy for one. The destroyers did not know that enemy cruisers were out or that British cruisers and light cruisers were out looking for them.[3] When the *Strongbow*, behind the convoy (the *Mary Rose* was six to eight miles ahead of the convoy), sighted two strange ships at 6.05 a.m., at about 2 points before the port beam, it was just daylight, with visibility not more than 4,000 yards. The *Strongbow* apparently took them for British light cruisers (they had been rigged to resemble ships of the 'Cleopatra' class), for she challenged them three times, flashing a recognition signal by highspeed morse, using a small searchlight. It was not until after the third challenge that the enemy cruisers, who were meantime closing at high speed, bluffed a reply. The *Strongbow*'s alarm gongs then sounded. Before the men could reach action stations, the *Brummer* had opened fire (6.15) at little more than 3,000 yards. The first two salvoes smashed

[3] 'The cruiser squadrons were sent out by C.-in-C. on information from Ad[ty], but important particulars were not sent [that the *Bremse* and *Brummer* were at sea?], which, if sent, would greatly have modified his dispositions. This is the old stupidity the Admiralty have been guilty of so often—not acquainting Commanders with the whole situation.' Richmond's diary, 8 December 1917; *Portrait of an Admiral*, p. 283, on the authority of Bellairs, who had recently been at the Admiralty. An intercepting force from the Grand Fleet and Harwich Force (3 cruisers, 27 light cruisers, and 54 destroyers) was at sea, the Admiralty having guessed that an enemy move was in the offing. This armada was 'searching for a force which so far as we could tell consisted of only one minelayer and a handful of destroyers . . .' Newbolt, *Naval Operations*, v. 151. The British forces were spread out, in the central part of the North Sea and off the south-west coast of Norway, that is, well south of the Scandinavian convoy route. The Admiralty had ruled out the possibility of an attack so far to the north. Yet they were aware, through Room 40 intercepts, that the *Bremse* and *Brummer* were at sea. 'We knew the call signs of the two ships,' Admiral James recalls, 'and by D/F we in Room 40 knew that they had moved north from Wilhelmshaven to Lister Tief [N. of Sylt] and were obviously about to carry out some operation. I remember Keyes, the Director of Plans, coming into our chart room and speculating on what these two ships were going to do. We did not of course have on our charts the position of any British ships: they were all shown in the charts in Operations Division. If the convoys had been shown in our charts, it is probable that Keyes or someone else would have seen the possibility that the *Brummer* and *Bremse* objective was a convoy.' 'My recollection is that Operations did not tell Beatty about these ships. But I do remember there was a devil of a row about this and Beatty came to the Admiralty for a meeting. I think these two ships were fitted as minelayers [they were], and so it did not occur to anyone in Operations that they might be going to attack a convoy. There is no doubt that the Admiralty were at fault in not warning Beatty about these two ships.' Admiral James's letters to the author, 31 May 1966, 19 March 1968. And see further, Hankey's statement, below, p. 334.

the *Strongbow*'s main steam pipe, which caused the ship to stop, and the W/T room and installations, which prevented the sending out of an S.O.S. She was overwhelmed by the fire of the enemy ships at a range of 2,000 yards and less. The cruisers then turned on the convoy itself and quickly sank nine of the merchantmen and, at 7.15, the *Mary Rose*, which had turned back after hearing firing astern, closed to between 2,000 and 3,000 yards, and put up a gallant fight. Finally, the raiders turned on the *Strongbow* again, practically finished her off—she fought until her guns were knocked out—and at 8.20 a.m. made for home, steering to the south-eastward. The *Strongbow* eventually sank at about 9.30 a.m., after her Captain had ordered her engine- and boiler-rooms to be flooded in order to sink the ship and thus prevent her capture by the enemy. The *Mary Rose* story was also a heroic one and in the finest British tradition. 'It is', the D.O.D. remarked, 'the nearest parallel to the *Revenge* that could be imagined, finishing with the 1st Lieut. ordering the Gunner to sink the ship.' For Pakenham the whole action was 'not less glorious to the Navy than that in which Sir Richard Grenville perished'.[4] The two trawlers with the escort were undamaged. One of them rescued most of the survivors from the *Strongbow*.

At the time of the attack there were two squadrons of British light cruisers in the approaches to the Skagerrak and three squadrons, plus the *Courageous* and *Glorious*, north of the Dogger Bank. Had the destroyers been able to send out a W/T message reporting the attack, the German cruisers might well have been intercepted by daylight. The principal point elicited at the *Mary Rose* Court of Inquiry was the apparent failure of the *Mary Rose*, despite her recognition of the hostile character of the light cruisers sighted, to report the presence of hostile vessels to Lerwick by W/T.[5] (One wonders, too, why she made no use of her torpedoes,

---

[4] Minutes of Hope (17 November) and Pakenham (28 October) on the reports of the *Strongbow* (28 October) and *Mary Rose* (26 October) courts of inquiry; Admiralty MSS.

[5] The *Mary Rose* Court of Inquiry and Court Martial (3 December) adopted a similar position, remarking on the gallantry that actuated her Captain (Lieutenant-Commander Charles Fox), but criticizing him for his 'ill-advised decision'. 'His action was evidently premeditated as he himself closed the enemy and was the first to open fire. The reasons for thus attacking are thus obscure, as it must have been evident that he would soon be put out of action, leaving his convoy unprotected, whereas if he had remained at long range, he might have drawn, some at any rate, of the enemy forces away from the convoy. Whilst doing this *Mary Rose* could have

though in a good position to do so. Her commander apparently forgot that he had such weapons.) Nor had any of the steamers transmitted a message. The action with the *Strongbow* had unfolded so suddenly and she was hit so quickly that she was unable to send out a W/T signal.[6] The consequence of the failure of any W/T signal to come through announcing the attack on the convoy was a delay in placing light-cruiser squadrons for interception. The first intimation that an action had taken place did not reach the nearest naval authorities (F. E. E. Brock, the Admiral Commanding Orkneys and Shetlands) until 3.50 p.m. on the 17th, when a signal was intercepted from the destroyer *Marmion* (one of the destroyers with the eastbound convoy from Lerwick which had come upon the escaped armed trawler *Elise* at 1.30 p.m.) to the Commodore (F). After delays, the news of the destruction of the convoy finally reached Beatty between 4 and 5 p.m. By then the raiders were well on their way home; all chance had gone of cutting them off during the long dark night of 17–18 October. The C.-in-C., nevertheless, attempted during the night to dispose his light-cruiser and cruiser squadrons to cut off the Germans.

---

furnished most valuable reports . . .' Beatty agreed with both the praise of the Captain's spirit and the criticism of his indiscretion. Report of *Mary Rose* Inquiry, H.M.S. *Inflexible*, 26 October 1917, and Beatty's minute of 31 October; Admiralty MSS. The *Strongbow* Court Martial (8 January 1918) was critical of the judgement of her Officer of the Watch (Acting Lieutenant R. W. James) and Captain (Lieutenant-Commander Edward Brooke). They 'should have endeavoured to keep out of range and called for assistance by wireless telegraph. The Court considers that this error in judgement did not amount to any offence under the Naval Discipline Act.' Admiralty MSS. The German account comes to the same conclusion: 'The heroic fight put up by the two British destroyers *Strongbow* and *Mary Rose* had been in the highest British tradition, but it had achieved nothing. On the contrary; in consequence of their determination to give battle, they had not been able to carry out their essential task, which was to report the attack and thereby facilitate effective and adequate counter-measures. If they had done this and later joined in the rescue operations after the withdrawal of the German cruisers, they would have done better service.' *Der Krieg in der Nordsee*, vii. 52.

[6] We now know that attempts were in fact made to send out a signal. The German Official History notes: 'Just as the *Mary Rose* was closing to attack the *Brummer*, a weak signal was heard. It was repeated on request from another station, but was jammed by the *Brummer*. If British observation stations had been alert then, it should perhaps have been possible to ascertain or at least suspect the position and time of the action. But this was not so, for throughout the forenoon British W/T traffic continued normally.' Elsewhere: 'It was vital for their unobserved breakthrough that none of the destroyers, patrol vessels, or steamers in the convoy succeed in sending out a distress signal. The German radio personnel in the *Brummer* and *Bremse* did some valuable work in successfully jamming every attempt to transmit.' *Ibid.*, pp. 48–9, 51.

There was bitter criticism of the Admiralty in the press, follow-ing the publication of a communiqué. It was, of course, unreason-able to expect that the Scandinavian convoys would have complete immunity from interruption. This was mentioned by Conservative journals like the *Spectator, Morning Post,* and *Daily Telegraph,* and by the leading Service organs, the *Army and Navy Gazette* and the *Naval and Military Record.* Their argument, hoary but sound, was that the sea is a large place, and it was absolutely impossible to prevent a few swift and powerful raiders from dashing out occa-sionally in darkness and mist, temporarily escaping detection, and overwhelming a convoy and its escort. (The defence of convoy HX.84 by the *Jervis Bay* against the battleship *Scheer* in November 1940 is a more recent instance of what has occurred a number of times in Britain's wars.) This, too, was the line that Geddes took in the Commons on 1 November. He pointed out the general immunity with which the convoy system had been carried out in Northern waters: they had convoyed over 4,500 vessels to and from Scandinavia since April. This was the first one to lose a single ship through surface attack.

Besides, as the *Naval and Military Record* brought out, the incident was of little strategic importance; it did not relieve Germany from the increasing pressure that the Royal Navy was applying. Indeed, as Newbolt suggests, 'In spite of its brilliantly successful execution, the raid must have been somewhat disappointing to the German Staff. The operation was obviously intended to act as a general deterrent to Scandinavian masters; yet in spite of the rapidity and ferocity with which it was carried out, it failed to deter them. In fact, it hardly caused a disturbance in the time-table of Scan-dinavian trade.'[7]

'Luck was against us' was the first reaction of Beatty, who lost no time in profiting from 17 October. He asked the officer com-manding the Grand Fleet flotillas to 'impress on all Destroyer Officers the paramount importance of being ready for immediate action at a moment's notice and the necessity of regarding every vessel sighted as hostile until her friendly character is unmistak-able'. One would have thought that the lesson of Jutland would have been sufficient! The C.-in-C.'s instructions went on: 'In the event of a convoy being attacked by enemy surface craft, the signal to scatter is to be made by escorting Destroyers. . . . The Destroyers

[7] *Naval Operations,* v. 157–8.

themselves, while using their utmost endeavours to damage the enemy, are not to engage superior forces. They are to use their speed to maintain a safe distance from the enemy; they cannot protect the convoy after it has scattered and Destroyers are not to be risked uselessly. Their most important duty is to report enemy vessels and position by W/T IMMEDIATELY.'[8]

On 22 October a conference was held at the Admiralty, with the C.-in-C. present. On 5 November definite proposals were made to the Admiralty for a revision of the whole Scandinavian convoy system. They were under consideration by a conference which met at Longhope on 10 December, and Beatty had just warned the Admiralty that the effective solution was to put the Scandinavian convoys under cruiser protection, when the enemy made a second surface attack on a Scandinavian convoy. Before that, however, there had intervened an unsatisfactory action in the Heligoland Bight.

2. THE 17 NOVEMBER ACTION

(Chart 5)

The intensified British mining activity in the Bight provided the Grand Fleet with its last real chance to weaken the High Seas Fleet appreciably. U-boats returning home always sent a signal when they were in the vicinity of the Shetlands with the time they would be at the end of a particular swept channel, so that they could be met by a sweeping flotilla. The British were continually laying minefields where these channels ended; the result was that the ends of the channels were continually being extended farther and farther into the North Sea. Eventually, the German mine-sweeping forces found themselves working to as much as 150 miles from the Jade—that is, within striking distance of British forces. To do their job, the sweepers and supporting craft had now to have protection against raids by British destroyers and light cruisers. At first a half destroyer flotilla, strengthened by one or two light cruisers, constituted the covering force. By June 1917 the Germans were sometimes keeping battleships in support near Heligoland, and from November 1917 this support of the sweeping forces became the main task of the High Seas Fleet: there was usually a whole battle squadron a considerable distance out.

[8] Beatty to J. R. P. Hawksley, Commodore (F), 19, 20 October 1917; Admiralty MSS.

Beatty had since August 1917 seen possibilities in this situation. By November N.I.D. had sufficient information on the enemy's sweeping and covering forces for the Admiralty to try to spring a trap on them. The plan was perfectly timed and the forces perfectly positioned, since the Germans had ordered a large sweeping operation that day in the very zone the British force was to examine.

The German force consisted of three minesweeping half-flotillas, two destroyer half-flotillas and two boats of another flotilla (total: eight destroyers), a barrier-breaker group (mine-explosion resistant trawlers) and, as the covering force, Rear-Admiral von Reuter and the 2nd Scouting Group (four light cruisers), with two battleships in support near Heligoland. The Grand Fleet striking force was composed of the *1st Cruiser Squadron*: the light battle cruisers *Courageous* (flag of Vice-Admiral T. D. W. Napier) and *Glorious* (four 15-inch guns each), and four screening destroyers; *6th Light Cruiser Squadron*: four light cruisers (*Cardiff*, flag of Rear-Admiral Alexander-Sinclair) and four screening destroyers; *1st Light Cruiser Squadron*: four light cruisers (*Caledon*, broad pendant of Commodore 'Titch' Cowan, of whom Beatty used to say, 'Well, I'm quite sure if Walter Cowan sees the enemy, he *won't* let them go!') and two screening destroyers; *1st Battle Cruiser Squadron*: four battle cruisers (*Lion*, flag of Vice-Admiral Pakenham, who was in charge of the whole operation), reinforced by the *New Zealand* and screened by nine destroyers. In support, a few hours' steaming away, was the *1st Battle Squadron*: six battleships and eleven screening destroyers. The key role was to be played by an admiral we have met before, at Jutland: the tall, handsome Napier, a good all-round officer, if hardly brilliant in any respect and lacking in initiative. He commanded the two light-cruiser squadrons as well as the 1st Cruiser Squadron, that is, the engaged forces. The plan, as summarized by Newbolt, was for the cruiser forces

to sweep across the North Sea to a point about half-way across the outer edge of the quadrant of mines in the Heligoland Bight. They were to approach this point from the western and southern sides of the large German minefield in the central part of the North Sea, and having reached it, were to sweep to the N.N.W. The 1st Battle Squadron was to take up a supporting position in the middle of the open water between the eastern edge of the German minefield and the north-western corner of the British mine barrier. The cruiser forces were to arrive at the general rendezvous on the mine barrier at 8.0 a.m.; the battle squadron was to be in its supporting position at the same time. . . .

As the squadron commanders were instructed to strike at a force of enemy ships on or near the outer edge of the mine barrier, it followed that if they found them, the British squadrons might be obliged to press on into the mined area in pursuit. If they were so compelled their movements would obviously be restricted by those minefields which they believed to lie within the zone of their operations.[9]

The British forces left Rosyth at 4.30 p.m. on 16 November; by 7 p.m. the cruiser squadrons were approaching the mine barrier in the Bight. The 1st Cruiser Squadron was in the lead, steering east; the 6th Light Cruiser Squadron, one to two miles on the port beam of the 1st Cruiser Squadron; the 1st Light Cruiser Squadron, three miles astern of the 1st Cruiser Squadron. Pakenham's battle cruisers were about 10 miles on the port quarter of Napier's flagship. Visibility on the surface was about $7\frac{1}{2}$ miles, the sea smooth and light, the wind westerly, force two. At 7.30 a.m. enemy vessels were sighted right ahead on a north-westerly course, and at 7.37 fire was opened. The Germans were taken by surprise. Their destroyers and minesweepers promptly made dense smoke-screens, and by 7.51 the German movements were hidden from sight. Von Reuter, aware that he was in the presence of a vastly more powerful British force, ordered a turn to the south-east at 7.53 through the British minefields towards his battleship support. 'Course was altered by our squadrons to penetrate the smoke-screens,' Napier reported, 'and occasionally an enemy light cruiser was a clear target for a short time, but on the whole they were indistinct in the smoke and firing was mostly at flashes in the smoke.'[10] It was not until 8.11 that Napier was aware that the Germans were retiring on a south-easterly course. He felt safe in pressing on, reckoning that the enemy were steaming through cleared waters. The action had now, Napier continued, 'settled down into a chase at ranges of 15,000 to 10,000 yards, the enemy still making heavy smoke, and steering down what was probably a swept channel as a pillar buoy was passed presumably marking an outer end.'

[9] *Naval Operations*, v. 165.
[10] Napier to Beatty, 5 December 1917; Admiralty MSS. This, his initial report on the action, is reproduced in Naval Staff, Admiralty, *Grand Fleet Gunnery and Torpedo Memoranda on Naval Actions, 1914–1918* (1922), pp. 55–6; Naval Library.

Napier's fire was beginning to tell when the Germans put up a fresh smoke-screen (8.20). At about 8.35, as Napier was approaching Line 'B' (so labelled by him on his charts: an imaginary line 12 miles beyond the rendezvous and marking 'the limit I had in mind of, at any rate, British minefields, and to which I could go if necessity arose'),[11] the harassed von Reuter performed his disappearing act once more behind a smoke-screen. Not daring to follow—the enemy might have altered course—Napier had his squadron make an 8-point alteration to port, that is, to a north-easterly course, at 8.40. Cowan and Alexander-Sinclair conformed. At 8.52, as the smoke-screen began to clear and Napier could see that the enemy had not altered course, he altered course 8 points to starboard and resumed the chase. He had lost five miles by the turn to port and was only able to re-engage the enemy at extreme range. Only the 6-inch of the 6th Light Cruiser Squadron and of the *Caledon* were at all effective. At 9.15 the enemy were out of range. At about 9.0 Napier was joined by the battle cruiser *Repulse* (rear flag of the 1st B.C.S., Rear-Admiral R. F. Phillimore, a little fire-eater), which had been detached by Pakenham at 8 a.m. to support the 1st Light Cruiser Squadron (Cowan). (Except for the *Repulse*, the 1st Battle Cruiser Squadron did not come into action.) But at 9.08, thinking that the enemy had been lost, Pakenham signalled that the cruiser squadrons were to give up the pursuit and rejoin his flag at the general rendezvous.[12] Napier disregarded the recall and continued the chase for another 12 miles.

The turning point of the action came at 9.32. Napier had reached Line 'C', the edge of what his charts labelled a 'dangerous area', an extensive mined area, British or German not specified (actually, a British minefield in the heart of the Bight that had been laid in 1915) and which he regarded as an absolute barrier. He turned his squadron sharply to starboard. From the time of sighting the Germans the three cruiser squadrons had acted independently. Napier appears to have made no operational signals. But now, at 9.40, he made this signal to the 1st Battle Cruiser Squadron and the 1st and 6th Light Cruiser Squadrons: 'Battle cruisers and cruisers should not go further through the minefield.

---

[11] Napier to Beatty, 16 December 1917; Admiralty MSS.

[12] Pakenham afterwards explained this signal to a mystified Admiralty as 'intended to direct procedure when action ceased. If action had already ceased, as was probable, obedience would be immediate.' Beatty to Admiralty (concurring in this explanation), 24 December 1917; Admiralty MSS.

Light cruisers use discretion and report movements.' And at 9.49 to the *Repulse*: 'Heavy draught ships should not go further into mine-fields.' The two light-cruiser squadrons, unaware of any such zone—their charts did not show it—continued right on, looking to the German light cruisers to guide them through the minefields. The *Repulse* was 'foaming along' not far behind. They had hopes of catching up with and dealing a decisive blow to the enemy. 'We really had great hopes towards the end', Cowan afterwards remarked.

Reuter's hopes were equally high, since he expected to draw the British into a pincers formed by his light cruisers and battleships.

'Up to this point [he wrote in his battle dispatch] the action had been fought with a calm that may well be called exemplary. Everyone manned his post, carrying out the duties assigned to him as in manœuvres. In spite of the tremendous impression caused by the mixed salvos and the ensuing effects of the enemy's fire . . . we were animated only by the fervent desire, filled only with the one thought: to destroy the enemy. This moment had arrived; calm yielded to a certain feverish expectation. It could only be a question of minutes until the fate of the enemy was sealed.' Von Reuter's intention was to draw the enemy on to pursue him on an easterly course through the English and German minefields and, thus, to get him between the light cruisers and the battleships. If the enemy took evasive action by proceeding on a north and north-west course, he could escape only across the mined areas . . . it was very likely he would suffer losses through mines. If, on the other hand, he withdrew to the westwards, this would bring him face to face with the battleships.[13]

The British force did not put itself into the noose Reuter had anticipated. Rather were both German and British hopes rudely shattered some ten or fifteen minutes later. At about 9.50 heavy-shell splashes began to fall round the British light cruisers and German capital ships came into sight to the south-east. They were the dreadnoughts *Kaiserin* and *Kaiser*, which had hustled up on receiving Reuter's report that he was engaged. Alexander-Sinclair lost no time in breaking off the engagement by ordering the two squadrons to turn 16 points to port. The *Repulse* covered their retirement to the north-west, which was not interfered with. They fell back on Napier, and shortly after 1 p.m. the entire British force was making for Rosyth.

[13] *Der Krieg in der Nordsee*, vii. 75.

The engagement on 17 November, the last big-ship action of the war, was a fiasco from the British point of view. Only Lord Fisher, who was elated over the performance of his much maligned light battle cruisers (the *Furious, Courageous,* and *Glorious* were generally known in the Fleet as the 'Helpless', 'Hopeless', and 'Useless'!), seems to have derived any satisfaction from the encounter. Not only had a British force of overwhelming strength failed to achieve its mission of cutting off and destroying the enemy's cruisers and minesweepers, but it had sustained severer casualties than it had inflicted. The German fire repeatedly straddled the British ships, yet made but seven hits—all on the light cruisers. (The Germans thought they had observed 18 hits.) The German light cruisers were hit but five times—only the *Königsberg* at all seriously: a hit by the *Repulse* at 9.58 that pierced the three funnels, causing considerable damage, and exploded over one of the boiler-rooms. She completed her repairs on 15 December. The Germans lost a patrol boat from the sweeping forces.

The smoke-screens that von Reuter had thrown out to hamper the British spotting and ranging, together with the proximity to large minefields and to Heligoland, had added greatly to the difficulties of the pursuit. In Napier's opinion, 'The outstanding feature of the action is that the gunnery difficulties are mainly due to smoke, artificial or otherwise, and that far from being exceptional conditions, they are much more likely to be the normal conditions for future occasions.' Also working against the accuracy of the British fire were the defensive tactics of the Germans throughout the action. They zigzagged often and occasionally made large turns-away. 'Their zigzags were successful in throwing off our shots; they caused misses for deflection, the effect of which was felt in the range spotting.' Also the large majority of shell fired by the British ships (82 per cent of the 3,170 4-inch and 6-inch fired) was Lyditte Common, which projectiles 'do not seem to have injured the enemy's vitals'.[14] The Captain of the *Repulse* stressed these considerations as affecting his gunfire: 'Only the flashes of enemy gunfire were visible as targets owing to the prevailing hazy weather and to the smoke screen being made by the hostile vessels. For this reason the fall of shot could not be spotted. . . . Another factor which mitigated against good shooting was the presence of enemy submarines [see below], and the absence of

[14] Napier to Beatty, 5 December 1917.

screening destroyers rendered it necessary to pay more attention to this menace than was conducive to satisfactory gunnery results.'[15]

Since the action was a chase, there had been no opportunities of firing torpedoes from the light cruisers or battle cruisers. Individual destroyers favourably placed for a torpedo attack at 6,000 yards managed to fire two torpedoes, which 'may have been successful'. They were not. The German light cruisers and destroyers fired about eight or ten torpedoes at ranges of 13,000–16,000 yards, one of which probably hit the light cruiser *Galatea* (1st L.C.S.) but did not explode. There were no U-boats in the action, although it was believed at the time that U-boats had fired torpedoes. The *Courageous* reported that she had sighted a group of U-boats in the midst of the German forces, and the *Repulse* claimed to have sighted two submarines.

A bitterly disappointed C.-in-C. criticized Napier for not having at once turned the 1st Cruiser Squadron towards the enemy light cruisers on sighting them, so as to get in the strategic position called for in the G.F.B.I.s, namely, between the enemy and their base. 'A determined effort to do this at the beginning of the engagement might have met with success and cut the enemy's line of retreat, forcing him into effective gun-range of the First and Sixth Light-Cruiser Squadrons, and possibly even of the Battle-Cruisers.' What Beatty undoubtedly had in mind (and what the Admiralty critique focused on) was Napier's turns to port (northward) between 7.30 and 8.0, although 20 miles clear of any minefields. Furthermore, when the action had developed into a chase, the high speed of Napier's squadron (better than 30 knots) should have been used to close the range. Instead, the *Courageous* and *Glorious* had pursued the enemy at 25 knots. Beatty also found it 'unfortunate' that the squadron had turned 8 points away and given up the chase at 8.40.

On the credit side, Beatty commended Phillimore for his 'determined support' of the light cruisers in their retirement before the enemy battleships. 'His action undoubtedly served as a deterrent to these supports which otherwise might have inflicted considerable damage on our Light-Cruisers.' He also praised Alexander-Sinclair and Cowan (as did Pakenham) for handling their squadrons 'with skill and determination in the difficult circumstances

[15] W. H. D. Boyle to Pakenham, 19 November 1917; Admiralty MSS.

[and] . . . for the resolute manner in which they persevered in the chase, notwithstanding the order given by the Vice-Admiral Commanding, Battle-Cruiser Force [Pakenham], at 0908 to rejoin his flag, and which they took upon themselves the responsibility of disregarding. It is assumed that this signal was intended by the Vice-Admiral to convey instructions as to where to rejoin him when their task was complete.'[16]

We can sympathize with Napier, who returned to harbour thinking he had done pretty well, all things considered.

Have you [he wrote] ever experienced the chill down your back when—after an exciting and tiring day's shooting, you return well pleased with yourself—and the house party immediately asks what is the bag. With a sudden revulsion you are obliged to admit it is only several pheasants and hares wounded and dying in their holes! This is somewhat our feelings on returning to harbour on 19th Nov.—and incidentally is much what we felt after that rotten entertainment called the Battle of Jutland. It seems that we are expected to sink them all, but we found that they were difficult to sink, especially when enveloped in smoke, with nothing showing except gun flashes. However, I am inclined to think they had a hammering, although I suppose we shall never know the details. Two destroyers and a submarine are, I think, tolerable certainties.[17]

As regards the first criticism noted above, Napier's general northward course between 7.30 and 8.0, the Vice-Admiral's explanation was not challenged. From the glimpses he had of the enemy through their smoke-screens, they appeared to be steaming to the north-westward across his bows in an attempt to escape to the west. It was not until some minutes after 8.0 that he realized that they were fleeing to the south-east. As for the second criticism, the alleged reduced speed during the chase, Beatty afterwards discovered that Napier's ships were not fast enough to catch the Germans or to clear the smoke-screens. Presumably he was refer-

---

[16] Beatty to Admiralty, 1 December 1917; Admiralty MSS. It was Napier, not Cowan and Alexander-Sinclair, who had taken it upon himself to disregard Pakenham's order. The Germans, too, had high praise for Cowan and Alexander-Sinclair: 'Only the conduct of the leaders of the 1st and 6th Light Cruiser Squadrons left nothing to be desired; they were least concerned with worries about mines, since their mine charts were the most incomplete and, unlike the charts of Admirals Pakenham and Napier, theirs did not show the extensive mined area to the west of List. [On the mine charts, see below.] But the decision of the day lay less with the leaders of the light cruisers than with those of the capital ships.' *Der Krieg in der Nordsee*, vii. 84–5.

[17] Napier to Tyrwhitt, 8 December 1917; Tyrwhitt MSS.

ring to the light cruisers, not to the *Courageous* and *Glorious*. But the general feeling was that Napier should have gone on on his own, that is, with his two battle cruisers, at full speed. Hope, Oliver, Wemyss, Jellicoe, and Geddes all fell on the hapless Napier for not having made use of the great speed of his squadron to get to a decisive range. Jellicoe found Napier's action in the early stages of the action in not closing the German light cruisers 'inexplicable'.[18]

Napier, called upon by the Admiralty to explain the 'inexplicable'—why he had not increased speed beyond 25 knots—submitted that

no cause was apparent for a further increase of speed. Speed was increased from 22 to 25 knots on sighting the enemy, as a matter of principle because it might be wanted and it is easier to drop speed than to work it up.

But the only reason for a further increase of speed would have been to close the enemy, and as shortly after this first increase enemy was seen on an opposite course to my own, it did not appear that this result would be achieved. Also the 6th Light Cruiser Squadron was just crossing my bow at a small angle and an increase would have hampered my movements. . . .

The course of the enemy, or of at least two of them, at about 0750 just before they were shut out by smoke screen, had been Northerly. I then altered course nearly straight for them; and the next momentary but very clear sight of them at about 0757 was of three enemy light cruisers on a Westerly course, or nearly opposite to my own course. I then altered course again nearly straight for them, and they were lost to sight again whilst turning what appeared to be about 16 points.

My chief consideration was to get through the smoke screen and determine what the situation really was, but nothing more became visible than what I have already described in my report of 16th December 1917, viz: occasional glimpses through the smoke of the enemy on varying courses—mostly gun flashes.

Napier's difficulty in appreciating the course the enemy were steering, and their subsequent line of retreat, was at best a partial

---

18 Hope's memorandum of 7 December 1917 and Admiralty minutes of 7–13 December; Admiralty MSS. The German Official History had this situation in mind when it commented: 'Minesweeping forces, closely supported only by light cruisers, encountered heavy enemy forces and found themselves in a situation which should have ended in the destruction of both minesweepers and light cruisers; if the enemy had acted with vigour, the *Kaiserin* and *Kaiser*, well to the rear, would have arrived too late to prevent it. . . . Correct tactical behaviour on the part of the German units, together with the weak and hesitant attack by far superior British forces, provided the essentials for this unexpected outcome.' *Der Krieg in der Nordsee*, vii. 83.

explanation. Oliver's pithy comment pointed to the weakness in the argument: 'The V.A.'s explanation, whilst covering the earlier stages of his movements, does not appear to explain why no increase of speed was made between 0859, when fire was re-opened, until course was altered on Line C and the action abandoned. This is possibly explained by his remark in para. 7 of his submission of 16th December, from which it is evident he did not realise that a chase was actually taking place.'[19]

After full consideration of the matter, the Board on 31 January 1918 closed the case by concurring with Beatty in his conclusion that 'although the circumstances at the time undoubtedly made it difficult to arrive at a proper appreciation of the situation, I consider that the Vice-Admiral, Light Cruiser Force, committed an error of judgement in the handling of the forces at his disposal'.[20] Napier was so informed on 8 February and that closed the matter.

The action could well have turned out better if the *Courageous* and *Glorious* had pressed on at their utmost speed. Had Napier

[19] Napier to Admiralty, 22 December 1917, and Oliver's minute, 28 December; Admiralty MSS. In para. 7 of his 16th December, Napier had written: 'When enemy were first sighted ahead they were steering to the Northward, and owing to their smoke screen their line of retreat was not known till some time afterwards. The mined area was on my Starboard Hand; I had no knowledge of any channels, and I did not consider the possibility of placing myself between the enemy and his base, which in open waters would have no doubt have been sound. Had the enemy's channel been known, it is possible such action might have met with success on this occasion, although not probable, and it is not possible to say what course the enemy would have pursued under the suggested conditions. It is reasonable to suppose that the enemy would have made off in a North-easterly direction, as the minesweepers did so far as is known.'

[20] Napier suggested to Beatty that, as he had failed, he ought to be relieved, but the C.-in-C., despite dissatisfaction with his performance, told him that he still had confidence in him and wanted him to stay. As the C.-in-C., with characteristic magnanimity, wrote to the Admiralty: '. . . although the circumstances at the time undoubtedly made it difficult to arrive at a proper appreciation of the situation, I consider that the Vice Admiral, Light Cruiser Force, committed an error of judgement in the handling of the forces at his disposal. I have pointed this out and have personally explained to him the result of his misjudgement. I am of the opinion, however, that the experience will be of the greatest value to this officer in any future similar engagement with the enemy. Opportunities of meeting the enemy have unfortunately been few and far between during the 3½ years of war, and those which have occurred have differed materially from one another and have demonstrated new points. Vice Admiral Trevylyan D. W. Napier, C.B., M.V.O., has hitherto shewn skill and judgement in command of light cruiser work, and notwithstanding the disappointing results which attended the recent operation in the Heligoland Bight, I should be very loath to part with his services. I therefore submit that the matter would be sufficiently met by an expression of Their Lordships' displeasure.' Beatty to Admiralty, 24 December 1917; Admiralty MSS.

rung down 'full speed', the two ships might have worked up to 34 or 35 knots, and easily to 32. The *Glorious* had attained 31.25 knots (mean speed) in her measured-mile trials. These results 'show that 32 knots could easily be obtained at the designed load displacement, and this has been confirmed on service'.[21] No measured-mile trials were carried out with the *Courageous*. This phase of the action was much discussed at the Staff College in a Course (1930–1932) that included not only Napier's son but also Curzon-Howe, who was Phillimore's Flag-Lieutenant, as well as a Lieutenant of the *Glorious*. Captain Creswell, who was the lecturer on this action, has observed: 'Curzon-Howe made us realise what a full load of offensive spirit there was on the bridge of the *Repulse* that day with "Ginger" Boyle (later Cork and Orrery), the Flag Captain, to back up Phillimore. But no real conclusion could be reached as to why Napier never went more than 25 knots. The main suggestion was that as a light-cruiser admiral he was accustomed to think of 25 knots as the battle speed and forgot how much faster he could go if he wanted to—which seems rather feeble.'[22]

Napier's experience pointed to the supply and use of aircraft for observation (aircraft, if carried on the larger ships for spotting purposes, could get over the enemy's smoke and direct the fire of the guns) and to the increase in the speed of the light cruisers by such means as reduction of weight and more frequent docking. Beatty drew these lessons from the action: (1) The speed of the 6th Light Cruiser Squadron, which was below that of the 1st Light Cruiser Squadron and 'certainly inferior' to that of the German light cruisers, needed investigation; (2) there was a need to experiment with smoke-screens, 'both from an offensive and defensive point of view'; (3) more practice in zigzagging under action conditions was required; (4) aircraft in action: 'Experiments on definite lines should be carried out in order to effect co-operation.'[23]

One result of the Admiralty investigation was to reveal what Newbolt calls the 'dangerously haphazard' state of the method of keeping the fleet informed of the position of minefields in the Bight. The extensive British minefields in the North Sea constituted at least as great an obstacle to the movement of British

[21] D.N.C. Department, Admiralty, *Records of Warship Construction During the War, 1914–1918*, 31 December 1918; Naval Library.
[22] Captain Creswell's letter to the author, 8 May 1966.
[23] Beatty's minute of 25 December 1917 on Napier's report of 5 December 1917.

warships there as did the German minefields. This huge British minefield, which was in patches, not a solid mined area, extending in a semi-circle from the Jutland coast to Dutch territorial waters near the Texel, served as a barrier to British vessels. This was a positive danger when minefield information was not updated for all officers commanding squadrons. Every month the Hydrographer of the Navy issued a chart showing the latest situation as regards British and German minefields in the Heligoland Bight. A copy of this mine chart went to the C.-in-C. Although it did not circulate in the Fleet, Pakenham had a copy of the latest chart, or had seen one. It differed in important essentials from that in Napier's hands. Beatty put the blame for this squarely on Pakenham. He should have provided the Senior Officers of the squadrons with full information of all minefields. 'The chart supplied to the Vice-Admiral, Light Cruiser Force, showing the position of the minefields, did not give as much information as was available; and for this the Vice Admiral Commanding, Battle Cruiser Force is responsible.'[24] Alexander-Sinclair and Cowan were without any up-to-date information. Only the C.-in-C. had a copy of the chart showing the positions of the German swept channels through the minefields in the Bight. Napier would have accepted the Official Historian's judgement: 'If he had possessed the information with regard to the minefields, and the German channels through them, which was supplied to him later, he might have foreseen the German line of retirement, and would certainly have been able to pursue them more vigorously.'[25] Or, as Madden said at the time, 'If the Admiralty expect chases over minefields, all concerned, Lt. Crs., etc. MUST have the charts. I told C.-in-C. this and he agrees; if charts had been on board, so that the situation could have been realized, that the minesweepers would have been followed, but whereas it is fairly safe for Lt. Crs. to follow Lt. Crs., it's not the same thing to follow light draft vessels who can pass over minefields.'[26] The Admiralty did take prompt steps to ensure

[24] Beatty to Admiralty, 24 December 1917; Admiralty MSS.
[25] Newbolt, *Naval Operations*, v. 177. *Ibid.*, pp. 165–8, has the details of the muddled minefield charts situation.
[26] Madden to Jellicoe, 24 November 1917; Jellicoe MSS. Hope made this point in his analysis (7 December): 'The question as to whether the heavy ships should have entered the area of mine-fields is a difficult one. The orders issued for the operation contained no instructions on this point. So long as our ships could remain on the track taken by the Germans they were comparatively safe, but if they were man-

that in future they would, direct from the Admiralty, supply all minefield information on a special chart, periodically corrected, to the flag officers of the Grand Fleet squadrons.

It had been an interesting day that gave much food for thought. That the failure on 17 November occurred nearly 18 months after Jutland had revealed serious deficiencies in staff work, co-ordinated action, and gunnery caused many to look askance at the Admiralty.

3. THE SECOND CONVOY INCIDENT
(Chart 6)

Scheer repeated his attack on the Scandinavian convoy on 12 December, this time on an eastbound convoy of one British and five neutral merchant vessels (8,180 tons), escorted by two destroyers (*Partridge*, *Pellew*, the latter in command) and four armed trawlers. After the convoy attack of 17 October, when available one or two armoured cruisers were detailed to patrol in the vicinity of the Lerwick–Bergen route. On 12 December the 'covering force' of the armoured cruisers *Shannon* (Captain V. B. Molteno) and *Minotaur* (2nd Cruiser Squadron, with the former in charge) were, with four screening destroyers, patrolling the convoy route between Lerwick and Norway. They were headed east, a good 60 miles westward of the convoy, when the Germans struck.

The enemy force of four modern destroyers (3rd Half Flotilla) was able to approach within five miles of the convoy, because, owing to a defective searchlight, the *Partridge* (which sighted the enemy at 11.45 a.m.) needed ten minutes to make the challenge, incorrectly replied to, to the unidentified ships. The Germans attacked at 11.55 a.m., as the convoy was approaching its eastern rendezvous, which was 25 miles south-west of the entrance to Bjornefjord. The two British destroyers were caught separated. Unaware that the *Shannon* force was at sea, as the action was about to commence the *Partridge* sent an urgent signal merely addressed

---

œuvred off this line they might easily have got into an unswept area. If a ship was mined and her speed reduced, she must have been lost, owing to the presence of strong German supports, as it would have been impossible for our supports to extricate her. The advantage of position was on the German side, as soon as our forces passed inside the minefields. It appears necessary for the Admiralty to issue definite instructions on this point, as it is not fair to an officer in command to have to make a decision involving such serious consequences when in the heat of an action.' Oliver concurred that flag officers 'should be given more information or else some definite instructions as to how far to carry on the pursuit'.

to the C.-in-C. It reported the engagement but gave no indication of strength or composition of the enemy.

The Official Historian writes: 'The British destroyers were no match for their opponents, and they were, moreover, in the leeward position. The north-west wind swept a blinding storm of spray into the faces of their gunners, and when the *Partridge* and *Pellew* were in the trough of the waves, nothing was to be seen of the enemy except their masts, and the tops of their funnels. The Germans made admirable use of their advantage; and, as usual, their fire was extremely accurate and rapid.'[27] All the ships of the convoy and escort, except for the *Pellew*, which was damaged and escaped only by the intervention of a rain squall, were sunk. It was all over by 12.40 p.m.

The *Shannon* had intercepted the *Partridge*'s first signal and at 12.15 p.m. she had picked up a second signal. This was incomplete due to German interference, but there was enough to make it clear that enemy destroyers were about 25 miles to the south-west of the entrance to Bjornefjord. Acting on the first message, the *Shannon* increased speed to 20 knots and moved to the scene of the disaster, while hustling her destroyers on ahead. The latter arrived at about 2 p.m. and spent a half hour rescuing survivors. By that time the German destroyers had been speeding homewards some two and a half hours. Pursuit would have been hopeless. Beatty, on receiving the *Partridge*'s first signal at 12.25 (passed to him by the *Shannon*, because German jamming prevented it reaching as far as Scapa), gave orders for the 5th Battle Squadron, the Battle Cruiser Force, and the 2nd and 4th Light Cruiser Squadrons to raise steam, since he believed that he might have to deal with a High Seas Fleet sortie. Soon afterwards, when he received the *Partridge*'s second message, also passed from the *Shannon*, concerning the German destroyers, he ordered (1.03 p.m.) the 3rd Light Cruiser Squadron (*Chatham*, *Yarmouth*, *Birkenhead*—Captain L. C. S. Woollcombe) to head in the direction in which the enemy were reported. This squadron, which formed a watching force to the southward, had been patrolling between the south-west coast of Norway and Bovbjerg, about 85 miles to the southward and eastward of the convoy and steering S.S.E. in the direction of Bovbjerg. But already, having intercepted the *Partridge*'s first signal to the C.-in-C. shortly after noon (it reached Woollcombe at 12.25), the

[27] Newbolt, *Naval Operations*, v. 189.

squadron was steaming northward to intercept the raiders. Throughout the whole of the afternoon they swept northward. There was a good chance of interception—if only the German ships had returned to the Heligoland Bight by the route they had left it. Instead, they had returned via the Skagerrak. Newbolt believes they 'most probably' passed astern of the British squadron at about 5 p.m., and this is what the British charts show.

What had gone wrong *this* time? A Court of Inquiry (Sturdee, de Robeck, Goodenough) met almost immediately. Beatty, the principal witness, took complete responsibility for the strength of the escort, but not for the sailing time of the convoy, which the Admiralty decided. The Court believed that 'the escort did their best to protect the convoy and were fought in a proper and seamanlike manner', and concluded that 'the cause of this regrettable incident was the continuation of a system of control of convoys which had previously proved ineffective for providing protection against attack by fast surface vessels. . . . The evidence shews that the responsibility is too divided and that no definite orders for guidance had been given.' Responsibility was divided between the C.-in-C., Grand Fleet, responsible for safeguarding convoys against attack by surface vessels, the Admiral Commanding Orkneys and Shetlands, responsible for safeguarding convoys against submarine attack, and the Admiralty, which was responsible for the convoy system. The Court of Inquiry's main recommendations were: (1) Assigning the control and immediate responsibility for the convoys to a flag officer afloat, under the C.-in-C., rather than as, at present, the Admiral of the Orkneys and Shetlands. It was impossible for an officer placed as he was to be able satisfactorily to supervise the work required. (2) Improving the W/T installations in escort destroyers. The destroyers in the 12 December affair had failed to keep in wireless communication, owing to jamming by German wireless, and the signal(s?) from the *Partridge* had failed to reach Lerwick and Longhope, though intercepted by the *Shannon* and her force. (3) Strengthening the escort, as through armoured cruisers.[28]

[28] Report of the Court of Inquiry to the C.-in-C., 18 December 1917; Admiralty MSS. Beatty did not see how the first recommendation would benefit the control of convoys. 'The control is largely based on communications which are obviously more efficient when the controlling authority is situated on shore with shore telegraph and telephone systems at his disposal.' Beatty's minute on the finding and minutes of the court of inquiry, 21 December 1917; Admiralty MSS.

'We do have the most cursed luck,' the C.-in-C. moaned. 'The *Shannon* and *Minotaur* should have been alongside the Convoy exactly at 12 o'clock after sighting the West-bound Convoy. Why they were not I do not know yet. I never anticipated that the Hun would send TBD's so far afield and the 3rd LCS could only have missed [them] going North by very little.'[29] Basically, as Beatty realized (and as the court of inquiry had brought out), the trouble lay in the extreme difficulty of covering a West- and an East-bound convoy which were at sea together, since they had the destroyers to arrange only one covering force. This stemmed from the Admiralty requirement that the Grand Fleet be in immediate readiness to proceed south should the High Seas Fleet raise steam. It would be better to have a large single convoy at a time, with a strong force in close support. This, too, was Madden's position.

What emerged from a conference of 15–20 December 1917 at the Admiralty, and one at Rosyth on 8–9 January 1918, was a new system for the Scandinavian convoys which went into effect on 19 January. Its more important features were: (1) The Admiralty were made responsible for the management of the convoys themselves, that is, for the selection of the convoy routes and for the deflection of convoys as necessary to avoid surface or U-boat attacks, informing the C.-in-C., Grand Fleet, and the C.-in-C., Coast of Scotland; the C.-in-C., Grand Fleet, was responsible for the provision and dispositions of the supporting forces, and was to inform the Admiralty and C.-in-C., Coast of Scotland, of these arrangements; the latter had the responsibility for deflecting convoys to avoid mines or submarines south of 58° N., and apart from the directions and decisions promulgated from the Admiralty for the conduct of this system, was responsible for the control of the Scandinavian convoys. (2) Convoys sailed every three days, instead of daily as hitherto (altered to every four days early in March, and to five at the end of April), so as to avoid having two convoys at sea at the same time. This relieved the Grand Fleet of the heavy strain of providing supporting forces frequently. (3) The western assembly point of the convoys was shifted from the far northern Lerwick to Methil (Firth of Forth), which shortened the total voyage from the south by about 80 miles, or ten to twelve hours' steaming, though bringing the convoys closer to the German bases. (4) A heavier supporting force would always be present in

[29] Beatty to Jellicoe, 14 December 1917; Jellicoe MSS.

the immediate vicinity of the convoy. It generally consisted, at first, of a battle squadron—reduced to a light-cruiser squadron by the end of June and later to two armoured cruisers. Was this measure adequate? Was not this dispersion of force, as Beatty was quick to recognize, 'a grave strategical risk', since there was always the danger of a more powerful enemy force surprising and overwhelming the strengthened covering force? As Captain Roskill has remarked, 'The only security against surprise lay in the Admiralty gaining foreknowledge of German intentions and movements. And that, for all the remarkably high standard of our naval intelligence throughout the 1914–18 war, the Admiralty could not guarantee.' In the event, as we shall see, the new system was a great success, although Scheer's sortie of 24 April 1918 with better luck might have made a prophet of Beatty by wreaking havoc on the British covering squadron.

'There is certain to be a dust-up about the whole business—people are in no mood for this sort of thing.' Commander Bellairs was right. The loss of the convoy, which was reported to the House of Commons on 17 December, raised the misgivings that had for some time been expressed as to the soundness of Admiralty administration to a point not very far removed from alarm. Questions were asked in the House of Commons. On 18 December the *Daily Mail* spoke of 'a humiliating reverse', the *Daily News*, of 'a disaster which will create indignation as well as deep concern in the public mind'; and the *Pall Mall Gazette* asserted that the affair had come so closely on the heels of a similar catastrophe that 'the public mind will have considerable need of reassurance as to the state of our commerce defences'.

4. THE DOVER STRAITS SIEVE

(*Chart 7*)

What a biographer of Jellicoe calls 'the final crisis' arose over the continued porousness of the Dover Straits. Vice-Admiral Sir Reginald Bacon had been in command of the Dover Patrol since April 1915, after several years in retirement. He had been one of the cleverest of Fisher's young men, an officer of tremendous energy and brilliant attainments on the technical side. A torpedo specialist, he had pioneered in the development of British submarines, and served as the first head of the submarine branch

(1901–4), the first captain of the first dreadnought (1906–7), and D.N.O. (1907–10). Oliver rated him 'about the ablest and cleverest officer I have ever known', and Hankey paid tribute to his 'extraordinary ingenuity, technical ability, and driving power'.[30] Bacon, whatever his talents, was a difficult person, he was not an inspiring leader of men, and he had never overcome the distrust of the Navy over the 'Bacon Letters'.[31] There were those officers who considered it a disgrace to the Service that Bacon had been allowed to hoist his flag again. Another Bacon handicap was that widespread curse of the Navy: he was a centralizer with no genius whatever for delegation. His Flag-Captain from October 1917, Evans, said that the Admiral 'planned and did many things with which I was quite unacquainted'. When Bacon was dismissed, he informed his successor that he had nothing to turn over to him— that it was a matter of experience, which was all in his head.[32] Finally, relations between Dover and Harwich were poor. Tyrwhitt never cared much for Bacon personally or his Dover Straits strategy.

Dover remained a difficult problem, as the Flanders U-boats continued to pass the Straits with ease and impunity, the mobile patrols and explosive mine-net barrage notwithstanding. In the latter part of the year the U-boats were sinking about 20 ships in the Channel every month. The D.N.I. informed Keyes, then Director of the Plans Division, in October that over 30 submarines were passing through the Straits monthly. The statement came from a German report on the passage of the mine-net barrage salved from *UC-44* (blown up on her own minefield off Waterford in October 1917). It showed that 190 passages had been made between 23 December 1916 and 6 June 1917, chiefly at night and on the surface. There were only eight reports of U-boats touching a net and eight reports of their being forced to dive to avoid patrols. Clearly, the barrage was absolutely ineffective in denying the passage of the Straits to the U-boats.

Bacon was long since aware that the net barrage was not effective, although he believed it was useful as a deterrent and in limiting the enemy's freedom of action. As early as February 1917

[30] Oliver MSS.; Hankey to Balfour, 31 October 1916, Balfour MSS.

[31] See *From the Dreadnought to Scapa Flow*, i. 83, 190–1.

[32] *The Naval Memoirs of Admiral of the Fleet Sir Roger Keyes* (London, 1934–5, 2 vols.), ii. 154.

he had proposed as a supplement a Varne Shoal–Cape Gris Nez vertical deep mine barrage to close the English Channel. (It was later extended, at his suggestion, from the Varne to the vicinity of Folkestone.) The Admiralty had accepted the scheme; it was to be commenced as soon as a sufficient number of the new mines were available. This was not until the autumn of 1917. In the meantime, Bacon's attention was absorbed in the project of a landing on the Flanders coast, whose capture would solve the problem of the Flanders boats by capturing their bases. When that possibility petered out, and at the same time the improved mines began to be available in quantity, Bacon shifted his gaze from the Belgian coast back to the Straits. On 8 October the Admiralty definitely approved the deep mine barrage, and work on it began on 21 November. It was completed by the end of December but was still being strengthened when the war ended, by which time over 9,000 mines had been laid in some twenty lines at depths of 30 to 100 feet below low water.

Meanwhile, in the last two months of 1917, a basic conflict developed between the Dover Command and the Naval Staff. On 13 November, Geddes appointed a Channel Barrage Committee with Keyes as Chairman to see what could be done to improve the barrier in the Straits. Two opinions quickly crystallized as to the best form of the deep minefield barrage. There was no dispute on the desirability of this barrage. The Plans Division and the Channel Barrage Committee (which was virtually its creature) favoured a brilliantly illuminated, day-and-night, closely patrolled deep minefield barrage, which would force enemy submarines to dive into the minefield. The illumination would be provided by searchlights in special stationary ships (converted lightships); until such ships were available, the minefield could be lit by flares and searchlights from patrol vessels. Bacon vehemently opposed this method of illumination: it would only light up the patrol boats and disclose the obstructive line. He would rather that U-boats hit the mines and go down without any sister boats in the vicinity being any the wiser. His scheme of 23 November proposed a different system of illumination: the use of powerful shore searchlights on both sides of the Channel (three each at Gris Nez and Folkestone, one a fixed beam, two, wandering beams) and the provision of three or four shallow-draught bulged vessels equipped with searchlights and guns and moored to divide the distance across the Straits. These searchlights would light up for the patrol ships (which would not be lighted up by this illumination) any U-boat which was on the surface. The Barrage Committee objected that the provision of bulged searchlight vessels would take at least two months. They 'could not afford to wait', writes Keyes, 'while special ships and devices were being constructed. During the month of October, 289,000 tons of shipping had been sunk in the Atlantic, and 62,500 tons in the Channel by enemy submarines, most of which had passed through the Straits of Dover; and although the losses in the Atlantic were at a somewhat lower rate at the moment, those in the Channel showed no signs of declining. The closing of the Straits was of immediate importance . . .'[33]

Bacon was against the massing of patrol ships at the barrage because he could not spare many ships for this duty; they were needed for other work. There was also the danger that the patrols, lit up by searchlights and flares, would only invite strong night-time destroyer raids on them. Accordingly, as he told Keyes (20 November), he proposed to have a patrol force of only five P-boats when the minefield was completed.

There were two lesser issues. One concerned shallow mines. Bacon wanted two lines of them, laid eight feet below water, to obstruct the passage of U-boats on the surface. Keyes asserted they would endanger the patrols, and that deep minefields alone would do the job, provided the whole area was powerfully illuminated at night.

Then there was the old mine-net barrage. The Dover Command wanted to strengthen and improve it by searchlights and flares in patrol craft. The Channel Barrage Committee wanted to scrap it as being useless. It relied on an N.I.D. report of late November which estimated that, to 14 November (and not including the transits in July, for which month figures were lacking), U-boats had traversed the Straits 253 times in 1917. None of the four U-boats destroyed in the Dover area during the year could be attributed to the mine nets.

These were the principal overt issues. Underlying the quarrel over the kind of barrage was Bacon's sensitivity to the Committee's 'interference' in matters he believed to be outside its competence. He afterwards described it as 'a fifth wheel' and a 'Committee of amateurs, so far as conditions of war in the Channel were con-

[33] Keyes, *Naval Memoirs*, ii. 123.

cerned', and its activities as 'the meddlings of an irresponsible committee!'[34] It is a fact that none of the Committee members had any Dover Straits or English Channel experience. Bacon especially resented the Committee's attempt to interfere in the disposition of the ships under his orders, which he strongly believed was the prerogative of the responsible officer at Dover acting in concert with the Admiralty. Jellicoe backed him up.

Bacon's personality enters into the picture. Indeed, we have here a classic example of how personality can be a determining factor in history. Late in November Bacon lectured the First Lord in successive letters. 'The reason for my writing is to say that if the Admiralty are wholehearted in the matter and will provide me with the material and follow my plan we can practically close the Straits but if the proposals are emasculated by makeshift light ships or fears—groundless—of loss of shipping it will be a failure. I think I know . . . more about conditions obtaining in the Straits than any other officer . . . if the Admiralty place their confidence in me I have no doubt of the final result.' A few days later: 'There is no reason if a little energy is used at the Admiralty the whole scheme should not be completed in two months and the Channel practically blocked but unless handled with energy matters will drift.' To a highly irritated Wemyss the letters 'disclose what is, in my opinion, an impossible attitude of mind on Admiral Bacon's part, and show the impracticability of carrying out in the Channel any scheme which does not originate at Dover. . . . after two and a half years of unavailing attempts to stop the passage of submarines (having a free hand the while), I consider it inadmissible to write such letters as those enclosed; and the matter is of so vital a nature as to necessitate the most careful consideration by the Board.' Bacon proceeded to dig his grave deeper with a frank revelation of his impatience with conflicting views. To the First Lord again: 'I own I like my own way. I own in some matters I have firm convictions. But then I know the place and am generally right!! I own I do not suffer fools gladly. . . . I have no use for the imperfectly informed. I hope perhaps that it is to some of the latter, of whom I have met a good many in the last few years, that

[34] Bacon, *The Concise Story of the Dover Patrol* (London, 1932), pp. 161, 163. It was Jellicoe's opinion that 'no suggestions of any proved value emanated from the Committee which had not already been put forward by Admiral Bacon and approved to be carried out as material and vessels were available'. Jellicoe's autobiographical notes.

I owe my evil reputation and this made the [Barrage] Committee wary. However all is right now . . .'[35] It was *not*.

Bacon suspected that one of the Committee's objectives was to secure his dismissal and have Keyes appointed to the Dover command. There was some basis for this feeling. It was Oliver's opinion that Keyes, ever since becoming D. of P., had 'devoted himself to engineering a plan to unship Bacon from the Dover Command on the ground that submarines still sometimes [*sic*] got through the Straits'.[36] There seems little doubt that Keyes did mount a campaign for Bacon's removal, though Oliver's assertion does scant justice to Keyes's genuine alarm over the ineffectiveness of Bacon's arrangements in the Straits. Keyes had an additional motive.

Our interim report [29 November] is a very strong indictment of Bacon and all his works. We *will* make Dover Straits unhealthy for submarines, but Bacon's presence adds to our difficulties, and I am afraid the Board *won't* kick him out. He was all over us when we went to Dover and apparently all out to help—but not really. However he is badly rattled and making an ass of himself. It will take him time to do it thoroughly and in the meantime I want to block Ostend and Zeebrugge. It *can* be done. . . . It is all very well urging other people to do things, if one has no responsibility oneself—and I have *none*.[37]

Keyes felt he 'had no choice but to fight an action, for what I regarded as essential to the conduct of the anti-submarine campaign and ultimate victory', since 'it was clear now that the Admiral had no intention of using searchlights or flares'.[38] His hands were strengthened by an N.I.D. report of early December showing that between 1 November and 9 December, 35 U-boats for certain and probably 15 others had passed the Straits, and that 21 boats had made the passage since the deep minefield had begun to be laid (21 November). This intelligence, together with the sinking of 11 ships in the Channel in the first week of December, brought matters to a head. On 14 December the Admiralty ordered Bacon to institute 'at the earliest possible moment' a strong patrol in the vicinity of the deep minefield barrage, if necessary reducing his

[35] Bacon to Geddes, 23, 26 November, Wemyss to Jellicoe, 5 December, Bacon to Geddes, 12 December 1917; Geddes MSS.
[36] Oliver MSS.
[37] Keyes to Beatty, 5 December 1917; Beatty MSS. Beatty had an equally low opinion of Bacon's work at Dover.
[38] Keyes, *Naval Memoirs*, ii. 134.

forces in other directions, and, pending the provision of the proposed special stationary ships fitted with searchlights, to have the
patrol vessels use their searchlights 'intermittently' (P-boats and
destroyers) and flares (drifters).[39] The Admiral's long reply (15
December) gave the authorities no satisfaction. 'The whole
matter,' he concluded, 'is one of compromise and difficulty, and
must be run on practical experience, and not on preconceived
notions.'[40] 'The above statement put, as politely as I possibly
could, the obvious fact that it was better to leave the defence of the
Straits to the Admiral who had local knowledge, experience, and
the whole responsibility entailed by the command at Dover than
to allow dabbling by a committee who had no local knowledge,
experience, or responsibility.'[41] He did strengthen the minefield
patrol on 15 December, and the next day he illuminated the old
South Goodwins–Snouw net barrage, but not the area of the new
lines. He was summoned to the Admiralty for a high-level conference in the First Sea Lord's room on 18 December. The upshot
was Jellicoe's explicit orders that Bacon institute a night-and-day
patrol of the deep minefield, and illuminated as the Admiralty had
directed him on 14 December. Bacon introduced these measures
the following day. Results were almost immediate. On the night
of 19 December, *UB-56*, forced to dive by the searchlights and
flares of the minefield patrol, was driven into the minefield and
blown up.

Bacon's *apologia* makes light of this first success:

. . . a system of lighting was evolved in London by means of flares
which lighted up intensely the vessels of the patrol line (which it was
highly desirable to keep in darkness), that blinded the observers in the
patrol (whose eyes should have been most carefully guarded from adjacent strong light), and which, compared with the [shore] searchlights,
had a very circumscribed area of illumination. The result of this grotesque system was that, after the lighting had been instituted, *only four
of the submarines which were sunk by the mine barrage were sunk at night-time.*
Just fancy that! In spite of one submarine having been sunk at night
before the minefield was even completed under the scheme I had in
force, during the next six months only four more were sunk at night
owing to the fundamentally unsound system of lighting and patrolling

[39] Naval Staff Monograph No. 18 (1922), *The Dover Command*, pp. 143–4.
[40] Bacon, *The Dover Patrol*, ii. 406–9, has the entire letter.
[41] *Ibid.*, p. 409.

that had been introduced, while during the same time nine were sunk in the day-time. Eventually searchlights had to be installed as I had originally proposed; but then it was much too late. . . . Had I been left in peace and been loyally supported, I have little doubt that our sinkings would have occurred earlier and been materially larger.[42]

For the Admiralty, at that time, however, as Keyes tells us, '*U-59* [*UB-56*] provided an overwhelming argument in support of the policy Plans Division had so insistently urged, and Sir Reginald Bacon had so strenuously resisted. *U-59* actually sealed Admiral Bacon's fate, for the First Lord—Sir Eric Geddes—had been watching the battle about the Dover Straits with the keenest interest.'[43] Jellicoe did not see eye to eye with the First Lord on this issue, and therein lay the catalytic cause of his dismissal.

---

[42] Bacon, *From 1900 Onward* (London, 1940), p. 262. The reasoning is set forth in greater detail in *The Concise Story of the Dover Patrol*, pp. 163–4. The crucial point is that the lighting up of the mine barrage would give away the whole scheme to the submarines.

[43] Keyes, *Naval Memoirs*, ii. 143.

XII

Jellicoe's Dismissal

(December 1917)

. . . Jellicoe was dismissed with a discourtesy without parallel in the dealings
of Ministers with distinguished sailors and soldiers.

SIR ARCHIBALD HURD, *Who Goes There?*

It would appear that when the public becomes too impatient because the
guns are not always firing, some of us have to be sacrificed.

SIMS to Jellicoe, 29 December 1917.

The French say that we, the English, are worse hunters of scapegoats than
they are themselves. All the French papers illustrate this by regretful articles
about Jellicoe. They are right . . .

LORD ESHER to Lord Derby, 29 December 1917.

When history comes to be written, you will have no reason to fear its verdict.

ASQUITH to Jellicoe, 31 December 1917.

1. IMMEDIATE BACKGROUND

THERE WAS towards the end of 1917 an ill-defined dissatisfaction with the status of the war at sea. As expressed by the well-known naval journalist and *Daily Mail* leader writer, H. W. Wilson, 'No one can feel the smallest confidence in the present Admiralty. If it does not fall soon, it will bring down our country with it.'[1] 'I am astonished,' Admiral Bayly wrote after a visit to the Admiralty in December, 'at the gloom with which people in London seem to be shrouded. The situation never looked healthier to me. . . . We beat Spain by sea pressure in Elizabeth's day and can do it again, though a little more singeing of the beard in Drake's manner would be better if we would only take a few more risks.'[2] Ah, but there was part of the rub: the Navy was doing nothing very spectacular. Important segments of the press were down on the Admiralty for this reason. The Admiralty were

[1] Wilson to Lord Fisher, 20 December 1917; *Fear God and Dread Nought*, iii. 491.
[2] Bayly to Jellicoe, 19 December 1917; Jellicoe MSS.

323

said to be subordinating the tremendous fighting power of the Navy to an unimaginative 'defensive' or 'passive' role, having no ideas of a naval offensive beyond the blockade. There was dissatisfaction over the still uncomfortably high shipping losses, and there was the long-standing annoyance over the Government's refusal to publish the weekly statistics of shipping losses by tonnage figures rather than by numbers of British, Allied, and neutral ships sunk. The convoy incidents in the autumn and the November action in the Bight were nearly the last straws.

The Liberal *Daily News* of 23 October summed up several of the strands in the criticism of the Admiralty. It wanted 'more evidence that caution is not the cover for lack of vision, absence of inspiration, failure to think in terms of war. It is not pleasing to reflect that the Baltic has become a German lake and that the submarine cannot be attacked at its source. We are lulled to sleep with assurances that the submarine menace has been got under. It has not been got under, and we are dwelling in a fool's paradise if we think it has. . . . And the question we have to ask is the question we have asked repeatedly. Is the best genius and are the best methods at our command being employed?' The Conservative *Globe* and *Saturday Review* were in the same camp. Three officers, all on the retired list, publicly joined in the agitation against the Admiralty: Admirals W. H. Henderson and Sir Reginald Custance in the press and Commander Carlyon Bellairs in Parliament. The Young Turks in the Fleet had never let up in their campaign to effect drastic changes at the Admiralty. 'Richmond and I,' wrote Captain Drax, 'are firmly convinced that our only certainty of salvation lies in clearing the Admiralty of all the old gang and putting it in charge of the "Intellectuals". Then, with close co-operation between them in London and the C.-in-C. afloat, we could achieve anything. . . . It is a pathetic thing to have to descend to the lowest forms of journalism in our efforts to save the Country from disaster. There appears however to be no alternative.'[3] The attacks upon the First Sea Lord and his direction of the Admiralty were so illustrative of the national penchant for giving short shrift to naval officers, as when, to cite a dramatic example, the public condemnation of Admiral Hawke in 1759 led to his being hanged in effigy—'at the very moment when', to quote

[3] Drax to Admiral W. H. Henderson (who often wrote for the *Daily Mail*), 29 August 1917; Dewar MSS.

Mahan, 'laborious effort was about to issue in supreme achievement' (Quiberon Bay).

Inevitably, the perennial demand for Lord Fisher's restoration was heard once more—for the last time. Behind the scenes George Lambert was trying (with some assistance from the *Daily Mail* and *Daily News*) to persuade Geddes to put the Admiral 'in charge of the engine'. Fisher was the man, despite his years, to use the Navy offensively. 'The test of a big man is the commotion he causes among the smaller fry.'⁴ The old sea dog himself was full of offensive schemes with Schleswig-Holstein as their main objective and making use of unstoppable 'amphibian Hippopotami', each holding 500 men, a thousand of which he was prepared to build in five months. Yet he knew that he was destined to remain 'an exile and an outcast'.

Jellicoe and the Admiralty were not without their champions. The two most influential Conservative newspapers, the *Morning Post* and *Daily Telegraph*, as well as the Liberal *Daily Chronicle*, expressed confidence in the Admiralty. The two main Service organs, the *Naval and Military Record* and *Army and Navy Gazette*, Carson, and a number of retired admirals of some distinction like Meux, Bridge, Ottley, and Beresford blasted the 'uninformed criticism' and were contemptuous of the 'cowardly' attacks on the First Sea Lord. Louder and more persistent, however, were the critics of the Admiralty.

Leading the pack baying at Jellicoe's heels was Lord Northcliffe's *Daily Mail*. Roy Jenkins has written of this powerful press lord: 'In an age of mass-literacy, before broadcasting, and with a House of Commons disorganised by coalition and too far removed from election to be effectively representative, Northcliffe exercised an influence greater than that of any newspaper proprietor before or since. Between them his two organs [*The Times* and *Daily Mail*] gave him a dominant grip on both ends of the London newspaper market. And their constant, unanswered denunciations of Asquith [autumn of 1916] . . . did much to undermine his position.'⁵ Substitute 'Jellicoe' for 'Asquith' and you have the situation in the autumn of 1917. The American Secretary of the Navy recorded a meeting in Washington. 'Had talk with Lord Northcliffe who was

---

⁴ Lambert to Geddes, 7 August 1917; Admiralty MSS. Geddes showed no interest; he thought Fisher too diffuse.

⁵ Jenkins, *Asquith* (London, 1964), p. 415.

evidently depressed & said he hoped we would build fire under English Navy. Jellico [*sic*] had but one thought and that was to preserve the great fleet.'⁶ Northcliffe's hostility may have stemmed partly from Jellicoe's refusal on a certain occasion in 1915 to permit a *Daily Mail* correspondent to visit a Grand Fleet squadron, then at Invergordon, to gather naval news from the ships. Given Northcliffe's inflated notions about himself and his newspapers, it would have been natural that he should thereafter harbour a grudge against the Admiral. There was a more immediate reason for the Great Man's animosity. As Jellicoe tells the story:

> Northcliffe came one day to the Admiralty in 1917 to see Sir E. Carson about air raids at Ramsgate and Sir Edward asked me to be present. Northcliffe arrived before Sir Edward and I received him. He became very abusive about the naval air force at Dover and said that they ought to stop the raids and that their organisation was bad, etc. Commodore Godfrey Paine, head of the R.N.A.S. at the time, who was present, did not mince matters in replying to Northcliffe and (in his usual somewhat heated manner!!) gave Northcliffe 'what for', pointing out that the R.N.A.S. did not pretend to stop air-raids. They were there for a totally different purpose. The responsibility for the attack of enemy aircraft over land was a military affair, but the R.N.A.S. gave, of course, all assistance possible. I think that Northcliffe mixed up the 1st Sea Lord and the head of the R.N.A.S. as he wrote Sir E. Carson after the interview an abusive letter about me which Sir E. shewed me. As a matter of fact Paine did all the talking as it was his arrangements that were being criticised. At any rate the Northcliffe Press consistently attacked me subsequently.⁷

Whatever the precise explanation, the *Daily Mail* became very outspoken from September in a barrage of leaders. The Navy was doing a poor job, it insisted. On 19 October, after referring to 'this humiliating display in the Baltic,' it asked the First Lord 'to consider very seriously whether the recent changes in Whitehall have gone far enough'. A leader of 30 October asked, 'What is Wrong at the Admiralty?' The answer given was that Jellicoe's abilities were of an administrative kind; he was not a strategist, and hence

⁶ Josephus Daniels's diary, 29 October 1917; E. David Cronon (ed.), *The Cabinet Diaries of Josephus Daniels, 1913–1921* (Lincoln, Nebraska, 1963), p. 228.

⁷ Jellicoe to Lieutenant-Commander Oswald Frewen, 8 July 1921; Frewen MSS. Three of the four airship raids made over the eastern counties during the first six months of 1917 involved Kent: 16–17 February, by one airship, which dropped bombs; 16 March, by four airships, which dropped bombs with no casualties and small damage; 16 June, by an airship, which killed three people at Ramsgate.

was not 'the right man in the right place'. Two days later: 'The heroism and devotion of our seamen could not be surpassed; but the magnificent qualities cannot be employed to the best effect unless the strategical direction is good. The best Navy in the world may be paralysed by feeble control. Our strategical direction— for which the First Sea Lord is primarily responsible—has shewn signs of weakness in three various theatres of war during the last few weeks.' These were listed as the Gulf of Riga, where 'the British Navy did not attempt a demonstration in aid of our Allies', the first convoy incident, when 'two German cruisers were allowed to sink two British destroyers and a large convoy of ships within a short distance of our coast and to escape scot free', and the submarine campaign, where 'the losses are again mounting steadily'.[8]

There can be no doubt that the steady tom-tom of press criticism weakened Jellicoe's position. This had been the situation in the spring. The difference now was that in Carson's place was a First Lord who had lost confidence in his chief professional adviser. Lloyd George's distrust, moreover, had not lessened with the passage of time. 'You kill him, I'll bury him', he is supposed to have said of Jellicoe to Northcliffe.[9] Speaking in the House of Commons on 19 November, Admiral of the Fleet Sir Hedworth Meux put the blame for the attacks on Jellicoe upon Lloyd George, who had nothing to say in reply. The King afterwards declared that the Prime Minister 'had his knife into him [Jellicoe] for some time and wished for a change'.[10] Beatty, whose attitude towards Jellicoe remained ambivalent,[11] held the same opinion. He was angered by the *Daily Mail*'s 'outrageous campaign vilifying the Admiralty in

---

[8] The Attorney-General, after a study of the *Daily Mail*'s vendetta against Jellicoe, believed there were legal grounds for prosecuting the newspaper under Regulation 27 of the Defence of the Realm Regulations. This forbade criticism of Departments or of responsible heads of Departments when the statements were likely to 'interfere with the success of His Majesty's Forces' (27a) or 'likely to prejudice the discipline or administration of His Majesty's Forces' (27c). 'I think on the whole that a magistrate ought to convict, and I think that he probably would convict. But it is not certain. . . . I should not refuse to direct a prosecution if in the opinion of the War Cabinet the objections of policy are superable.' Sir F. E. Smith to Geddes, 31 October 1917; Admiralty MSS. The Government did not pursue the matter.

[9] Hamilton Fyfe, *Northcliffe: an Intimate Biography* (London, 1930), p. 185.

[10] George V to Beatty, 10 February 1918; Beatty MSS.

[11] On the one hand, he was in a dither over continuing frustrations in his relations with the Admiralty. For instance: 'I hope the condition of the sailors, etc. is going to be improved at once. . . . All my time is spent fighting the Admiralty instead of the Enemy, first on one thing and then on another.' 'The poor old Admiralty is still

general and the unfortunate Jellicoe in particular', and figured that 'somebody in the Government was at the bottom of it. L.G. probably, or it would not be permitted'.[12] Jellicoe had no doubts 'that Northcliffe was pressing the P.M. to get rid of me, the P.M. was pressing Geddes, the latter wanted to avoid trouble and so tried to get away from the Admiralty but failing this carried out the desire of Northcliffe'.[13]

Jellicoe attributed Lloyd George's hostility to these factors: 'My consistent support of the policy of concentrating our military efforts on the Western front, and my criticism of the secondary Eastern campaigns as placing a strain on our naval and shipping resources which resulted in heavy losses elsewhere, undoubtedly tended to inspire Mr. Lloyd George (a convinced Easterner) with hostility towards my views, and was no doubt one of the factors leading up to my dismissal from the Admiralty at the end of 1917. A second factor was my opposition towards futile bombardment operations (including the bombardment of Heligoland) during 1917 . . .'[14] These charges have substance, and to them we should add the differences over merchant-ship convoy during 1917, the clash in personalities, and Lloyd George's belief that the Admiral was played out. 'I knew in my bones that Jellicoe was tired out, and believed that with fresh measures we could hold on.'[15]

---

going down hill, but what a long hill it is with never a bottom to it. Everybody says the same chaos and disruption reigns supreme and it will for some time yet.' Beatty to Lady Beatty, 18 September, 9 December 1917; Beatty MSS. On the other hand, he appreciated Jellicoe's administrative talents and had on various occasions urged him not to resign. He had been 'greatly relieved' that Jellicoe had stayed on despite the Burney affair. Above all, he did not want to see Jellicoe removed as a result of the pressure of the politicians. The Navy always closed ranks when it was a case of a difference between a sailor and the politicians.

[12] Beatty to a friend, 30 November 1917; Chalmers, *Beatty*, pp. 321–2. 'This is against all fair play,' the C.-in-C. protested in the same letter. 'He cannot reply, and as long as he occupies the important and responsible position he does, he is entitled to some measure of protection against the Press. . . . It is destroying confidence in the Directing Powers of the Great Service, and causing a feeling of disquiet and uneasiness in the higher direction which must have a baneful effect.'

[13] Jellicoe's autobiographical notes.

[14] *Ibid.* The latter reason was the one singled out by the C.I.G.S. 'Jellicoe was always pouring cold water on L.G.'s fervent imagination and bringing him down to the earth, and L.G. did not like it.' As noted by Repington in his diary of 23 to 30 December 1917 after a conversation with Robertson. Repington, *The First World War*, ii. 160.

[15] Diary, 24 August 1919; *Lord Riddell's Intimate Diary of the Peace Conference and After, 1918–1923* (London, 1933), p. 113.

It was Newbolt's belief that Jellicoe's run-down physical and mental condition, the product of the strains and stresses of his Grand Fleet command, followed by overwork at the Admiralty, was the decisive factor in his dismissal. Jellicoe 'had borne for nearly three and a half years the burden of the naval war. It was a burden in itself great beyond all experience . . . there was among those who met him frequently at the council table no doubt that the strain was bearing hard upon him, and could not be further prolonged with justice to him or advantage to the Service.'[16] It is a truism that physical fitness and stamina, and a goodly measure of equanimity, are extremely important in a war leader. There is a considerable body of evidence that Jellicoe was physically fit and under no great mental strain during 1917. His elder daughter is absolutely certain that she cannot remember him being ill in 1917 or, indeed, hearing any discussion about his health at the time. Mrs. O'Neill, who was in very close touch with her aunt, Lady Jellicoe, all through 1917, remembers that Lady Jellicoe never showed any anxiety about the Admiral's health. As Mrs. O'Neill puts it, 'He seemed always his usual shrewd, quietly observant self, though with much to do.'[17] The onetime First Lord, McKenna, denies that Jellicoe was tired out by the end of 1917. 'The suggestion that Jellicoe was suffering from strain is new to me and quite ridiculous. I saw him constantly at the time and he certainly showed no indication whatever of unusual fatigue.'[18] Dreyer, who, too, was in regular touch with Jellicoe at the time, confirms this. 'He was physically very fit, running about a mile in the Mall every morning before breakfast. His mind was as active and quick as ever, and his executive ability and initiative were fully efficient. He was only fifty-eight.'[19] Up to a point this evidence is convincing.

It is safe to say that, clinically speaking, Jellicoe was not in exceptionally poor health during his year as First Sea Lord. He was absent from the Admiralty on at least three occasions due to

---

[16] *Naval Operations*, v. 203. Similarly, Lord Salter, *Memoirs of a Public Servant* (London, 1961), p. 89, Lord Hankey, *The Supreme Command*, ii. 656, and Captain Stephen Roskill's letter in *The Times*, 19 November 1964, and his 'The Dismissal of Admiral Jellicoe', *Journal of Contemporary History*, October 1966.

[17] Lord Jellicoe's letter to the author, 24 February 1968.

[18] McKenna to Bacon, 21 August 1936; Bacon, *The Life of John Rushworth, Earl Jellicoe* (London, 1936), p. 386.

[19] Dreyer, *The Sea Heritage*, p. 224.

sickness (influenza, neuritis, and a bad cold), and once because the doctors insisted that he needed a few days' rest. But these ailments were not of a serious or chronic nature, and he lived until nearly 76 (1935). It was rather, it seems to me, that fatigue, which has been defined as 'a weariness resulting from bodily or mental exertion', had taken its toll. 'Fatigue,' Dr. Hugh L'Etang has remarked, 'tends to be the fate of the ambitious, the conscientious, or the idealistic.' It is 'the conscientious' that applies to Jellicoe, who always tried to do too much himself. (See above, pp. 56–7.) To the extraordinary physical stress must be added extraordinary mental stress. Jellicoe had been under unremitting strain as C.-in-C., Grand Fleet, for the first 28 months of the war, as he organized and prepared the fleet for battle, all the while trying to reconcile two seriously contrasting factors. One was the knowledge that he could lose the war in an afternoon; the other was the assumption of the populace, and to some extent of the Fleet, that if he did his job properly, there would be a second Trafalgar and the virtual annihilation of the High Seas Fleet. The reconciliation was well-nigh impossible with a fleet which had no battle experience and with so many untested factors to be considered, unless the High Seas Fleet came out definitely asking for trouble. The latter was most unlikely, though he tried to believe it to ease the strain of his dilemma—even then on the assumption that it would be at the High Seas Fleet's best moment and the Grand Fleet's worst. As First Sea Lord he found the strains of 1914–16 intensified. Commanding an intensely loyal and admiring fleet was one thing; operating in the jungles of Whitehall during the most critical year of the war was something else again. In 1917 Jellicoe was, mentally and physically, a very tired man. As Balfour noted, 'It may be that Jellicoe is now an over-tired man. He certainly has every right to be. No one has done harder work since the outbreak of war.'[20] Overly tired men are never at their best, for excessive fatigue has an adverse effect on judgement. In short, Jellicoe's ability to grapple with his problems as First Sea Lord was sapped by the cumulative mental and physical pressures of three years and a by-product of these—the intensification of his latent pessimistic streak to the point where he saw all problems through the darkest of glasses.

[20] Balfour to Carson, 3 January 1918; Balfour MSS.

In any case, the root cause of the Prime Minister's lack of confidence in Jellicoe was not his health—not directly. Rather was it the conviction that under Jellicoe the Admiralty was slumbering. It is probable that he had appointed Geddes First Lord with the intention of giving Jellicoe a good shake-up. Milner was echoing Lloyd George's sentiments when he wrote:

Our men are splendid, but our naval policy has been far from admirable. *Every single great improvement, since I have known anything about it,* has been *forced upon them from outside.* How long did they pooh-pooh convoys, forget mines? Are they even now open-minded enough about the use of submarines against submarines? etc., etc., etc. . . . If it had not been for Carson, for you, for Geddes, should we have ever got a move on? We have got a move now, with difficulty, *but it must be kept up.* The Germans will certainly have fresh surprises for us. We must be quick to counter them.[21]

In August the Prime Minister went up to the Fleet and canvassed Jellicoe's abilities with various Admirals. Beresford learned that 'suggestions were thrown out that one of these Admirals should accept the position of First Sea Lord'.[22]

Ultimately, Jellicoe's fate was in Geddes's hands, although the First Lord would not have proceeded without the Prime Minister's blessings. The legality of the First Lord's power to dismiss a First Sea Lord was not open to question; it dated from an Order in Council of 1869. When Lloyd George put Geddes at the head of the Admiralty, the latter, as already mentioned, made his feelings about Jellicoe's retention clear. He 'stipulated that Jellicoe should not be immediately removed. Geddes knew that Jellicoe had the confidence of the senior officers in the Navy, and that it would therefore be a distinct advantage to secure his co-operation if that were at all possible. He promised to tell me without delay if he found that he could not work with or through him.'[23]

An early source of friction arose out of the future of the R.N.A.S. The intensified competition between the Army and Navy for aircraft, the Navy's dissatisfaction over the Haig's employment of a few R.N.A.S. squadrons on purely military duties, and, most immediately, the public grumbling following the successful daylight

[21] Milner to Lloyd George, 23 November 1917; Lloyd George MSS.
[22] Beresford to Jellicoe, 16 August 1917; Jellicoe MSS.
[23] Lloyd George, *War Memoirs*, iii, 1177.

raids of German bombers on London in the summer of 1917, caused the War Cabinet to order an investigation of the problems of air warfare. Lloyd George was the nominal chairman of the committee, whose actual chairman was the energetic and brilliant South African soldier-lawyer-statesman, Lieutenant-General Jan Christiaan Smuts, a member of the Imperial War Cabinet. The Committee's first report (19 July) dealt with the organization of air-raid defences. The more significant second report (dated 17 August, but available a week earlier) was the climacteric as regards the development of maritime air power. It recommended the fusion of the R.N.A.S. and the R.F.C. into a new Service, to be known as the Royal Air Force, under an Air Ministry and Air General Staff. The Air Staff would 'from time to time attach to the Army and the Navy the Air units necessary for naval and military operations, and such units shall, during the period of such attachment, be subject, for the purposes of operations, to the control of the respective naval and military commands'. In other words, except during operations, naval aircraft and their crews would be under a different ministry (Air) from that responsible for the conduct of operations at sea (Admiralty). The Smuts Committee operated on the central premise that the future of air power lay mainly in strategic bombing, a policy that could not be effective if there were independent Navy and Army air services.

The Committee's recommendations made imperfect sense. It was, as Haig pointed out, basically unsound 'to depart from the principle that the authority responsible for handling a service in the field should be charged with its training'.[24] Jellicoe fought hard against the Smuts proposals. As he expressed his feelings subsequently, 'The idea seemed to me simply ludicrous and I objected to it in the strongest possible terms and on every occasion.'[25] He resented the fact that Geddes, ignoring the objections of his responsible adviser on such matters, referred the question to Beatty, who had endorsed the conclusions of the Smuts Committee (15 August). He saw no reasons why 'the R.F.C. or any other Air Service could not perform the majority of duties now entrusted to the R.N.A.S.' A week later, having read a Naval Staff critique of the Committee's proposals, which the Staff claimed were

[24] Haig to Robertson, 15 September 1917; Jones, *The War in the Air. Appendices*, p. 15.
[25] Autobiographical notes.

'fundamentally unsound', the C.-in-C. charged the Admiralty with being 'too parochial in their outlook on the conduct of the war'.[26] 'From that time on,' says Jellicoe, 'Sir Eric Geddes, in spite of my arguments, favoured the idea, or only weakly opposed it.'[27]

Geddes stated the Admiralty's case, which had been strongly influenced by the Geddes–Beatty position, at the War Cabinet of 24 August. 'The Admiralty were very strongly impressed with the difficulties of co-operation and limitation of responsibility in regard to an Air Service operating with fleets or squadrons which is not in every way a part of the Naval Service. . . . the introduction of a third Ministry for the Air would exaggerate the complications of the co-operation which already existed in joint undertakings where the Army and Navy were both concerned. . . . there is a definite future for an aerial offensive apart from the Army and the Navy. It did not, however, appear to them practicable that such operations should take place over the sea without being part of the naval operations and under naval command.' The Admiralty preferred that the R.N.A.S. be left as it was, for the duration, anyway; but they were prepared to accept the principles of the Smuts Report, subject to the provision of certain safeguards, for example, that the Air Ministry provide the Fleet with the machines, while the Navy continued to train its own pilots and observers. The War Cabinet accepted the Report in principle and directed that legislation be prepared to implement it.[28] The denouement will be treated in the concluding volume. Here we are primarily concerned with the relations between Geddes and Jellicoe: the controversy over naval aviation was one of the first storm signals. The first convoy incident came next.

On 26 October there was a special meeting in the Cabinet Room of the Prime Minister, Geddes, and his two immediate predecessors, Carson and Balfour, on the First Lord's initiative, for the

---

[26] S. W. Roskill, *Naval Policy between the Wars*, Vol. i, *The Period of Anglo-American Antagonism, 1919–1929* (London, 1968), p. 238. Beatty came to regret his error exceedingly when he became First Sea Lord in 1919. His seemingly supine attitude in the summer of 1917 is beyond rational explanation, since he possessed a lively appreciation of the role that air power had come to play in sea warfare. Years later he observed that 'the decisions given many years ago were considered by the Government of the day to be the best compromise that could be made pending experience'. Beatty's letter in the *Daily Telegraph*, 13 February 1936.

[27] Autobiographical notes.

[28] W.C. 223. The Smuts Report is in G.T.-1658: 'Committee on Air Organisation and Home Defence against Air Raids (2nd Report)'.

specific purpose of discussing the question of Jellicoe's supersession. Geddes afterwards used the fact of the meeting as 'evidence of the care and deliberation with which I came to the decision which caused the recommendation I made to you on the 24th [21st?] December'.[29] We do not know exactly what transpired at this meeting, beyond the fact that Geddes had stated that it was time Jellicoe left the Admiralty, and that he had made much of the *Mary Rose* disaster. 'It appears,' Hankey noted, 'that from the Ad[ty] inquiry it has transpired that the latter had been fully warned by highly secret, but absolutely reliable information, of the probability of the recent attack on the Norwegian convoy, and had neglected to act. Geddes regards this as an example of Jellicoe's lack of energy, if not timidity, and wants to replace him by Ad[l] Wemyss.'[30]

It is probable (as Balfour thought at the time) that Geddes delayed asking Jellicoe to resign so long as the press campaign was at its height. He did not wish to give the impression that the press criticism had forced his hand. Moreover, essentially a kind-hearted man, he could not make up his mind to let Jellicoe go. '. . . my courage failed me,' he told Lord Riddell, 'and I wanted to return to France to deal with transport. I did not like to take the responsibility of parting with Jellicoe and other Admiralty

---

[29] Geddes to Lloyd George, 8 March 1918; Lloyd George MSS. Geddes afterwards claimed that at this conference Carson and Balfour had approved the course that he took two months later. This was, at any rate, what the Sea Lords informed Jellicoe on 28 December that Geddes had told them two days before. Jellicoe had at once put the matter to Carson. In no time Balfour and Carson were bombarding Geddes with indignant letters of protest. Both positively denied they had made the statement attributed to them. Apparently they had spoken frankly about Jellicoe's shortcomings, but without recommending his dismissal. On the contrary, they maintained, they had said he was irreplaceable. Geddes denied that he had claimed their support. As he wrote to Carson: 'What I have said . . . is—that my opinion of Admiral Jellicoe was not come to hastily and that I had some $2\frac{1}{2}$ months ago, I thought, consulted my two immediate predecessors about it and that from the interviews I felt that my opinon of him was confirmed. . . . I have always understood that . . . you saw no one better than Admiral Jellicoe to be 1st Sea Lord. I have never stated or implied anything to the contrary.' Geddes to Carson, 29 December 1917; Carson MSS. (Belfast).

[30] Diary, 26 October 1917, on Balfour's authority; Hankey MSS. (Balfour afterwards recalled that Geddes had made 'some very unfavourable comments on the procedure of the First Sea Lord in connection with the attack on a convoy in the North Sea'. Balfour to Geddes, 8 March 1918; Jellicoe MSS.) The 'Ad[ty] inquiry' does not refer to the *Mary Rose* inquiry (its report was issued that day, 26 October), which contains nothing on 'highly secret' information (Room 40 intelligence) in Admiralty possession.

leaders.'[31] That is, Geddes delayed making an unpleasant decision, hoping that another First Lord would pick up that burden.

Several incidents in the last weeks of the year were sources of conflict that brought matters to a head. The first was over Napier's conduct in the action of 17 November. In response to Beatty's report on the engagement, Jellicoe proposed that Napier be directed to explain his movements and that Beatty report on certain points in which his own orders were not clear. 'Sir E. Geddes agreed, but having been told later by Admiral Beatty during a visit to the Fleet that he, Beatty, disapproved of Napier's action, obviously wished to find a scapegoat, and to act against him quickly. During the next week or so Sir E. Geddes frequently referred to the matter with impatience, and wished to hasten the report, and said that in his opinion Admiral Beatty was trying to shield Admiral Napier and that this was having the effect on him (Geddes) to make him all the more determined to make a scapegoat of Napier. I said this was unjust and wrong and that he must await the receipt of the report.'[32]

The loss of the second Norwegian convoy put a further strain on Geddes's relations with Jellicoe.[33] An infuriated First Lord asked Jellicoe (15 December) to order an immediate inquiry by a court composed of very senior flag officers whose names would be reported to him, Geddes, for approval. All the facts were to be brought out. If Jellicoe refused to order such an inquiry, Geddes would send Lord Fisher up to conduct the inquiry. This, Jellicoe remonstrated, would only cause much ill feeling in the Fleet. 'I can hardly believe that the suggestion is serious. Such a step would go some way to destroy the confidence of the officers of the Fleet in the Admiralty. Lord Fisher has not been to sea since about 1902 and he has absolutely no experience of modern warfare but what is more to the point the Navy would not trust his judgment and impartiality.' He proposed instead that a telegram be sent to Beatty. 'The 1st Lord altered my telegram, made it offensive to

---

[31] Diary, 24 August 1919; *Lord Riddell's Intimate Diary of the Peace Conference and After*, p. 113. Similarly, 'Eric did not relish the prospect [of dismissing Jellicoe] and still hankered after his true love, the development of transportation for the armies.' Geddes, *The Forging of a Family*, p. 242.

[32] Jellicoe's autobiographical notes.

[33] The principal sources for what follows (the second convoy incident) are Jellicoe's autobiographical notes and the Geddes MSS. Bacon, *Jellicoe*, pp. 374–84, reproduces much of this material.

Beatty (without my knowledge) and followed it with a still more offensive personal one from himself in which he said that nothing but a full and searching enquiry would satisfy the public!' The first telegram (over Oliver's name) to Beatty, dated 15 December, read as follows, with Geddes's amendments to Jellicoe's draft telegram italicized by the present writer:

234. URGENT.
My 830. You are requested to order an immediate enquiry into all the circumstances connected with the attack on the Scandinavian Convoy on 12th instant, *the absence of adequate protection*, and the escape of the enemy vessels.

A point on which information is necessary is the dispositions made for the defence of the convoys against surface attack and how far they were carried out.

A Flag Officer of standing belonging to the Grand Fleet should preside and the names of the officers composing the Court should be telegraphed *for approval and for public announcement by First Lord on Monday* [17 December] *in Parliament.* As soon as all necessary arrangements for the Court of Enquiry have been made *and names approved* you are at liberty to proceed to Rosyth.

The following day Geddes sent Jellicoe the draft of a statement on the subject that he proposed to make in the House of Commons.

It was worded [Jellicoe continues in his autobiographical notes] so as to throw blame on Sir D. Beatty, and in such a way as to give the idea that the loss of the convoy was a disaster of the greatest magnitude as well as preventable. I objected to this wording, altered it a great deal, and sent it back.[34] Most of my alterations were adopted but not all, and the announcement [House of Commons, 17 December] was not a very happy one. The following Saturday (December 22nd) I visited the

[34] 'It seems to me superfluous [so read Jellicoe's minute to Geddes, 16 December] to say that the C.-in-C. is responsible, and it conveys the *impression* that the Admiralty is trying to shield itself. The remaining portion of the draft where I propose alterations, seems to imply that there is something that might be hushed up unless a very strong court is formed. In any case an Enquiry would naturally be ordered by the C.-in-C., and it is rather an insult to naval officers to give an impression that they are not likely to make a full and accurate report and to record their opinions faithfully. Should anything arise from a first court indicating that blame might be attached to officers in high position anywhere, it is always possible to convene a second one or to order a court martial. . . . The original draft implies that protection against surface attack is *regularly furnished.* This is not the case at present, though I am trying to devise means to do it as soon as possible. I thought it was agreed that a statement in Parliament magnified the business rather too much as compared to a Press communiqué.' Geddes MSS., which also have Geddes's draft statement.

Fleet at Rosyth and found Sir D. Beatty furious about the telegram which I then saw for the first time as sent by Sir E. Geddes. . . . I told Admiral Beatty that I should tell the 1st Lord on my return that I agreed with his (Beatty's) view and that the telegrams as sent (particularly the personal one) were insulting. I did so on my return and the 1st Lord did not like my frankness. . . . After my departure from the Admiralty he sent Beatty a written apology.[35]

The next incident had to do with a New Year honour for Duff. Jellicoe recommended him for a K.C.B.

Geddes discussed the matter with me and asked if I had recommended him for his services afloat or at the Admiralty. I replied the latter. He said that he objected to his manner, and I said I was recommending him for his services not his manner. Geddes then said he did not like his manner to him or the wording of some of his minutes. I then said that I feared he did not realise that the Sea Lords were his colleagues and not his subordinates and that it was both their right and their duty to state their opinions quite clearly and frankly, realising of course that he was the responsible minister. After some further talk he agreed to put forward Duff's name.[36]

Finally, there was the Dover Straits problem, which turned out to be the immediate cause of Jellicoe's dismissal. In spite of the apparently amicable settlement arrived at on 18 December, Geddes, Wemyss, and Keyes were not happy with the prospects in the Dover area so long as Bacon remained in command. 'Half-measures,' in Keyes's words, would continue. Thus, the Admiral's insistence on maintaining the mine-net barrage would not leave him with sufficient ships for a close patrol of the deep minefield. Wemyss's intervention proved decisive at a meeting in the Admiralty on 20 December which an officer described as 'turmoil amongst the Gods in Olympus':

[35] Beatty was furious over the First Lord's usurption of his authority by dictating the composition of the court of inquiry. It implied, moreover, that the C.-in-C., his dispositions open to criticism, might pack the court with his own supporters. When Geddes visited the Grand Fleet soon afterwards, Beatty minced no words: he and his flag officers had felt deeply insulted by the Admiralty order. Eventually, on 9 January 1918, Beatty extracted a letter of apology from Geddes for the wording of the convoy telegram which he read to the assembled flag officers in his cabin. The letter assured the C.-in-C. that it was not 'intended to convey—either directly or by inference—any lack of confidence in yourself, or any desire to subject your own dispositions to a Court of Enquiry'. Geddes MSS.

[36] Jellicoe's autobiographical notes.

The Intelligence Department [wrote Wemyss] satisfactorily proved to me that the enemy did pass the Straits successfully and almost unchallenged. Sir R. Bacon on the other hand maintained that they did not, that his system of nets was satisfactory and that the proof of this lay in the fact that no ship had ever been torpedoed in his area. He brushed aside as puerile my contention that naturally the enemy left alone an area that he wished to pass unmolested and took other areas for his nefarious activities. Towards the end of December I brought the subject very insistently before both the First Lord and the First Sea Lord, and my contention was that Bacon was not being successful in his antisubmarine measures, that we should leave no stone unturned to try and stop the passage of these craft and that we had better try somebody else and go on changing until we found somebody who could.[37]

Jellicoe would not countenance Bacon's dismissal: he had alway' carried out the wishes of the Board as quickly as was possible; he was the best man for the job and he had done 'invaluable works in the Dover Patrol. Besides, loyalty to old friends was one of Jellicoe's failings (or virtues). Wemyss 'came away feeling that matters could not go on in this manner. The First Lord was in the disagreeable position of finding his two principal technical advisers in direct opposition to each other on a matter which was essentially the First Sea Lord's responsibility whilst he, I knew, agreed with me, the junior.'[38] Geddes's decision was that Jellicoe must go if Bacon were to go and the U-boats were to be stopped from negotiating the Straits at will. There can be little doubt that the immediate and direct cause of Jellicoe's leaving was the impending sacking of Bacon.[39]

Jellicoe had no doubt afterwards that 'all these incidents, together with the differences of opinion between the Prime Minister and myself, led to my supersession'. He might have added the report of the Court of Inquiry on the second convoy disaster, which contained some frank criticism of the Admiralty, and what Balfour termed 'a certain incompatibility between the two men, Jellicoe and Geddes.

Geddes himself stressed other, more general, considerations. One statement of his motives is contained in an unused speech

---

[37] Wester Wemyss, *Wester Wemyss*, p. 365, quoting the Admiral's unpublished memoirs.
[38] *Ibid.*, pp. 365–6.
[39] This is confirmed by Captain A. C. Dewar, who had got it from Beharrell, the Director of Statistics, who was close to Geddes. A. C. Dewar to K. G. B. Dewar, 27 October, 17 November 1960; Dewar MSS.

intended for delivery in the House of Commons early in March 1918 as a rejoinder to Carson's expected speech on behalf of Jellicoe: 'After close association with Lord Jellicoe for two months as Controller, and daily association for 5 months as First Lord, I arrived at the conclusion, deliberately and regretfully . . . that Lord Jellicoe did not evidence progressive adaptability and effectiveness in decision.'[40] Also, Geddes thought that Jellicoe allowed himself to become too much immersed in office detail and that, as he told Balfour (7 March 1918), Jellicoe, 'with all his great ability and experience (perhaps partly in consequence of them), found it difficult to carry decentralisation as far as in your opinion decentralisation was rendered necessary by modern conditions'.[41] There is one other first-hand clue as to Geddes's motivations. He claims that some time between the special 26 October meeting in the Cabinet Room and 24 December he had discussed the situation with Jellicoe, 'and told him that he thought either he [Geddes] or Lord Jellicoe ought to leave the Admiralty in the national interest as their views as to the organization of the Naval Staff and as to personal [personnel?] appointments appeared irreconcilable'.[42]

On 21 December Geddes informed the War Cabinet of his keen desire to relinquish the Admiralty for the co-ordination of Allied land and sea transport. They would not hear of it: he could not be spared 'in view of the gravity of the shipping situation'. Later that day, according to Lloyd George, Geddes saw him and told him

that he had come to the conclusion that he could not give of his best at the Admiralty if Admiral Jellicoe remained there as First Sea Lord. Bonar Law, Geddes and I then went into the whole matter, and Geddes explained that while he was on the best of terms with Jellicoe, and had the highest regard for him, and had no intention of trying, as a civilian, to override the Admirals in technical matters, he felt that he could make

[40] Geddes, 'Notes made for use in debate on Navy Estimates, 6 March 1918 on Dismissal of Lord Jellicoe'; Geddes MSS. He did not use the above material in the debate. His first draft had included the words 'carefully, patiently', before 'deliberately and regretfully'.

[41] Balfour to Geddes, 8 March 1918; Jellicoe MSS. This is Balfour repeating what Geddes had told him. The 'your' is Geddes.

[42] In a statement prepared for the Prime Minister on 28 April 1918 at the latter's request for use in the Commons the next day, but which was not needed. Geddes MSS. For the difficulties over personnel and the Staff, see above, Chapter VIII. The difference over whether to allow Bacon to stop at Dover was the culminating one as regards personnel.

no progress there with Jellicoe. Wemyss, on the other hand, was a man who would give opportunities to the younger men, and was on the best of terms with Beatty. During the time he had been at the Admiralty as Deputy First Sea Lord, Wemyss had encouraged the active brains in the Planning Division and indeed throughout the Admiralty.

Bonar Law agreed with me that in the circumstances a change was now desirable. We had as a matter of fact thought so for a long time, but had undertaken to give Geddes an opportunity to make up his own mind, and after six months' trial he had come to the same conclusion that we had previously reached—a conclusion shared by Sir Douglas Haig . . . Haig happened to be in London about this time and expressed his mind freely about the desirability of change.[43]

2. RESIGNATION AND AFTERMATH

Geddes later wrote: 'I made the announcement to Lord Jellicoe —a very disagreeable duty to perform—in the way I thought least likely to offend his feelings.'[44] It took the form of sending this bolt from the blue to Jellicoe on 24 December:

After very careful consideration I have come to the conclusion that a change is desirable in the post of 1st Sea Lord. I have not, I can assure you, arrived at this view hastily or without great personal regret and reluctance.

I have consulted the Prime Minister and with his concurrence I am asking to see the King in order to make the recommendation to him. The Prime Minister asks me to tell you that, in recognition of your past very distinguished services, he proposes to recommend to His Majesty, that a Peerage should be bestowed upon you.

I have thought that you would prefer me to convey this decision to you in writing; but should you wish to see me I shall of course be at your disposal at any time. My regret at having to convey this decision to you is the greater in view of the very cordial personal relations which have existed between us throughout.

---

[43] Lloyd George, *War Memoirs*, iii. 1179–80. The date of the Geddes-Lloyd George-Bonar Law conversation is given as *24* December in the statement referred to in the preceding footnote. However, Geddes here speaks of the meeting taking place in the evening, and the best information we have is that Geddes's letter to Jellicoe (see below) reached the Admiral at 6 p.m. on the 24th.

[44] 'Notes made for use in debate on Navy Estimates, 6 March 1918 on Dismissal of Lord Jellicoe'. The letters exchanged between Geddes and Jellicoe are in the Geddes and Jellicoe MSS. Both, as well as the Duff, Carson (Belfast), and Balfour MSS., have material pertaining to the circumstances of the dismissal and the immediate aftermath.

Geddes's letter was placed in Jellicoe's hands at 6 p.m., Christmas Eve. (This was just after a representative group of his Grand Fleet Captains had left Mall House, after presenting him with a beautiful silver model of the *Iron Duke* as a token of the esteem and affection with which the Captains regarded him.) He replied that evening: 'You do not assign a reason for your action, but I assume that it is due to a want of confidence in me. Under these conditions you will realise that it is difficult for me to continue my work, as action taken by me may commit my successor and may be contrary to your own views. I should therefore be glad to be relieved as soon as possible, and if you prefer that Admiral Wemyss should take my place temporarily I am ready to go on leave to facilitate matters.' Geddes replied that night, accepting his suggestion that he go on leave. Lloyd George's reaction to the news of the resignation, which Geddes telephoned to him on 25 December, was: 'It's a good thing.'

Geddes motored to Sandringham on Christmas Day to get the King's *pro forma* consent to the change. His Majesty was 'greatly surprised, but had to give my approval. I hope it is all for the best.' He wrote to Jellicoe that he had agreed to the change 'with great regret'.[45] He approved a peerage for Jellicoe, and this was offered to him by Geddes that evening. Wemyss took over on 27 December.

Although in public Jellicoe carried himself with calmness and restraint, he did not disguise his true feelings in private correspondence. He had not resigned, he told friends and associates, but had been '*dismissed* curtly' or 'kicked out', and without being given any reason at all. He was not sorry to be relieved from a 'thankless job'. At first he thought that the reason was, as he put it to Beatty, that 'I have recently had to take exception to [Geddes's] method of dealing with senior officers, yourself amongst them, and although I have no doubt the country will be told I am war weary, lacking in the offensive spirit, etc., I incline to the opinion that the true reason is that I will not agree to the Navy being run by an autocrat like a Railway!!'[46] His 'only fear' was that Wemyss 'will not stand up to him' and if so 'there is great danger ahead'.[47] A month

[45] King George's diary, 25 December 1917, and his letter to Jellicoe the same day; Windsor MSS.
[46] Jellicoe to Beatty, 25 December 1917; Beatty MSS.
[47] Jellicoe to G. H. Hoste, 29 December 1917; Jellicoe MSS.

later, though still in the dark as to why he had been forced out, he gathered from what Carson and others had told him that 'the change was due to Northcliffe's pressure on the Prime Minister, passed on to Geddes'.[48]

The bombshell burst in the press on the morning of 27 December, the Admiralty statement ending: 'It is hoped that his services and experience may be made use of at a later date in another important appointment.' Jellicoe, who saw the statement before its release, thought the last sentence was 'unnecessary' and had 'the appearance of being intended to "make it easy for me" '. The news was not entirely unexpected, given the rumours as far back as September that the First Sea Lord would retire shortly. *The Times* and the *Daily Mail* were, of course, delighted, the latter declaring that 'the sole and sufficient ground for our objections to him as First Sea Lord was the conviction that the naval guidance of the war in his hands was losing in initiative, flexibility, and prevision'. The *Spectator* and the *Saturday Review* rejoiced. Declared the latter, 'We cannot say that, either as Commander-in-Chief or First Sea Lord, Sir John Jellicoe has been a success. . . . The sea is a big place, we know, and it wants a big man to command it.' The *Morning Post, Daily Telegraph, Globe, Daily Express,* and *The Observer* were non-committal on the wisdom and justice of the ouster, although on 7 March 1918 the first-named wrote that Jellicoe 'was most discourteously treated, and the whole business wears an ugly complexion'. At the other end of the political spectrum, the *Westminster Gazette* and *Daily Chronicle* were non-committal, whereas the *Daily News*, the *Nation*, the *New Statesman*, and, with qualifications, the *Manchester Guardian* welcomed Jellicoe's departure: the Admiralty record in recent months did not inspire general confidence; a more aggressive naval policy was wanted. Among the few journals to express regret were *The Navy* (organ of the Navy League) and the *Army and Navy Gazette*. The *Naval and Military Record* was non-committal, preserving a judicious calm.

Jellicoe's supersession came as a complete surprise and shock to the Navy. Many senior officers were furious at the way he had been treated. Some, like Beatty (and, incidentally, the King), appear to have been less concerned with the dismissal itself than with the 'ruthless' way in which it was effected. Thus, Beatty was 'truly amazed' to hear of Jellicoe's departure. 'The manner of your

[48] Jellicoe to Beatty, 24 January 1918; Beatty MSS.

342

dismissal was apparently in keeping with the usual way they have at the Admiralty of dispensing with officers who have given their whole lives to the service of the country.' 'So they have got rid of you at last,' Bayly wrote. 'Well I am very glad indeed that you stuck to your post, and shewed that you were not afraid of them and of their intrigues.' Colville, C.-in-C., Portsmouth, 'knew the d——d politicians would do it sooner or later. Words fail me old chap to say how disgracefully you have been treated and not even given a reason by 1st Lord in his letter!! . . . Oh, how these politicians remind me of the child who daily digs up the plant to look at the roots.' Burney thought the dismissal 'perfectly scandalous and wicked'; it was 'a great shock' to de Chair and to Tyrwhitt; Leveson felt 'as if one of the props of our Maritime Empire had been brutally kicked away'; Madden described his feelings as 'mutinous and explosive and very bitter'. Lord Milford Haven (the onetime First Sea Lord, Prince Louis of Battenberg) could not 'find words to express my disgust and indignation! . . . We are now ruled by lawyers and journalists.' Other retired Admirals of high standing like Bridgeman and Callaghan wrote in a similar vein, as did civilians who had been connected with the Navy. Carson was angry, Churchill heard the news 'with great regret', Graham Greene was 'grieved and dismayed', and Hankey was 'most awfully sorry . . . and I should like to say how much I have admired the way you have tackled the difficult problem with which you were confronted and literally put a new face on the submarine warfare'. Sims was 'distressed . . . particularly when the efforts of all your anti-submarine measures are showing such promising results of complete success'.[49]

Most of the captains and junior officers in the Grand Fleet felt no differently. There was a feeling of fury concerning his shameful treatment. 'And so another great man goes down under the sea of Mud of the Gutter Press. . . . In England no one who is a gentleman can succeed.' This was Lieutenant-Commander Oswald Frewen's reaction.[50] The ships' companies, in Madden's opinion, were 'even more annoyed at your removal than their Seniors. . . .

[49] All this correspondence of the last days of December 1917 is in the Jellicoe MSS. The former First Sea Lord, Sir A. K. Wilson, still toiling at the Admiralty, thought the dismissal was 'a disgraceful concession to an unscrupulous press agitation . . .' Admiral Sir Edward E. Bradford, *Life of Admiral of the Fleet Sir Arthur Knyvet Wilson* (London, 1923), p. 246.

[50] Diary, 27 December 1917; Frewen MSS.

Beatty has never replaced you in their affections altho he is much liked and respected. A Parson last Sunday preached on Christ as the rejected of men and finished by referring to your rejection by the Politicians, who he described as fools, which greatly pleased the men.'[51]

Of course, the Young Turks in the Grand Fleet were overjoyed. 'Jellicoe has fallen,' Richmond noted. 'One obstacle to a successful war is now out of the way.'[52] So far as can be determined, reaction at the Admiralty was divided. Some officers felt that Jellicoe had been treated badly; others thought a change was overdue.

The Liberal leaders Asquith, McKenna, and Runciman were distressed at Jellicoe's leaving, but decided it would be useless to press the question in the Commons in view of indications that no worthwhile result would be obtained. Jellicoe agreed: 'it was more dignified to say nothing at all on the subject at any rate whilst the war lasted'. On 6 March 1918, nevertheless, the House of Commons spent several lively hours in debating the circumstances under which Jellicoe had left the Admiralty. The discussions left the country no wiser, since Geddes, who defended himself with characteristic imperturbability, gave no hint whatever as to the reasons that had prompted his action.

The Government's offer of a peerage struck the Service as an attempt to damp the criticism over Jellicoe's dismissal. Of the Grand Fleet Admirals consulted by Madden, only Leveson thought that Jellicoe ought to accept the peerage. 'All others considered it an insult. Sir A. Wilson refused one when he was dismissed [1912], here is the precedent.'[53] Madden agreed with them. The peerage 'is bound to come in time and please don't receive it at Geddes' hand—and bad for service to feel its most trusted men can be turned out at a moment's notice and squared by a peerage.'[54] But Jellicoe had already accepted a peerage (26 December), as Viscount Jellicoe of Scapa, feeling that, as it was intended as a tribute to the Navy, he had no right to refuse; also so that he would have a platform from which to speak out 'if things went wrong and foolish action with the Navy was taken'; finally, 'for the sake of my children, as History might never know the truth and might say

[51] Madden to Jellicoe, 1 January 1918; Jellicoe MSS.
[52] Diary, 28 December 1917; *Portrait of an Admiral*, p. 290.
[53] Madden to Lady Jellicoe, 28 December 1917; letter in the possession of the late Dowager Countess Jellicoe.
[54] Madden to Jellicoe, 27 December 1917; Jellicoe MSS.

I was kicked out, apparently justly, as no honour was conferred.'[55]

All the naval members of the Board but one (Heath, Halsey, Tothill, Paine, Oliver, and Duff) came to Wemyss and protested against Jellicoe's dismissal, for they all liked him very much and felt that he had been 'kicked out without warning like a housemaid'. They at first contemplated resignation out of sympathy and protest. They quickly changed their minds when they realized, as Halsey put it, 'that we cannot possibly bring you back and we may do great harm to the Country'.[56] They almost went through with the resignation a few days later over Geddes's claim that he had had the support of Balfour and Carson, and the latter's contradiction. They pulled back ('very much against their inclination', said Duff) after receiving Jellicoe's sane advice that their resignation would do no good and would be bad for the country—Geddes would bring in Sea Lords who would do his will, men without knowledge of the Admiralty—after a plea from the civilian memberk of the Board (Lytton, Pretyman, and Macnamara) that for patrisotic reasons they had to remain, and, finally, after Geddes's insistence (4 January) that 'the appointment and removal of the Sea Lords individually is entirely a matter for His Majesty and His Majesty's Government'. There was another angle. Duff wrote later: 'A mis-managed affair, owing to the Sea Lords not pulling together, and arguing without acting. My view was, that we ought to resign in a body simply on the ground that we considered the dismissal of Jellicoe disastrous. The line actually taken of arrogating to the Sea Lords the right to interfere in the appointment or of the dismissal of the 1st S.L. put us entirely in the wrong, and the politicians were quick to seize it.'[57] Calm was restored by 5 January, though relations remained strained. Halsey was quite determined, he told Jellicoe, never to have Geddes inside his house.

Jellicoe naturally felt disappointed at being idle at such a critical state of the war. Geddes had Jellicoe on his conscience, which would help explain his eagerness to find him a job. He offered him the post of C.-in-C., Plymouth (that is, the Devonport command) on 3 April 1918, in succession to Sir Alexander Bethell. (This was

[55] Autobiographical notes.

[56] Halsey to Jellicoe, 26 December 1917; Jellicoe MSS.

[57] Duff's note on an envelope containing copies of the memoranda between the Sea Lords and Geddes; Duff MSS. Duff himself had been in a particularly ugly mood. On 28 December he 'gave a verbal resignation and received a verbal dismissal, on which I quitted the Admiralty on leave'. The First Lord was able to coax him back.

interpreted by many as an attempt by the Government to silence the storm of criticism which arose at his leaving the Admiralty.) When Jellicoe realized that, in order to make room for him, Bethell was to be forced to vacate the job eighteen months before the normal three years of such appointments, he would have none of it, despite Wemyss's persuasive powers and Bethell's advice to accept the offer. He wrote to the First Lord that he could not accept an appointment which involved 'depriving a brother Flag Officer of his appointment before its proper termination, when that officer so far as I am aware has filled it with credit. My feelings on this matter are strengthened by the circumstances under which I took over the command of the Grand Fleet.'[58] We shall see that Jellicoe nearly became Mediterranean Admiralissimo that summer. With the failure of that scheme there vanished his last opportunity to resume an active part in the war at sea. During 1918 the Admiral spent much of his time writing his *The Grand Fleet, 1914–16* (published early in 1919) and making public speeches on the Navy's role in the war. On 18 November he agreed to head a special mission to Canada, Australia, and New Zealand for the purpose of drawing up a scheme for the naval defence of the Empire.

Jellicoe had been less successful as First Sea Lord than as C.-in-C., Grand Fleet. For long he saw a solution to the U-boat only through the ineffectual method of cutting down all oversea commitments except in France, at the same time hoping, dolefully, for the best from various ineffectual measures, which he worked hard to organize. He had been dangerously slow to appreciate the value of a general convoy system, even after its introduction; yet, once finally converted, he had done everything possible to extend convoy and to make it efficient. The provision of the vast quantity of *matériel* essential to the success of convoy was his achievement. When he left the Admiralty, he had the satisfaction of knowing that the back of the U-boat campaign had been as good as broken. He was a great gentleman, sincerely loved by all who served with him. Yet, when all has been said, as in the case of Lord Fisher in 1910 it was just as well that Jellicoe left Whitehall when he did. It was time for a change: he had lost the confidence of important segments of the Service, at Whitehall and

[58] Jellicoe to Geddes, 10 April 1918; Admiralty MSS. For the last reference, see *From the Dreadnought to Scapa Flow*, i. 433–4.

afloat, to say nothing of the Prime Minister, the First Lord, and part of the press. This is *not* to condone the squalid way in which his dismissal was engineered. The war at sea went better in 1918 partly because of the healthier First Lord–First Sea Lord and First Sea Lord–Grand Fleet relationships.

Other changes at this time saw Oliver, the D.C.N.S., leaving the Admiralty in January to take over the command of the 1st Battle Cruiser Squadron. (He was succeeded by Fremantle.) Oliver's departure was not connected with Jellicoe's dismissal, having been arranged by Jellicoe and Beatty early in December. Beatty had asked for Halsey but had switched to Oliver when Jellicoe said they could not spare Halsey—he was too difficult to replace—and suggested Oliver. '. . . he is not only absolutely first class in handling ships, but has a very fine knowledge of gunnery in all its branches and is quick to pick up new ideas.' Wemyss and Everett, who had served with Oliver, 'entirely share my views. I don't want to keep him here and ruin his future career. Hope has been at the work for some time now and the advent of Wemyss and Keyes makes it possible to let Oliver go.'[59]

Bacon shared Jellicoe's martyrdom—or so Jellicoe and his friends always considered it. He was summarily recalled on 28 December and superseded by his chief critic, Keyes, on 1 January. A. K. Wilson and Churchill were among those who found the Oliver and Bacon changes distressing. 'It is madness,' thought the onetime First Lord. 'They cannot be replaced—particularly Oliver. The position is most serious.'[60] Wilson considered Bacon 'far the best man in the Navy for that particular work. I think Oliver will also go, so we shall have lost the three ablest men in the Navy.'[61] Haig, too, was sorry to see Bacon go, as the Admiral had worked 'wholeheartedly' with the soldiers and no difficulties had arisen. Bacon himself took his dismissal in a calm and gentlemanly manner, holding no animosity towards anybody. He saw the justification of his command in the fact that in the three years, 1915–17, only five merchantmen were torpedoed and one lost by gunfire of the 88,000 vessels that had passed through the Straits— that is, through the strip of water between Beachy Head and the Downs to which the traffic was restricted.

[59] Jellicoe to Beatty, 11 December 1917; Beatty MSS.
[60] Diary, 1 January 1918; *Lord Riddell's War Diary, 1914–1918*, pp. 303–4.
[61] Bradford, *Wilson*, p. 246.

For three years we had fought the enemy with our guns and with our brains. The situation had changed from one of great possibilities to the enemy and danger to this country, to one of comparative safety for our interests afloat. This change had been effected by relentless and unremitting exertions on the part of the Dover Patrol. We had maintained sea communications with the Armies in France without intermission, in spite of destroyers, submarines, mines, and aircraft, and our commerce had passed as freely and with almost equal security to and from the Thames as it did in peace time. We may well claim that the work of the Dover Patrol in 1915–16–17 drew the teeth of the enemy in occupation of the Belgian coast and cancelled the potential value to the Germans of these bases during the remainder of the War.[62]

What Bacon fails to mention is that the U-boats were getting through the Channel on to Britain's arterial trade routes. Yet, in other respects his command had been a success, and he certainly deserves some of the credit for the success of the Dover barrage in 1918. The deep minefield was his idea; it was not the intensive system of patrol alone, but the minefield and patrol *together* that proved so successful in 1918. Bacon had justification for his keen resentment afterwards at the lack of official recognition of his achievements at Dover, the most exacting and arduous command of any flag officer in the war except for the C.-in-C., Grand Fleet.

The year had ended on the depressing notes of reverses in the North Sea and the retirement of the country's most respected Admiral from any direct connection with the war. On the more encouraging side, Germany's supreme effort to destroy Allied shipping through unrestricted submarine warfare had failed. Although Allied losses remained high, the U-boat threat was at last being contained. The United States was making her naval weight felt. In November an American battle squadron joined the Grand Fleet and placed itself under Beatty's command. The effect of the Allied blockade on German morale, particularly that of the German people, was becoming pronounced.

The ledger had another side. As the New Year opened, the probability of obtaining a decision on land in 1918 was remote. Italy and Russia were tottering; France had been bled white. It was not wildly improbable that Britain and America would have to finish the war practically by themselves. The whole Allied cause was coming to rely more and more upon the British Navy, yet to many

[62] Bacon, *The Concise Story of the Dover Patrol*, p. 297.

348

naval officers as well as civilians it was evident that the Navy had failed to meet adequately the needs of the situation. Few at the Admiralty and in the Fleet talked of the war ending before 1919 at the earliest. One of the more astute Captains feared that in the spring of 1918 the U-boats would make 'a terrific effort to defeat us finally. It is very possible they will compel us to choose between famine in England and checking the flow of American troops to France. Either course spells ruin.'[63]

The year 1917 ended with the ledger appearing to show the assets and liabilities approximately equal. The final balance that was to be struck before the end of 1918 was hidden by the prospect of another difficult year. In the meantime the British could recall with satisfaction the Abbé Sieyès's words after the Reign of Terror: 'I survived.'

[63] Drax to Bellairs, 14 November 1917; Bellairs MSS.

Index

All officers and titled people are indexed under the highest rank and title attained. Ships are indexed under 'Warships', British and German.

INDEX

Beatty, Adm.—*cont.*
attributes, 25–6, 27, 58; marital stresses, 26; improves B.C.F.–main fleet relationship, 27; and his staff, 27–28, flag officers, 28–9; wins confidence of Grand Fleet, 29–30, 344; ideas on tactics, 30–9, strategy, 40–2, 45–6, 47, 171, 172, 180, 236–40, 255; and dreadnought margin, 42; concern over battle-cruiser strength, 43, 44; and *matériel* weaknesses, 44–5; itches for action, 46–7; relations with Carson, 55; on Jellicoe, 58, 112, 173, 193, 197–8, 214, 328n., Burney, 59; urges use of submarines *v.* U-boats, 83–4; suggests mine barrage, 86–7, 180; urges copying German mine, 88; criticizes Admiralty, 99, 112, 172, 327–8n.; opposes Fisher's recall, 111; relations with Jellicoe, 40–2, 112n., 123, 198, 203n., 217, 218, 327–328; urges adoption of convoy, 119, 141–2, 157–8; and Grand Fleet destroyers, 123–4; admires Lloyd George, 153; on Custance's strategic ideas, 169–70; and 'Young Turks', 170; on Churchill's strategic ideas, 170n.; and Richmond's strategic ideas, 171; on Halsey, 174, Tothill, 175, May Admiralty reorganization, 179–81, U-boat menace, 185, 256, 289; supports Jellicoe's strategic ideas, 203n.; on Geddes administration, 214, Graham Greene, 215, work of Plans Division, 222n., Wemyss's appointment to Deputy First Sea Lord, 223, bombardment of Heligoland, 231; and blocking scheme, 234n., 235, naval air offensive schemes, 236–40, Russian Baltic Fleet, 242, German attempt to seize Scheldt, 248, strategy *re* Holland, 248–50, strategy *re* Norway, 251–2, 254; suggested as First Sea Lord, 255n.; opposes laying up part of Grand Fleet, 274; and 17 October convoy incident, 295n., 297, 298–9, Heligoland Bight action, 300, 305–10, *passim*, 335; on Cowan, 300; and 12 December convoy incident, 312–14, *passim*, 335–7, new Scandinavian convoy system, 314–15; on Bacon's work, 320n., Smuts Committee recommendations, 332–3, Jellicoe's dismissal, 342–343; and Oliver's joining Grand Fleet, 347
Beatty, Countess (Ethel Field, m. 1st Earl, ?–1932): relations with husband, 26–7
Beharrell, Sir John George (1873–1959): 57; Director of Statistics, 176n.; takes over weekly appreciation,

197; issues review of A/S campaign, 279–80; on Jellicoe's dismissal, 338n.
Bellairs, Cdr. Carlyon (1871–1955): agitates against Admiralty, 324
Bellairs, R.-Adm. Roger Mowbray (1884-1959): 33n.; 295n.; on 12 December convoy incident, 315
Benson, Adm. William Shepherd (1855–1932): opposes convoy, 187
Beresford, Adm., 1st Baron (Charles William de la Poer Beresford, 1846–1919): confidence *re* U-boats, 108, 109–10; rallies behind Carson, 199; supports Admiralty, 325; on Lloyd George *v.* Jellicoe, 331
Bethell, Adm. the Hon. Sir Alexander Edward (1855–1932): and Jellicoe succeeding him in Devonport command, 345–6
Bethmann Hollweg, Theobald von (1856–1921): and launching of unrestricted U-boat warfare, 51
Birkenhead, 1st Earl of (Frederick Edwin Smith, 1872–1930): on Northcliffe's vendetta *v.* Jellicoe, 327n.
Blackett, Baron (life peer) (Patrick Maynard Stuart Blackett, 1897–   ): 136
Boyle, Adm. Sir W. H. D.: *see* Cork and Orrery
Brand, Adm. the Hon. Sir Hubert George (1870–1955): Beatty's Captain of the Fleet, 27
Bridge, Adm. Sir Cyprian Arthur George (1839–1924): supports Admiralty, 325
Bridgeman, Adm. Sir Francis Charles Bridgeman (1848–1929): on Jellicoe's dismissal, 343
Brock, Adm. Sir Frederic Edward Errington (1854–1929): and Longhope Conference, 141, 143–4, 17 October convoy incident, 297
Brock, Adm. of the Fleet Sir Osmond de Beauvoir (1869–1947): 141; as Beatty's C.O.S., 27–8; critical of Admiralty, 173; on Beatty's air offensive scheme, 240
Brooke, Lieut.-Cdr. Edward (1885–1919): and 17 October convoy incident, 297n.
Browning, Adm. Sir Montague Edward (1863–1947): 173
Burney, Adm. of the Fleet Sir Cecil, 1st Bt. (1858–1929): as Second Sea Lord, 58–9; dismissed, 216–18; on Jellicoe's dismissal, 343
Bywater, Hector Charles (1884–1940): in public controversy over strategy, 169

352

Fleet, 347; on Oliver, 347, Bacon's dismissal, 347
Jutland, Battle of: 20, 298, 306, 311; airships in, 7; seaplane reconnaissance in, 12, 18; tactics, 31–9, *passim*

Kenworthy, Lieut.-Cdr. J. M.: *see* Strabolgi
Kerensky, Alexander Fedorovich (1881–): hopes for British naval help in Baltic, 243; British, French views on, 244n.
Kerr, Adm. Mark Edward Frederic (1864–1944): on naval airmen, 23
Keyes, Adm. of the Fleet, 1st Baron (Roger John Brownlow Keyes, 1872–1945): 347; and 'Young Turks', 170; on Jellicoe's influence on Third Ypres, 206n.; appointed D. of P., 221; and command of Baltic force, 243; on Baltic strategy, 244n.; and lack of offensive spirit at Admiralty, 254, 17 October convoy incident, 295n.; conflict with Bacon, 317–22, *passim*; on blocking Zeebrugge, Ostend, 320; succeeds Bacon, 347

Lambert, Adm. Sir Cecil Foley (1864–1928): 59
Lambert, 1st Viscount (George Lambert, 1866–1958): campaigns for Fisher's recall, 111, 325
Law, Andrew Bonar (1858–1923): 208; in War Cabinet, 62; in Committee on War Policy, 202; supports Geddes *vice* Carson, 207; and Jellicoe's dismissal, 339–40
Leslie, Sir Norman Alexander (1870–1945): 151n.; on Admiralty attitude towards convoy, 119; gives Henderson information on shipping entering, clearing UK ports, 150; and credit for convoy system, 154–5; attributes, 155; on relations with Henderson, 165–6; and convoy system organization, 264
Leveson, Adm. Sir Arthur Cavenagh (1868–1929): 28n.; on Jellicoe's dismissal, 343, Jellicoe accepting peerage, 344
Leyland, John (?–1924): in public controversy over strategy, 169
Lloyd-George of Dwyfor, 1st Earl (David Lloyd George, 1863–1945): 54, 55, 172; on Carson as First Lord, 56; establishes War Cabinet, 61–2; appoints Shipping Controller, 64; reduces Salonika force, 68–9; and Fisher's recall, 111; on Admiralty attitude to convoy, 115, 119, 123–4, 151, 167; on shipowners' war profiteer-

ing, 128; attributes, 152–3; use of informants in Navy, 153–5; and Carson's pessimism, 155, Jellicoe's pessimism, 155, 193, 208; Hankey's influence *re* convoy, 155–6; delays taking action on convoy, 157; makes plunge, 157–9; visit to Admiralty, 160–4, 192, 195; and defensive outlook of Admiralty, 165, reform of Admiralty organization, 165, 174, 176–8, 192, Geddes's appointment as Controller, 175, 176n.; optimistic *re* U-boats, 185; directs Admiralty to increase destroyers for convoy, 189; on Admiralty reluctance to extend convoy, 192; loses faith in Jellicoe, 192–5, 197–9, 203, in Carson, 192; favours more aggressive naval strategy, 194–5, 203; wants Staff 'offensive' section, 195; decides to replace Carson, 199; sets up Committee on War Policy, 202; challenges Jellicoe's pessimistic prediction, 204; and Haig's Flanders offensive, 204, 206, Haig's campaign *v.* Jellicoe, Carson, 206; proposes Board changes, 207; accepts Milner plan to replace Carson, 207; finally decides on Geddes *vice* Carson, 208–9; on Geddes, 213; association with Geddes, 215n.; and dismissal of Graham Greene, 215–16, Burney, 216–18; attempts to oust Oliver, 216–18, 223–4; and Geddes-Jellicoe relations, 218, 331; continued dissatisfaction with Jellicoe, 224; favours naval bombardment of German naval bases, 230, 231, 328; on defeat of U-boat menace, 256, 289; and Jellicoe's dismissal, 327–8, 331, 333–4, 339–40, 341, 342; and air warfare, 332
Longmore, Air Chief Marshal Sir Arthur Murray (1885–): 24; and aircraft carrier development, 13; promotes torpedo-carrying aircraft, 20, 22
Luckner, Cdr. Count Felix von (1881–1966): commands surface-raider *Seeadler*, 100–1
Ludendorff, Gen. Erich Friedrich (1865–1937): and launching of unrestricted U-boat warfare, 50, 51
Lytton, 2nd Earl of (Victor Alexander George Robert Bulwer-Lytton, 1876–1947): 56, 265n.; optimism *re* U-boats, 108–9; and Sea Lords' threat to resign, 345

McKenna, Reginald (1863–1943): and entry, clearance shipping statistics, 151; on Jellicoe's health, 329, Jellicoe's dismissal, 344

[1] Abbreviations: A.C.: aircraft carrier; B.: pre-dreadnought battleship; B.C.: battle cruiser; Cr.: armoured cruiser; D.: dreadnought; L.C.: light cruiser; S.C.: seaplane carrier; S.M.: submarine; T.B.D.: destroyer.

THE MAPS
Large-scale versions of the maps that follow
may be seen and downloaded from the book's page
on the publishers' websites.

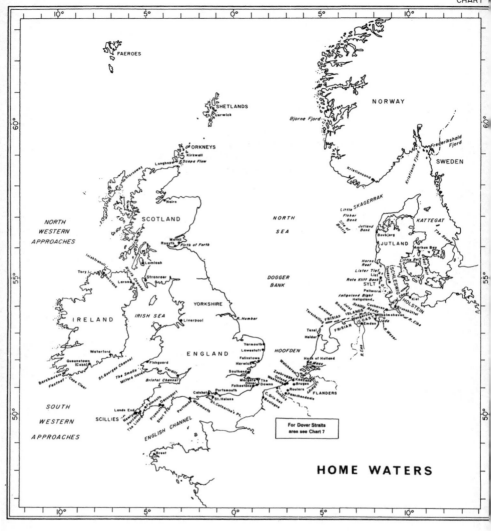

FAEROES

NORWAY

SHETLANDS
Lerwick

Bjorne Fjord

Frederikshald Fjord

SWEDEN

ORKNEYS
Kirkwall
Longhope Scapa Flow

Kristiansand

SKAGERRAK
Little
Fisher
Bank

KATTEGAT

Nairn

SCOTLAND

NORTH
SEA

Jutland
Bank

Bovbjerg
The Skaw

JUTLAND

Aarhus Bay

Little Belt
Kiel

Inishtrahull

May Isl
Rosyth Firth of Forth

Horns
Reef
Lister Tief

SCHLESWIG-HOLSTEIN

Tory Is.
Lough
Swilly

Lemlash

Larne

Stranraer

DOGGER
BANK

Lief
Rote Kliff Bank
SYLT
Pellworm

Tonning
Cuxhaven
Brunsbüttel

NORTH
WESTERN
APPROACHES

YORKSHIRE

R. Humber

Heligoland Bight
Heligoland.

IRELAND

IRISH SEA

Liverpool

Ameland
Terschelling FRISIAN ISLANDS
FRISIAN

Borkum
Juist
Norderney

Emden

Wilhelmshaven R. Weser
Wangerooge
R. Jade
R. Ems

R. Elbe

Waterford

Queenstown
(Cobh)

Berehaven
Fastnet Cape Clear

ENGLAND

HOOFDEN

Texel
Helder

Hook of Holland
M. Maas

R. Ems

Yarmouth
Lowestoft
Felixstowe
Harwich

Fishguard
Cardiff
The Smalls
Milford Haven Bristol Channel

Southend

Zeebrugge
Westkapelle Ostend
Blankenberghe

Bruges

Margate The Downs
Ramsgate
Whitstable
Dover
Folkestone

Roulers
C. Gris Nez
Passchendaele

FLANDERS

Catshot
Portsmouth
St. Helens
Boulogne

SOUTH
WESTERN

Lands End
Newlyn
Penzance
Falmouth
Plymouth Torbay
The Lizard Start Pt. Portland
SCILLIES

Weymouth
St. Catharine's Pt.

For Dover Straits
area see Chart 7

APPROACHES

ENGLISH CHANNEL

Brest

HOME WATERS

THE BALTIC

FRANCE

SPAIN

PORTUGAL

BALEARIC
ISLANDS

C. St. Vincent

Straits of Gibraltar   Gibraltar

C. Spartel

ALGERIA

TUNISIA

MOROCCO

MEDITERRANEAN

CHART 2

SHIPPING LOSSES:
WESTERN APPROACHES,
CHANNEL AND EAST COAST

•————Ship sunk by U Boat
✦————Ocean Convoy Assembly Port

Plan (i)   Five Months of Restricted S/M Warfare
           Sept. 1916–Jan. 1917.

Plan (ii) 1st Quarter of Unrestricted S/M Warfare
           Feb.–April 1917.

Plan (iii) 2nd Quarter of Unrestricted S/M Warfare
           May–July 1917.

Plan (iv) 3rd Quarter of Unrestricted S/M Warfare
           Aug.–Oct. 1917.

Plan (v)   4th Quarter of Unrestricted S/M Warfare
           Nov. 1917–Jan. 1918.

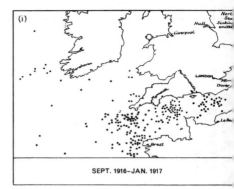

SEPT. 1916–JAN. 1917

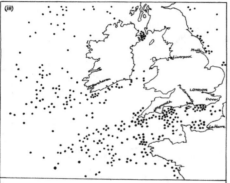

MAY –JULY 1917

April. First Scandinavian Convoys run.
May. First two experimental Ocean Convoys run.
June. Four N. Atlantic (Homeward) Convoys run.
July. Regular Homeward N. Atlantic Convoys begin.

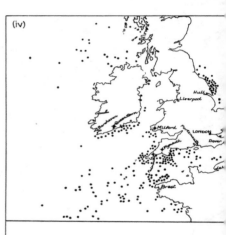

AUG.–OCT. 1917

Aug. Homeward S. Atlantic and Gibraltar Convoys started.
Mid. Aug. Outward Convoys (dispersing in 12°–15° W.) started.
Sept. Convoys organised on a Speed and Destination Basis.
All except fastest (20 knots) and slowest (below 7 knots) in
    Ocean Convoy.
Mid Oct. Outward Gibraltar Convoys kept together until arrival
    at Gibraltar.
Oct. Through–Mediterranean Convoys started.

CHART 3

(iii)

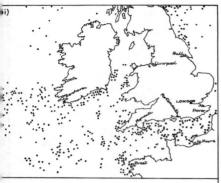

FEB.–APRIL 1917

No Ocean Convoys: No Coastal Convoys
French Coal Trade Convoys Running (Night Sailings).
Of 2583 Ships sailed in F.C.T.C's in March and April, 5 only
    were sunk. – 0·2%

(iv)

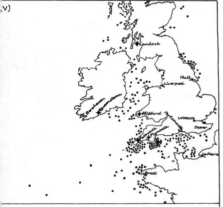

NOV. 1917–JAN. 1918

Ocean Convoy System now fully developed
Queenstown given up as Convoy Assembly Port (2.1.18).
Milford used as Convoy Assembly Port instead.
V.A. Milford starts local convoys to Ireland and Anglesey in
    Dec. 1917, and convoys suffer no losses.

**RAID ON
SCANDINAVIAN CONVOY**

17–18 October 1917

CHART 5

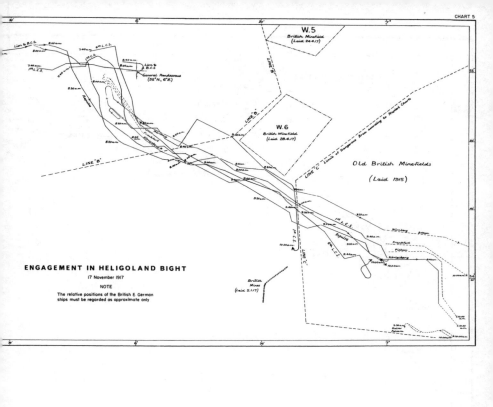

ENGAGEMENT IN HELIGOLAND BIGHT

17 November 1917

NOTE

The relative positions of the British & German
ships must be regarded as approximate only

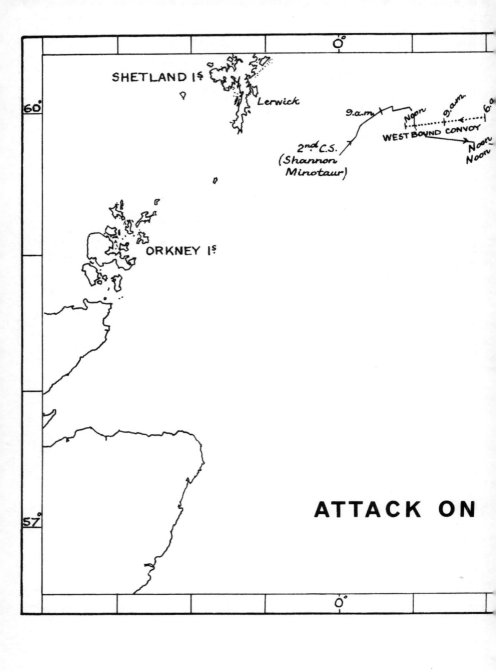

SHETLAND IS

Lerwick

60°

9.a.m.   Noon   9.a.m.   6.a

WEST BOUND CONVOY

2nd C.S.   Noon
(Shannon   Noon
Minotaur)

ORKNEY IS

ATTACK ON

57°

0°

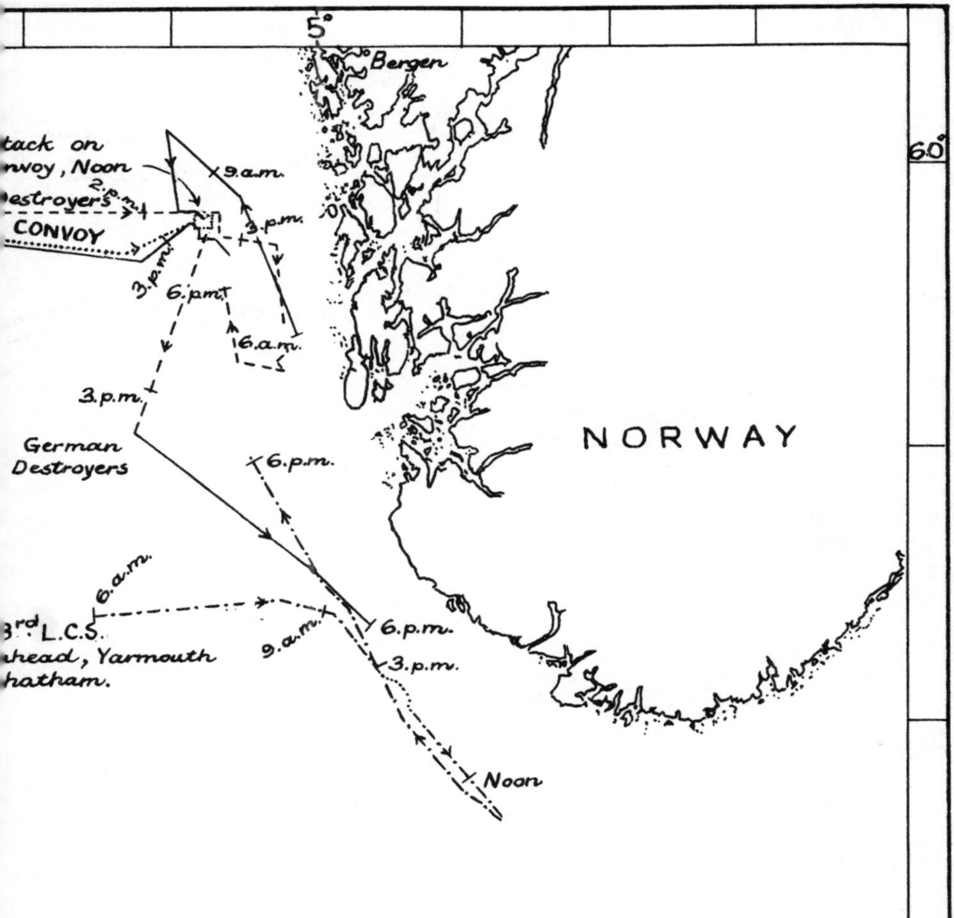

CHART 6

5°

Bergen

60°

tack on
nvoy, Noon
2
estroyers 4
CONVOY

×9.a.m.

3.p.m.

3.p.m.

6.pm.t

6.a.m.

3.p.m.

German
Destroyers

6.p.m.

NORWAY

6.a.m.

3rd L.C.S.
head, Yarmouth
hatham.

9.a.m.

6.p.m.

3.p.m.

Noon

WEGIAN CONVOY

mber 1917

57°

5°

Bovbjerg

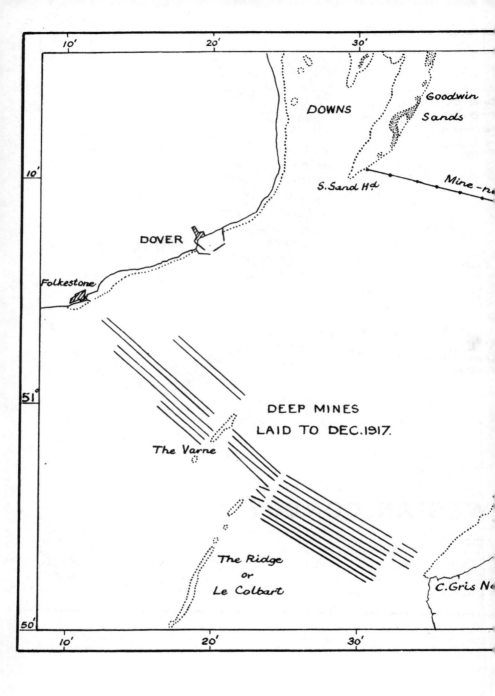

CHART 7

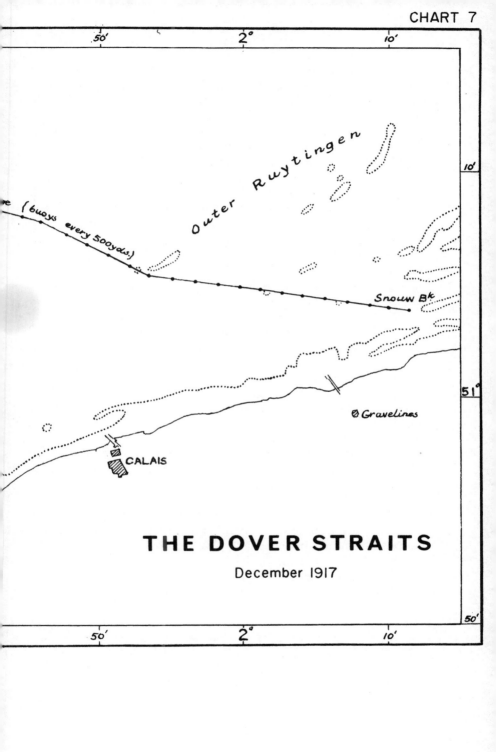

THE DOVER STRAITS

December 1917